THE IRISH MIND
EXPLORING INTELLECTUAL TRADITIONS

... When a man sits down to write a history — ... he knows no more than his heels what lets and confounded hindrances he is to meet with in his way, — or what a dance he may be led, by one excursion or another, before all is over. Could a historiographer drive on his history, as a muleteer drives on his mule, — straight forward; — for instance from Rome all the way to Loretto, without ever once turning his head aside either to the right hand or to the left, — he might venture to foretell you to an hour when he should get to his journey's end; — but the thing is, morally speaking impossible: For, if he is a man of the least spirit he will have fifty deviations from a straight line to make with this or that party as he goes along, which he can no ways avoid. He will have views and prospects to himself perpetually soliciting his eye, which he can no more help standing still to look at than he can fly; he will moreover have various Accounts to reconcile: Anecdotes to pick up: Inscriptions to make out: Stories to weave in: Traditions to sift: Personages to call upon: Panegyrics to paste up at this door; Pasquinades at that: — All which both the man and his mule are quite exempt from. To sum up all; there are archives at every stage to be looked into, and rolls, records, documents, and endless genealogies, which justice ever and anon calls him back to stay the reading of: — In short, there is no end of it . . (Laurence Sterne, The Life and Opinions of Tristram Shandy*).*

By the same author

Dialogues with Contemporary Continental Thinkers (Manchester U.P. 1984).
Poétique du Possible (Beauchesnes, Paris, 1984).
Myth and Motherland (Field Day Publications, 1984).

Edited and coedited by the same author

The Black Book: An analysis of 3rd level Education (Denian Press, Dublin, 1977)
Heidegger et la Question de Dieu (Grasset, Paris, 1981).
The Crane Bag Book of Irish Studies (Blackwater Press, Dublin, 1982).

For my daughter, ANNA SIMONE

THE
IRISH MIND

Exploring Intellectual Traditions

Edited by
RICHARD KEARNEY

Wolfhound Press

U.S. DISTRIBUTOR
DUFOUR EDITIONS
CHESTER SPRINGS,
PA 19425-0449
(215) 458-5005

Paperback reprint 1985, 1987
First published 1985

Wolfhound Press
68 Mountjoy Square,
Dublin 1

British Library Cataloguing in Publications Data

Kearney, Richard
    The Irish mind: exploring intellectual traditions.
    I. Ireland—Civilization
    I. Title
    941.5   DA925

    ISBN 0-86327-013-1
    ISBN 0 86327 047 6 pbk

The illustration on the cover, titled 'Openings', is by Irish artist Anne
Madden. Reproduced by kind permission.

Typesetting by Print Prep, Dublin.
Printed and bound by Billings & Sons Ltd., England.

EPIGRAPH

We wish the Irish mind to develop to the utmost of which it is capable, and we have always believed that the people now inhabiting Ireland . . . made up of Gael, Dane, Norman and Saxon, has infinitely greater intellectual possibilities . . . The union of races has brought a more complex mentality.

Ireland has not only the unique Gaelic tradition, but it has given birth, if it accepts all its children, to many men who have influenced European culture and science, Berkeley, Swift, Goldsmith, Burke, Sheridan, Moore, Hamilton, Kelvin, Tyndall, Shaw, Yeats, Synge and many others of international repute. (A.E. (George Russell), *The Irish Statesman*, 1925).

ACKNOWLEDGMENTS

I wish to express my gratitude to all who participated in this collective exploration of the Irish mind. These include not only those whose work is published in this volume but also my wife Anne, my brother Timothy, and my friends Anne Madden, Barre Fitzpatrick, Ronan Sheehan, Kevin Barry, Patrick Masterson, Dorothy Cross, Seamus Heaney, Gerard McNamara and Willy Kelly, whose incisive comments and suggestions kept the project open to new paths of investigation while preventing it from straying too far afield. Parts of two chapters in this book, 'Early Irish Ideology and the Concept of Unity' by Proinsias MacCana and 'The Concept of the Hero in Early Irish Mythology' by Tomás Ó Cathasaigh appeared in earlier, shorter versions in *The Crane Bag*, Vol. 2, Nos. 1 and 2, 1978.

INTRODUCTION

I
AN IRISH INTELLECTUAL TRADITION?
Philosophical and Cultural Contexts

Surprisingly, there has never been a study specifically devoted to Ireland's contribution to the world of thought.[1] Content with the cliché that this island was inhabited by irrational dreamers of dreams, we have tended to ignore the intellectual adventures of the Irish mind over the centuries, at the level of mytho-poeic, metaphysical, political, aesthetic and scientific thought. We have heard much of the *images* in Irish cultural history (and so we should), but little or nothing of its *concepts*. This publication hopes to redress the balance and to challenge the colonial and racial stereotype of the "thoughtless Celt".[2]

The existence of an Irish mind has frequently been contested; but the main lines of the argument reached their most explicit form in the nineteenth century.[3] This was expressed as both a negative and a positive discrimination. The former was vividly epitomised by the colonialist portrayals of the Irish as brainless savages. In 1836, Disraeli, the Prime Minister of England, stated: "The Irish hate our order, our civilisation, our enterprising industry, our pure religion. This wild reckless, indolent, uncertain and superstitious race have no sympathy with the English character. Their ideal of human felicity is an alternation of clannish broils and coarse idolatry. Their history describes an unbroken circle of bigotry and blood." The British historian, Charles Kingsley, provided further justification for the cultural and military suppression of his Irish neighbours when he composed this racist portrait in 1860: "I am daunted by the human chimpanzees I saw along that hundred miles of horrible country. I don't believe they are our fault. I believe that there are not only many more of them than of old, but that they are happier, better and more comfortably fed and lodged under our rule than they ever were. But to see white chimpanzees is dreadful; if they were black, one would not feel it so much, but their skins, except where tanned by exposure, are as white as ours."[4] So much for the colonial calibanisation of the Irish.

The positive discrimination against the Irish mind was more subtle, more benevolent, and for this very reason, more effective. This discrimination derived from the conviction, perhaps best summed up by

7

Matthew Arnold and his Victorian peers, that the Irish were great fantasisers, great pedlars of ballads, mysteries and dreams, but ultimately incompetent when it came to translating dream into decision, when it came to responsibly ordering and organising their boundless fancies. Accordingly, Arnold could enthusiastically commend the "Celtic soul" for its readiness to revolt against the despotism of fact; but he never recognised the existence of a Celtic *mind*. Thinking minds were the prerogative of Angles and Saxons. This racial discrimination was manifested in Arnold's unambiguous opposition to the Home Rule for Ireland Bill of 1886. Commenting on this cultural prejudice, one critic caustically remarked: "By means of it, Celts could stay quaint and stay put."[5]

Both these positive and negative strategies of discrimination had as their attendant aim the provision of an ideological vindication of colonial domination in Ireland. The Irish Revival, when it finally flowered in the early decades of this century, operated on a number of fronts—linguistic, literary and political—to counteract the colonial prejudice against, among other things, the Irish mind. The revival's campaign to liberate the Irish from their incarcerating colonial self-image was pursued with the idea of reconquest, but reconquest not only of territory but more fundamentally of mind.[6] This is clearly one of the reasons why Douglas Hyde insisted that the Gaelic League was primarily "an *intellectual* movement" to repossess Ireland's dispossessed culture.

The Irish—Catholic, Protestant and Dissenter—have over time come to espouse some of the intellectual, or rather anti-intellectual, prejudices of their historical opponents. An Irish philosopher, Garrett Barden, has remarked that, "in the dialectic of master and slave, the slave's image of himself is precisely that − an image. His speech is taken from him not only by the master but by himself . . . he is a slave because he identifies with his servile discourse . . . Speech or will is the fundamental possibility of thinking through and overcoming servile discourse."[7] This book hopes to contribute something to the cultivation of such an intellectually liberating speech. The task is not an easy one, however, for the colonial image of the master has been adopted by a considerable section of our population, including some of our most influential authors and critics. The early Yeats, for example, while still under the influence of Arnold's cultural apartheid, enthused about an Ireland whose socio-political inferiority to the English was compensated for by its "poetic . . . idyllic and fanciful" life of the Spirit![8] "Poetry," he declared in *Hopes and Fears for Irish Literature* (1892), "has nothing to do with thought, nothing to do with philosophy." (A sentiment he had the good sense to later revoke − to the benefit of both his thought and his poetry.) But Yeats is not an isolated example. Frank O'Connor spoke of the Irish "choosing the imagination over the intellect;"[9] Seán O'Faoláin endorsed the thesis that early Irish texts "revealed a total inability of the Irish mind to form a concept;"[10] and Seán Ó Tuama declared: "One doubts if we have added anything of real importance to sociological or theological or philosophical or aesthetic thought."[11] (Though to be fair, Ó Tuama is regretting rather than sponsoring this doubt.) It is perhaps time to question the validity of such self-wounding affirmations. We must reclaim the idea of ourselves.[12]

But if an Irish mind does exist, what *is* this mind? What are the distinguishing characteristics, if any, of its historical expression? These questions may best be broached by situating the debate within philosophical and cultural contexts. When we have suggested some conceptual frameworks for our argument we may be better prepared to engage in a general presentation of the essays contained in this volume.

The Philosophical Context
I begin with an hypothesis. The Irish mind does not reveal itself as a single, fixed, homogeneous identity. From the earliest times, the Irish mind remained free, in significant measure, of the linear, centralising logic of the Graeco-Roman culture which dominated most of western Europe. This prevailing culture was based on the Platonic-Aristotelian logic of non-contradiction which operated on the assumption that order and organisation result from the dualistic separation of opposite or contradictory terms.[13] Hence the mainstream of western thought rested upon a series of fundamental oppositions — between being and non-being, reason and imagination, the soul and the body, the transcendentally divine and the immanently temporal and so on.

Could it be that the Irish intellectual tradition(s) represent something of a counter-movement to the mainstream of hegemonic rationalism which Jacques Derrida has termed "logocentrism"? Could it be that the Irish mind, in its various expressions, often flew in the face of such logocentrism by showing that meaning is not only determined by a logic that centralises and censors but also by a logic which disseminates: a structured dispersal exploring what is *other*, what is irreducibly diverse.

In contradistinction to the orthodox dualist logic of *either/or*, the Irish mind may be seen to favour a more dialectical logic of *both/and*: an intellectual ability to hold the traditional oppositions of classical reason together in creative confluence. This would not mean, as the colonial prejudice presumed, that the Irish abandoned order for disorder or reneged on conceptual rigour to embrace formless chaos. The highly complex ideologies of life and death articulated by the symbolic systems of neolithic Newgrange or Celtic mythology, to take some of the most ancient instances, do not bespeak primitivistic unrule. As the recent research of such anthropologists as Lévi-Strauss, Dumézil and Eliade enables us to recognise, the symbolic systems of such early Irish culture testify to an alternative order and organisation.[14] We have here not meaninglessness but another kind of meaning, not confusion but another kind of coherence. Lévi-Strauss makes this point succinctly in *Structural Anthropology*, when he states that "the kind of logic in mythical thought is quite as rigorous as that of modern science". But is there any evidence to suggest that this more openended and para-doxical logic has been reformulated in later, post-mythic Irish intel-lectual traditions?

The Cultural Context
Which modern Irish intellectuals, if any, have acknowledged the cultural possibility of this *other* quality of mind? To begin with some modern writers: Joyce, for one, repeatedly insisted that his own work was not a surrender to a capricious anarchy of word play, but a challenge to the reader to discover different and deeper models of understanding. In this regard, Joyce might well have sympathised with the psychoanalytic belief in the existence of a "non-casual and synchronistic order" in those regions of consciousness suppressed by logocentrism. Joyce sub-verted the established modes of linear or sequential thinking in order to recreate a mode of expression which would foster rather than annul heterogeneous meanings, which would, in his own words, permit us to have "two thinks at a time." To cite some common examples, Joyce could refer to Dublin as "lugly" (simultaneously communicating his ambiguous perception of his native city as both lovely and ugly); Dublin is, as he reminds us in *Finnegans Wake*, "doublin". Yeats wrote of a "beauty born out of its own despair" and referred to the 1916 Rising as a "terrible beauty". Wilde boasted that in his art "a truth was that whose contradictory was also true." And this fecund double-mindedness is also a decisive factor in Beckett's own aesthetic maxim: "Where we have *both* darkness *and* light, there we also have the in-explicable. The key word of my work is *perhaps*."

Thomas Kinsella has, more recently, adverted to the decisive role played by psychic ambivalence in Irish culture in his essay "The Divided Mind" (1972). Whereas the English writer, says Kinsella, can easily identify with the continuous tradition of English literature, "an Irish poet has access to the English poetic heritage through his use of the English language, but he is unlikely to feel at home in it." Kinsella observes that the real condition of Irish culture in the nineteenth cen-tury preceding Yeats was silence – the silence surrounding the demise of the Irish language and of half of the famine-stricken population. Moving back into the eighteenth century Kinsella discovers, in contrast, the voices of those Gaelic poets resurrected for posterity in Corkery's *Hidden Ireland* and *An Duanaire: Poems of the Dispossessed* (translated by Kinsella and Ó Tuama). Before them again, Kinsella points to a literary tradition stretching back some thousand years. "In all this," writes Kinsella, "I recognise a great inheritance and simultaneously a great loss. The inheritance is certainly mine but only at two enormous removes – across a century's silence and through an exchange of worlds

... I recognise that I stand on one side of a great rift and can feel the discontinuity in myself. It is a matter of peoples and places as well as writing – of coming from a broken and uprooted family, of being drawn to those who share my origins and finding that we cannot share our lives." Hence a *double* vision which characterises the Irish mind as discontinuous, divided and, at times, *comic*. For perhaps there also exists an Irish comic vision, as Vivian Mercier has argued, extending from the medieval bards to Swift, Shaw, Wilde, Joyce and Beckett – a comic intellectual heritage typified by an ability to respond creatively to dislocation and incongruity?[15]

(The question arises, however, as to whether this double vision is a quality *inherited* by the Irish mind or a quality *imposed* on it by divisive historical circumstances – e.g. the various invasions, the break between the Gaelic and Anglo-Irish traditions and so on. In other words, is the ambivalence of the Irish mind something which produces or something which is produced by history? In all probability it is a dialectical combination of both. But in thus suggesting the possibility of some intellectual disposition towards history, I would insist that this be understood as a *cultural* phenomenon which develops and alters as history progresses, and *not* as some innate racial characteristic.)

In the case of many Irish writers, notably Joyce and Beckett, the double vision assumed the focus of exile or estrangement, the unmistakable sentiment of residing on the outside or periphery, of being *other* – for better or for worse. Joyce's experience of exile, for example, was not only geographical but also cultural and linguistic. Even though he wrote in English, Joyce was mindful of the fact that he was never quite at ease with its vocabulary; and this uneasiness perhaps also accounts for his exceptional capacity to deconstruct and reconstruct it. Joyce often exulted in the knowledge that his writing was a Trojan horse in the city of the Anglo-Saxon tongue. As Stephen Dedalus ruminated after his exchange with the English Dean of Studies in *A Portrait of the Artist*: "The language in which we are speaking is his before it is mine . . . I cannot speak or write these words without unrest of spirit. His language *so familiar and so foreign*, will always be for me an acquired speech. I have not made or accepted its words. My voice holds them at bay. My soul frets in the shadow of his language." Joyce could only inhabit the English language as an exile. But if he was not at home in English, he was not at home in his native culture either. Joyce derided familiarity whenever it took the form of narrow chauvinism – those "nets of nationality, language and religion" which Stephen deplores – and chided the ideology of insular nationalism as a pale "afterthought of Europe." But while he felt himself a foreigner in Ireland, he prided himself on being an Irishman in foreign lands. After only three years in Europe, Joyce wrote to his brother Stanislaus: "The Irish are the most intelligent, most spiritual and most civilised people in Europe". "If once it could assert itself," he continued, the Irish mind "would contribute a new force to civilisation." Throughout his life and work Joyce retained a dual fidelity to both the foreign and the familiar. He wanted to Europeanise Ireland and to Hibernicise Europe – no less.[16] John Montague provides this portrait of Joyce's bifocal vision: "He is the first great artist of his race in the English language, the master forger of his race . . . his feats grow and grow like an interlaced Celtic manuscript, corrections and additions serpenting along the margins . . . His whole being is a blackness, a bottlefield of contradictions. An Irishman who retains his British passport, he loathes British officialdom, and is obsessed with the land he left behind . . . Sadness and gaiety, seriousness and anarchic humour, he makes his contradictions dance."[17]

This Joycean counterpointing of the foreign and the familiar is arguably one of the most recognisable watermarks of the Irish intellect. Seamus Heaney, a Northern Irish poet who migrated South, at once exiled and at home, haunted by borders and partitions, exposed to the cultures of coloniser and colonised, Catholic and Protestant, Gael and Saxon, has also practiced an art of making contradictions dance. The following statement of his intellectual position is instructive in this regard: "I am convinced that one can be faithful to the nature of the English language and at the same time to one's own non-English origins. This is a proper statement for our poetry. In the Sweeney story (which I translated from the Irish) we have a northern sacral king, Sweeney, who is driven out of his home in County Antrim. There is a sort of schizophrenia in him. On the one hand he is always whinging for home, but on the other he is celebrating his free creative imagination. Maybe here there was a fable which could cast a myth across the swirl of private feelings in me. But one must not forget the other side of the poetic enterprise, which is precisely the arbitrariness and the innocence of the day to day poetic impulse . . . This inner impulse has to be preserved, however essential the outward (mythic) structures may be for communication, community and universal significance . . . Yeats and Kavanagh point up these contradictions: Yeats with his search for myths and sagas, the need for a structure and a sustaining landscape; Kavanagh with his need to be liberated and distanced from it, the need to be open, unpredictably susceptible, lyrically opportunistic . . . You need both."[18] Derek Mahon, speaking for and from the Northern Protestant tradition, makes a similar plea for the validity of a double cultural residence: "I still consider myself in the tradition of Louis MacNiece, that is an Irish poet who is no more at home in the specific culture of Ireland than in the English culture imparted by a Protestant education and a London residence. The tensions are, I hope, fruitful."[19] And extending the analysis of intellectual dialectics to the Irish visual arts, Louis le Brocquy describes how his own painting attempts to articulate a "secret logic of ambivalence". He explains: "It would appear that this ambivalent attitude

. . . was especially linked to the prehistoric Celtic world, and there is further evidence that it persists to some extent today . . . I myself have learned from the canvas that emergence and immergence—twin phenomena of time—are ambivalent; that one implies the other and that the matrix in which they exist dissolves the normal sense of time, producing a characteristic stillness."[20] One recalls here the spiral mandala and interlacement motifs which recur in Newgrange, the Celtic crosses and the *Book of Kells*.[21] Le Brocquy leaves us with the following thought-provoking question: "Is this the underlying ambivalence which we in Ireland tend to stress; the continued presence of the historic past, the indivisibility of birth and funeral, spanning the apparent chasm between past and present, between consciousness and fact . . . day-consciousness/ night-consciousness, like (Joyce's) Ulysses and Finnegan"? It is certain that Joyce's own choice of the word "wake," where the antithetical worlds of life and death overlap and embrace, is no accident.

Finally, several Irish philosophers and scholars appear to bear witness to parallel preoccupations of mind. It is a curious, if much neglected fact, that two of Ireland's most reputed thinkers, John Scottus Eriugena in the ninth century and Bishop George Berkeley in the eighteenth, reacted against the mainstream logocentric philosophies of their time in an effort to espouse heterodox currents of thought. In Eriugena this decentralising scruple was marked by a resistance to the Latin orthodoxy of his time (in particular the primacy of substantial being). Eriugena turned instead to the marginal Eastern spirituality of thinkers like Maximus the Confessor and the Pseudo-Dionysius. For his pains he was branded a heretic by Pope Honorius III in 1225. Berkeley was no less iconoclastic in his response to the established mechanist-materialist philosophy of British empiricism (inaugurated by Hobbes and Locke). Looking beyond the colonial curtain to the anathemised thought of the continent, Berkeley fashioned an Irish version of Cartesian idealism. For Berkeley, as for Eriugena, this radical movement towards the intellectual *other*—French metaphysics for Berkeley, Oriental theology for Eriugena—also involved a surmounting of confessional divides between Catholic and Protestant for the former, between Oriental and Roman for the latter. In short, both Irish thinkers considered themselves alien to the prevailing philosophical orthodoxies and responded by embracing what were for them *alternative* modes of thought.

The pattern of intellectual exodus towards 'otherness' recurs in the experience of certain Irish scholars as a *peregrinatio* to foreign lands. One could mention here Eriugena's emigration to Laon in France to translate, write and teach philosophy; St Columban's holy quest for the "solitude of contemplation" at Lake Constance in Switzerland; the European wanderings of Sedulius Scottus, St Cilian and Clement Maelcomer (whose teachings were also condemned by Rome). So pro-

found indeed was the impact of these emigré Irish scholars between the
sixth and ninth centuries that one German abbot was prompted to pro-
claim: "How can we ever forget Ireland, she fills the church with her
science and her teaching."[22] The *peregrinatio* cult may, in reality, have
been necessitated by the Viking invasions of Ireland, but in cultural
memory it was recorded as a spiritual movement outwards to alien
lands.[23] Moreover, this link between Irish and Continental spiritualities
re-emerged between the seventeenth and nineteenth centuries, when
many Irish priests and intellectuals, unable to study in Ireland due to
penal colonial regulations, travelled abroad to receive their education
in the Irish Colleges established in Paris, Salamanca, Rome, Crakow
and other continental cities.

No formal distinction has been made in the preceding account
between the poets and the philosophers; both testify to what would
seem to be common, if fluctuating, characteristics of the Irish mind
– *decentredness, double-vision, exile* and so on. The conventional
practice of rigidly separating the artist and the thinker, imagination and
reason, must be questioned if we are to fully appreciate the integrity of
the Irish mind.

*   *   *

Poets, philosophers, and other creative thinkers are not, however, the
only representatives of the Irish mind. The characteristics of this
mind have also found *negative* intellectual expression. For example, the
logic of ambivalence, the ability to have 'two thinks at a time', can
equally manifest itself in our own particular brand of 'double-think',
our peculiar relish for moral equivocation and evasiveness, for having
it both ways: *Tadgh an dá thaobh*. No culture, Irish or otherwise, is
above critical approach. In the third part of this introduction, I will
return to the question of the need to discriminate between positive
and negative, authentic and inauthentic, expressions of mind.

II

PRESENTATION OF THE TEXTS
Commentary and Methodological Considerations

This book presents a critical survey of Irish intellectual history under five main rubrics: *mythopoeic thought, philosophical thought, literary thought, political thought* and *scientific thought*. Our selection of studies does not claim to be comprehensive, but it does intend to represent significant aspects of Irish thinking.

Mythopoeic Thought
In the first of these sections Brendan Purcell, a philosophical anthropologist, explores the complex ideology of life and death expressed by the symbolic motifs of the neolithic passage grave at Newgrange, County Meath. The stone inscriptions and architectural cyphers of Newgrange are some of the earliest records of Ireland's pre-Celtic period dating back to 3200 BC. An archaeologist who visited Newgrange in the last century is reported to have exclaimed: "What marvellous manuscripts, if only we could read them!" – a sentiment which calls to mind Montague's lines in *A Lost Tradition*: "All around, shards of a lost tradition/The whole countryside a manuscript we had lost the skill to read." It is fortunate that the recent anthropological insights made available by such philosophers as Eliade, Voegelin and König have provided scholars like Purcell with the methodological key to decipher one of the earliest manuscripts of our lost heritage. By attempting the first hermeneutic recuperation of Newgrange's cosmic symbolisations of time, place, partnership, totality and narrative, Purcell takes an exploratory step towards the intellectual retrieval of this archaic culture. His analysis thus serves to complement the archaeological

studies of Newgrange carried out by O'Kelly, Herity, Eogan and others. Herity and Eogan concluded their monumental *Ireland in Prehistory* (1977) with a call for "a new philosophical understanding of the actual and potential archaeological evidence." Purcell's study represents a timely, if inevitably partial, response to this call.

In the second essay of this section, entitled "Early Irish Ideology and the Concept of Unity", Proinsias MacCana delves into a further layer of our cultural lineage. Probing the loam of old and middle Irish texts spanning the pagan and Christian periods, MacCana adverts to the "conservative" and "mythic" cast of "native Irish thought", particularly as evidenced in the ancient Celtic concepts of sovereignty and unity. He argues that these characteristics have more in common with Indian culture—which represents the other, outer surviving limit of Indo-European civilisation—than with the Graeco-Roman rationalist culture which came to dominate most of Western Europe. In this respect, the structural anthropology of George Dumézil has proved of paramount assistance in discerning the continuities between Indo-European and Irish ideology (e.g. the structural parallels between the Fifth Veda and the Irish narratives of Eochaid). This study traces the developing role of the druids and *filí* (poet-seers) up to the seventh century AD and beyond, demonstrating how the "native institutions and modes of thought survived the change of religious orthodoxy relatively unscathed," largely thanks to the complementary co-existence of the pagan and Christian ideologies. In this way, the early Irish intellect was able to obviate the logocentric polarisation into the *logos* of scientific reason and the *mythos* of poetic discourse which tended to prevail elsewhere in Europe. MacCana points out that this unusual nonconformity to logocentric polarisation cannot be explained away by claiming that written prose (which is said to have accounted for the emergence of Greek thought) was absent from Irish culture. Ireland produced one of the first written vernacular literatures in Western Europe. The Christian authors of early Christian Ireland, from the seventh to the ninth centuries, were more concerned to refine and reformulate what they had inherited from the pagan oral tradition than to replace or supplant it. Thus Eriugena, for instance, was able to combine a capacity for abstract speculation learned from the Latins and Greeks with that indigenous talent for concrete thinking so typical of Indo-European ideology. In a similar vein, the ancient Celtic ideology of order, involving a subtle equilibrium between spiritual/cultural cohesion and socio-political diversification "sustained more than a millennium of Christianity, and remained a living force in Irish tradition centuries after Vikings and Normans had shaken the social premises on which it was founded." This is a fine example of how ideas can sometimes out-live their historical conditioning. MacCana's study serves two main functions: (i) it establishes the existence in early and medieval Ireland of a "comprehensive and internally coherent system of politico-religious doctrine and speculation preserved and interpreted by the druids;" (ii) it shows how such a system, and in particular the old druidic ideology of cultural unity and political differentiation, "outlasted profound social and linguistic change" to furnish some of the more perduring features of the Irish mind.

In "The Concept of the Hero in Irish Mythology" Tomás Ó Cathasaigh invokes the claim of Vico, the first philosopher to make the inter-rogation of myth intellectually respectable, that "the first science to be learned should be mythology or the interpretation of fables." Ó Cathasaigh draws from some of the most recent researches in philoso-phical anthropology, depth psychology and the comparative history of religious ideology, to reveal how our mythological texts possess concep-tual structures and motifs "unique in Western Europe". These texts which contain "the native ideology of Ireland" require a critical "elucida-tion and interpretation" which will enable us to "uncover and to restate in abstract terms the configuration of the ideological patterns which underlie the myths." Ó Cathasaigh's analysis operates according to Dumézil's hermeneutic dictum that it is the "reader's task to perceive the providential design which has arranged the events in the order in which the work presents them . . . Yet it is the design that justified these events and gives them meaning." The basic tenet of Ó Cathasaigh's argument is that Irish myth is structured in terms of a dialectic between man and God mediated by the tertiary category of the hero. The two examples selected for detailed scrutiny are Cú Chulainn, the martial hero, and Conaire Mór, the king-hero. The author also explores the com-parative content of pagan and Christian ideology in these heroic myths. He concludes that "while celebrating the achievements of the hero, Irish myth asserts the precariousness of man's position in the cosmos."

These three studies give us cause to ponder the implications of Mircea Eliade's claim that "myth itself, as well as the symbols it brings into play, never quite disappear from the present world of the psyche — it only changes and disguises its operations."[24]

Philosophical Thought

The second section of the book deals with Ireland's philosophical thinkers. The three studies included here extend from Scottus Eriugena in the ninth century to George Berkeley and the counter-enlightenment philosophers of the eighteenth and nineteenth centuries.

Dermot Moran examines the original and innovatory contribution to speculative metaphysics made by Eriugena's concepts of nature, God and man. Eriugena can be said to have translated the Irish ideology of the human/divine relationship from mythology into metaphysics, sub-stituting the mediational category of nature for that of the hero. His central thesis "on nature" (*Periphyseon*) as a pantheistic mediation between divine transcendence and human immanence is pithily summed up in the following passage: "It follows that we ought not to understand God and the creature as two things distinct from one another, but as one and the same. For both the creature, by subsisting, is in God; and God, by manifesting himself in a marvellous and ineffable manner creates himself in the creature." Natural creation serves to synthesise the orders of eternity and time, dualistically segregated by logocentric metaphysics. Moran remarks that while Eriugena was deemed to be one of the greatest metaphysicians of all time, and certainly the finest philosopher writing in Latin between Augustine and Anselm, he inaugurated no continuing metaphysical tradition in his native Ireland, nor indeed on the Continent where he taught and died. And yet, though branded a heretic and repeatedly censored down through the ages, his thought has survived to the present day as a record of one of the most adventurous speculative systems to be found in western philosophy. Perhaps one of the reasons for Eriugena's failure to establish an eponymous philosophical tradition, along the lines of Augustine, Aquinas or even Descartes, was an indigenous antipathy to doctrinaire schools of any description. More probable still is the ex-centric and unconventional nature of his theories which transgressed the orthodox mainstream of "Roman realism," reaching instead from the western periphery of his native culture to the eastern periphery of oriental mysticism. It was Eriugena, we must not forget, who made the first comprehensive translation of both the Pseudo-Dionysius and Maximus the Confessor from Greek into Latin on the invitation of King Charles the Bald of France.[25] He was considered one of the few philosophers in Western Europe at that time with a sufficient knowledge of Greek for the task.

Moran's study responds to the present need for a re-evaluation of Eriugena's contribution to the history of human thought. He suggests that Eriugena's cosmological system of creation, fall and redemption enunciated in the *De Divisione Naturae* was restated, though not in any continuous or casual way, by both the twelfth century renaissance and the mystical revivals of Meister Eckhart and Nicholas of Cusa. He also suggests some significant parallels between his speculative idealism and the modern idealist thesis, given common currency by Descartes, Berkeley, Kant and Hegel, that divine truth reveals itself in and through man's creative ideas. (It is worth remembering that one of the theories which earned Eriugena papal censorship in 1210, 1225 and again in 1681 when his works were placed on the *Index Librorum Prohibitorum*, was his insistence upon the pivotal role of man's free and creative intellect.) Nor should we neglect to mention in this regard the curious fact that Eriugena's system has been variously invoked by such modern Irish writers as Shaw and Joyce.[26]

Rejecting any effort to prove the "Irishness" of Eriugena's thought by recourse to unsubstantiated biographical conjecture, Moran recommends the more credible procedure of a cultural comparison between the Irish and Oriental mystical ideologies of the early middle ages. In this way, he contends, we may come to appreciate the real significance of Eriugena as an "Irishman who became a European intellectual" and "set the categories of a new age."

In his study of Berkeley, Harry Bracken argues that Ireland's most celebrated philosopher is an "Irish Cartesian" attuned to the continental tradition of modern idealism, rather than a "British empiricist", as has been commonly supposed. Born in Kilkenny in 1685, Berkeley attended Trinity College in Dublin. Though he did make several trips abroad—for example, to England (where he met Addison and Steele), to the Continent (where he is reputed to have met Malebranche) and to Bermuda (where he attempted to found an interracial college for the New World)—Berkeley lived and worked and thought in Ireland for most of his life. He referred to Newton as "a philosopher of a neighbouring nation" and dissociated himself from Locke and the empiricists with the famous retort: "We Irish do not hold with this!" Yeats was, understandably, partial to Berkeley's defence of the creative powers of the mind against what he saw as the reductive onslaught of the materialist philosophies. He even went so far as to assert that Berkeley's revolt against mechanistic reductionism (of ideas to empirical sensations), represented the "birth of the national intellect". There can be little doubt that Yeats romanticised Berkeley's philosophy and exaggerated his nationalist credentials. But he was correct in affirming Berkeley's profound empathy with Continental idealism and in particular with the idealist thesis of intellectual creativity formulated by Descartes and Malebranche.

David Berman extends the discussion of Berkeley's intellectual background and influence to include a critical overview of the "golden age" of Irish philosophical debate in the seventeenth and eighteenth centuries. His study pays special attention to the sixty-year period between 1690 and 1750 which witnessed the emergence of such thinkers as Toland, Browne, King, Hutcheson, Molesworth, Shaftsbury, Clayton, Synge, Dodwell, Berkeley, Skelton, Ellis and Burke.[27] "During this period," says Berman, "these Irishmen wrote originally and influentially, and Swift's writing records their popular diffusion." These thinkers constituted what may be considered a modern Irish tradition in philosophy which Berman suggests is largely counter-enlightenment in character. Caught in the interplay of enlightenment and counter-enlightenment doctrines, modern Irish philosophy divides into two main tendencies: the *liberal* devoted to rational tolerance and the *traditionalist* devoted to supra-rational fideism. As a proponent of the former, Berman singles out John Toland, the Donegal heretic who wished to promote a new attitude of tolerance by returning to the pre-sectarian religion of the ancient Irish, "the western latitudinarians" as he described them in *Nazarenus* in 1718. Amongst the traditionalist philosophers Berman numbers Peter Browne, Edward Synge and William King — counter-enlightenment thinkers whose fideistic privileging of spiritual mysteries over commonsense experience may even have indirectly derived from the negative theology of the Pseudo-Dionysius, first introduced into western philosophy by Eriugena.

One could also count amongst this counter-enlightenment fold the Irish thinker, James Usher. Born in 1720 and educated in Trinity College, Usher's seminal essay on philosophical aesthetics, *Discourse on Taste* (1767), celebrates the "shadowed ideas not in experience" but innate in the human mind "which fling inexpressible charms" over the objects of our perception. Usher insists that our ideas of beauty, truth and the *summum bonum* are not reducible to empirical sensation or association, as Locke maintained. They are differentiations of an original divine idea which we can only encounter in a state of exalted pleasure and enthusiasm: a state which Usher, like Burke after him, calls the "sublime". "The soul of man," he writes, "naturally pays homage to unseen powers. He feels obscure hopes and obscure fears, which become a religious passion . . . the source of the sublime sensation."[28] This sublime passion is one that ceaselessly "wanders and is astray for its object"; and as such, it bequeaths us "an orphan's mind" in anxious search of a divine consummation whose "completion lies in the dark." Usher thus refutes what he refers to as Locke's "ludicrous explication" of our ideas of beauty, goodness and happiness in the mechanist terms of empirical experience. The experience of the sublime does not "attend on sensible ideas", as British empiricism taught, but on a fugitive, unknown, presence which reveals itself to the poetico-religious mind as something "forever near" and yet "forever hidden".[29] In short, Usher, like Eriugena and Berkeley before him, instances a proclivity of the Irish mind towards metaphysical idealism.[30]

Berman champions Berkeley as the thinker who best synthesised the liberal and traditionalist tendencies in modern Irish philosophy. In a contentious conclusion to his essay, he also explores the ways in which the writings of Swift and Burke incorporated some of the theological and epistemological theories of the Irish counter-enlightenment,[31] which, he infers, may have been deployed at times as an ideological strategy by the Anglo-Irish ascendancy to preserve their cultural, political and religious powers.

(In our own century, the most notable disciple of this Berkeleyan heritage is perhaps Arland Ussher (1899-1980)—no relation to James Usher—who described his life-work as an attempt "to hammer out a new aesthetic philosophy, which should carry on the work of the great Irish thinker, George Berkeley."[32] Ussher sums up the guiding principle of his anti-empiricist metaphysics as follows: "The world consists of the thoughts of a Mind. But up to Berkeley, mind was regarded as transcendent, external, like Paley's clockmaker. Since Berkeley we've come to regard it as immanent . . . What people call fact is unreal; only the whole, the continuum, is real — of which man is the microcosm."[33])

Political Thought

The third section of this volume opens with Seamus Deane's critical reassessment of Edmund Burke's liberal philosophy. Deane locates the beginnings of an Irish liberal tradition in the free-thinking works of Molesworth, Toland and Molyneux, published at the end of the seventeenth century. Though he acknowledges fitful reappearances of this tradition in the United Irishmen of the 1790s, in the Irish socialists of the late nineteenth century and in Connolly, Mellows and Cruise O'Brien in our own century, Deane's basic thesis is that the fate of this intellectual movement was ultimately determined by Burke's political writings. Deane argues that Burke's brand of liberalism, not unlike that of Mill and Morely, attempted to offset revolutionary upset by diffusing the combustible alliance of widespread political disaffection and radical intellectualism, as witnessed, for example, in the French Revolution. Burke dismissed Rousseau as the "founder of the philosophy of vanity" and warned against Voltaire's "infidel" cast of mind. Yet Burke shared with Montesquieu (the one thinker of the French Enlightenment he esteemed) and the early Irish liberals a fundamental distrust of any effort by an individual or elite to impose a totalitarian ideology of statism. Against the model of the monopoly state, Burke advocated the model of mixed, pluralistic government which would democratically reflect the people as a nation. So that while it is true that Burke's conservative liberalism expressed itself as a defence of the *status quo*, in particular the British Constitution, it is equally true that he was, on occasion, able to find common cause with the more radical republican liberalism of Toland, Molesworth and Molyneux. He shared with this latter group a profound antipathy to any form of centralised, authoritarian power. For Burke this meant that all forms of disruptive revolution must be avoided as they lead to the despotic rise of a military dictator. (Burke had Cromwell, amongst others, in mind.)

Burke saw himself as being at once a defender of reason and an enemy of rationalism. The form of rationalism he most deplored was that scientific logocentrism which sacrificed the rich multiplicity of human existence to the abstract systematisations of cold, cut-and-dried ideology. He would not brook those fanatical ideologues who dispensed with living *men* out of some putative commitment to *mankind*. In this respect, Burke might be seen as ratifying Eriugena's original synthesis of concrete and speculative thinking and also, indeed, his reverence for the mystery and meaningfulness of nature. Burke refused to sponsor any brand of theoretical reason which did not remain faithful to the human complexity of practice, feeling and creative imagination. He would only subscribe to those political ideas and ideals which safeguarded the liberties of independent minds in civil society. Accordingly, he vigorously repudiated all forms of totalitarianism where, in his own words, "individuality is left out" and "the state has dominion and conquest for its sole objects — dominion over minds by proselytism, over bodies by arms."

By the 1760s Burke had, significantly, defected from the intolerant Protestant ascendancy whose bigotry he denounced as a "malignancy" and a "monster of plebeian oligarchy". He pleaded instead for justice and liberty for *all* Irishmen, regardless of race or creed. He opposed all forms of ascendancy sectarianism and was deeply horrified by the Penal Code against Catholics, which he considered quite as heinous as the power ploys devised by colonial Indianism and revolutionary Jacobinism. This uncompromising dissidence was in large part due to his liberal humanitarian scruples. But Deane suggests that it also served to express his conviction that the disabused response of the Catholic oppressed could easily culminate in divisive anarchy and revolt. In championing the cause of Irish Catholics, Burke may be said to have anticipated the radical republican liberalism of the United Irishmen. Furthermore, in stressing the venerability of cultural pluralism, national heritage and spiritual mystery, Burke also anticipated the Irish Revival's preoccupations with a native cultural identity. Deane sums up Burke's liberal ideology as follows: "Power, not concentrated but dispersed; loyalty, not commanded but won; complexity conceded to, simplicity of system avoided."

Perhaps one of the most welcome features of Deane's analysis is its departure from the litany of Burke studies which have neglected the Irish dimensions and context of his thought.[34] Deane adds credence to the claim that Burke is Ireland's first real political thinker, even though he had few followers in Ireland. It was not his particular brand of conservative liberalism that set the tone for Irish liberation in the nineteenth century and afterwards. This derived more from O'Connell's Benthamite liberalism and, on the revolutionary side, from the republican and Jacobin liberalism of the United Irishmen.[35]

Liam De Paor reminds us in his essay that the first Irish experience of republican ideology was at the receiving end of Cromwell's sword. When English republicanism was thus foisted upon this country, Irish political thought was essentially aristocratic and traditional, taking most of its conceptual precedents from the middle ages. It is against this historical and colonial backdrop that De Paor charts the ways in which "the Protestant republic first came to Catholic Ireland."

After the Cromwellian invasion, the Irish saw themselves as "the disinherited of lost glory", promulgating a "propaganda of the dispossessed" and sustained by a belief in the messianic return of the true prince from exile in Europe. But this ideology of dispossession had the curious effect of making Irish conservatism radical: Jacobitism eventually begat Jacobinism. Tone learned the principles of radical republicanism neither from England nor his native land but from the continent Robespierre, not Cromwell, was his mentor of emancipation. As De Paor puts it: "It was a desperate country, and modern Irish repub-

licanism springs from a seedbed of ideas not planted in Ireland . . .
The philosophers refined their ideas. Their message came to liberate
the discontented in a very simplified form: the present scheme of
things had no divine, or even human, sanction but was rotten and corrupt; it should be swept away and a new scheme devised." The Dublin
manifesto.of the United Irishman circulated in 1791 details the conceptual genesis of Hibernian republicanism as follows: "Dieu et *mon*
Droit! is the motto of kings. — Dieu et la liberté! exclaimed Voltaire,
when he first beheld Franklin his fellow-citizen of the world. — Dieu
et *nos* Droits! Let Irishmen cry aloud to each other. — The cry of
Mercy — of Justice — and of Victory."

Irish republicanism differed from its enlightenment counterpart
in France in its absorption of a strong dose of romantic nationalism.
The United Irishmen, for example, substituted the concrete notion
of Nation for the abstract notion of the General Will. De Paor recounts
the failure of the republican ideology of Tone and Davis to ultimately
override the confessional divide between Dissenter, Catholic and
Protestant, and the ethnic division between Gael, Dane, Norman
and Saxon. This was partially due to the colonial siege mentality
of the Protestant planter, but it also resulted from the romantic
aspiration of the Catholics to restore their ancient Gaelic nation.
So that by the dawn of this century, Irish republicanism had become
synonymous with revolutionary separatism. De Paor states accordingly:
"In 1916 the republic was openly proclaimed . . . By the time of the
twentieth-century upheaval, the republicans were returning to ideology. Both Pearse and Connolly attempted to set their separatist aspirations in a framework of general theories of society and they were not
alone. Pearse indeed attempted to define the republican tradition
itself, somewhat eclectically, pronouncing the true succession to be
Tone, Davis, Mitchell and Lalor. But the emphasis in this succession
was on breaking the connection with England and the transmission of
a need of revolutionary nationalism". De Paor's essay also includes an
analysis of the origins and evolution of the Unionist ideology in Ireland,
comparing it to its republican counterpart. De Paor identifies two main
strands of Unionist thinking: (i) the eighteenth-century Unionism of
the New•Light Northern Presbyterians which had close links with the
Scottish enlightenment and was not always inimical to republicanism;
(ii) the modern Unionism derived on the one hand from the imperialist
ideology of the late nineteenth century (related to the Home Rule
debates) and from social Darwinism on the other.

Desmond Fennell's survey of socialist ideology in Ireland covers
both the utopian socialist experiments of the eighteenth and nineteenth centuries and the democratic nationalist socialism of the Irish
Labour movement in our own century. In these intellectual movements
he counts such figures as Thompson, Doherty, O'Connor, Bronterre,
O'Brien, Vandaleur, Davitt, Devoy, Russell (AE), Connolly and Larkin.

Fennell analyses how these Irish socialists drew in an eclectic and often original way from English utilitarians such as Bentham, from utopian socialists such as Owen, Proudhon and Fourrier and on occasion from the revolutionary communism of Marx – in order to enunciate socialist projects, mainly of a cooperative or trade union character, tailored to the specific needs of the Irish rural and urban experience. Though the Irish socialist theoreticians and practitioners never actually constituted an unbroken intellectual tradition, most of them did share–like the liberal Burke–a profound distrust of state monopoly. George Russell expressed this decentralising sentiment succinctly when he remarked that "Governments in great nation-states, even representative governments, are not malleable by the general will. If Irish self-government, which all the Irish socialists sought in one form or other, were really to be government by the people then the national assembly governed by general interests" would, Russell insisted, have to be founded upon localised "councils, representative of classes and special interests." In this context Fennell usefully draws our attention to the often ignored fact that Connolly propounded a similar ideal of "cooperative commonwealth" based on decentralised syndicalist models. Fennell offers an account of the way in which radical Irish thinkers, notably Connolly, conceded the necessity in Ireland for a socialist commitment to national and non-sectarian (albeit frequently religiously motivated)[36] social liberation. Connolly was determined to cultivate a specifically native brand of socialist theory. To this end, he actually took the bold step of reinterpreting Irish revolutionary nationalism in socialist terms. He maintained that primitive, self-governing communities had already existed in Ireland under the Gaelic clan system up to the seventeenth century, and "that an Irish socialist republic would therefore be a restoration, in contemporary terms, of this native Irish principle." Consequently, Connolly not only rewrote Irish labour history from the seventeenth century forward, highlighting the socialist contributions made by Thompson, the Young Irelanders and radical Fenianism, but he also recorded the revolutionary implications of cultural movements such as the Irish language and literary revivals. In short, what Yeats and others did for Irish culture by "inventing" a literary tradition, Connolly did for Irish politics by invoking an indigenous heritage of radical thought. He was, of course, greatly assisted in this task by unorthodox socialists like AE, capable of combining a talent for concrete praxis (e.g. his cooperative diary scheme) with a flair for metaphysical speculation, typified in his quaint dictum that "nations evolve around certain ideals as part of the cosmic plan."[37]

Fennell also observes the decline of Connolly's socialist tradition in Ireland due to the fact that its sporadic attempts to resurface in the Irish workers' league, in the radical wings of the Labour party or in the I.R.A. (e.g. Mellows, Gilmore, O'Donnell, MacBride, Johnston, Goulding and MacGiolla) all proved ultimately impotent "in the face of the double-edged fact that the mass of the labour movement and its formal leadership were committed to state paternalism and that Fianna Fáil was on the way to making this the socio-economic orthodoxy of the state."

Perhaps it is still possible to retrieve the submergent tradition of Connolly's socialist ideology, with full cognisance of its national and international implications. E.P. Thompson is one English intellectual who acknowledges, more explicitly in fact than most Irish intellectuals, the Irish contribution to the British radical movements of the late eighteenth and nineteenth centuries. He suggests that we would do well to reclaim our original heritage of political thought and recognise the international role it could play in overcoming the ideological hegemonies of east and west: "Ireland must act to end the power blocks . . . The Irish sell themselves short. I don't think they act and behave as they could do, as a nation of influence with an incredibly long significant history in western civilisation. Ireland has allowed itself to shrink into smaller stature. This also goes together with self-preoccupation; and self-preoccupation with one's own problems and sufferings doesn't make for good internationalism."[38]

* * * * * * * *

These three main tendencies in Irish political thought—liberal, republican and socialist—cannot be said to comprise a single or uniform intellectual tradition. It is undeniable nonetheless, that at certain historical junctures all three have been known to overlap or intertwine, e.g. with Tone and the United Irishmen, with Russell, Connolly, Mellows and others. It is also true that all three ideologies shared a pronounced disinclination for orthodox models of political thought—generally of English provenance—and an equally pronounced inclination to readapt foreign, usually French, ideological precedents to specifically Irish concerns. One could cite here Burke's liberal adaptation of Montesquieu; Tone's republican adaptation of Robespierre and Voltaire; Connolly's socialist adaptation of Marx, Fourier and the French utopianists. The fact that these ideological transplantations were all in some respect marked by an emphatic hostility towards centralised orthodoxy cannot be fully explained as merely a separatist reaction to British colonialism. Might this habitual phenomenon of political decentralisation and dissent (or "segmentation" as MacCana refers to it in its early Irish manifestation) have something to do with recurring political attitudes of the Irish mind?[39] This was not, in any case, too far-fetched an hypothesis for such a committed realist as Connolly.

Aesthetic-Literary Thought

The fourth section of this book investigates the intellectual achievements of certain Irish writers. Since we have already outlined some key pre-occupations of the Irish literary mind, our comments here can be brief.

Elizabeth Cullingford writes about Yeats's "unknown thought", a phrase Yeats himself employed to convey his belief that ultimate truth retains its inexhaustible fascination for the questing and questioning mind precisely because it remains, in part at least, irreducibly other, beyond the reaches of positivistic possession. Cullingford documents Yeats's transformation of the ideas of neoplatonism, mysticism, Continental idealism and modern political theory into an original confection of literary thought and thinking literature. Apart from some intemperate anti-intellectual posturings in his early Arnoldian phase, Yeats recognised the essential poverty of an Irish culture devoid of contemplative and critical intellect. "With Irish literature and Irish thought alone have I to do," declared the more mature Yeats; and in his poem *To Ireland in the Coming Times* we find him praying that "the thought of Ireland (may) brood/Upon a measured quietude." Cullingford discerns in Yeats several of those distinguishing features of the Irish mind inventoried in our opening analysis: (i) a dialectical rapport between the experiences of marginality or exile—in Yeats's case in England—and of cultural identity; (ii) a determination to resist the logocentric opposition between intellect and imagination, theory and praxis, abstract and concrete, in favour of "embodied truth"; (iii) a deep suspicion of British empiricism and positivism accompanied by a conspicuous preference for Continental idealism, depth-psychology and mysticism (the unorthodox logic of paradox); (iv) a conviction that this alternative logic of *both/and* could best express itself in a comic double vision wherein the antithetical claims of soul and body, eternity and time, transcendence and immanence, could, like the dancer and the dance in *Among School Children*, accede to the "brightening glance" of unity-in-difference.

The three subsequent essays on Irish literary thought indicate how several of these distinguishing features are also to be found in the works of other Irish writers. John Jordan reveals the manner in which dramatists such as Wilde, Shaw and O'Casey succeeded in creating a vibrant theatre of ideas by wedding national literary idioms with international philosophic ones — adopted mainly from the Stoics, Schopenhauer, Nietzsche, Butler and Swedenborg in the case of Shaw, and from the great socialist thinkers such as Morris, Kropotkin and Marx in the case of Shaw, Wilde and O'Casey. Not that the intellectual charge was always transmitted from abroad. O'Casey certainly learned as much about socialist ideology from Connolly as he did from Marx; and as Jorge Luis Borges has remarked, the "flavour of liberation" which Shaw's work inherited from the "sages" bears an uncanny affinity to the metaphysical heresies of John Scottus Eriugena.[40]

In "The Mind of James Joyce", Mark Patrick Hederman traces Joyce's intellectual itinerary through the medieval school of Thomism, the renaissance school of Bruno and Vico and the psychoanalytic school of Freud and Jung. Hederman argues that Joyce collapsed the traditional opposition between literature and philosophy and that the resultant synthesis of creative intellect enabled him to break from the logocentric categories of paternalistic domination (the causal, predetermining creator of theology; the manipulative omniscient author of aesthetics; the censoring superego of psychology) to embrace a new and liberating mode of paternity. This new order found apt expression in Joyce's invention of an "acausal" or "nighttime" language capable of at least "two thinks at a time". Joyce recognised that in such a novel order of thought, the old, logocentric "order is othered." This *othered order* is not to be considered as illogical or even prelogical – however convenient an assumption for the anti-intellectual – but as post-logical; meaning, very simply, that *Finnegans Wake*, for example, is not less but more coherently structured than the traditional logic of linear causal narrative and non-contradiction. As Joyce himself explained: "In writing of the night . . . I felt I could not use words in their ordinary relations and connections. Used that way they do not express how things are in the night, in the different stages – conscious, then semi-conscious, then unconscious."[41] And so he wrote the *Wake*, his "Jungfraud messongebook", where, as he put it, "the forms prolong and multiply themselves, where the visions pass from the trivial to the apocalyptic, where the brain uses the roots of vocables to make others from them which will be capable of naming its phantasms, its allegories, its allusions." Here the "othered" thought patterns work "nichtthemerically" – a multivocal term which convokes the key ideas of *night-time, non-thematic, numerically* and *nichts* (nothingness). This last connotation of the preoriginal void or "nichts" provides us with a further clue to the aesthetic of creative intelligence which typifies the Joycean mind. In Joyce's comic rewriting of the Johannine logos—"In the Buginning is the Woid"—we rediscover the same obsession with a non-logocentric metaphysics of creation which Borges has attributed to both Shaw and Eriugena in his own suggestive conspectus of Irish intellectual history. Commenting on Shaw's enigmatic admission, "I understand everything and everyone and I am nothing and no one," Borges wrote: "From the nothingness, so comparable to that of God before creating the world, so comparable to that primordial divinity which another Irishman, Johannes Socttus Eriugena, called *nihil*, Bernard Shaw educed almost innumerable persons or *dramatis personae*."[42] Borges might also have been commenting here on the intellectual disposition of Joyce himself.

Joyce was clearly aware of, not to say fascinated by Eriugena's original contribution to metaphysical thought. In *Finnegans Wake* he delights in punning on "erigenal" and "original"; and in a passage replete with allusions to beehive huts and monastic abodes he hails Eriugena as "the most pure human being that ever was called man, loving all up and down the whole of creation..."[43] Joyce championed Eriugena's heretical subversion of logocentric metaphysics in a lecture entitled "Ireland, Island of Saints and Sages", delivered in Trieste in 1907. Here he commemorates the great "heresiarch ... Scottus Eriugena, Rector of the University of Paris, a mystical pantheist who translated from the Greek the books of the mystical theology of Dionysius, the pseudo-Areopagite, patron saint of the French nation. This translation presented to Europe for the first time the transcendental philosophy of the Orient."[44]

In my concluding study of Beckett's "demythologising" intellect, I attempt to show how Beckett developed the Joycean conflation of literature and philosophy into a radical rewriting of some of the cardinal movements of western thought—in particular, Cartesian idealism, mystical theology and contemporary Continental hermeneutics. But Beckett's literary demythologising of certain reified fictions of western logocentrism, is motivated not by a desire to dispense with fiction but to make it still possible, to be able to go on creating new images, thinking new thoughts, producing new myths, in a world where the creative mind seems almost everywhere in retreat. "I can't go on, I'll go on," is Beckett's own two-thinking response to this dilemma.

The Irish writers under discussion in this fourth section all illustrate, in their distinct ways, the Heideggerian plea that the thinker (*Denker*) and the writer (*Dichter*) abandon the rival camps, to which they have been for so long confined, and finally acknowledge their common allegiance to the 'creative' mind—not just for the sake of their respective vocations but for the sake of the human society which has created them and is recreated by them.

Scientific Thought
In the fifth and final section, Gordon Herries Davies provides an informative survey of Irish thinking in the realm of science. The stereotype of the 'mindless Irish' frequently found expression in a radical opposition between so-called 'native' romantic fantasy and 'foreign' scientific reason. Herries Davies challenges this *cliché*. He demonstrates that Ireland can boast of distinguished contributions to astronomy, geophysics, electromagnetism, mathematics, botany, chemistry, geology and natural history. The author documents the achievements of some fifty Irish scientists in the eighteenth and nineteenth centuries, most notably Kirwan, Molyneux, Callan, Cooper, Griffith, Conway, Walton and Hamilton.

These scientific thinkers, who often combined creative imagination with a rigorous commitment to empirical data, flourished in such institutions as the Royal Irish Academy, The Dublin Society and the Royal College of Science for Ireland, providing research of international importance in conferences and journals which drew the attention and collaboration of some of the finest scientists overseas. (In 1864, for instance, the Natural History Society of Dublin sent its journal to 109 libraries outside the British Isles.)

In the face of such impressive evidence of the national and international significance of Irish scientific thinking, Herries Davies asks why Ireland has chosen "largely to ignore the very considerable achievements of those of her sons who have devoted themselves to science?" Part of the answer, he suggests, may be that some of our historians felt "more comfortable in discussions of banking, battles and bishops, than in dealing with problems concerning basalt, bionomials and brachiopods". He also asks if this conspicuous omission or erasure in our contemporary historical awareness of the Irish mind, might not have something to do with the fact that most of Ireland's scientists in the nineteenth century were drawn from the Protestant, Anglo-Irish Ascendancy and might so be dismissed as 'non-Irish'?

In this respect, Herries Davies' study stands as a rebuke to the racist revisionism of D.P. Moran and his ilk who argued that 'the Gael must be the element that absorbs' all other minority cultural traditions, lest 'pagan, alien and un-Irish philosophies' corrupt our national being. Herries Davies comes close to AE's affirmation of a cultural pluralism where all the children of the island be cherished equally, irrespective of the 'purity' of their racial genes or religion: "We do not want uniformity in our culture, but the balancing of our diversities in a wide tolerance. The moment we had complete uniformity our national life would be stagnant".

Reminding us of the remarkable attainments of Ireland's scientific thinkers, Herries Davies concludes: "It needs to be emphasised that Richard Griffith's geological map of Ireland is just as much a manifestation of the Irish creative genius as is Orpen's *The Holy Well* – that in Salmon's *Conic Sections* we see an Irish mind at work just as surely as we see De Valera's mind at work in Ireland's 1937 constitution. De Valera himself would hardly have been unaware of such facts; let it be remembered that he harboured a deep admiration for that greatest of Irish mathematicians, William Rowan Hamilton".

*   *   *

This volume does not claim to be comprehensive. Its aim is to isolate and identify some of the more salient accomplishments of Irish thought throughout the centuries. Its method of selection is philosophical, following a hermeneutic guideline which confines interpretation to linguistic texts capable of conceptual analysis. The function of such philosophical hermeneutics (i.e. science of interpretation) is to reflect upon the scripts of the past and to translate them into the concepts of a contemporary understanding.[45]

This methodological limitation of our inquiry to specifically conceptual-ideological texts expressive of the Irish mind inevitably entails omissions. The Irish mind has expressed itself historically in several other important areas which exceed the hermeneutic competence of our present analysis: the visual arts or architecture; social or religious institutions and socio-economic history; the decisive, if eclipsed and often neglected, role of women in Irish society as both creators and transmitters of cultural heritage[46] and so on. Several of these areas have been dealt with in Robert O'Driscoll's *The Celtic Consciousness.* The Irish visual arts, architecture and archaeology have been investigated by such scholars as Anne Crookshank, Bruce Arnold, Maurice Craig, Michael Herity, George Eogan and others.[47] And the whole complex question of socio-cultural history, analysing the continuities of Irish life and society from the early Celtic period to the medieval and modern Christian periods is currently being explored by Proinsias MacCana and Liam De Paor. Such studies cover some of those crucial episodes and transitions in Ireland's cultural history which our own analysis has been unable to explore—for example, the cultural dichotomies which occurred between what we have termed the "mythopoeic" and "metaphysical" systems of expression, or between the early medieval speculation of Eriugena and the modern idealism of Berkeley and the Irish counter-enlightenment. I am thinking particularly of those dichotomies in the native Gaelic order occasioned by the arrival of Christianity and by the Anglo-Norman, Cromwellian or Elizabethan conquests. There is no doubt that such historical factors have conditioned or reflected the modalities of Irish thought. To take a single crucial factor—the emergence of an Irish Christian culture—one might cite the influence of the Christian church on the literature written in Ireland down to the twelfth century; the church's assimilation to the local environment and its relations with ecclesiastical and secular learning abroad; the interaction between faith, asceticism and scholarship as expressed in the numerous ecclesiastical commentaries or the *Hibernensis* legal tracts of the seventh and eighth centuries; the impact of the church reforms of the eleventh and twelfth centuries and the Norman conquest, both of which in their different ways affected the structures of native learning, notably by breaching the insular independence of its patrons, displacing the older monasteries from their predominant role as mediators of literature and scholarship, and introducing new continental orders of Cistercians and friars with their own network of cultural and ecclesiastical connections abroad. All these factors—and many others besides—have gone into the shaping of Irish cultural history and have in their several ways influenced Irish intellectual attitudes and responses; but to investigate them all adequately would be to write a socio-cultural history of Ireland, which is not our purpose nor within our competence. In short, this volume is not intended to be in any sense an all-embracing survey of the evolution of Irish culture or society. Its more modest objective is to examine a number of decisive individual thinkers or philosophical movements which appear to have special significance for the historical development of *intellectual* activity in Ireland and which may help to explain some of its peculiar strengths and limitations.

III
THE PROBLEM OF INTERPRETING THE PAST
The Hermeneutic Debate

There are only facts – I would say: No, facts are precisely what there are not, only interpretations. (Frederick Nietzsche, The Will to Power).

The slamming of the door on the long galleries of historical consciousness is understandable. It has a fierce innocence ... But it is an innocence destructive of civilisation ... without the true fiction of history, without the unbroken animation of a chosen past, we become flat shadows.

(George Steiner, *After Babel*)

The traditional devices for constructing a comprehensive view of history and for retracing the past as a patient and continuous development must be systematically dismantled ... History becomes 'effective' to the degree that it introduces discontinuity into our very being (Michel Foucault, Language, Counter-Memory, Practice*).*

How are we to distinguish between the Irish mind the poets and philosophers have invented and the Irish mind as it really existed in history? In a way, this kind of question presupposes an artificial opposition. But it may usefully be employed to clarify the fundamental problem of trying to interpret the meaning of our intellectual history, of trying to make sense of our past by creating or recreating a tradition.

Seamus Deane has argued elsewhere that we should divest ourselves of the cultural myths of the Irish Revival, and particularly the myth, endorsed by Yeats, of a native Anglo-Irish tradition comprising Berkeley, Burke, Goldsmith, Sheridan and other ascendancy intellectuals.[48] Yeats regrouped these disparate minds under the common banner of anti-modernism. He attributed this anti-modernist quality to the Irishness of their intellectual endeavours, which for him amounted to a concerted hostility to the "filthy modern tide" unleashed by eighteenth-century English philosophy. "Born in such a community," commented Yeats, "Berkeley with his belief in perception, that abstract ideas are mere words, Swift with his love of perfect nature, of the Houyhnhnms, his disbelief in Newton's system and every sort of machine, Goldsmith and his delight in the particulars of common life that shocked his contemporaries, Burke with his conviction that all states not grown slowly like a forest tree are tyrannies, found in England the opposite that stung their own thought into expression and made it lucid."[49] Deane ascribes Yeats's "mythologising" of the past to his intellectual and aesthetic need for coherent "arrangements of history" (for a *continuous* tradition), identifying this with an Hegelian rage for retrospective order. But while Deane credits the aesthetic force of such "historical fictions", he deems it a betrayal of what he calls "the brute facts of history": the signal feature of our *discontinuous* tradition as "an inheritance of colonial history". Hence his plea for the abandonment of the fiction of continuity.

I would not dispute the content of Deane's analysis, only some of his methodological presuppositions. Is not history always translated into story (the French use the same term for both: *histoire*) as soon as it is interpreted by the human mind? And how can history have meaning except through human interpretation? That is, except through its being written or recounted? Deane seems to oppose the fictive claims of myth to the truth claims of sociological analysis. He does not wish to privilege either. He simply exhorts us to acknowledge them as two mutually exclusive orders: one pertaining to imagination, the other to reality. But is not the "realist" methodology of sociological history itself a fictional construct of the mind? Does the scientific reliance upon empirical verification not itself presuppose the positivistic myth of *truth as an objectively observable fact*? In short, is not the abandonment of all myths itself a kind of myth?

I would suggest that what we are dealing with in the Yeatsian hermeneutic of an Irish intellectual tradition is not so much an *unreal* historical fiction to be pitted against the "social literalism" of *real* historical truth, as a myth of one order (Yeats's romantic interpretation) opposing a myth of another order (the enlightenment positivist interpretation). *Both* are hermeneutic constructs. History is never literal; it is a *figurative* reading of events by means of human thought and language. And it is precisely because history is figurative that it is subject to the ethical laws of hermeneutic transfiguration or disfiguration, of liberation or distortion.[50] Every reading of history involves a choice between different interpretative models.

Irish intellectual history, like any other, can be interpreted in a variety of ways. Four of the most obvious hermeneutic models are: (i) an Anglo-Irish ascendancy reading; (ii) a nationalist/republican reading; (iii) a positivist/enlightenment reading; (iv) a socio-economic or Marxist reading. The existence of these rival hermeneutics simply testifies that history is a carrier of multiple, and often conflicting, readings of the same historical phenomena. And one cannot appeal to the putatively *neutral* court of fact—the way it *really* was—without in turn resorting to a particular mode of *interpretation* (i.e. the hermeneutic of positivism). Facts are devoid of meaning until they are interpreted by human thinking and praxis. "Tradition," as Terry Eagelton reminds us, "is the practice of ceaselessly excavating, safeguarding, violating, discarding and reinscribing the past . . . history is not a fair copy, but a palimpsest, whose deleted layers must be thrust to light."[51]

This is not to deny that it is the ethical duty of the critical, discernin mind to discriminate between hermeneutic rivals. (What, after all, is this publication but an attempt, amongst other things, to debunk the myth of the mindless Irish.) But one cannot discriminate and debunk by presuming privileged access to some pre-interpretative experience. History cannot pre-exist hermeneutic invention.[52] And here we must restore to this word, invention, the double etymological connotation originally carried (before its romantic idealist distortion) by the Latin *inventio*, meaning both *creation* and *discovery*: the hermeneutic projection of that reading which resides in latent or potential form in the events of history. Historical meaning is neither exclusively subjective (as the romantic idealist claims) nor exclusively objective (as the positivist empiricist holds). It precedes the division into such extremes of subjectivism and objectivism. The meanings of our past emerge from a reciprocal act in which interpreter and what is interpreted each contribute to the identification of a pattern. This is perhaps the single most revolutionary discovery of contemporary philosophical hermeneutics as formulated by Heidegger, Ricoeur and the Frankfurt school.

*   *   *

Deane asserts that Yeats's interpretations of an Anglo-Irish intellectual tradition "can only be understood as myths, as versions of history converted into a metaphor." I agree. But I would reread the "only" in this sentence as denoting a condition of possibility rather than of disqualification. This is not to suggest that we should dispense with the critical duty to demythologise cultural myths and metaphors whenever they assume a reactionary or perverse guise. But in discharging our hermeneutic duties we should not delude ourselves into thinking that such a critique can ever lead us back to some pristine, pre-interpreted world of fact. An authentic hermeneutic demythologises the dehumanising myths of history in order to recreate new and more liberating ones.[53]

Deane does, however, appear to recognise implicitly the unavoidable existence of the hermeneutic circle when he concedes that the Yeatsian Revival myths "survive because they have no serious competitors" (presumably no serious alternative myths); or when he regrets that the influence of the Joycean hermeneutic "on Irish modes of thought has been negligible compared with that of Yeats and even Synge."[54]

What hermeneutic competitors to the Yeatsian reading might we consider? First there is Joyce's critical rereading of the Irish Revival tradition of the heroic imagination. The main target here is, as Deane observes, Stephen Dedalus who prides himself, like Yeats and Wilde, on being a "priest of the eternal imagination", a *salvator mundi* transmuting the daily bread of history into the hieratic word of art. Through his deflation of Stephen's aesthetic pretensions (ironically played off against the more humane and life-embracing aesthetic of Bloom and Molly), Joyce repudiates the imperial wilfulness of the romantic hero at war with history. But by presuming that history, in this context, comprises a "literal" world of "class problems, economics, bureaucratic systems and the like"—Deane finds himself, paradoxically, invoking the old dualism between subjective imaginings and objective "brute facts", which he lauds Joyce for trying to surpass. What this dualistic presupposition fails to adequately appreciate is that the "brute facts" of class exploitation and economic bureaucracy are themselves products of dehumanising political ideologies. As Habermas and the Frankfurt school have taught us, capitalism and communism are themselves derived from hermeneutic rereadings of history.[55]

*   *   *

While Deane and Kinsella interpret Irish intellectual history in terms of a hermeneutic of discontinuity, other critics such as Frank O'Connor and Vivian Mercier have chosen to reaffirm a hermeneutic of continuity – albeit from a perspective different to that of Yeats. In the *Irish Comic Tradition* (1962), Mercier advances a retrospective overview of Irish culture ranging from early Gaelic to late Anglo-Irish literature. He isolates the comic character of the Irish mind as a recurring feature of our tradition. But Mercier's unfamiliarity with the Gaelic tradition left him vulnerable to the charge of under-estimating the basic disruption in Irish culture occasioned by the break-up of the Gaelic tradition. The hermeneutic of continuity may not, however, be so easily dismissed. Frank O'Connor, one of Ireland's most eminent translators from the Gaelic,[56] also promoted the idea of a continuous Irish cultural tradition. In *The Backward Look* (1967), O'Connor composed a critical survey spanning the entire course of Gaelic and Anglo-Irish literature. His argument for continuity stems from the conviction that both literatures share a common *retrospective* vision: whence the title. "I am not sure," he writes, "that any country can afford to discard what I have called the backward look, but we in Ireland can afford it less than any other because without it we have nothing and are nothing." His study is divided into two parts: the first dealing with Gaelic literature down to the seventeenth century, the second with Irish literature in

English from the seventeenth century to the present with special emphasis on Yeats, O'Casey, Synge, Stephens and Joyce. O'Connor's reading is facilitated by his omission of any serious reference to the literature written in Irish since the revival.[57] Notwithstanding this, he does make a strong case for a certain kind of cultural continuity: a sort of continuity in discontinuity. Speaking of the structural composition of the *Táin*, for example, O'Connor sees it as a multi-layered excavation site with a transversal vein of reinterpretations: "Some I cannot identify at all, but I think I can isolate a seventh century substratum in archaic verse; an eighth century rendering of this in good narrative prose, which more or less corresponds with what the lawyers were trying to do at the same time with the charted laws; definitely there is a ninth century layer, very elegant, but less vigorous than the earlier strata; and finally, as the influence of the Norse invasions become felt, there is a recrudescence of the oral element . . ." and so on. O'Connor's account illustrates the hermeneutic lesson that meaning can only be historically constituted and transmitted as a palimpsest of ever receding, ever recurring readings. There is no original *arche* that could be recovered as some sort of pure prelinguistic presence. History is an endless text incorporating a horizonal context of *possible* readings which can only be actualised by each interpretation. History is thus an interplay of multiple re-inscriptions: a play of re-creation. As the old Irish epigram on pilgrimages to Rome reminds us: "The King you seek there,/ Unless you bring Him with you, You will not find him."

O'Connor finds interconnections everywhere in the "immense mass" of a thousand years and more of Irish literature, in both English and Gaelic. He divines links between the literary revivals inaugurated by Ferguson, Mangan, Hyde, Pearse and Yeats and the 1916 Rising; and between both of these and the ancient Celtic saga tradition. Emphasising Ireland's Indo-European roots, O'Connor concludes that we are "a people of The Book," and as such can "no more escape from the burden of tradition than the Jews have been able to escape from the Pentateuch."[58]

Is it a mere coincidence that O'Connor, like Deane and Kinsella, is both a critical and creative writer? Probably not. These three interpreters of our cultural tradition have successfully combined intellectual and poetic sensibilities. This bifocal hermeneutic fidelity exemplifies one of the central hypotheses of this introduction – that the Irish mind has succeeded, in several important respects, in eschewing the orthodox dualism between intellect and imagination, between conceptual and aesthetic creativity which has been a hallmark of the western logocentric tradition.[59]

It is not, of course, being suggested that the Irish mind is the only European instance of non-logocentric expression. One could, no doubt, cite examples of other European—not to mention non-European—cultures which resisted, transcended or simply remained on the periphery of Graeco-Roman logocentrism.[60] It is undeniable, however, that the Irish mind is one of the most sustained examples of such intellectual difference and dissent.

*   *   *

Some might object that the debate concerning the conflicting readings of Irish intellectual history and in particular the rival interpretations of continuity and discontinuity is simply not worth such expense of time, space and energy. Seán O'Faoláin, for one, has expressed the view that the main trouble with modern Ireland stems from that "old curse and bore", our "revered, unforgettable indestructible, irretrievable past . . . the underground stream that keeps on vanishing and reappearing."[61] O'Faoláin attributes such preoccupations to the mesmerising atavisms of "myth and mystique" epitomised in what he calls the "atrocity" of nationalism. The curse and bore of the past is also evinced, he insists, in our political ineptitude and inability to govern ourselves: "All our life-ways remained for far too long based on social structures dependent on the primitive idea of the local ruler, while Europe was developing the more powerful concept of the centralised state." Against this intellectual self excoriation, so typical of that post-colonial servility which repudiates its own past, I would invoke the pronouncement of Sir Samuel Ferguson that we should attend to the records of our past in order that we may liberate our minds by "living back in the land we live in."[62]

But can we *look back* without anger or nostalgia? Can we *live back* without resorting to the opiates of racist nationalism or reactionary conservatism? Or to put it in more pertinent terms for our present purposes, how may we *think back* in order to think forward in an intellectually emancipating manner?

The first assumption to be dispelled is that the past constitutes some abstract evolutionary chain leading from the bad, to the better, to the best (the progressivist illusion); or indeed from the best to the bad (the regressivist illusion). We might take our cue here from the philosopher Walter Benjamin who wrote in the thirties: "In every era the attempt must be made anew to wrest tradition away from the conformism that is about to overpower it."[63] Benjamin recognised that the only way to confront such conformism is to think through the tradition in a critical and creative fashion. The deletion of the past from our minds is the best recipe for enslavement to it. Or as Arland Ussher, the contemporary Irish philosopher, remarked: "The sentimentalist would like to look at the past as a mere picture hung upon the wall. But the past is throbbing with a secret life, like a dragon's egg."[64] One of the most insidious kinds of conformism to overpower the sense of Irish tradition is, I have been arguing, the racist stereotype of the heroic, thoughtless Celt (a stereotype which has been variously deployed for colonial and also chauvinistic nationalist reasons). Accordingly, history must be continually reinvestigated and revised not just that we may expose its stereotypes, but so that we may restore its forfeited or discarded fragments. Corkery's "hidden Ireland", Kinsella's and Ó Tuama's "poems of the dispossessed" or Montague's "lost tradition" are retrieved from oblivion only by an initial acknowledgement of loss. In similar fashion, the neglected heritage of the Irish intellect can only be reclaimed by challenging the prejudices which occasioned such neglect.

Tradition is not just some homogeneous totality, it is a multilayered manuscript with each layer recording some new crisis, rupture or spasm which has altered the course of history. Consequently, while historicism —as advanced by the liberal humanists or the Second Marxist International—tended to read history teleologically as a causally determined sequence of events, a more authentic hermeneutic will, in Benjamin's words, "brush history against the grain," thereby salvaging its repressed lineages, unmasking reactionary ideologies and reminding us that "there is no cultural document that is not at the same time a record of barbarism."[65] To ignore or to disregard our past is, ironically, to remain in corrosive collusion with it. The past is thus taken for granted and robbed of its critical potentiality to challenge the imposing ideologies of the present. The question of tradition is too often consigned to quarantined remoteness, or misconstrued as an exclusive dialect of the tribe to be purified by the elect. In this regard one must be equally wary of the Eliotic view of tradition as a pantheon of eternal monuments that "form an ideal order among themselves," an order which is "complete before (any) new work arrives."[66] More authentic is the view that tradition is a seedbed of multiple readings which subvert any pretension to univocal self-identity or self-completion.

In the field of Irish intellectual history which concerns us, this means accepting our tradition as a medley of rupturing, irregular and often suppressed perspectives, a tradition which comprises such diverse claimants as the pre-Celtic ideology of Newgrange; the Celtic ideologies of old and middle Irish myth; the medieval, Christian vision of Eriugena; the dispossessed mind of the Gaelic 'hidden' Ireland; the Anglo-Irish ascendancy tradition of Berkeley, Swift, Burke, Shaw, Wilde, Yeats and many of our scientific thinkers; the political ideologies of Irish socialism, republicanism and liberalism; the nationalist aesthetic of the Fenian poets, Mangan, Davis and Pearse; the self-scrutinising critical modernism of Joyce, Beckett and many of our contemporary writers.

To interrogate this plurality of conflicting interpretations is to open ourselves to those other, often occluded possibilities of being ourselves from which our constricting present may have alienated us. Hence the necessity for an openended hermeneutic which Benjamin describes as a "science of history whose subject matter is not a tangle of purely factual details, but consists rather of the numbered group of threads that represent the weft of the past as it feeds into the warp of the present."[67] Such a hermeneutic disengages us from the reifying predeterminism of history; it sidesteps both the historicist cult of a pre-ordained continuum and the post-modernist cult of arbitrary fragmentation, in order to engage us with genuine questioning. There is, I suggest, no better hermeneutic guide to the present work than Benjamin's own blueprint: "For successful excavation a plan is needed. Yet not less indispensable is the cautious probing of the spade in the loam; it is to cheat oneself of the richest prize to preserve as a record merely the inventory of one's discoveries, and not this darkjoy of the place of the finding itself. Fruitless searching is as much a part of this as succeeding, and consequently remembrance must not proceed in the manner of a narrative or still less of a report, but must, in the strictest epic or rhapsodic fashion, assay its spade in ever-new places, and in the old ones delve to ever deeper layers."[68]

Richard Kearney

PART I

1

Brendan Purcell

IN SEARCH OF NEWGRANGE:
LONG NIGHT'S JOURNEY INTO DAY

Ireland has been inhabited from about 7,500 BC, very shortly after the end of the last Ice Age, according to recent discoveries at Mount Sandel (Derry), Carrowmore (Sligo), Lough Boora (Offaly) and Randelstown (Meath). Some 4,000 years later the northern half of the country was inhabited by the Neolithic-A people, well-organised agriculturists and stockbreeders with comfortable cottage-sized dwellings, whose (court) tombs are almost completely undecorated.[1] However, it was the people of the Boyne Culture, coming perhaps from Brittany towards the end of the fourth millenium BC, whose four major cemeteries, at Newgrange and Lough Crew in Meath, and at Carrowkeel and Carrowmore in Sligo, mark the first deep expression of a unique, native or "Irish" mind. The Boyne people belonged to a Far Western European neolithic civilisation which extended from Iberia, Brittany and Britain to Denmark and Sweden. Yet they transformed and expanded their spiritual and artistic heritage with a controlled freedom which has produced one of the most original and exciting bodies of prehistoric symbolism extant in the history of archaic humankind. Michael Herity has noted that their artistic richness remained unequalled in Ireland until the coming of the Celts some 1,500 years later: "Significantly it was the Celts who showed their appreciation of this culture by weaving their own mythical recon-struction around it."[2]

If we can presume that the three mounds of New Grange, Knowth and Dowth, now dated at c.3200 BC, constitute the deepest expression of the Boyne people's search for the mystery of their existence, we have to ask ourselves how we can go in search of their search. For their history, since they belonged to the same family of humankind as we do, is a piece of our own history, even if we are separated by over five thousand years. Whatever insight, wisdom, meditation, tragic anguish and happiness they developed or achieved through their symbols and rites is a development and achievement for our humanity too. Ruaidhri de Valera quoted a nineteenth century archaeologist's response to seeing the stone circles at Lough Gur: "What marvellous manuscripts if we could only read them."[3] Is there any way we can make Newgrange's illuminated manuscripts of finite stone transparent for the transfinite divine-cosmic reality which engendered them?

In fact, the past thirty years have brought about a completely changed situation with regard to our possible grasp of the symbols of Newgrange which still beckon to us across five millennia. Four factors have contributed to this. Thanks to the magnificent work of M.J. O'Kelly on New Grange and of George Eogan on Knowth, the most basic requirement for understanding these expressions of neolithic experience, their excavation and restoration, has been largely achieved.[4] Secondly there has been the discovery by Alexander Thom, Gerald Hawkins and others that many sites in Brittany, England and Scotland were deliberately constructed from 3,500 BC to 1,500 BC in astonishingly accurate alignments with specific solar and lunar positions.[5] Professor O'Kelly's discovery of the solar alignment of New Grange in 1969 indicates the relevance of this second level of mathematical and astronomical archaeology to the Irish sites as well. A third level in the understanding of Newgrange has been made possible by a remarkable advance in the study of archaic symbols and the experiences which engender them. Particularly relevant are Marie König's exploration of the late paleolithic (30,000 to 10,000 BC), mesolithic (10,000 to 4,000 BC) and neolithic (4,000 to 1,000 BC) symbols, along with Mircea Eliade's examination of neolithic and post-neolithic archaic cultures.[6] Finally, the work of Eric Voegelin has put the study of archaic experience and symbolisation on a completely new basis by placing it in the context of a range of equivalent answers, cosmological, philosophical and revelational, to the constant question arising throughout history regarding the mystery of existence.[7] Since the first, archaeological level, is being documented, and the hard work of measurement and correlation required for the second, mathematical and astronomical level, is only beginning, the present essay will attempt an elucidation of the depth-experience of existence still expressed through symbols and silent rite at the Bend of the Boyne in terms of the revolution in understanding of archaic symbols and their underlying cosmology.

This elucidation, which has the character of an extended interpretative hypothesis, will examine five preliminary groupings of Boyne Culture symbols. Drawing on the categories employed by König, we will discuss Newgrange in terms of its symbolisation of place, of time, of partnership between place and time, of the whole, and of story.[8] Because of the wealth of symbols to be examined, this quite preliminary presentation will resemble a neolithic "dictionary" of particular symbols, or a neolithic "grammar" of specific usages and symbol-combinations. However, of any symbols of the mystery of existence it can be said that "their meaning can be understood only if they evoke, and through evocation reconstitute, the engendering reality" in the interpreter, in this case of the Irish neolithic vision of existence.[9] All an exploration of this sort can do, with the help of the interpretative context drawn

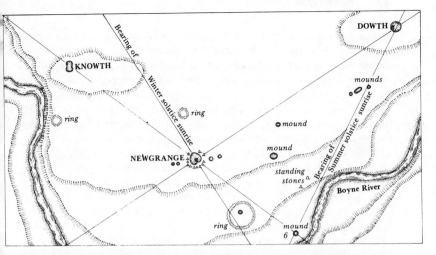

Knowth, Newgrange and Dowth. Reproduced from *The Boyne Valley Vision* by Martin Brennan (Dolmen Press Ltd.) by kind permission.

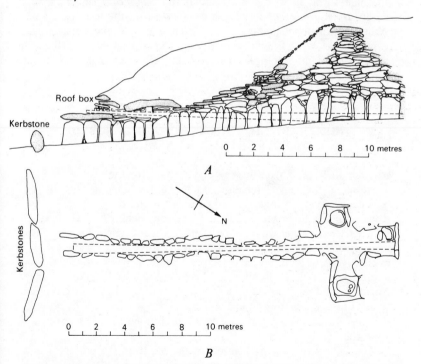

Inside New Grange. The dashed lines indicate the path of the sun's rays at midwinter solstice. Based on a diagram in J. Patrick, 'Midwinter Sunrise at Newgrange', *Nature*, 249 (1974) and reprinted in *Sun, Moon and Standing Stones* by John Edwin Wood (Oxford University Press, 1978)

principally from König, Eliade and Voegelin, is to help the interpreter a little on the upward path towards reconstituting in himself or herself the spiritual outburst which gave rise to Newgrange.

To introduce our exploration, a bare statement of its guiding presuppositions, drawn from Voegelin's own work on archaic symbolisations, will be necessary. We can presume that the people of the Boyne Culture, like other archaic peoples, were aware that they belonged to the whole community of being, including humans, society, the world and the gods. They would also have seen a certain hierarchy of lastingness and passing away, in that as individuals they were outlasted by their own society, which in turn was outlasted by the world, which itself was outlasted by the gods, or even created by them.[10] Earth, along with the unchanging rhythms of her plants and animals, and the heavens, with their unchanging cycles of the sun, moon and stars, would have been the overwhelmingly powerful and more lasting partners in the community of being. By attunement to these more lasting partners, humans could open their ephemeral existence to participation in some form of everlasting being. Herity and Eogan conclude their study, *Ireland in Prehistory,* with a statement on the need for "a new philosophical understanding of the actual and potential archaeological evidence."[11] What follows is an attempt to point towards the direction such a new philosophical understanding of Newgrange might take.

I

HOMEWARDS TO THE CENTRE OF THE WORLD: SYMBOLS OF PLACE AT NEWGRANGE

Whether they came from nearby or far away, for the people who had constructed the three immense tumuli in the Bend of the Boyne, Newgrange must have represented their Jerusalem, their Athens or their Rome, the spiritual centre of their lives. Approaching New Grange, the first barrier they met would have been the Great Circle, which then had thirty-five, but is now reduced to twelve massive standing stones. That circle (which in fact, like New Grange mound, is ovoid in shape) most impressively marked the boundary between the sacred and the profane. Not only did the circle signify a divine presence within the sacred place, it also protected people from the danger they would incur by entering that place unsanctified, without having performed the right gestures of approach.[12]

The same ritual of marking off the sacred from the profane would have been repeated even more emphatically by the three huge stones guarding the entrance to the passage. Having been allowed to proceed thus far, there is now the upward slope of the long passage (in Knowth and Dowth there are sill stones to make entrance a more difficult ritual,

Five shallow grooves on R21, at centre of Newgrange.

while the Knowth passages are much longer)[13] recalling what Eliade has written about rites of ascent: "The transcending of the human condition by entering a sacred place, by some ritual consecration, or by dying, is expressed concretely as a 'passage', a 'rising', an 'ascension'. Death means transcending the human state and 'passing to what is beyond'. In those religions which place the other world in the sky or in some higher sphere, the souls of the dead trudge up mountain paths, or clamber up a tree."[14] The ascent is made at least ritually tortuous by its deliberately constructed bends, bringing to mind the archaic notion of the labyrinth, which expressed a gradual initiation undergone to approach the centre more worthily.[15]

The centre of what? The primary place or home of man is the earth, one of man's great partners in the community of being. As in many archaic cultures, the Boyne people may have considered the earth as a mother, "that is, as giving birth to living forms which it draws out of its own substance. The earth is 'living' first of all because it is fertile. Everything that comes from the earth is endowed with life, and everything that goes back into the earth is given new life. What we call life and death are merely two different moments in the career of the earth-mother as a whole: life is merely being detached from the earth's womb, death is a returning 'home'."[16] The earth is often symbolised as a four-sided figure, as a square or as a lozenge. The four sides would represent the four quarters or points of the sun's most extreme movements over the earth at the midsummer and midwinter solstices and at the equinoxes.[17] It is at least possible that the numerous squares and lozenges at Newgrange are earth-symbols.

The passage is also the shaft of what opens out to become a cross-shaped chamber. König has noted many examples of right-angled and diagonal crosses from 30,000 BC onwards, and regards them as symbolising the earth, with the additional significance of the centre represented by their point of intersection.[18] Certainly there are many indications of possible centre symbolisation at the fifth point where the four parts of the cross meet. While direct continuity of traditions between the Boyne people and the Celts would seem almost impossible to establish, it is interesting that the Old Irish name for Meath, *An Mhidhe*, the county where Newgrange is located, meant "the centre" or "central area". Nora Chadwick notes that in the *Táin* there are four peoples, from the four provinces. Yet the provinces were known as "fifths", *cóiceda*, as if there were a fifth province, "though only four divisions are certainly known, the fifth being disputed."[19] Possibly this "fifth" was less a political area than a symbol of cosmic order, only later becoming an actual fifth province, Meath. The symbolism of the "fifth" as a centre occurs almost universally, from the Aztecs to ancient China. For the Chinese, the fifth, central point, was not only the horizontal axis of the empire, but also the vertical axis through which heaven contacted the earth through the emperor, who was thereby filled with celestial wisdom which radiated outwards to the subject kingdoms in the form of imperial decrees.[20]

The corbelled vault rising vertically above the horizontal cruciform axis both in New Grange and in Knowth East would seem to express an experience of the intersection of the heavens with the earth. And since the burial remains were grouped in the three chambers around the centre, the underworld was presumably considered as intersecting there too. Herity quotes Molyneux, who in 1726 spoke of "a slender quarry-stone, five or six feet long shaped like a pyramid which originally stood in the central chamber."[21] This would have intensified the symbolism of the centre as a vertical as well as a horizontal axis.

An expansion of the symbolisation of the earth as four-sided may be found in the variations on the number 12, as, for example, three squares, one inside the other. König takes these boxed squares to symbolise the three places — heaven, earth and underworld — that go to make up the whole world.[22] This might be the meaning of the three triple squares-within-squares on the left, and the large triple square on the right, of the entrance stone at New Grange which is almost bisected by a vertical line. Perhaps they are to remind us that we are coming to the centre of the world, where the three regions, heaven, earth and underworld inter-sect. What Eliade has to say about the symbol of the mountain at the centre of the world may help us to appreciate how the Boyne people could have felt about their three holy mountains: "The mountain, because it is the meeting place of heaven and earth, is situated at the centre of the world, and is of course the highest point of the earth." Because they are the place of meeting between the different regions, mountains are "the point through which the Axis of the World goes, a region impregnated with the sacred, a spot where one can pass from one cosmic zone to another."[23]

Again, Eliade, discussing the symbol of the centre, has remarked that "Hell, the Centre of the Earth, and the 'gate' of Heaven are therefore found on the same axis, and it is through this axis that passage from one cosmic region to another is possible."[24] Would not this explain the importance of the Newgrange mounds for their builders? "Every human being tends towards the centre and towards his own centre, which con-fers on him integral reality, 'sacredness'. This desire, profoundly rooted in man, to find himself at the very heart of the real, at the centre of the world, where contact can be made with heaven, explains the prolific use of 'centres of the world'."[25]

Finally, a word about the Boyne people's use of stone as the most important medium for safeguarding their most sacred place, ensuring that it would always enable man to enter into communion with the divine-cosmic source of life. For Eliade,

> the hardness, ruggedness and permanence of matter was in itself a hierophany in the religious consciousness of the primitive. And nothing was more direct and autonomous in

the completeness of its strength, nothing more noble or more awe-inspiring, than a majestic rock, or a boldly-standing block of granite. Above all, stone *is*. It always remains itself. Rock shows him something that transcends the precariousness of his humanity. Stone [at burial grounds] was a protection against animals and robbers, and, above all, against "death", for, as stone was incorruptible, the soul of the dead man must continue to exist as itself.[26]

II

NEW YEAR CELEBRATION:
SYMBOLS OF TIME AT NEWGRANGE

While it is now accepted that the Far Western European neolithic civilisation had a highly developed capacity for astronomic observation, the real question we are faced with is — for what purpose? John Wood, in his survey of this neolithic astronomy is quite clear that its accuracy far exceeded the approximate time measurement required for agriculture.[27] We have already explored how the Boyne people, through attuning themselves to the centre of the earth sought communion with the lastingness of divine-cosmic presence. We may also presume that, in common with other archaic peoples, they desired attunement to the special times in the courses of the sun and the moon, which by their invarying constancy were transparent for the everlasting being of the heavens.

In his chapter on the sun in *Patterns in Comparative Religion,* Eliade details the complex and sometimes apparently contradictory activities and attributes of the sun in archaic cultures, as source of life and as associated with death: "Throughout the north, the gradual shortening of the days as the winter solstice approaches inspires fear that the sun may die away completely. The falling or darkening of the sun becomes one of the signs of the coming end of the world, of the conclusion, that is, of the cosmic cycle, generally to be followed by a new creation and a new human race."[28] The sun is also linked with the dead, whom it accompanies to the underworld through the western 'gate of the sun': "Unlike the moon, the sun has the privilege of passing through hell without undergoing the condition of death; but it can also guide souls through the lower regions and bring them back next day with its light."[29] There are also close links between the sun and kingship. In many parts of the world, kings were supposed to be descendants of the sun, and were themselves called "suns", "children of the sun".

These insights from later archaic cultures may help us to understand the gigantic drama between the sun and the earth's centre re-enacted on that most important sun-day which is the first day of the solar new year. Here, at the centre of the world where heaven, earth and underworld intersect, the Boyne people expressed their experience of the mysterious

K69, "Calendar Stone", Knowth. From *The Boyne Valley Vision* by Martin Brennan (Dolmen Press) by kind permission.

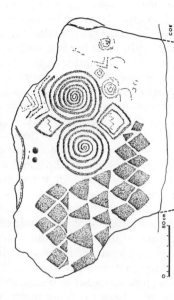

K1, entrance stone to Newgrange. Reproduced by kind permission of Claire O'Kelly.

K52, Kerbstone at back of Newgrange. Reproduced by kind permission of Claire O'Kelly.

K67, Kerbstone at east side of Newgrange. Reproduced by kind permission of Claire O'Kelly.

answer to their search for participation in everlasting order. Here they deployed all their artistic, technological, astronomic and measuring skills to elevate midwinter sunrise into a cosmic *YES* between sun and earth at the zero point of their mutual forsakenness. After the longest night of the year, at sunrise on the shortest day, the direct rays of the sun burst through the narrow roof-box over the entrance, along the winding passage, to the inner chamber, which explodes into light for nearly twenty minutes. Cutting through the heart of all reality, when darkness seems to have finally enveloped the world, light shines. At the time when sun and earth seem closest to the condition of death, the promise of a new year of life draws for both of them. If death had overtaken the people's king, then, in this place at this time, a renewal of kingship is promised through attunement to the silent rebirth of the whole cosmos.

What of the second most brilliant inhabitant of the heavens? Given the enormous difficulty of calculating the solar year exactly (Alexander Marshack notes that, e.g. North American Indians measured time "solely by days, by sleeps, by moons, and by winters. There is no Indian word synonymous with our word year"[30]), it is possible that the moon rather than the sun was the most important cosmic partner when the Boyne people wished to attune themselves to the order of the heavens. Marshack has indicated the ability of paleolithic people from 30,000 BC to construct a system of notation for calculating lunar periods of varying lengths; for example, his examination of hollow eagle bones from a 12,000 BC site at Le Placard has uncovered a complex series of marks representing computations for six months on each side, with what seem to be special markings for a month marking the "turning" of the year.[31] König links the frequent variations on three-symbols with the paleolithic experience of time in its aspect of death and regeneration. This is because of the three moon-phases, each of nine days (leaving two or three days before the beginning of the new month). Common symbols are three straight lines, three dots, three red ochre daubs on stones shaped like a lunar crescent, and especially triangles.[32]

The triangle is one of the most frequent representations at New Grange, and may symbolise the three phases of the moon : birth, fullness, decline. Stonehenge (begun c.2800 BC) which is an expression of the same neolithic civilisation to which the Boyne people belonged, along with its four principal alignments to midsummer and midwinter sunrise and sunset, also has eight principal alignments to moonrise and moonset at the extremes of its greatest and least arcs.[33] It would seem rather unlikely that Newgrange had not some equivalent lunar alignments, the establishment of which, however, will require the same standards of accuracy as have characterised the Stonehenge correlations. Martin Brennan has suggested a clear lunar reference in Knowth kerbstone 69, which he calls the calendar stone. This stone has a series of nine crescents, seven circles and two crescents, and nine more crescents, in a huge semicircular arc and diameter. At the centre of the diameter is a spiral covering two further crescents, possibly indicating the "dead" fourth phase of the moon's cycle. "Attention is thus focused on the western horizon on the thirtieth day, when the new crescent may appear."[34]

The frequent use of single and multiple circles and arcs at Newgrange may also express specific attunements to time. König suggests that such symbols, which are common in paleolithic and mesolithic rock-carvings in the Île-de-France caves, refer to the cyclic rotations of the sun, moon and stars. All of these describe a semicircular bow in the sky and may be presumed to pursue a similar course under the earth, to return to sight once again.[35] By attuning themselves to the glimpses into the eternal Now manifested by the special moments marking the daily, monthly and yearly cycles of solar and lunar waxing and waning, rising and setting, dying and reappearing, the Boyne people could hope for periodic renewals from their own falls into disorder and ultimately from death.

III
THE MARRIAGE OF EARTH AND HEAVEN AT THE ROYAL CENTRE: SYMBOLS OF PARTNERSHIP AT NEWGRANGE

While it would be impossible here to detail all the symbolic motifs to be found at New Grange, we can list a few of the most frequently occurring groupings of symbols. Still invoking our interpretative convention of preferring the "the profounder to the flatter meaning" ([8] above), we can suggest that combinations of three-symbols and four-symbols represent partnership or "marriage" of the eternal heavens with the transfinite earth, and that combinations of three-symbols or three and four-symbols with five-symbols signify partnership occurring at the centre of the earth, which may have the added significance of representing the origin of royal power.[36] As a help to the evocation within us of the engendering reality underlying these symbols, we can remind ourselves of what C. O'Kelly and M. Herity have noted of the highly developed artistic imagination of the Boyne people, who have created several characteristic symbolic "languages" for the different tombs at Newgrange and Loughcrew.[37] These people were perhaps highly stratified (given the marked contrast with the simpler graves, lacking in personal ornamentation, of the so-called Neolithic-A people who seem to have coexisted with the Boyne people[38]). Compared to these others, Herity notes that "the jewellery of the passage grave people showed an unprecedented awareness of personal elegance." He considers on this basis "that the clothing worn by these people was similarly refined."[39] When it comes to determining what he speaks of as their "formal religion", he remarks that "the details remain shadowy."[40] Yet every archaic society has its holy places and holy times. It is enough to recall the four major Irish Celtic festivals, *Beltine* (May 1) and *Samain* (November 1), *Lugnasad* (August 1) and *Oimelc* (February 1), where the first two divided the year into two six-month periods, which were then divided by the second two, to get some idea of how the Boyne people may have, with a different calendar but similar festivities, celebrated their time together at the centre of their world where they felt most at home with their gods.[41] We cannot recreate the colour and sound, the fun and carnivalia that no doubt accompanied these celebrations of cosmic liturgy. Still, the present writer's vivid memories of the gloriously contrasting accents of profundity and gaiety, ritual and spontaneity, that marked the popular liturgies during the Pope's visit to Ireland in September 1979, do not seem inappropriate as indicating a modern Irish equivalent.

The partnerships suggested here are best imagined as occurring within a living cosmic liturgy.

(i)   *Earth and heaven* symbols: One of the most common grouping of symbols at New Grange is that of triangles (symbolising, perhaps, the re-ordering power of lunar rebirth) and squares or lozenges (perhaps symbolising the earth). These can be found, e.g. on K52, the kerbstone diametrically opposite the entrance stone, on K67, a kerbstone on the east side of the mound, on roofslab 17, and on three of the corbel stones in the east recess of the chamber, C12–13, C14, and C16. König regards seven-symbols, if expressing a synthesis of place and time, as "the foundation stone of culture", and gives as examples from the Île-de-France a cross with the ends of two of its arms joined to form a triangle, four points carved within a triangle, and from Lascaux, a square divided into seven areas.[42]

A possible variation on the same theme is provided by the zigzag or snake-in-lozenge representations on K67, and on L19, a standing-stone on the left side of the passage near the centre. For Eliade, this is a common neolithic motif, in which the snake has both a lunar and a phallic significance of regeneration, and the lozenge represents both the earth and the vulva. Together they express "an idea of dualism and re-integration",[43] in the sense, perhaps of a cosmic marriage of heaven and earth.

(ii)   *Earth and heaven and centre* symbols: a particularly beautiful and meditative expression of the intersection of place and regenerating time at the centre is perhaps to be found in a tapestry in stone on C16 in the east recess. Here are picked out five rows of figures, consisting of three rows of triangles and two of lozenges, while the unpicked surface, in a chessboard effect, yields another five rows, two of triangles, two of lozenges, and a bottom row of triangles.

Another possible expression of the partnership of time and place at the centre is the examples of a square or rectangle divided by a diagonal cross into four triangles. This motif, of a four-sided figure divided into four triangles intersecting at a fifth point is given great prominence at

Newgrange by being carved into a row of eight such figures across the lintel stone over the roof-box above the entrance, through which the first sunrays of the New Year pass on their way to the centre. There is also the dynamic group of triangles and lozenges which spring upwards from R21 at the central intersection. Some of these triangles, in addition, form irregular four-sided figures divided by diagonals into rough Maltese crosses. König considers the four triangles to represent the three phases of the moon, along with the "fourth" phase of its two or three dark days.[44]

A somewhat different expression of the same experience may be found in one of the most massive motifs of all in the Boyne Culture, that of the cross-in-circle of the cruciform passage graves to be found in all three of the more or less circular mounds, a motif graphically expressed in one of the Dowth symbols, of a cross-in-circle. This key symbol of cosmic integration was still available in the early Bronze Age,[45] and was perhaps still understood and adapted by the builders of the Irish high crosses almost four millennia later.

Finally, if there were thirty-five stones in the Great Circle, their number is unlikely to have been without symbolic significance, perhaps that of the penetration of the royal centre by the renewed and renewing power of earth and heaven, indicated by a number symbolism of $(3 + 4) \times 5$.

(iii) *Heaven and (royal) centre* symbols: A third recurring group of symbols at New Grange, expressing another aspect of dense interpenetration and close partnership between the characters of the cosmic drama, signifies perhaps the direct renewal of the royal power at the centre by the heavens. A particularly dynamic interaction between the three horizontal grooves cut into R12, a standing-stone half-way along the right side of the passage, and five horizontal grooves on R21 facing the centre at the end of the passage, occurs whenever someone journeying towards the centre, ritually unites the three grooves of R12 with the five grooves of R21.

Those sunrays continue through the centre to strike C10, with its magnificent three-spiral, one of the masterpieces of all neolithic expression. Its relevance here is that it is made up of five raised bands and five shallow channels throughout, possibly symbolising the graceful renewal of royal power by its attunement to the eternal Now.

In the second edition of her *Guide*, Claire O'Kelly notes that the most constant measurement obtained between those stones in the Great Circle diametrically opposite each other is 340 feet, or 125 megalithic yards (a constant unit of measurement discovered by Thom in neolithic monuments in Brittany and Scotland).[46] Again there may be a deliberate number symbolism here, this time of $5 \times 5 \times 5$, indicating a belief that every single point within the circle is intensely impregnated with the power of time renewing the cosmos through its royal centre.

C16, interweaving of triangles and squares. Reproduced from *The Boyne Valley Vision* by Martin Brennan (The Dolmen Press). By kind permission.

Lintel over roof-box. Photo by kind permission of Claire O'Kelly (*Illustrated Guide to Newgrange*)

C10, Triple spiral.

Tedavnet 'broach': cross in circle. Photo: Commissioners of Public Works.

IV
BELONGING TO COSMIC ONENESS: SYMBOLS OF THE WHOLE AT NEWGRANGE

As Voegelin has remarked, "The cosmos is not a thing among others; it is the background of reality against which all existent things exist."[47] How did the Boyne people express their experience of the cosmos as the all-embracing oneness underlying the earth and its fruitful garden of plants and animals, the bright eyes of the heavens' light- and life-giving inhabitants, their own society and their kings? König has proposed one possible meaning for the symbol, common since paleolithic times, which is both most undifferentiated and yet most perfect, the sphere, as the primary symbolisation of the cosmos as a whole.[48] Perhaps this was the explanation for what Herity refers to as the "numbers of carefully made balls, like children's marbles, of chalk, clay and stone" found among the cremated burials in Irish passage graves, including New Grange.[49]

Much more noticeable are the ovoid granite stones found interspersed in the white quartz facing-wall of both New Grange and Knowth. Eliade's remarks on the cosmological significance of the egg gives a clue to the possible meaning of these egg-shaped symbols:

> The ritual power of the egg bears not so much on birth as upon a *rebirth* modelled on the creation of the world. Otherwise there could be no explanation for the important place eggs hold in the celebration of the New Year and the feasts of the dead . . . At the New Year, when the world is re-created, the dead feel themselves drawn towards the living and can hope to return to life. The basic idea is not that of ordinary birth, but rather the repeating of the archetypal birth of the cosmos . . . Clay eggs have been found in a great many tombs in Russia and in Sweden; with good reason Arne sees them as as emblems of immortality.[50]

A similar type of experience of cosmic rebirth may be expressed in the oval shaped "altars" or settings of pavement to be found close to the entrance of New Grange and to both the Knowth entrances.[51]

By far the most impressive ovoids or somewhat spherically shaped symbols are the three great mounds of New Grange, Knowth and Dowth, each of which both from inside and from outside may have represented the whole cosmos for the Boyne people.[52] The very prodigality of the "microcosmic" eggs embedded in the "macrocosmic" eggs of New Grange and of Knowth seems to express a cosmic cheerfulness and trust in the accessibility to everyone of wholeness in the renewal of the whole. These three huge mountains, each covering about an acre, each visible to the other two at a distance of a mile, must have conveyed an enormously reassuring sense of thankfulness that contact was being made with the underlying oneness of the whole, a oneness they must have yearned to belong to completely.

V
PASSING THROUGH DEATH TO THE HEART OF BEING: THE DRAMA OF NEWGRANGE

But how did they rise to participation in this cosmic reunification? While we have had to examine their possible modes of symbolisation motif by motif, we can presume that like other archaic societies, the Boyne people expressed their own self-interpretation of existence in the form of myth, their own unique "symbolisation of society and its order as an analogue of the cosmos and its order."[53] Since the New Grange entrance stone, K1, and the back stone, K52 diametrically opposite, contain the mound's principal symbols in dense interaction, it is not unlikely that they declare in concentrated form the essence of the people's myths. We have come across many varying nuances of what seems to be the key theme in that myth, the death and rebirth of the cosmos, and man's attunement to it and its reordering power. The plain person's guide to this significance of the mounds was perhaps the white quartzite facing on all three mounds, rendering these abodes of darkness dazzling cathedrals of light. Chevrons or zigzag lines are one of the most common symbols at New Grange, woven into its many patterns, often, as in one of the roof-stones of the Knowth East passage, forming a whole tapestry of row upon row of chevrons. König has suggested that the vertical rows of chevrons in the Île-de-France caves, sloping alternately downwards (towards the underworld) and upwards (towards the heavens), symbolise the victory of life over death, so that the Newgrange symbols may have this meaning too.[54]

Given the central position of New Grange at the base of the triangle formed by the three mounds, it is possible that the Boyne people wrote the final act of their cosmic drama along the axis uniting K1 to K52, an axis horizontally open to the four quarters of the earth at the centre-point of the passage, and vertically intersected three times, (by the vertical lines bisecting K52 and partly bisecting K1, and by the vault at the centre). While K1 almost certainly, due to its south-easterly orientation towards midwinter sunrise, signified attunement to cosmic life, the back stone, K52, which appears to be aligned to the moment which marks the beginning of the sun's dying away, at midsummer sunset, may be New Grange's "door of death", facing northwest and leading nowhere. Again, as with the chevrons, the significance could be in the polar opposition of life and of death.

In this, the Boyne Culture, like many archaic cultures, could have understood the mystery of cosmic existence as originating in two opposed cosmic forces, not only in the opposition of life/death, but of male/female, darkness/light, day/night, and so on. Another expression of this duality could be the linked two-spirals or juxtaposition of two spirals to be found at Newgrange. In general, the symbol of the spiral, a motif particularly developed in Ireland,[55] with its representation of recurrence about a centre while at the same time conveying a movement outwards from and returning to the centre, suggests a meditative expression of the cyclical order of being in terms of its divine-cosmic origin.[56] What then of the three-spiral, the most beautiful and mysterious of all the Newgrange symbols, which lies at the heart of the intersecting and perhaps opposed polar axes of life and death, heaven and earth? As we know, none of the Boyne people's symbols can be traced with certainty to their experiential origins because of the non-existence of literary sources, yet there are some possible equivalents worth exploring.

Voegelin has referred to the obviousness of the number three "wherever the problem of origin is expressed in terms of procreation," in terms of the procreating couple and its offspring. But a non-representational three-symbol such as the Minoan fleur-de-lis could express a deeper grasp of the problems, symbolising perhaps, "the sex differentiation, representative of becoming, and the originating unity, representative of being."[57] Much later, about 500 BC and apparently independently of each other, three of the most advanced cosmological civilizations, Persia, India and China seem to have been impelled by a desire for contact with a oneness underlying the polar opposition of archaic duality. Zoroaster, the Upanishadic mystics and Lao Tzu advanced to a spiritual breakthrough in which they experienced and articulated that single unifying cosmic principle underlying and grounding a polarity of two lesser co-principles of cosmic order.[58]

The fire-dance at the centre of the world at the dawn of each New Year, culminating in the embrace of heaven and earth at the three-spiral, symbolically unique in human history, may express an Irish spiritual outburst equivalent to the Minoan mytho-speculation. The five bands of the three-spiral may have indicated the golden thread of royal mediation through which the people could participate in this manifestation of the divine-cosmic ground of being. In and through their loving-suffering agon of attunement to the central place of the cosmos, at its own anxiously awaited time of rebirth, the Boyne people touched ecstatically for a few boundless timeless moments the everlasting cosmic oneness at the heart of being. Radiating outwards from that oneness, renewing their kingship, sanctifying every corner of the earth's four quarters, eternalising every moment of cosmic time, bestowing hope and dignity to the people's otherwise mere mortality, was the happiness of belonging to the ultimately kind cosmic ground, the source of peace beyond the struggle between life and death.

Proinsias MacCana

EARLY IRISH IDEOLOGY
AND
THE CONCEPT OF UNITY

Sometime in the second half of the twelfth century one of the scribes
of the *Book of Leinster* recorded there a recension of *Táin Bó Cuailnge*
"The Cattle-raid of Cuailnge" that had been compiled earlier in the
same century. And having copied the long heroic narrative of the *Táin*
he went on to copy the hortatory tail-piece which, in one form or
another, was a familiar feature of learned Irish storytelling – as it had
once been of ancient Indian storytelling:

> A blessing on everyone who shall faithfully memorize the
> *Táin* as it is written here and shall not add any other form
> to it.[1]

But then, as if this abbreviated invocation of the story's magic potency
had reminded him of its rank paganism, he immediately deferred to
Christian orthodoxy by adding another codicil, this time in Latin and
pedantically formal, disclaiming any personal interest in or responsibility for the narrative he had so faithfully transcribed:

> But I who have written this story, or rather this fable,
> give no credence to the various incidents related in it. For
> some things in it are the deceptions of demons, others
> poetic figments; some are probable, others improbable;
> while still others are intended for the delectation of foolish
> men.

This nice instance of medieval diglossia neatly epitomises the disparity
between the cultural contexts of the two languages, Irish and Latin. On
the one hand we have to do with a culture which is coeval with the Irish
language and receives its only verbal expression through it, first orally
and then from the late sixth century onwards both orally and in writing.
It is a mythopoeic culture, innocent of secular chronology and locating
people and events in the past by reference to genealogical filiation or to
the reigns of famous kings, whether legendary or historical. On the
other hand there is the Roman and international culture which was
introduced to Ireland with Christianity and the Latin language and

which extended its influence with the spread of monasticism and the monastic schools from the first half of the sixth century onwards. It is the creation of a church rooted in finite time by the central fact of the incarnation and by its residual inheritance from imperial Rome, and in consequence it brought with it to Ireland a view of time and history, of secular and sacred, of artistic and religious categories, that was radically at variance with that of native Irish society. The events and phases of the Irish past, real or legendary, were fitted within the chronological framework of world history as formulated by Christian historians like Eusebius and Orosius, and monastic scribes began to make brief notes of significant happenings in the form of annals, which in the course of time developed into a relatively full chronological record of Irish political and socio-cultural history. Latin, which was almost exclusively the language of monastic history until the middle of the ninth century, provided continuing if not total access to the universal learning mediated by the Church and at the same time acted as a partial filter against the mythic cast of native thought and tradition. "The white language of Beatus" (*bêlre bán biait*), as Latin is called in an early Irish legal tract, could be used not merely as a linguistic reference but also as shorthand for scriptural or canon law, or, in a still broader sense, for the whole range of ecclesiastical learning. It embodied a culture and patterns of thought foreign to those inherited from pre-Christian Irish society. Its ideology was exogenous, "universal" and, at least in a relative sense, innovational, whereas that of Irish was by contrast indigenous, self-contained and largely conservative.

The conservatism of early Ireland is a commonplace of historical commentary. Those concerned with the ordering of society set much store by time-hallowed precedent and by the maintenance of cultural continuity, and their preoccupation with the past was as pragmatic as it was philosophical. The kingship of each Irish kingdom was a reflex, or a replica, of the sacral kingship that was already old when the Indo-European community took shape, and even when Irish rulers owed their accession more to force of arms than to hereditary right they were always careful to legitimise their claim by reference to the primal myth and ritual of sovereignty. The simple political structure over which they presided lacked institutionalised machinery for enforcing the administration of justice, and in the absence of appropriate state sanctions the only power that could command permanent respect for the rule of law was the power inherent in immemorial custom, confirmed as it was by the wisdom of countless generations and by the sacred prestige of the professional class who were its custodians and interpreters. This fairly numerous yet exclusive corporation of priests, poets and lawmen controlled the whole range of sacred tradition—myth and ritual, epic, onomastics, genealogy, origin legend and law—and it is largely in consequence of their jealous safeguarding of tribal or national memory that the surviving records of Old, Middle and even Modern Irish preserve so much that is archaic, some of it every bit as old as the oldest testimony to Indo-European ritual and institutions.

Like extreme conservatism anywhere, the conservatism of druids and *fili* (the fraternity of poet-seers and savants associated with the druids) discouraged change and innovation in so far as they disturbed the stability of social and cultural norms, but where change was inevitable the native orders showed a remarkable capacity to live with it, to temper its novelty and to assimiliate it as quickly as possible to their own system of perennial verities. The coming of Christianity is itself perhaps the most striking instance of this. It might so easily have transformed or even eradicated the existing learning and institutions associated with paganism, and it did in fact bring about a confrontation with organised paganism which led to the extinction of the druidic order and the suppression of certain of the more unacceptable features of druidic doctrine and ritual; but when the dust had cleared away, say by the seventh century, it could be seen that the *fili* had assumed the mantle of the druids—discreetly adjusted to contemporary circumstance—and that native institutions and modes of thought had survived the change of religious orthodoxy relatively unscathed. The subtle *modus vivendi* which had evolved during the first century and a half of the Christian mission—and which continued to the period of church reform in the eleventh and twelfth centuries and, in a more restricted form, to the aftermath of the Elizabethan conquest—permitted the complementary coexistence of two ideologies, one explicitly Christian, the other implicitly and essentially pagan. In matters theological and doctrinal the former was backed up by the universal authority of the church, yet whenever its exponents—the clerics and other monastic scholars—extended their activities to encompass the several areas of profane learning they were immediately subject to the pull of traditional categories of knowledge and the ways of thinking that accompanied them. The attraction was all the stronger in that the monastic *literati* were themselves sprung from this traditional culture, and many of them must have belonged to those very families which over numberless generations produced the *fili* whose status and vocation were bound up with the responsibility of maintaining it. Against this kind of pervasive influence the civilisation opened up by the Church and by Latin could make only limited headway, affecting certain facets of the external expression of the Irish mind rather than its conceptual or analytical capacity.

The effect of the use of writing in the vernacular is a case in point. One knows that when a rich and cultivated oral tradition is introduced to writing it can be transformed in various ways. The very fact of its being recorded in more or less permanent form enables the actual process of composition to be accompanied by a continuing exercise of retrospection, elaboration and reference, which may in turn lead to a greater variety of style and complexity of thought than is possible in oral narrative or discourse. As has often been pointed out, the first and the essential step towards the achievement of Greek philosophy and science was the adoption of writing. In mastering its potential the Greeks perceived the limitations imposed by oral or poetic discourse, and set forth a clear opposition of style and significance between the *logos* that was the written language of science and reason and the *muthos* embodied in oral tradition:

> Prose composition—medical treatises, historical accounts, the speeches of the orators and the dissertation of the philosophers—represents not only a different mode of expression from that of oral tradition and poetic composition but also a new form of thought. The organisation of written discourse goes hand in hand with a more rigorous analysis and a stricter ordering of the conceptual material. As early as in an orator such as Gorgias or a historian such as Thucydides, the measured interplay of antithesis in the balanced rhetoric of written discourse functions as a veritable logical tool. By separating, positioning and opposing the fundamental elements of the situation to be described, term for term, it allows the verbal intelligence to obtain a grip on reality. The elaboration of philosophical language goes further, not only in the degree of the abstraction of concepts and in the use of ontological terminology (for example of Being, as such, or of the One), but also in its insistence on a new type of rigorous reasoning. . . . In form it is opposed to *muthos* in all the ways that argued demonstration differs from the narrative of the mythical story; and in fundamental significance it is also opposed, to the extent that the abstractions of the philosopher differ from the divine powers whose dramatic adventures are the subject of myth.[2]

However, like causes do not necessarily produce like consequences. Irish, a language like Greek with a rich and respected oral tradition, began to be written about the middle of the sixth century and thereafter produced the earliest written vernacular literature in Western Europe—and the most abundant until the twelfth century—yet this did not bring Irish literature and learning significantly closer to the spirit of rationalist and scientific enquiry which it led to in Greece. New genres or disciplines introduced with Latin had to struggle continually, and often ineffectually, to escape the pervasive influence of *muthos*, and history, like hagiography, tended to be conceived in the same terms as the traditional narratives of gods and heroes. Commentators relate the elaboration of Greek thought to the emergence of a written prose which permitted the development of an abstract language far removed from the epico-poetic timbre of oral tradition;

yet Irish not merely had an extensive written prose but was somewhat exceptional in using prose rather than verse for the epico-mythic narrative, and still it never experienced the need to extend its use still further and to make of it a vehicle for a new kind of rigorous and speculative reasoning.

One reason for the disparity (apart from the fact that the Greek achievement is distinguished by its uniqueness) is the control exercised by the native men of learning, the *fili*, whose responsibility and corporate interest it was to maintain the traditional integrity of social organisation and the traditional concepts on which it depended. With certain exceptions they had little active part in the creation of a written literature, which was mainly the work of the monastic scriptoria, but the oral literature which constituted the official legacy of the past was virtually their monopoly, and this, be it remembered, must have been much more extensive and socially more effective than what has been transmitted in writing. It was not for nothing that the *fili*, some of whom must have been able to read and perhaps even to write already in the early Irish period, nonetheless accorded a certain very definite priority to the oral mode, as did the druids of Gaul before them or the Brahmans of India; the spoken word was not only in some respects more exclusive, as Caesar suggests, but it was also regarded as a living dynamic medium by contrast with the static character of writing, and it never wholly lost the magic associated with solem oral pronouncement in traditional societies.

Oral language is, by its very nature, more suited to narrative, description, ritual and imagery than to speculative discourse, and in the Irish context it would appear that this limitation was, by and large, accepted for the written literature as well. During its creative period, from about the seventh to the early tenth century, the authors of this literature were seemingly more concerned to refine what they received from oral tradition than to replace or transform it. In the event they produced an extraordinary harvest of lyric verse and of spare sinewy prose admirably adapted to hero tale or straight historical narrative; but in reading this literature one is generally conscious—and senses that its authors were still more conscious—of its continuing relationship to the oral tradition from which it is largely derived; only fleetingly did it achieve the kind of autonomy that written Greek had already attained by the fourth century BC, and for the specific reason that those who wrote it assumed for the most part the same basic postulates as those who cultivated the oral tradition. And this applied even to those monastic scholars writing in Latin, despite their access to foreign models, in so far as they belonged to the same native cultural environment as the composers and transmitters of oral literature, as in fact most of them did.

It has sometimes been remarked that one of the admirable qualities of the Irish language (and literature) in all its periods is its peculiar concreteness of expression and imagery. It has also often been remarked by ethnologists that primitive thinking in general is more concrete than that of more literate and intellectual societies. The connection between the two has been made succinctly by the great German Celticist Rudolf Thurneysen in a review of the edition of an early Irish tract on grammar:

> The Irishman sees the grammatical schemata as concrete realities. There are few documents that give us so deep an insight into the mind of the early Irish—so completely different from our own—as these tracts, and yet they spring from the learned classes, acquainted with Latin grammarians. Only by comparison with them can we judge the powerful intellectual achievement a Johannes Eriugena has accomplished in the ninth century, schooled of course by the translation of Dionysius the Areopagite; he too erects a similar pyramidal construction, though it is logically built on a capacity for abstraction learned from the Greeks, without any loss of the Irish capacity for concreteness. Such a work in the Ireland of his day would have been impossible and remained incomprehensible. Apart from their piety the Irish certainly brought abroad with them their inclination to scholarship, which was not very widespread on the continent, and made them welcome as schoolmasters; but to develop their powers was something they could only do in closer proximity to the Mediterranean.[3]

Thurneysen refers here to grammar and philosophy, but as Frank O'Connor remarks, "He might have said with equal truth that a book like Bede's *History of the English Church* would in the Ireland of that time have been impossible and remained incomprehensible."[4]

The trouble is, if trouble it is, that the mode of theoretical thinking which has long been familiar throughout the educated world and which has its origin in the speculation of the Greeks did not take root in Gaelic Ireland. This was not, as we have seen, through lack of literacy nor indeed through any inherent inability to deal in theoretical concepts, but rather because traditional ideology (even in its somewhat restricted para-Christian form) and the social order were so closely intertwined as to be mutually dependent. The druids may have been extinguished as a religious and moral establishment by the Christian church but they left behind them a deep-rooted system of cultural values that flourished and eventually faded with Gaelic society itself. It is no longer possible, of course, to construct any adequate idea of the totality of the detail of their teaching in the pre-Christian period, for the simple reason that our only record of it was made by Christian redactors who could, and doubtless did, censor it by extensive omission as well as by revision. So far as the continental druids are concerned, it is clear that Posidonius and some later Greek and Latin writers exaggerated their intellectual sophistication as philosophers and theologians, but it is equally clear that the extant literature understates the form and content of druidic teaching in Ireland. It is idle to imagine how it might have developed had it passed into writing without the intervention of Christianity, but one can be fairly certain that here as in so many other instances Ireland would have found itself closer to India than to Greece, and that such druidic philosophy as might have emerged would have subordinated itself to the reality of the sacred in a way familiar to the Indians, but quite foreign to the rationalist spirit of the Greeks.

Until recently the very idea that the Irish druids might have been capable of producing a system of thought remotely comparable with that of India would have seemed inconceivable to most Celticists. Apart from the suppressed premise—to which most philologists were inherently prone—that any form of sustained and systematic thought was impossible in a non-literate society, there was the related assumption that the written remains of early Irish literature offer a reasonably full and accurate reflection of the pre-Christian socio-religious ideas of the learned and priestly classes. Neither supposition has much substance: the first has been effectively disposed of by Paul Radin and other anthropologists and the second is disproved not merely by its general improbability but also by the internal evidence of the extant literature; it is true that Irish monastic scribes and redactors were exceptionally liberal in recording native non-Christian tradition, but they were writing several centuries after the dissolution of druidism as the organised religion of the Irish people, and this remove in time combined with the need to uphold Christian orthodoxy made it quite impossible for them to reflect adequately the integral system of druidic teaching. Yet despite all the evidence of revision and suppression there remains a great deal of material bearing upon native institutions and ideology—sacred kingship, the otherworld, cosmic division and the provinces, status and functions of druids and *filid*, and so on—which presupposes the earlier existence of a complex system of socio-religious doctrine and practice consciously maintained and applied during many centuries. Georges Dumézil, who has done more than any other scholar to reveal the continuities of Indo-European ideology in Irish and other conservative traditions, has this to say of one particular instance of analogous tales of kingship in India and in Ireland:

> Certainly we have here, conserved on the one side by the Druids, on the other in the unwritten "fifth Veda" from which the post-Vedic narratives of India in large part derive, a fragment of Indo-European politico-religious philosophy, that is, some of the speculations made by the Indo-Europeans on the status and the destiny of kings. . . . As is typical in accounts from medieval Ireland, which no longer rely upon a religion or even upon a living ideology, the

story of Eochaid, of his daughters Medb and Clothru and
his grandson Lugaid, is still more laicized and worked over
as literature ["plus littérarisée"] — despite the marvels
which are still found in it. But the "lessons", as we have
seen are the same.

Noting that the Indian analogue is in this case more structured than
the Irish he continues:

One may suppose that this latter, cut off from Druidic
philosophy like all the epic texts and conserving from the
ancient symbols only the interplay of figures and their
behaviour, has reached us in an impoverished form. But
the Indian comparison does afford a glimpse of its primary
significance, its value as a structure.[5]

There are many such survivals in Irish literature, some of them like
this one cast in an epic mould and therefore more or less secularised,
or *littérarisé*, others embodying ritual or institutional forms and therefore more likely to retain their original religious definition as applied or
canonical texts, but taken in the aggregate—and making due allowance
for defective and selective transmission—they can hardly be seen other
than as the residue of an earlier comprehensive and internally coherent
system of politico-religious doctrine and speculation preserved and interpreted by the druids. Most of these survivals were in the form of myth
and epic narrative or were closely connected with specific ritual or
quasi-legal contexts, and as a result they perished in large measure
together with the learned literature and with the aristocratic society
which engendered it. But there were others which, while linked to
traditional ritual and institutions, had at the same time a much wider
cultural resonance and which for that reason have outlasted profound
social and linguistic change to become part of the image of the "typical"
Irishman particularly as it is perceived by the greater world outside.
Take for example what one might call the motif of Irish, or Celtic,
generosity, which goes back as far as the classical authors of antiquity
and is still not quite extinct even in the age of commercialism and the
Common Market. One can easily and validly explain it as a varying
blend of external preconception and internal reality, yet at the same
time one cannot wholly dissociate it from the functional role of liberality in early Irish and Celtic society, where, as an integral part of the
communal honour-system it was more a social imperative than a personal virtue and where a ruler's open-handedness was one of the ritual
touchstones of his worthiness for office. But to pursue this and kindred
topics further would lead us towards modern sociology and away from
medieval ideology. Instead we shall concern ourself in the present
context with an instance of cultural continuity which has more to do

with political organisation and action and has the advantage of being more susceptible to clear demonstration.

*　　　　*　　　　*

One of the commonplace notions about the Celtic peoples in general, the Irish in particular, is that they were chronically incapable of unity of purpose and, as a corollary to this, that they lacked the sense of nationality (and *a fortiori* that of nationalism). Like most ethnic clichés this one is not wholly without substance: whatever of the second of its two assumptions—and we shall return to that presently—the first seems to be amply substantiated by the chronicle of Irish history, which from the annalistic perspective is little more than a catalogue of battles, burnings and killings and of continual strife and dissension, even in the face of external aggression. The inability of the Irish to make common cause against a common enemy becomes the more obvious in the context of the modern concept of nationalism, and it is significant that from the sixteenth or seventeenth century onwards the Irish themselves seem to betray a growing if still intermittent consciousness of this disunion as a defect, a negative factor in native society — as in the disillusioned realism of the poet who deplores *an dream bocht silte nár chuir le chéile* "the poor and ineffective mob who did not stand together."

And here surely we come close to the nub of the matter. One salutary lesson we have learned from anthropologists (and from some good cultural historians) is not to import our own inherited system of motivation and classification into our description of alien societies — and naturally this holds as true for the diachronic as for the synchronic dimension. In the primitive Irish view of things political cohesion and centralism were not in themselves necessarily a social good, nor did this attitude change radically with the rise of expansionist dynasties within the historical period. The underlying principal was one of coordination rather than consolidation. Over-kings there were, and provincial kings, but in the earliest documented situation the king *tout court* was the king of the petty or tribal kingdom, the *tuath*, and he and his kingdom constituted the central nexus, both ritual and political, in Irish society. One's *tuath* was one's *patrie* and beyond its boundaries one became an outlander, a foreigner (Old Irish *deoraid),* and however much this definition was overlaid by the effects of political expansionism within the historical period the concept of local loyalty and autonomy long remained an essential element of the Irish understanding of social organisation.

But kingdoms were not islands even in the earliest period for which we have documentary evidence, and relations were maintained, through the persons of king, over-king and king of a province, by a system of treaties, bonds of allegiance — and by fighting. The structure of early

Irish society was such that one could no more do without one's enemies than one could do without one's friends and in consequence the character and the effects of warfare were limited accordingly. Modern police and "security" forces, struggling to cope with urban unrest, are busy devising what they sometimes refer to as "harmless weapons"; by the same euphemism one might almost describe the endemic warfare of early Ireland as 'harmless', for, while it could be barbarous, its primary aim was not unlike that of the modern riot weapon: to sting and to stun but not to kill. It was not designed to destroy people or to annex territories, but to assert status or to claim redress for real or assumed breaches of established relations. Like the later faction fights it had a strong element of ritual, but it was essentially less destructive because it was less rigidly patterned and because in the long run its purpose, at least in theory, was to uphold social order and to bond the tribal kingdom. As in India the newly elected monarch had to carry out a successful cattle-raid as an integral part of the protracted ceremonial of royal inauguration, so in Ireland, though the procedure is less formally defined in the extant texts, he had to perform the *crech ríg* or "royal prey", and the whole symbolism of this ritual expedition underlines the normative and conservative function of the cross-border cattle-raid.

Two factors contributed towards this convention of limitation, one practical, the other ideological. Cattle-reiving in a cattle-rearing society can be a source of profit as well as of honour, but one thing it requires is that there be foreign or enemy territory within easy reach, and this in itself is frequently sufficient to neutralise the lust for territorial conquest. Secondly, where war was governed by the heroic ethic, as was largely the case in early Ireland, it often constituted its own justification and, as with the Indian *dharmavijaya* or "righteous conquest", it had for its reward honour and glory rather than annexation of territory. Where one or other of these factors operates — or both — there is almost always a tendency to limit the consequences of war — notably in regard to its extent, duration and range of target — by a body of restrictive convention or a more or less developed code of chivalry. One of the most demoralising effects of the Norse invasions, as D.A. Binchy has pointed out, was that they brought the Irish face to face with an enemy who ignored the traditional conventions: "Hence war as waged by the invaders was more 'total', to use a modern term; ancient taboos were ignored; no holds were barred. Before long the native kings themselves were using these ruthless and efficient fighters as allies in their own quarrels, and, inevitably, came to adopt the new tactics."[6]

Viewed then in purely Irish or even in Indo-European terms the obvious political disunity of the country did not entirely lack a social rationale. Moreover the Vikings themselves demonstrated most dramatically if unintentionally that it could function as an effective mechanism of defence against foreign aggression — at least until such time as the aggressors could mobilise sufficient forces and sophisticated weaponry to wage a war of total conquest: given the cellular, un-centralist structure of Irish civil organisation and the absence of complex organs of administrators it was possible to win victory after victory and slay king after king without achieving effective control over any considerable part of the country. In the event the Norse invaders faced up to the realities of the situation and, conscious of their own priorities, set about establishing a string of posts and trading settlements around the coast which were to stand for all time as the Achilles heel of the native order.

This is what happened on the level of historical fact; equally significant, however, if less tangible, was the psychic reaction produced by these events in the popular consciousness, in so far as this can be gauged accurately from their reflex in the literature. The Scandinavians do not figure as such outside the strictly historical and more particularly annalistic tradition before the eleventh century, but there can be little doubt that they are already present, disguised under the name Fomoire, in a number of earlier texts. These Fomoire are the race of demonic beings who exist somewhere beyond the sea, a perpetual menace to the familiar world of everyday reality. According to the account of the several mythical settlements of the country in *Leabhar Gabhála Éireann*, "The Book of the Conquest of Ireland", they opposed Partholán, leader of the second immigration, in the first battle that was fought on Irish soil and they strive continually to subvert cosmic order as re-presented by legitimate rule and sovereignty within the confines of Ireland. When the pagan, marauding Norsemen appeared around the Irish coast, the shock-waves created by their violent irruptions must have had a profound effect upon the whole populace in the vicinity of their landings and far beyond, and while the clerics, nobles and secular men of learning would have been only too well aware of the mortal character of the terror that threatened them, for the mass of the people, beset by report and rumour, it was all too easy to confuse these ravaging gentiles with the mythic forces of anarchy. And so, one should not be unduly surprised to find that, when the cycle of Fionn mac Cumhaill and his brotherhood of roving hunter-warriors develops a prolific written literature from the twelfth century onwards which obviously draws heavily on popular and semi-popular oral tradition, one of the motifs which keep recurring in it is that of the Fianna defending the Irish shore against the Lochlannaigh, as the Norsemen are generally known in the non-historical literature. Here we have the fusion of myth and history, the assimilation of the historical event to the mythic analogue that is a characteristic feature of a people *admodum dedita religionibus* — and what is important from our immediate point of view is that the dominating theme is the security and integrity of the land of Ireland as a whole, not of one or other of its constituent parts. As the divine Lugh, paragon of kingship and vindicator of the central sover-eignty of Tara, had routed the hordes of Fomoire in the great mythic battle of Mag Tuired, so did Fionn mac Cumhaill and the Fianna repel the attacks of the marauding Lochlannaigh.

One could of course argue, if one wished, that in the latter case the notion of Fionn as the protector of Ireland is tied up with the elaboration of the propagandist fiction of the high-kingship as a political reality, particularly from the ninth century onwards, but while this was doubtless a contributory factor it was not a prime cause: the idea of Ireland as a single entity goes back much further in time, and indeed without its prior existence the political exploitation of the "high-kingship" would not have been possible. Here, as in so many other instances in the Irish past, history converges with mythic tradition and draws support from it. D.A. Binchy has stressed the enhanced reputation of the over-king of the Uí Néill dynasties as a result of their obstinate resistance to the Norsemen and the increased prestige of the Tara monarchy as the main focus of that resistance, and he sees here "a striking parallel with the fortunes of the House of Wessex, which, alone among the English kingdoms, maintained an unbroken resistance to the Danes, and eventually became the nucleus of the national monarchy."[7] He also observed that the Norse invasions evoked among the native population "that sense of 'otherness' which lies at the basis of nationalism". Yet if this was a notable step towards political unity, it was also by the same token a step towards the secularisation and politicisation of a spiritual datum of long standing. In ideological terms the sense of national identity and the concept of unity were already old when the Vikings first drew up their long ships on the Irish shore.

Eoin MacNeill once wrote that the Pentarchy — the division of Ireland into five provinces ruled by five kings of equal status — "is the oldest certain fact in the political history of Ireland", a statement so well supported by tradition as to be almost axiomatic. The corollary of this — as has since been argued with convincing logic by D.A. Binchy — is that the "high-kingship" as a political reality is late and largely spurious. However, if the pentarchy thus helps to discredit the notion of a supreme political monarchy, at the same time (by the kind of paradox that is not unfamiliar in the Irish context) it also has the effect of highlighting the underlying conceptual unity of the country. The word for a "province" in Irish is *cúigeadh*, Old Irish *cóiced*, literally "a fifth", and *cúig cúigidh na hÉireann* is still a familiar synonym for "the whole of Ireland"; and as the fraction presupposes the whole, so the five provinces, though politically discrete, are conceived as mere fractions of a single all-embracing totality coterminous with the land of Ireland. The pattern of a central province enclosed by four others representing the cardinal points cannot be explained otherwise than as a historical reflex of an ancient cosmographic schema, and one which has striking analogues in several of the "great traditions" of the world. This cosmography is implicit in many incidental details of the extant tradition, though only one fairly extended exposition of it survives, in a Middle

Irish text on "The Disposition of the Manor of Tara". This defines the extent of the provinces and their attributes and it declares that a pillar-stone with five ridges on it, one for each of the five provinces, was erected at Uisneach. The central province was known as Mide (from an older *Medion* "Middle") and within it stood the hill of Uisneach, supposedly the centre of Ireland, or as Giraldus Cambrensis puts it: *umbilicus Hiberniae dicitur, quasi in medio et meditullio terrae positus.*[8]

Here we have one of the most fundamental constituents of Irish, and indeed of Celtic ideology: the cult of the centre. The very notion of a centre naturally presupposes a circumference and an encompassed unity, and it is both remarkable and significant that the Celts should have re-created this cult wherever they established themselves as a distinct community or nation with reasonably well-defined borders. We have it on Caesar's authority that the Gaulish druids held an assembly at a holy place in the lands of the Carnutes which was believed to be the centre of the whole of Gaul, and to it came people from all parts to submit their disputes to the judgment of the druids. It seems likely that the *drunemeton* "oak-sanctuary" at which the council of the Galatians met had a similar role to the "holy place" of the Gauls, as no doubt had the great assembly, *Mordháil Uisnigh*, which is said to have been held at Uisneach on May-day. The social and ideological significance of such assemblies cannot be disregarded. Ferdinand Lot declared that the Gaulish gathering maintained a kind of ideal unity, both judiciary and political, among the Gauls, comparing its role to that of the temple of Delphi among the Greeks: "The Gauls had thus a sense of *celticité* as the Greeks had of Hellenism, in spite of the rivalries and wars that took place within these two nations. This the Romans understood full well, and they made use of the abolition of human sacrifice as a pretext for the persecution they carried out against druidism until it was exterminated."[9]

It should be said at once that Lot's comments conceal a fair amount of academic controversy and uncertainty: was the pursuit of the Gaulish druids as ruthless and thorough-going as some of our sources suggest, what were the real motives which inspired it, and what was the real extent of the druidic participation and influence in politics? For example, as part of the critical re-evaluation of the classical commentaries on the Gauls, especially Caesar's, it has been argued that the social and political importance of the druids has been exaggerated (as also indeed their religious and speculative sophistication). How one interprets the evidence in this regard depends very much, I fear, on one's scholarly background and presuppositions; certain it is that many of those who have cast doubt on Caesar's account — and not entirely without justification be it said — have been fortified in their conclusions by an almost total ignorance of the culture and social organisation of the insular Celts.

Essentially the druid was a religious not a political figure, but the distinction was easily blurred where the political structures were as simple as they were in primitive Ireland and no doubt had been in the other Celtic communities. In the small individual kingdom the few governmental functions required were at the disposal of the king and, given that the chief-druid of the *tuath* was the king's "chaplain" and counsellor and the interpreter of the law, it is inevitable that he should have exerted some influence on political policy within the *tuath* and, perhaps especially, in relations with neighbouring kingdoms; just how great his influence was in any particular instance must have depended as much on his adroitness and strength of personality as on the political power conferred by his office. By and large those who would make light of the druids' political role are those who believe that the Romans in seeking to suppress the druids were motivated by the desire to eradicate barbarism rather than to quell political opposition. The problem is that barbarism may mean different things to different people. For some, mainly the classically oriented, it was marked by savage practices, such as human sacrifice, which were incompatible with Roman civilisation, and this they deemed sufficient justification for its suppression. But historical situations can rarely be adequately interpreted in such simple terms. The civilising (or proselytising) impulse is a characteristic feature of empire-builders wherever they appear and no doubt it affected Roman policy regarding the druids, but it would be naive to suppose that a sodality like the druids, enjoying high social status and control over law, religion and sacred tradition, would not have been seen as a main source and organiser of opposition to the Roman conquest. Whatever of nationalism, cultural or political, professional solidarity and self-interest alone would have given them sufficient cause to defend the native ideology and institutions with which their own existence was wholly bound up, and the Romans, in common with other colonising powers before and after, were only too well aware that conquest to be permanent required acculturation and that a native learned class of prestige and influence could seriously hinder both one and the other. "Dès la conquête terminée," observed Joseph Vendryes, "le druidisme devait porter ombrage aux vainqueurs, parce qu'il représentait une force d'opposition. C'est en lui que s'incarnaient les traditions nationales. Il fallait le supprimer pour romaniser le pays."[10]

A millennium and a half later the same suspicion and animosity coloured the attitude of the British government towards the Irish "rhymers" who were the lineal descendants of the druids, and ultimately for the same reason: consciousness of cultural identity and commitment to its preservation is not overtly political, even among a professional elite, but they have profound political implications and a political potential which, given the right circumstances — the threat of foreign domination for example — can easily be transformed into an active and even decisive force. This is why the Romans and English distrusted druids and *filí* and acted more or less effectively to neutralise them.

The fact is, of course, that the *fili* of the fifteenth and sixteenth centuries, whatever of the Gaulish druids, lacked the capacity for effective political action on a national scale. The element of "realism" introduced by the Vikings does not appear to have seriously disturbed the basic assumptions which shaped the *fili*'s view of society and their own role within it; if indeed these assumptions were temporarily cast into doubt by the Vikings' lamentable lack of respect for convention, then they were certainly reaffirmed in the period of retrenchment which followed the Norse invasion and the reform of the Church. For the *fili* themselves personified the web of paradox and ambiguity that materialises so easily where the two planes of reality, the secular and the sacred, converge. According to the view of the world by which they were conditioned the spiritual concept of a national unity did not require an exact reflex in the realm of secular politics: in other words religious concept and political structure did not necessarily coincide. We have seen that the cosmographic schema of the four quarters and the centre occurs in several major traditions as well as in Irish, but, as Alwyn Rees has remarked,[11] in many respects these do not accord with actual political and geographical structures.

In Ireland, Tara was the ritual centre of sovereignty and consequently the king of Tara enjoyed a special prestige, but he was not in any real and practical sense king of all Ireland. Ideally, no doubt, religious and political entities would have formed a complete correspondence, but in practice, circumstances would as surely have hindered its full realisation. If we assume that Tara was established as the seat of sacred kingship *par excellence* by the Gaelic colonisers who seized dominion over large areas of the northern half, those who came to be known as Uí Chuinn "descendants of Conn Cétchathach", then obviously its spiritual precedence could only have become a political precedence in so far as the Uí Chuinn or their later representatives succeeded in gaining effective control over the whole of Ireland. This they failed to do. In particular, the province of Munster came under the sway of a different set of Gaelic colonisers who, while they shared for the most part the same cultural heritage as the northern overlords, yielded nothing willingly to them in terms of political power.

Thus, while in principle one might expect the two orders to tally, they do not do so in practice, through the pressure of personal, tribal and dynastic interests (but also perhaps, as we shall see, because there is an inherent tension and conflict between the political and cultural-religious spheres in many pre-modern societies). It is true that some scholars have found difficulty in accepting this. Faced by the discrepancy between the religious concept of unity and the reality of political disunity, they have sought to resolve it by discounting the former. Joseph Vendryes laid great stress on the local character of Irish, and Celtic, religion. He pointed to the some four hundred deity names attested in Gaulish inscriptions, noting that the great majority of them occur only once. He also pointed to the formulaic oath which occurs a number of times in the tales of the Ulster cycle: *tongu do dia toinges mo thuath* "I swear to the god to whom my tribe swears", and related it to the name of the Gaulish deity *Teutates* mentioned by Lucan. The conclusion he arrived at was that Celtic religion lacked universal deities and was characterised by local cults and tribal deities. In this he was echoed by his brilliant student Marie-Louise Sjoestedt.

It seems to me that both of them have in this instance misread the evidence and have as a result greatly exaggerated the inorganic character of Celtic religion. The features on which they base their conclusions come into clearer focus when we take account of the syncretism of Gaulish religion as represented in epigraphy and plastic art, the inadequacies of the Irish written tradition as a record of pagan belief and practice, the use of multiple names for a single deity, the confusion of divine epithets with deity names, and so on. That two such perceptive scholars should have so erred by taking the evidence at its face value requires some explanation. Perhaps the most likely one is that they were influenced by the teaching of their close neighbours in the Sorbonne school of sociology and most especially by the views of Emile Durkheim, father of modern comparative sociology, who maintained that religion was essentially a social phenomenon and that "primitive gods are part and parcel of the community, their form expressing accurately the details of its structure, their powers punishing and rewarding on its behalf."[12] Durkheim's theories in this regard were accepted widely, if not universally, and naturally they have been especially influential among French scholars. Vendryes and Sjoestedt can hardly have been unaffected by them, and if this has led as 1 suspect to their partially misrepresenting the character and structure of Irish religion it is not that Durkheim's views are wholly incorrect or irrelevant to the Irish situation, but that they have operated as an unstated and unquestioned premise and been applied without sufficient regard to the peculiarities of the context and to the deficiencies of the extant corpus of evidence. Irish religion is not unstructured, as Sjoestedt would have it ("we seek for a cosmos and find chaos"), but it is structured differently from Irish society, and to the extent that the two correspond it is not so much that religion reflects society as that it itself furnishes an ideal model towards which in given circumstances actual political structures may evolve or be consciously directed (as in the case of the Uí Neills' exploitation for their own expansionist ends of the cult of the central kingship of Tara). And the fact remains that despite the large ambitions of certain kings and dynasties, the impressive unionist and centralist theory so richly supported by myth and ritual was virtually impossible to translate into practical reality because, traditionally, there was no close correspondence between religious and political structures.

This disparity between the political and the cultural-religious is not in any way peculiar to Ireland. In universal terms one may see it as a particular manifestation of the combination or tension of oppositions which, like some complex system of systole and diastole, seems to be essential to the whole of human life and culture and which, as in the case of living speech, creates a fruitful interplay of conservation and change, of irregularity and uniformity: "L'humanité," as Claude Lévi-Strauss puts it, "est constamment aux prises avec deux processus contradictoires dont l'un tend à instaurer l'unification, tandis que l'autre vise à maintenir ou à rétablir la diversification."[13] But there are, and have been, other societies as well as Ireland in which this conjunction of opposites appears to express itself with particular clarity as a contrast or inequality of political and cultural-religious structures, and in some indeed this is so much the norm that the degree of political and administrative centralism stands more or less in inverse ratio to that of religious and cultural unity. M. Fortes and E.E. Evans-Pritchard have discussed the several variations on this relationship which they found among a number of African peoples in modern times:

> We may, therefore, ask to what extent cultural heterogeneity in a society is correlated with an administrative system and central authority. The evidence at our disposal in this book suggests that cultural and economic heterogeneity is associated with a state-like political structure. Centralized authority and an administrative organization seem to be necessary to accommodate culturally diverse groups within a single political system, especially if they have different modes of livelihood.

Naturally, centralised government may be found in societies of homogeneous culture, but:

> A centralised form of government is not necessary to enable different groups of closely related culture to amalgamate, nor does it necessarily arise out of the amalgamation.

It is a matter that has universal relevance for the analysis and classification of social organisation:

> Herein lies a problem of world importance: what is the relation of political structure to the whole social structure? Everywhere in Africa social ties of one kind or another tend to draw together peoples who are politically separated and *political ties appear to be dominant whenever there is conflict between them and other social ties* [my italics]. The solution of this problem would seem to lie in a more detailed investigation of the nature of political values and of the symbols in which they are expressed. Bonds of utilitarian interest between individuals and between groups are not as strong as the bonds implied in common attachment to mystical symbols. [14]

Its relevance for the Irish situation in particular is obvious, for when Fortes and Evans-Pritchard speak of "culture" and "other social ties" they include among these myths, rituals and all the other "mystical symbols" to which they attach such importance for the effective ordering of society. Basically what they are saying is that where there is cultural diversity unity must be maintained through centralist state-like structures, but that where there is cultural homogeneity these may be dispensed with. The position in early Ireland was that each individual kingdom was small enough not to require such structures, while in the country as a whole cultural-religious homogeneity was such that centralised government was unnecessary.

As in so many other contexts, here again one of the most striking analogues to the Irish situation, despite the glaring discrepancy in scale, is that of India. In the period before independence apologists for the Indian nationalist movement were much concerned to demonstrate the cultural homogeneity of the country as a justification for their claim to self-government. For that very reason their arguments and conclusions are suspect, or at least would be so if they were not confirmed by a good deal of informed objective opinion. When Radhakrishnan declares that "there is an inner cohesion among the Hindus from the Himalayas to Cape Comorin," he is saying in effect what virtually every serious student of India has said: that despite its teeming variety the huge continent of India shares in the same flexible, tolerant, comprehensive culture engendered of Hinduism. In the words of the *Oxford History of India,* "India beyond all doubt possesses a deep underlying fundamental unity, far more profound than that produced either by geographical isolation or by political superiority. That unity transcends the innumerable diversities of blood, colour, language, dress, manners, and sect."[15] It was most definitely not a political unity; indeed a stable, enduring political unity was something never achieved, even under the powerful Mauryan Empire, yet such was the integrating force of India's dominant culture that she was able to absorb an endless variety of peoples and traditions in a way that is hardly paralleled elsewhere in the world.

This almost axiomatic sense of belonging to a single comprehensive cultural environment colours the whole mainstream of the literary tradition, and what I said of Irish literature in this regard might be said, and indeed has been said, of its Indian counterpart: "The Indian epics and legends, in their manifold versions, teach that the stage for the gods was nothing less than the entire land and that the land remains one religious setting for those who dwell in it."[16] One of the many scholars who have stressed this capacity for integration is Louis Dumont ("By putting ourselves in the school of Indology, we learn in the first place never to forget that India is one . . ."). He views it in terms of a conflict between *dharma* "the moral law, moral and religious duty", and *artha* "material gain, the pursuit of the useful". *Artha* is the negation of *dharma*, but since society continues to be ruled by *dharma*, the art of politics is thus dissociated from the realm of values (a dissociation which is not unknown much nearer home, though lacking perhaps the same philosophical justification as in India). *Dharma* and *artha* must coexist, but they need not, and in a sense they cannot, coincide:

> It is not in the political sphere that the society finds its unity, but in the social regime of castes ... The system of government has no universal value, it is not the State in the modern sense of the term, and as we shall see, the state is identical with the king. Force and interest work only for strife and instability, but these conditions may thrive without anything essential being put in question; much to the contrary, *social unity implies and entertains political division* [my italics].[17]

Early Indian society differed profoundly from the modern African societies discussed by Fortes and Evans-Pritchard, but clearly the principle succinctly enunciated by Dumont has relevance for the question posed and answered tentatively by them. When they say that "bonds of utilitarian interest between individuals and between groups are not as strong as the bonds implied in common attachment to mystical symbols," what they are saying in fact is that *artha* has less binding force than *dharma*, though naturally these precise terms are very much culture-bound and the social context to which they refer is infinitely more complex than the African one. The dissociation of *dharma* and *artha* has even more relevance for early Irish society – not surprisingly in view of the cultural affinities between Ireland and India. It may lack the explicit documentation and elaborate rationale that it has in India, but it is implicit in the very fabric of history and tradition.

In both India and Ireland, then, culture–in the sense of belief, ritual and general tradition–was the transcendent force operating towards unity, but it was able to do so effectively only because there was in both countries a learned and priestly class which could assert the claims of orthodoxy. The druid or *file* had his local affiliations but at the same time he, and he alone, had free and untrammelled passage across tribal boundaries throughout Ireland. He had therefore, like the brahman, the mobility as well as the professional status and cohesion to propagate an accepted culture to all parts of the land and all segments of the population irrespective of ethnic origins. It might indeed almost be said of him, as has been said of the brahman, that "the destruction of tribal culture was a logical outcome, if not the conscious goal, of his ideology." In his residual role as priest and adviser to his royal patron the *file* was above all distinguished as praise-poet. This was one of his primary functions during the historical period, since praise-poetry was the medium *par excellence* for validating a rightful king and for setting forth in exemplary fashion the ideals of conduct which he should strive to maintain, and it is perhaps not surprising, in the light of what has already been said, that the topos of unity should crop up fairly frequently in these formal poems, some of which may have been odes composed for the occasion of the prince or chief's inauguration. In a poem addressed to Niall Óg Ó Néill, who was inaugurated chief of Tír Eoghain in 1397, the poet Tadhg Óg Ó hUiginn begins with the declaration:

> From the north comes succour;
> from Eamhain all quarters are joined in union;
> let the men of the north take Tara,
> they who came to her aid in the past.

and ends with a stanza that echoes and confirms the cosmographic allusion in the phrase *gach aird* "all points of the compass, all quarters":

> Niall Ó Néill of the nine fetters
> brings peace to the lands he unites;
> having established the five equal divisions,
> he goes forth to inspect the borders of Ireland's
>   territory.

Most of the examples of the theme of unification as a panegyric motif occur in the post-Norman period which saw the establishment of the hereditary schools of poetry run by a number of distinguished learned families. The work of these learned poets is dominated by praise-poetry — though this preponderance of the genre in the later as compared with the earlier period may be somewhat exaggerated by the fact that it was more consistently recorded; during the Old and Middle Irish period, when the writing of secular literature seems to have been virtually confined to the monastic scriptoria, it was hardly to be expected that panegyric verse should enjoy priority, whereas the position was quite the opposite from the thirteenth century onwards when the learned lay families themselves assumed responsibility for writing the poetry and began to compile "poem-books" (*duanairí*) which brought together the formal verse of individual poets or groups of poets or verse composed for individual patron families. This would help to account not only for the higher concentration of praise-poetry in the post-Norman period but also for the higher frequency of the unity theme as a praise motif. It is true that one might also explain the latter as a reflex of a growing unease and foreboding among the poets, who now saw the social order on which they depended being gradually eroded and threatened with total dissolution, but the rather formalised manner in which the motif is used in most instances also suggests something less topical and it seems reasonable to accept that it is in fact a very old ingredient of native praise-poetry which, for the reasons I have suggested, is better documented after the twelfth century.[18]

That it acquired a new and more urgent relevance during this period, and especially from the mid-sixteenth century onwards, is beyond question. For as long as Gaelic society remained relatively intact, so long could the combination of spiritual unity and political disunity continue without serious risk, since both were encompassed within a common, universally acknowledged ideology. So far as the poets were concerned, raiding and skirmishing among native chieftains was little more than a well-tried social lubricant that conferred certain benefits and carried few dangers for the system. This is why Eleanor Knott can write in the following terms of the poetry of Tadhg Dall Ó hUiginn, who died in 1591:

> He shows in most of his poems a calm acceptation of the contemporary strife, as though it were the natural order. Poetry flourished on it, and for him, like most bardic poets, the profession was the thing. The apprehensions and sorrows which troubled Irish poets of a slightly later period did not affect Tadhg Dall. Shadows palpable enough to us in his own poems portended no disaster to him. We may take him as a typical figure, thoroughly adapted in mind and customs to the existing order; utterly unaware of the imminent dawn of a new world.[19]

Warfare and strife were indeed part of "the natural order". So also was the traditional independence and mobility of the *file*, who, notwithstanding that he often formed close bonds of friendship and loyalty to a single patron, still set great value upon his own freedom to choose the subjects of his encomium. It is this, combined with a liberal dash of professional self-interest, that accounts for the apparent opportunism and cynicism of the poets some of whom seem to opt for the highest bidder and to measure their praise more in terms of profit than of merit – a failing which is neatly ridiculed by one of their own number, Gofraidh Fionn Ó Dálaigh, who flourished in the fourteenth century.

But by the late sixteenth century the poets were faced with a very different kind of reality, one in which war was fraught with calamitous and possibly irrevocable consequences. The expansion of English power in Ireland meant cultural suppression as well as military conquest, and the ultimate outcome could only be the extinction of the native order. The poets, who were after all better placed than most, including their patrons, to take a global view of contemporary events, saw the signs and read them clearly. Tadhg Dall Ó hUiginn himself realised the inappropriateness of the traditional dissipation of energy and in his poem urging Brian Ó Ruairc to engage the English in all-out war he counsels a different mode of action; I quote from the convenient summary by Standish Hayes O'Grady:

> . . . in the sword alone all hope lies now, and the state of
> affairs is such that never were the five provinces less inclined
> to peace; but all will not serve unless there be union: from
> north to south, from sea to ocean; the components of a
> great and (supposing concord to prevail) a feasible army are
> recited: the poet's immediate hero being (according to the
> consecrated figure of speech) held forth as chief commander
> of the host.[20]

The nobles of Ireland, says the poet, "are being driven to the outskirts
of Ireland, while troops of English are at its very centre (*'na glé-
mheadhón*)," in other words the foreigner has established himself
at the sacred spot which symbolises the unity of the country. The
phrasing is eloquent in its brevity.

A hundred years later Dáibhí Ó Bruadair is scandalised by the bick-
ering and dissension of the Irish leaders, declaiming his message with all
the passion and solemnity that only he can bring to bear on such a
subject. There is no cause to wonder, he says, that the English are
successful, for they hold firm by their compact, unlike his fellow-
Irishmen whose alliance falls apart at the pluck of a hair. The substance of his plaint is summarised in the title assigned to this poem
in several of the manuscripts; it reads in translation: "The Shipwreck
of Ireland, composed by Dáibhí Ó Bruadair on the misfortunes of
Ireland in the year of the Lord 1691 and how the sins of her own
children brought ruin and dispersion upon her in the month of October
of that year: *Regnum in se divisum desolabitur.*"[21] Again in his poem
to Patrick Sarsfield (no. 22) he shows himself preoccupied with the
same anxiety:

> O King of the world, Thou who hast created it
> and everything that stands upon it,
> redeem the land of Fodla from the peril of this
> conflict
> and join her peoples together in mutual love

— to which a scribal note in one of the manuscripts adds the disillusioned comment, *Agus fáríor ní dearna* "But alas! He did not."

By the time of Dáibhí Ó Bruadair the great dissolution of the
native order had largely been accomplished, a circumstance which goes
some way to explaining the sombre cast of much of his verse. He realised the full implications of the cultural changes brought about by
military defeat and the imposition of British rule and he was close
enough to the old dispensation to appreciate in a way that was impossible for those who came after how much had been lost and never
could be regained. The symbols of unity are occasionally invoked by
later poets, but they have become mere stereotypes emptied of real
significance, either in the political or in the cultural sphere. Through-

out the visible history of Irish tradition the palpable mark of the cultural unity of the island was the learned, literary language fashioned and cared for by endless generations of druids and *fili*; now this linguistic cohesion was shattered, and with its shattering came the end not perhaps of a culture but certainly of an ideology. *Things fall apart; the centre cannot hold* — the atrophy of the archetypal symbolism of the centre and of the cosmographic vision of totality of which it is a part signifies the collapse of a subtle equilibrium between cultural cohesion and political segmentation that was, it would seem, already old when the Celtic peoples were born. This perhaps more than any other single event or innovation marks the end of traditional Irish society and—from the ideological point of view—the reversion from order to chaos.

*   *   *

These notes on the traditional concept of unity are not intended to be exhaustive nor do they follow through to the end the possible implications of the topic. One might, for instance, trace out the extremely important role of the land, the actual soil of Ireland, as the material basis for the concept of national unity, and the tensions and complications which later arise within Irish republican nationalism when "the people" — an entity which figures hardly at all in Irish tradition — becomes an integral part of the complex from the eighteenth century onwards. One might also reflect on the curious contradiction between the traditional view that cultural unity could dispense with political unity and the modern nationalist view which glorifies political unity in the face of cultural disparities.

But the primary motivation of republican nationalism lies further back in the English conquest and plantations of the sixteenth and seventeenth centuries and these had already by dint of suppression and expropriation profoundly altered the traditional concept of nationhood. That it survived the seventeenth century only as an etiolated memory is in the circumstances hardly surprising. What is much more remarkable is that the principle of discrepant political and cultural organisation, whose existence is endlessly implied in the literature but never explicitly described — unlike the Indian theory of the relationship of *artha* and *dharma* which it so much resembles — should have outlived the druids who propagated it as part of their ideological system, sustained more than a millennium of Christianity, and remained a living force in Irish tradition centuries after Vikings and Normans had shaken the social premises on which it was founded.

Tomás Ó Cathasaigh

THE CONCEPT OF THE HERO
IN IRISH MYTHOLOGY

Giambattista Vico claimed, as long ago as 1725, that "the first science to be learned should be mythology or the interpretation of fables."[1] Vico's words, and the work of modern mythologists in many fields — anthropology, depth psychology, the history of religions and literary criticism — have left little impression on the intellectual life of Ireland. Yet our manuscripts contain mythological texts whose abundance and archaic character make them unique in Western Europe. Insofar as our mythology has been at all rediscovered, credit must rest largely with our creative writers, and notably with Yeats whose use of myth in the creation of literature was hailed as "a step toward making the modern world possible in art."[2] The use of myth by Anglo-Irish writers stands in marked contrast to the practice of modern writers in the Irish language. There is a chiastic pattern here: Anglo-Irish writers trying to create a national literature in English have drawn upon the resources of the indigenous tradition, whereas those writers whose aim has been to create a modern European literature in Irish have for the most part turned away from traditional themes. Perhaps in their case the burden of the past was too strong in the language itself to allow them to exploit Irish myth for their own purposes.

But it is not primarily as a quarry for modern creative writers that Irish mythology lays claim upon our attention, but rather as a rich and complex body of material which is there and which calls for elucidation and interpretation. It is in that mythology that we can discover the native ideology of Ireland, for although the early Irish material includes a valuable wisdom literature the abstract formulation of philosophical and theological theories was not the Irish way. It was in their myths that they explored the nature of men and the gods, and a central task of criticism must be to uncover and to restate in abstract terms the configuration of the ideological patterns which underlie the myths. As the great French mythologist Georges Dumézil has put it: "A literary work does not have to set forth a theory: it is the hearer's or the reader's task to perceive the providential design which has arranged the events in the order in which the work presents them and with the results which it describes. Yet it is the design that justifies these events and results, and gives them a meaning."[3]

This "providential design" must be established by close study of the texts, but the general observation may be made that Irish myth is concerned above all with the relationship between man and the gods, and that the myth of the hero is used as a vehicle for exploring this relationship. In this respect, Irish myth shares the character of mythological systems in general. The situation can be stated in structuralist terms: a basic opposition in Irish myth is between man and god, and this opposition is mediated in the person of the hero. "Opposition" is used here in the sense of the discrimination of paired categories, and it is the structuralist view that every mythical system is built upon a sequence of such oppositions which are mediated by a third category which is abnormal or anomalous. [4] The hero belongs to this third category: he is at once the son of a god and of a human father; he is mortal and he lives out his life among men, but otherworld personages intervene at crucial moments of his life. The myth of the hero is exceptionally well represented in Irish sources, and the space at my disposal here allows only of a selective treatment. It seemed best to choose two of the more remarkable heroes of Irish tradition for extended discussion, and the two who are dealt with are the martial hero, Cú Chulainn, and the king-hero, Conaire Mór. In each case I concentrate on a single tale: for Cú Chulainn I restrict myself in the main to the early version of his 'Conception Tale', and for Conaire Mór to 'The Destruction of Da Hostel'. The necessarily summary account of these two texts may perhaps give some indications of the thematic content of the Irish versions of the myth of the hero, while the commmentary is intended to elucidate the ideological framework within which they may be interpreted. Having considered the two texts, we go on to two other topics, one of which is thoroughly pagan, while the other shows an admixture of pagan and Christian elements. The first of these is the role of the god Lug in relation to mortal heroes, the second the election to kingship of Corc of Cashel.

The early version of *Compert Con Culainn* ("The Conception of Cú Chulainn") tells how a flock of birds repeatedly grazed to the roots the plain of Emain Macha, the ancient capital of Ulster. The warriors of Ulster gave chase to the birds and pursued them in nine chariots, Conchobor's daughter Dechtine serving as his charioteer. In the evening, three of the birds led the pursuers to the edge of Bruig na Bóinne (Newgrange), where night came upon the Ulstermen. It snowed heavily and the Ulstermen sought shelter. They found a new house where they were made welcome by a couple. The man of the house told them that his wife was in labour. Dechtine went to her and a boy-child was born. At the same time, a mare outside the house dropped two foals, and these were given to the child. By morning both the house and the birds had disappeared, and all that remained with the Ulstermen at the edge of Bruig na Bóinne were the child and the two foals. With these the warriors returned to Emain Macha.

Dechtine reared the child, but he fell ill and died. Then a man came to Dechtine in her sleep and said that he was Lug son of Eithniu. He told her that she would be pregnant by him; it was he who had brought her to Bruig na Bóinne, it was with him she had stayed the night, and the boy she reared was his son. It was that boy he had placed in her womb, and his name would be Sétantae.

Conchobor betrothed Dechtine to one Sualdaim mac Roich, but she was ashamed to go pregnant to Sualdaim's bed and carried out an abortion. Then she slept with Sualdaim: she conceived again, and bore a son, Sétantae, who was later given the name Cú Chulainn.[5]

The theme of the "waste land", with which *Compert Con Culainn (CCC)* opens, occurs frequently in Irish tradition: the laying waste of the land is the ultimate sanction of the gods. In *CCC* the land is laid waste by otherworld birds; in other texts this is done by otherworld horses and pigs; and the fruits of the earth will of themselves dry up when the land is ruled by an unrighteous king, who is unpleasing to the gods. The theme of the waste land implies the need for a fecundating hero who will restore vegetation to Emain Macha. In Irish tradition the fecundating role of the hero is seen most clearly in the lives of the king-heroes, who ensure the fertility of land and beast and man by their wise and judicious rule: we shall see presently that Conaire Mór exemplifies this. Cú Chulainn, on the other hand, is essentially a martial hero, the defender of his people against the enemy invader. But it has been argued that in the *Táin,* when he defends Ulster against the ravages of its Connaught enemies while Conchobor and the Ulstermen are undergoing their winter sleep, Cú Chulainn exemplifies the vigorous young male as the vital force in nature, and that this scenario represents an ancient vegetation myth, the basic theme of which is "the triumph of life and fecundity over death and decay, as suggested by seasonal change."[6] The occurrence of the theme of the waste land in *CCC* lends weight to that interpretation. In the immediate context of *CCC,* however, the theme presages the decisive intervention by the otherworld in the affairs of Ulster. It also has the function of inducing the Ulstermen to give chase to the birds, which lead them to Bruig na Bóinne.

Bruig na Bóinne is a localisation of the otherworld, one of the *síde* to which the gods were consigned when men came to share dominion of the land in Ireland. Thus, these *síde* (the singular is *síd*) were the abodes of the gods: they were located in the mounds of the earth (both natural formations and prehistoric tumuli), under the lakes, and on the islands of the ocean. The world of the *síde* was distinct from that of men, but contact between the two was frequent, and especially at Samain (November 1) when the *síde* were believed to be open, and their denizens free to wander abroad at will — beliefs which have persisted down to modern times. The prominence of the *side* on the landscape doubtless contributed to the constant awareness among Irish country people of the imminence of the otherworld. Bruig na Bóinne, in particular, was originally the whole necropolis on the Boyne, but the name became specially attached to Newgrange, which is but one of the tumuli there. In our text, the Lord of Bruig na Bóinne is Lug, the Irish reflex of a Celtic god who is commemorated in the names of a number of continental cities such as Lyons (from an earlier Lugudunum), Laon and Leyden. We have seen that when he later comes to Dechtine in her sleep, Lug explains that it was he who brought her to Bruig na Bóinne. And he brought her there, not on an errand of doom, but so that Sétantae might be brought into the world. Thus, Bruig na Bóinne is here the telluric womb from which emerges the saviour-hero of Ulster.

Cú Chulainn shares with mythical personages everywhere the characteristic of dual paternity: he is at once the son of a god (Lug) and of a human father (Sualdaim). What is remarkable in the case of Cú Chulainn is that he is conceived three times: in one manuscript text of *CCC* he is said to have been "the son of three years". The number three is of course everywhere invested with symbolic significance, and triplicity of gods and heroes is a very common theme in Irish myth. Cú Chulainn's threefold conception is one of the many expressions of this notion. Another one which may be noted here is the theme of threefold death, of which we have a number of examples in Irish texts and which will be mentioned again in connection with Conaire Mór. Triplicity is a feature also of Celtic iconography, both in Ireland and on the continent, its most striking expression being the head with three faces. In the particular case of Cú Chulainn, his triplicity is related to his destiny as a warrior, for his martial career is marked by a number of encounters with triple adversaries of one kind or another. One such encounter is his initiatory combat in which he ventures forth and defeats the three formidable sons of Nechta Scéne. This has been identified as a variant of an ancient mythical exploit in which a god or hero slays an adversary who is endowed with some form of triplicity: Dumézil compares Heracles, who conquers the three-headed Geryon, and who was conceived in one night three times as long as normal. [7]

But perhaps the most interesting feature of the threefold conception in *CCC* is its structural sequence. The boy is first begotten in the otherworld by Lug upon his otherworld consort; then at Emain by Lug upon Dechtine; and finally by Sualdaim upon Dechtine. There is thus a progression from fully divine to fully human parentage: in this sequence the hero recapitulates in his own life the history of man, since, if we may judge from the occurrence of deity names in their pedigrees, the Irish apparently believed themselves to be descended from the gods. Furthermore, this sequence gives us a singularly clear example of the manner in which the hero mediates between the gods and men: the second (or middle) conception, linked to the first by Lug and Dechtine respectively, mediates the opposition between the divine and the human. In this case at least the "meaning" of the triplicity of the hero is inseparable from the structure of the narrative.

The manner of Cú Chulainn's conception and birth marks him out for greatness. He is destined to save his people from the ravages of war: how he accomplishes this is shown in the *Táin*. There is a whole cycle of texts about Cú Chulainn telling how he was initiated into warrior status, how he overcame great obstacles to win Emer as his wife, how he journeyed to the otherworld, how he killed his only son, and, finally, how he met his tragic death. Taken together, these episodes make up Cú Chulainn's heroic biography from conception and birth to death. Rather than follow up these texts here, however, we turn now to our second hero.

Conaire Mór (Conaire the Great) is depicted in our sources as a prehistoric king of Tara. His biography is heroic, and it follows much the same basic pattern as that of Cú Chulainn. But Conaire is destined to be king, and, in contrast to the martial ethic which informs the cycle of Cú Chulainn, Conaire's life is presented in terms of the pacific ethic which was the basis of the Irish ideology of kingship. I have already referred to the fecundating role of the king who ensures the fertility of man and beast and land by his wise and judicious rule. The characteristic of the king which ensured fertility in this way was known as *fír flatha* ("Prince's truth"). "Truth" in this context is a broad term, embracing the notions of wisdom and justice, and, as well as fertility, it also secures seasonable weather and amity among men. In short, it is a cosmic force, and the doctrine of *fír flatha* places the king at the centre of the cosmos. This is the doctrine which is expressed in heroic terms in the life of Conaire Mór.

Our text for Conaire Mór is *Togail Bruidne Da Derga (TBDD)*.[8] The title is conventionally translated "The Destruction of Da Derga's Hostel", but the *bruiden* or "hostel" in question is a localisation of the otherworld. (It may be noted in passing the this *bruiden* gave its name to Bohernabreena, near Tallaght in County Dublin.)[9] It is in Da Derga's hostel that Conaire met his death, and the title of our tale is in keeping with the fact that much the greater part of it is devoted to that event and to those which led up to it. *TBDD* is nonetheless a biography of Conaire, dealing in turn with his conception and birth, his boyhood, his elevation to kingship, the Golden Age enjoyed in Ireland during his reign, and turning only then to the tragic story of his death. All of this resolves itself into three sections, which we shall consider in turn: the making of a king, the golden age, and the tragedy of a king.

The Making of a King

Conaire's mother Mess Buachalla was brought up in humble circumstances, but she was the daughter of a king and a beautiful goddess who was born in a *síd*. Mess Buachalla married Eterscélae king of Tara, but on the night before her marriage she saw a bird on the skylight coming to her. The bird left his "bird-skin" on the floor and ravished her. He told her that she would bear his son and that he should be called Conaire. So it came to pass, and Conaire was brought up as the son of Eterscélae. He was reared with three foster-brothers. Now Conaire had three "gifts" *(buada)*, the gift of hearing, the gift of seeing and the gift of calculation, and he shared these gifts with his foster-brothers, giving one gift to each of the three.

When Eterscélae died and a successor was to be chosen, Conaire was told by his foster-father to go to Tara. He set out and when he reached Dublin he saw great speckled birds, which he pursued as far as the sea and onto the waves. They then cast off their bird-skins, and one of them identified himself to Conaire as Nemglan "the king of your father's birds". Nemglan instructed Conaire to go along the road to Tara stark-naked, bearing a stone and a sling. Meanwhile, it had been prophesied at a "bull-feast" (a solemn divinatory rite) that the person who arrived in this way would be the future king. So when Conaire appeared he was recognised as king. His nakedness was covered with royal raiment, he was placed in a chariot, and he bound the hostages of Tara (an act which signifies their submission to him). But the people of Tara objected to him, since he was young and beardless. Conaire refuted this objection, however, saying that a king was not disqualified by youth, provided that he be generous, and that it was his right from father and grandfather to bind the hostages of Tara. This utterance was greeted with enthusiasm by the people ("'Wonder of wonders', they cried"), and Conaire was invested with the kingship. Then the taboos of Conaire's reign are listed: these are prohibitions which were laid upon Conaire (perhaps by Nemglan, but the text is ambiguous at this point), and so long as they are honoured Conaire's reign is marked by prodigious peace and prosperity.

The begetting of Conaire Mór represents an otherworld intervention in the affairs of Tara. We are reminded of the otherworld birds in *CCC*, who summon the Ulstermen to Bruig na Bóinne. In *TBDD* the birds have a more direct role: Conaire is begotten by a god who appears in the guise of a bird; he is called to his destiny by the king of his father's birds, Nemglan; and his reign is called "the bird-reign" *(én-flaith)*. This otherworld intervention is an integral part of the election of Conaire to kingship, and it seems right to compare the sequence summarised above with the scenario which Dumézil has traced in the traditions concerning the primitive Hindu king Pŕthu. There were three stages in the election of Pŕthu: designation by the gods, recognition by the wise men and acceptance by the people.[10] These three elements occur in *TBDD:* Conaire is designated by the very manner of his conception; he is recognised as king when he arrives on the road to Tara in fulfilment of the diviner's prophecy; and he is accepted by the people when he successfully meets their objection to his youth and beardlessness. Each of these stages has its proper place in the structure, but it is in the last one that Conaire establishes his right to the kingship. This he does by delivering a true judgement on the matter of his own eligibility for kingship, a judgement which reveals his understanding that it is essential for a ruler *(flaith)* to be generous – a notion which is reflected in the Modern Irish *flaithiúil* "generous". This true judgement shows Conaire to be possessed of *fír flatha*, which, as we have seen, is the distinguishing characteristic of the rightful king.

The Golden Age

TBDD describes the state of peace and plenty which was enjoyed in Ireland during the reign of Conaire Mór. The ideal conditions which characterised his reign (and also that of Cormac mac Airt) are reminiscent of the otherworld in its beneficent aspect as it is depicted in Irish texts. They represent two different responses to the paradisal yearning, the otherworld being separated in space, the Golden Age in time from the storyteller and his audience. In Old Irish the word for "peace" is *síd*, which is a homonym of the word which (as we have seen) denotes a habitation of the gods. These homonyms were originally one and the same: I have argued elsewhere that the homonymy reflects the nexus between the otherworld and conditions in this world, as mediated in the person of the king. The otherworld is the source of the king's cosmic truth *(fír)* and peace is its symptom; the state of peace secured by the kings of the mythical past, whose kingship was sanctioned by the otherworld, is seen as a re-creation of the paradisal condition; and, as a material correlative to these abstract connections, the king would seem often to have been consecrated upon a *síd*. [11]

The Tragedy of a King

The golden age of peace and plenty depicted in *TBDD* is a measure of the beneficent role of the rightful king. In fulfilling this role the king is constrained by his *gessi* (taboos), and by the requirement to maintain the order based on cosmic truth. Conaire's tragedy is that he is faced with a conflict between his duty in these respects and his love for his foster-brothers, and that he puts love before duty. What happened is that Conaire's foster-brothers took to thieving in order to see what punishment the king might inflict upon them and how the theft in his reign might damage him. Conaire repeatedly refused to punish them. They were therefore emboldened to advance in crime from theft to marauding, the significance of this being that one of the taboos laid upon Conaire was that there should be no marauding during his reign. By failing to punish his foster-brothers for their earlier and less serious crime, Conaire caused the violation of one of his own taboos. And then, when the foster-brothers and their companions in crime were brought before him on the charge of marauding, Conaire delivered a false judgment, decreeing that the others should be slain by their fathers, but that his foster-brothers should be spared. Conaire saw the injustice of his judgment and revoked it, saying, "The judgment which I have given is no extension of life for me." He ordained instead that all the marauders should be spared and banished overseas. Ironically, even the revised judgment proved "no extension of life" to Conaire, for in due course the marauders whom he had spared returned to destroy him in the *bruiden* of Da Derga.

All of this provides us with an Irish example of an old Indo-European theme which Dumézil has called the "sin of the sovereign", "which destroys either the raison d'etre of sovereignty, namely the protection of the order founded on truth . . . or the mystical support of human sovereignties, namely the respect for the superior sovereignty of the gods and the sense of limitations inherent in every delegation of the divine sovereignty. The king falls prey to one or other of these risks, which are at bottom reducible to the same thing."[12] Dumézil was not aware of the occurrence of this theme in Irish tradition, but his formulation stands as an excellent summary of Conaire's "sin" in *TBDD*, save that Conaire falls prey to both of the "risks" described by Dumézil. The taboos which have been laid upon him constitute in effect a contract with the otherworld, and his transgression of one of these taboos destroys the respect of the otherworld personages who have delegated sovereignty to him. In failing to punish his foster-brothers, and later in delivering a false judgment, Conaire destroys the respect for the order founded on truth.

No sooner has the king's judgment been given and the marauders departed than we hear that the perfect peace has broken down which had been enjoyed during Conaire's reign. The otherworld now takes on its malevolent aspect, and Conaire proceeds to transgress all the taboos which have been laid upon him. He sets out from Tara and finds that he cannot return, for the lands round about are full of raiders coming from every side, men roam about naked, and the land is all on fire. This is a sign that the law has broken down there. And so Conaire turns away and he takes the path which leads him to his doom in the *bruiden*. He encounters a number of malevolent otherworld beings on his way to the *bruiden*, and in the meantime his foster-brothers and their allies return to Ireland. They assail Conaire in the *bruiden*, which they set on fire three times. Conaire's head is cut off, and the severed head is given a drink of water which has been taken by his servant Mac Cécht from Uarán Garaid on the plain of Croghan in County Roscommon after a tour of the rivers and lakes of Ireland. The severed head thanks Mac Cécht, and Conaire dies.

Conaire dies by decapitation, but the elements of fire and water are also present: the *bruiden* is set on fire, and Conaire dies only after water has been poured into his throat and gullet. I suspect that we have a variant here of the motif of three-fold death. This is well-represented in Irish sources, and in its classic form comprises death by wounding, drowning and burning. Although Conaire is not drowned and it is not explicitly stated that he is burned, the elements of iron, water and fire are brought into play in the account of his death.

There is another instance of triplicity in *TBDD* which is made explicit, and which has a bearing on the interpretation of the text, namely the fact that Conaire's foster-brothers are three in number. Irish tradition presents examples of trios which are merely triplications of a single personality. Perhaps the best known of these is the trio in the Deirdre story: the three sons of Uisniu are at all times found together, and among them only Naoise has a definite personality. Áinle and Ardán are but shadows of Naoise, and they die when he dies.[13] The three foster-brothers in *TBDD* (who are themselves blood-brothers) are a somewhat different trio, for they are identical in appearance and dress, not only among themselves, but also with Conaire: the text says that all four were identical in their clothing, their weapons, and the colour of their horses. Moreover, it will be recalled that Conaire distributed his gifts (*buada*) to them: each one of them represents an aspect of his triple self and together they are his equal. These three personages are cast in Conaire's image and in *TBDD* they use his own "gifts" to destroy him: it is scarcely too much to suggest that they may be taken to represent the evil side of his nature. In this way they are a projection in corporeal form of "the enemy within". They too die at the destruction of the *bruiden*.

The "providential design" (to use Dumézil's term) which gives meaning to the tragic events of *TBDD* is that of the Irish ideology of kingship, and it will be clear by now that the otherworld is central to that ideology. Many Irish texts give expression to the underworld legitimation of sovereignty, but this notion is nowhere more explicitly stated than in *Baile In Scáil* ("The Phantom's Vision").[14] This tells how Conn Cétchathach was brought to an otherworld abode where he met a couple — a girl sitting on a chair of crystal and wearing a golden crown, and a man sitting on a throne. The man identifies himself to Conn as Lug and tells him that he has come to Conn to tell him the span of his sovereignty and of that of every prince that will come of him in Tara for ever. The girl is identified as the Sovereignty of Ireland, and she has a golden cup from which she gives Conn a drink of ale at Lug's instructions. And then she asks who next should be given a drink from the cup, and Lug names Conn's successor, and so the dialogue continues and we are given a list of those who will follow Conn in the kingship of Tara.

This text is a version of the sovereignty myth, which has to do with the espousal of the king to the goddess of sovereignty, and it shows that the kingship of Conn and his descendants at Tara has been conferred at the behest of the god Lug. It will be remembered that Lug was the divine father of Cú Chulainn, and now we find him presented as legitimator of the Dál Cuinn kings of Tara. The key to Lug's role is to be found in the story of the battle of Mag Tuired (now Moytirra, in County Sligo), *Cath Maige Tuired*.[15] This tale tells of the war of the gods, and in it we see Lug successively attaining pre-eminence in the domains of sovereignty, martial vigour and agricultural practice: those who are acquainted with Dumézil's work will recognise here the three terms of the tripartite structure which that scholar has established for Indo-European ideology.

Lug may be described as the hero among the gods. His heroic deeds in relation to kingship, martial vigour and agricultural practice were performed in the time of the gods, which preceded the appearance of man in Ireland. When men did come to share dominion of the land, the gods, as we have seen, retreated to the *síde*. Thenceforth, great deeds were to be performed by mortal heroes, such as Cú Chulainn, who differ from Lug in that, however great their achievements in life, they must die, and when they are dead they are dead.

What then is the relationship between the mortal hero and his divine predecessor who still inhabits the *síde*? It can be said, in the first place, as de Vries has argued, that the hero raises himself to the level of the gods.[16] Having performed his deeds in the time of the gods, Lug is by definition anterior to the mortal heroes: it follows that the other heroes are perceived within the system as replicating (in some measure) the heroic achievements of Lug. In the field of kingship, the great hero is Cormac mac Airt, who is the exemplary model of *fír flatha;* the Golden Age which was enjoyed in his reign was not brought to an end by any sin of the kind committed by Conaire Mór. In the field of martial vigour, Cú Chulainn is the outstanding figure. But the connection between Lug and Cú Chulainn or Cormac is not solely that of exemplary model and replicator. We know from *CCC* that Lug was progenitor to Cú Chulainn. And *Baile In Scáil* attests a connection of a somewhat different kind between Lug and Cormac. The latter was one of the Dál Cuinn kings of Tara, and one of those upon whom the drink of sovereignty was conferred at Lug's behest. In this act, Lug effectively bestows his otherworld consort, the Sovereignty of Ireland, upon Cormac for a stated period of years. As her spouse for the time being, Cormac is Lug's surrogate as king of Tara, while Cú Chulainn, for his part, is an incarnation of Lug.

*   *   *

What we find in the early Irish narrative texts is mythology and ideology refracted through literature, and it is worth noting that this literature would not have come down to us were it not for the labours of monastic scribes. Early Irish literature stems from the fruitful interplay of two sets of institutions, the native orders of learning and the monastic schools. The texts contain many survivals from Celtic and

Indo-European culture, and these elements clearly must have been transmitted orally until such time as they were transferred into the written record. The written literature had its beginnings in the monasteries in the seventh century, and continued to flourish in them until the twelfth, and what survives to us today is the remains of that literature. The early Irish texts owe much to the vigorous oral tradition which not only preceded the written literature but continued unabated alongside, but the ecclesiastics' contribution to their extant condition must have been crucial and continuing. The creation and survival of the early Irish narrative texts show that the early Irish churchmen were not only open to, but deeply involved in the extra-ecclesiastical lore of their country.

It will be appropriate, therefore, to end with an instance of syncretism: this is an account of the election to the kingship of Cashel of Corc mac Láire (Corc son of the Mare), in which the basic pattern is similar to that of the election of Conaire in *TBDD,* but which is realised in partly Christian terms.[17] The designation by the gods here takes the form of designation by angels; the recognition of Corc by the wise men is here entrusted to swineherds to whom it has been revealed in a vision, though there is also a druid who discovers that Corc is to be king by means of druidic divination; the people assent to Corc's accession by answering "Amen" to his response to a blessing. As Dillon pointed out, this blessing, apart from a pious invocation, "is rather pagan than Christian in expression". This blessing and the king's solemn response to it show the power of the spoken word, as did Conaire's pronouncement on his eligibility to kingship. Finally, we may note that the king is bound to preserve his prescriptions, namely that he have truth and mercy; such a prescription *(buaid)* "is a thing or act which brings good luck, and which is therefore a duty or prescribed conduct, the reverse of *geis*";[18] we are reminded of the *gessi* which were laid upon Conaire.

The story of Corc also bears comparison with *Baile In Scáil,* for here the angels reveal the names of the kings who are to succeed Corc in the kingship of Cashel. In contrast to *Baile In Scáil,* however, this text shows the kings to have been legitimated by God, of whom the angels are of course messengers.

Corc of Cashel mediates between his people and God. The other texts which I have been discussing exemplify some of the ways in which Irish tradition presents the destiny of the hero who mediates between man and the pagan gods. The world-view of these texts is an anthropocentric one: man is the centre of the cosmos, and the fruits of the earth and the workings of the elements are contingent upon the physical and moral excellence of the king – and, in texts where the martial ethic prevails, upon that of the champion. But the hero is subject to constraints from within and without, and otherworld personages intervene at all the crucial moments in his career. These interventions may be benevolent or malevolent, reflecting the contradictory aspects of the otherworld. A benevolent god may function as progenitor and helper, a malevolent one as villain and destroyer. The burden of heroism is a heavy one, and is ultimately unenviable. While celebrating the achievements of the hero, Irish myth asserts the precariousness of man's position in the cosmos.

PART II

4

Dermot Moran

NATURE, MAN AND GOD
IN THE PHILOSOPHY OF
JOHN SCOTTUS ERIUGENA

It follows that we ought not to understand God and the creature as two things distinct from one another, but as one and the same. For both the creature, by subsisting, is in God; and God, by manifesting Himself, in a marvellous and ineffable manner creates Himself in the creature.

John Scottus Eriugena, *Periphyseon,* vol. 3, 678c

This is why I pray to God to rid me of God, for my essential being is above God in so far as we comprehend God as the principle of creatures. . . . And if I myself were not, God would not be either: that God is God, of this I am the cause. If I were not, God would not be God. There is, however, no need to understand this.

Meister Eckhart, *Beati pauperes spiritu.*

Apart from Berkeley, Johannes Scottus Eriugena (also known as John Scotus Erigena or John the Scot) is Ireland's most important philosopher. He has been called the greatest philosopher writing in Latin between Augustine and Anselm, one of the greatest metaphysicians of all time, the "father of speculative philosophy", the first scholastic.[1] Yet, despite this high evaluation of his position, he is generally regarded as an outsider to the main western tradition in philosophy, whose philosophy spawned no movement, whose achievement stands alone, an isolated beacon of light in the prevailing darkness of the age.[2] It was not until the nineteenth century that the serious study of his works began, and then it was because of the similarity perceived between his system and the idealist philosophies of the German writers who saw him as their precursor, an enlightened rationalist struggling against blind subservience to authority.[3] In the twentieth century the true subtlety and brilliance of his system has been appreciated for its own sake, but, more often than not, among specialists in the history of philosophy rather than among general students and readers. Translations of his works are not readily available, he is rarely the subject of post-graduate dissertations; his greatness is generally acknowledged, his works generally ignored.[4] There is a pressing need for a revaluation of his contribution to philosophy and for a new recognition of the imaginative adventure which his system expresses — a speculative critique of ideas not at all irrelevant to present day philosophical debates on the nature of the universe, or the significance of human existence. I hope that this essay may at least stimulate an appetite for the exploration of Eriugena's intellectual world.

I
LIFE AND WORKS (THE IRISH BACKGROUND)

John was born in Ireland in the early ninth century. He emigrated to France possibly to escape the Viking raids which were gradually destroying the monastic golden age of this island, and he first appears in history as philosopher-grammarian at the court of Charles the Bald.[5] This period in France is generally known as a time of educational reform and *renovatio,* and yet even in this climate John was noticed for his breadth of learning and the boldness of his cosmological interpretations in his commentary on the writings of an obscure Neoplatonist, Martianus Capella.[6] Because of his knowledge of Augustine and his obvious dialectical skills, he was enlisted by Hincmar, Bishop of Rheims and Pardulus, Bishop of Laon, into the theological dispute raging at the time over the question of freewill and predestination, a controversy which had been sparked off by the Saxon monk, Gottschalk.[7] Scottus wrote an enthusiastic and idiosyncratic rebuttal of Gottschalk which insisted that evil and sin belong more properly to the realm of non-being than to being. Hence evil and sin are unknown to God who knows only His own volitions which are necessarily good. God did not create hell as a place of punishment; rather hell is a state of mind which the sinful bring about in themselves of their own doing.[8] This rebuttal of Gottschalk's double predestination *(gemina praedestinatio)* theory was severely condemned by the French bishops and by the councils of Valence and Langres, but Scottus himself seems to have been untouched by this censure, presumably because he was a favourite of the king. Thus we find him, soon after his theological disputes, engaged by Charles as the official translator of the writings of the Pseudo-Dionysius, a mysterious eastern Christian who wrote in Greek, thought by Charles to be St Denis, patron saint of France.[9]

Eriugena's theological speculations on predestination had already led him away from the standard interpretation of Augustine and the Christian literature of the Latin west; the impact on him of Dionysius and the Greek eastern Christian tradition marked him off from the western tradition even more. A new world had been opened up and Eriugena's philosophical efforts were now directed towards constructing a vast synthesis of the learning of Greek east and Latin west, reconciling Augustine and Dionysius, Roman realism with eastern mysticism.

The result of this undertaking was Eriugena's masterpiece, the dialogue *On the Division of Nature,* a complete account in five books of the nature of God and creation, fall and redemption, heaven and hell, so far as human reason could grasp them. It was this work which inspired much of the cosmological thinking of the twelfth century Renaissance.[10] However it later became linked with the pantheistical teachings of David of Dinant and Amaury of Bène and was condemned with their writings in 1210 and again in 1225.[11] This papal condemnation obscured Eriugena's influence in the thirteenth century, although his translations of Dionysius and his homily on the Prologue of John's Gospel remained in circulation. In the fourteenth and fifteenth centuries he had some influence over the mystical doctrines of Meister Eckhart and Cardinal Nicholas of Cusa, although the latter regarded his doctrines as too dangerous for general consumption.[12] Finally, when the first printed edition of his works appeared from Oxford in 1681 it was placed on the *Index Librorum Prohibitorum.*

The reasons for Eriugena's condemnation are not clear, especially as these condemnations come so long after his death, and also because his teachings were not that different from other writers such as Cusanus who escaped censure. But it is absolutely clear that the curt dismissal of his work contained in the condemnations, and repeated in the early manuals of scholastic philosophy, is a complete misrepresentation of the complex dialectical arguments which he employs and the careful manner with which he presents his conclusions, backed up by the best authorities of the eastern and western traditions.

The accusation of heresy excluded Eriugena from the main western philosophical tradition for many centuries. Yet even in his own time he was regarded as an outsider, a *vir barbarus,* as the Vatican Librarian termed him, an *advena,* merely a "famous Irishman" *(Scotum illum).* [13] He stood out as a stranger in France. Presumably he coined the name, Eriugena, to express this curious phenomenon, an Irishman versed in philosophical wisdom. Yet he is equally a stranger to Irish tradition. He did not write in Irish (although Eriu- is considered to be Old Irish) nor refer to Irish events or customs. He wrote in a Latin which has hardly anything insular or Hibernian about it.[14] All of this troubles those who would seek to claim Eriugena as an exclusively "Irish" philosopher,' meaning by that someone who advocated an Irish or Celtic way of life, or whose ideas have something of the Celtic twilight about them, a precursor of George Russell perhaps. "Irish" traits have been adduced – his love of nature, his resistance to authority which reminds one of Columbanus, his use of the imagery of sea-voyaging and peregrination which recalls Brendan the Navigator (or Walafrid Strabo's remark that wandering was "second nature" to the Irish).[15] His love of learning might suggest a schooling in the famous monasteries of early Ireland. Yet none of these traits provide us with concrete evidence of his "Irishness".

Several writers have tried to explain his fascination for things Greek by suggesting a Greek education for him in the Irish schools. The controversy has raged since the 1930s and the present *status quaestionis* reflects a compromise.[16] There is no evidence to suggest that Eriugena learned his Greek in Ireland, indeed he himself claimed to be a novice in these matters until King Charles asked him to translate Dionysius. At the same time, Greek learning on the continent was carried on in the main at Irish centres, and there is no evidence to suppose that Scottus could *not* have learned his Greek in Ireland.

We are left with something curious: a pre-established harmony, as it were, between Eriugena's mind and the mental attitude of the Neo-platonic Christian writers of the Greek tradition. When he had to choose between Latin and Greek authorities he chose the Greek, when he had to decide between realism and idealism, he chose idealism.[17] How is this to be understood? Instead of worrying about Eriugena's actual contact with Ireland, it would be more fruitful to engage in a comparative analysis of the structures of the Greek and Celtic-Irish cultures of the early middle ages, in order to find some clues to the apparent convergence between them on spiritual matters. I am not talking here about the distinguishing features of the Celtic church, its date for Easter, or the shape of the tonsure and such like; rather I am suggesting that the categories of sainthood and deification *(theosis)* be compared, or the Greek contemplation *(theoria)* with the imaginative visions *(fís)* of Irish literature. Eriugena's concept of the otherworld, and the nature of punishment as a fantasy which torments the mind, could be compared with the Irish Christian understanding of these things – not so much the dogma, but the popular literary portrayal of these matters. Eriugena's commentary on the scriptures should be compared with surviving Irish commentaries. It is only in this way that the true nature of Eriugena's relation to his Irish background can be assessed. We are no longer dealing here with random biographical facts, but are at the more important task of cultural comparison, which will be of enormous value to those who wish to understand Eriugena's true standing as a philosopher.

To sum up, it is somewhat misleading to portray Eriugena as a complete outsider to the western or even to the Irish traditions. His work transcends the narrow categories which are most often used in textbooks on the history of philosophy. Rather than attempting to fit him in to the narrow mould of western Aristotelian-Thomistic or Augustinian traditions, he should be conceived as the founder of a new philosophy, an originator like Plotinus or Descartes, whose work itself sets the categories of the new age. Similarly with his Irish heritage, there is no point in seeking in Scottus some Anglo-Irish Revival concept of Irishness or even some classical Celtic criterion, instead we should see Eriugena as establishing a most significant cultural motif – the Irishman who became a European intellectual, indeed a figure of world status. His philosophy should be judged, as all philosophy must, on its own merits alone. In Eriugena's case we must seek to understand the speculative idealism which informs all his major concepts, a speculative idealism so forceful that it does not recur again with such vigour until we come to the writings of the eighteenth century Irish philosopher Berkeley.

II
THE MEDIEVAL COSMOS AND THE RENAISSANCE IDEAL OF MAN

In order to understand Eriugena's philosophy we must first situate him in the medieval world. He is a writer of the Carolingian *renovatio*, a time when the liberal arts were the basis of the educational curriculum[18] and there was a strong, if fashionable, interest in things Greek. It is often described as a time of humanist inquiry in contrast to the general decline of the tenth and eleventh centuries; but the Carolingian revival is rarely seen as a full renaissance of thought and letters as it later developed in Italy.[19] Generally speaking, the medieval world is contrasted with the modern post-Cartesian world along the following lines: the medievals accepted the primacy of faith over reason, they conceived of the cosmos as a finite well-ordered structure exhibiting a hierarchy of perfection and value, with God occupying the highest position, the angels below Him, and below them the planets, until we come to man who occupies a central but lowly place above the irrational animals and the vegetable and mineral strata.[20] The moderns, on the other hand, begin with the primacy of the human intellect and its own self-certainty (the Cartesian *cogito*); they accept the independent and self-validating nature of reason itself, championing the individual's moral autonomy and freedom of conscience against the authoritarian dictates of a dogmatic scholasticism. They assert the infinity and boundlessness of the world and the homogeneity of space, rejecting totally the hierarchical world of the medievals.[21] To the moderns, medieval philosophy is speculation based not on rational principles but upon received opinions. It is the moderns who recognise the need for the critical revaluation of the role of reason itself, who make a "Copernican revolution" and begin not with God as true object of our knowing but with man's indubitable presence to himself.[22] Thus, Ernst Cassirer names Cardinal Nicholas of Cusa as the "first modern thinker" because "his first step consists in asking not about God, but about the possibility of knowledge about God".[23]

In general, then, the medieval world was broken apart by the developments of the new science and the new philosophy of writers such as Cusanus, Bruno, Descartes and Newton. The new emphasis on critical reason and subjective self-awareness had the consequence of making all reality into mere external objectivity, reducing the whole medieval hierarchy of being into homogeneous extended matter, limitless extension radically distinct from the unextended perceiving subject. Thus the modern world gives rise to a new concentration on *human* nature, now seen as the epistemological measure of all things. This liberation of man from nature represents a considerable advance on the medieval position, which saw man as an integral part of the natural chain of beings. Pico della Mirandola is often seen as the harbinger of this new non-medieval confidence in man and his unlimited rational powers, although he expresses his new understanding in the traditional language of hierarchy and order:

> O great liberality of God the Father! O great and wonderful happiness of man! It is given him to have that which he chooses and to be that which he wills. As soon as brutes are born, they bring with them "from their dam's bag", as Lucilius says, what they are going to possess. . . . At man's birth the Father placed in him every sort of seed and sprouts of every kind of life. The seeds that each man cultivates will grow and bear fruit in him. If he cultivates vegetable seeds, he will become a plant. If the seeds of sensation, he will grow into brute. If rational, he will come out a heavenly animal. If intellectual he will be an angel, and a son of God. And if he is not contented with the lot of any creatures but takes himself up into the centre of his own unity, then, made one spirit with God and settled in the solitary darkness of the Father, who is above all things, he will stand ahead of all things. Who does not wonder at this chameleon which we are?[24]

There is no doubt that Pico is asserting that man lives in a hierarchical universe. But much more importantly, he is saying that man is not limited to a single position in that universe, he has the freedom and the power to range across all the levels of created being; and still more, he has at the centre of his consciousness the ability to transcend his created nature altogether and can enter into complete unity with God.

Pico's recognition of the infinite capacity of the human will and intellect is the beginning of a new interest in consciousness in western philosophy. Now, not only God but man also is in touch with the infinite. Instead of abasement before the infinite omnipotent God, man proclaims that he too can be infinite and omnipotent, can become one with God in *theosis.* [25] This movement reaches its historical culmination in Sartre's pronouncement in *L'Être et le Néant:* man's project is to be God.[26]

We have simplified the contrast between medieval and modern world views for a particular purpose, namely, to show the critical position occupied by Johannes Scottus Eriugena in the transition between

medieval and modern worlds. If Pico, Cusanus and Descartes are har-
bingers of the modern world, it is mainly because the traditional
portrait of the middle ages as a time of dull scholasticism (a portrait
painted by the Renaissance and canonised in the official histories of
philosophy by the Hegelian *Lectures on the History of Philosophy)*
has gone largely unchallenged.[27] It is only in the twentieth century
that the importance of such writers as Scottus Eriugena and the medieval mystics has been recognised in its true role. Eriugena, the
Victorines, the English and German mystics were all instrumental in
anticipating the so called "modern" view of man as the real centre of
the world.[28]

Until recently this philosophical movement has been understood as
a fringe development outside of the main Aristotelian-Thomistic
tradition of the thirteenth century flowering of scholasticism, and as
such it has been seen as obscure, figurative, fantastical. If, however,
we read the Neoplatonic philosophy of Scottus and his successors not
as an aberration of the true tradition but as the first stirrings of the
modern understanding of philosophy, then this imaginative, figurative
tradition begins to make sense. For it is in Scottus, for example, that
we have the hierarchical tradition at the same time both propagated
and subverted.[29] We have the theological discussion of God's nature
dismissed in favour of a negative theological approach which concentrates on human knowledge and its limits.[30] We have authority
reinterpreted until it comes to be understood as nothing other than
vera ratio, right reason.[31] We find an infinite world proclaimed and a
Cartesian *cogito* whereby man, like God, can know with absolute
certainty *that* he is, but cannot circumscribe his nature so as to be
able to say *what* he is.[32] We find human nature understood as a perfect
image of God such that human beings have the potentiality to be both
omnipotent and omniscient, and can of course in deification become
one with God himself. In fact, all of the features of the modern world
which we sketched above are to be found, not just prefigured but laid
out in detail, in Scottus' massive cosmological epic of the *Periphyseon,*
the dialogue *On the Division of Nature.*

So far we have attempted to situate Eriugena's philosophy at the
theoretical (rather than historical) intersection of the medieval and
modern conceptions of the world. It is now time to turn our attention
to the *Periphyseon* itself in order to examine more closely Eriugena's
understanding of the nature of man and the world.

III
THE MEANING OF NATURE IN ERIUGENA

Eriugena's point of departure is novel. He sets out by defining his area
of investigation as *nature,* which for him includes all that is, and all that
is not.[33] By this he means that nature includes not only being (material

or spiritual) but also those things which escape the intellect because of their superiority to it (e.g. God transcends the mind). Thus nature is a term which includes both creation *and* God. From this beginning he is able to sketch out the four possible logical options offered by considering nature in relation to creation. We can, he says, conceive of nature as uncreated and creating (i.e. God as creator), as created and creating (i.e. the "Platonic ideas" or "primary causes" as Eriugena calls them upon which the created world is modelled and from which it is derived), as created and not creating (the visible spatio-temporal world which is what we usually mean by the term *nature),* and as uncreated and uncreating (nature as unrelated to creation – that is either pure nothingness or else God considered apart from creation).[34]

These four possible interpretations of nature are seen by Scottus as expressing successive *moments* in the being of God and the world, related according to the Neoplatonic sequence of procession and return.[35] God is the name Christians give to the inaccessible one who dwells beyond being and from whom all being derives. When God creates the world, He wills the primary causes into being and these causes are conceived of as contained in the word or *verbum,* the utterance (*clamor*) of which gives rise to creation.[36] The primary cause in their turn "flow forth" into their effects, which gives rise to the spatio-temporal world of creatures in all their particularity. These effects are themselves unproductive of anything lower and depend totally upon their causes to which they "revert" or return.[37] Below this region of created effects lies the realm of *non-being.*[38] Ultimately, however, when the cycle of procession of causes into effects has terminated and all the effects have returned to rest in their causes, then the cycle of creation is complete and the absolute non-being of the fourth level becomes indistinguishable from the manner of existence of the inaccessible One.

Although this brief description of the cycle of nature conveys the impression of a temporal sequence, Eriugena more properly conceives of the four "levels" of nature as four "aspects" or ways of viewing the absolute unity of the One. The four divisions of nature are ways in which the human rational mind orders the manifest appearances of this world in relation to the One which, above time and space, is their origin.[39]

Eriugena's metaphysics, then, is an attempt to reconcile the Christian understanding of the creation with the understanding of the One developed by Neoplatonist philosophers.[40] The Christian Neoplatonists exploited the parallels between the Biblical myth of creation and the Platonic understanding of the dependence of this imperfect world upon the perfect realm of the forms (or causes) and ultimately on the One itself. The Christian Platonists, whom Eriugena read in the original Greek, conceived of God as the One of Plotinus (as developed from the concepts of the One in the hypotheses of Plato's dialogue *Parmenides*). This One is above being, beyond the good, beyond the realm of intellect or the intellectual light, dwelling in an inaccessible darkness, unknowable and unfathomable. This conception of God (as wholly transcendent) satisfied the Greek demand that God should be unsullied by the world, even to the extent of not knowing about it. At the same time all other beings flow forth from the One and depend on it for their existence. All things achieve their identity by attempting to imitate the primal unity of the One at a lower level. Everything which exists is a unity of some kind, and the more integrated is the unity, the closer does the thing come to the One.[41] Thus the lower level unities imitate the higher and the whole chain or procession of being is linked together by a pattern of imitation and striving upwards by which each thing tries to become more self-integrated. The One, itself, of course, is un-affected by this striving. The result of this striving is that the world must be seen as possessing a triadic structure of unity-procession-return.[42]

This Neoplatonic metaphysics struck the Christians as similar to the truth of Christian revelation in two ways. *First*, the triadic structure paralleled the paradise-fall-salvation sequence of Christian myth. All creatures were originally one with God in paradise, then they fell through the sin of Adam (which the Neoplatonists and Eriugena see as a disruption of the original unity in which man's total consciousness was centred on God, brought about by man turning his gaze upon himself, thus giving rise to the phenomenon of human self-consciousness).[43] The aim to achieve salvation is understood as a process through which man will recover his primordial unity with God by purifying his self-conscious acitivity until it is once again God-centred.

The *second* parallel with the Neoplatonic triad is expressed by the nature of the One itself, since for the Christians the One is also a Trinity. According to Eriugena God is in Himself hidden and unknown, dwelling in inaccessible darkness; but when He utters the Word which gives rise to creation, He makes himself manifest at the same time in the Person of the Word, the second Person of the Trinity.

This movement of self-manifestation from darkness to light is a procession similar in kind to the procession of things from the One.[44] The second procession from the Son to the Holy Spirit is understood by Eriugena as overseeing the procession of the primary causes (contained in the Son as *verbum* and *sapientia*) into their spatio-temporal effects, and of course at the same time is responsible for the reversion of those effects upon their causes.[45]

From the Greeks then Eriugena inherited a very unusual theory of creation. Creation is to be understood as the self-manifestation of God, the process by which He makes His hidden nature manifest.[46] As such it is a timeless event, inseparable from the Trinitarian procession from Father to Son. The whole of the created universe is to be understood as unfolding within the Trinity, at no stage is creation to be seen as an alienation or separation of things from God. If the fall had not taken place, it is implied, all things including man would have evolved in their own mysterious manner in the bosom of God Himself. Eriugena's God is not static but dynamic, manifesting, unfolding and explicating Himself in spirals of divine history. The famous triadic spirals of the chi-rho page of the Book of Kells might be taken as an illustration of this divine dynamism.

The fall however disrupts this cycle. The fall is, like creation, a timeless event. Man in his prelapsarian condition was one with God, indistinguishable from him, omnipotent and omniscient like him, because man was the perfect image of God. Man fell from this unity because he became obsessed with his own self-image and self-consciousness and sought to impose human rather than divine meanings on things. The fall never took place in historical time; rather, for Eriugena, it expresses the metaphysical possibility that man can achieve unity with God if his freewill is utilised correctly. Eriugena has no time for the more literal interpretations of the Bible which sought to blame the devil or Eve for original sin. All human beings are separate from God so long as their freewills are self-centred rather than directed towards the infinite, endless will of God.

Eriugena understands man as possessing a boundless freedom of choice, the perfect mirror of God's infinite and boundless freedom. In Greek, God's boundlessness is expressed by the term *anarchos* which means without limit or without ruling principle.[47] Thus we can say that Eriugena's perfect man is *anarchic* in character, totally free because he is ruled by nothing other than God's will which is itself total freedom:

> Thus, just as the Divine Essence is infinite, so human substance made in Its image is bounded by no definite limit.
> *Periphyseon,* vol. 4, 772a[48]

> For if human nature had not sinned and had clung without change to Him Who had created it, it would certainly be omnipotent. Whatever in the universe it wished done would necessarily be done, since it would not wish anything to be done except what it understood that its Creator wished.
> *Periphyseon*, vol. 4, 778b[49]

Eriugena took this doctrine of the potential omnipotence and omniscience of human nature from the Greek writers, notably Gregory of Nyssa.[50] In the *Periphyseon* Eriugena quotes long passages from Gregory of Nyssa's tract *De Hominis Opificio*, a work which explained the concept of human nature as made in God's image in terms of the complete identity between image and archtype. For Gregory and Scottus, an image resembled its archtype or exemplar in *all* aspects, they differ only in being numerically distinct. Thus Eriugena quotes Gregory:

> For if God is the plenitude of good things, and man is an
> image of God, the image must resemble the Primal Exem-
> plar in this respect also, that it is the plenitude of all good
> . . . In this respect also it is the image, in that it is free
> from all necessity, and is subjected to no natural or material
> authority but possesses in itself a will which is capable of
> obtaining its desires.
>
> *Periphyseon,* vol. 4, 796a[51]

How far this is from the usual humility of medieval statements about
man! Man is asserted here as being free from all external authority and
all necessity. As the image of God, he mirrors God's perfect freedom
and power. Indeed it is difficult to speak about God without recognising that in fact we are also speaking about human nature — a fact which
Feuerbach and Marx will utilise in their critique of religion. But for
Eriugena, the transcendence of God protects religious utterance from
the total conflation of the divine with man. God is always an unknown
darkness above the world, it cannot be said *what* He is. But what
about man? Can we understand human nature and grasp its essence?
If human will is really infinite and boundless then perhaps it is equally
impossible to say what man is. Let us now turn to a more detailed
examination of Eriugen'a concept of human nature and its self-
knowledge.

IV
THE DEFINITION OF MAN

After our cursory examination of Eriugena's understanding of nature,
we were led to a consideration of his theory of creation and the concept
of human nature involved therein. We must now look more specifically at human nature from the standpoint of knowledge in general
and self-knowledge in particular, because, for Eriugena, the return
of all things to the One is brought about by man when he purifies his
self-understanding and "reverts" upon himself and upon his cause
(i.e. God) in the right manner. Self-knowledge then is the lynch-pin
of the entire system, as it is also, of course, for the systems of Descartes and the rationalists who followed him.

Eriugena conceives of man as being essentially a mind. Man is
mens, spiritus, animus or, in Greek, *nous*.[52] In itself it is without sexual
differentation into male or female, and indeed, at the highest level, all
human minds are one.[53] This pure mind has several levels of awareness or contemplation. The highest is that by which it contemplates
the hidden darkness of the Father (the One). He calls this "motion"
of the soul "simple" because it "surpasses the nature of the soul herself and cannot be interpreted" (*Periphyseon*, vol. 2, 572d).[54] At this
level the soul both knows itself and also by recognising itself as un-

bounded and infinite, it transcends itself towards its source. Eriugena can only speak about this level of contemplation in terms of negatives, because, of course, it is merely a transcendent ideal for man in this fallen, sinful state. The second level of the soul is represented by rational knowledge, which has divided up the primordial unity of the first level into cause and effect.[55] This second rational level of the self Eriugena considers to be born from the highest intellectual contemplation, in a manner akin to the way in which the Son is generated from the Father:

> For just as the wise artist produces his art from himself in himself and foresees in it the things he is to make . . . so the intellect brought forth from itself and in itself its reason, in which it foreknows and causally pre-creates all things which it desires to make.
> *Periphyseon,* vol. 2, 577a-b [56]

Thus Eriugena conceives of the mind as a hidden transcendent unity which then creates (manifests) itself in the form of the rational mind we know and understand. Just as God is a transcendent "non-being" above the being of creation, so also the human mind is understood to have a hidden depth which acts to produce the rational and sensible minds. It is this third motion of the soul which links the mind with the outer world and the phantasies of sense.[57] Eriugena sees the sense level as a further descent from the highest hidden level of the mind. Indeed he sees the *nous* or mind of man as being responsible for the creation of the body:

> For (the mind) is made from God in the image of God out of nothing, but the body it creates (itself), though not out of nothing but out of something. For by the action of the soul . . . it creates for itself a body in which it may openly display its hidden actions which in themselves are invisible, and bring them forth into sensible knowledge.
> *Periphyseon,* vol. 2, 580b [58]

Eriugena then makes high claims for the nature of man's mind. Not only does it have a hidden perfect side (this is reminiscent of Plotinus's belief that part of the soul remains in the One and does not fall into the alienating realm of sense) which Eriugena says is immortal, omniscient and omnipotent; but the mind also is active in the creation of the realms of reason and sense. Mind gives man a body so that he can articulate his inner thoughts in signs, actions and language, and so that he can receive the phantasies of the world about him. Of course Eriugena makes it sound as if the mind does this freely and willingly, as if it could prevent itself from so doing; and this indeed is what he intends. The fall of man is essentially a fall of the mind into sense, which man chose of his own free will to perform. Fallen human nature then is temporal and spatial, it operates in the realm of sense knowledge and in the corporeal physical realm. Man at this level is a rational animal.[59]

But even understood as a rational animal Eriugena believes man to be the pinnacle of creation. Following Maximus he sees man as spanning the two worlds of the sensible and the intellectual.

Maximus argues that man "contains within himself all creation"[60] because he spans the two worlds of sense and intellect, and joins them together in his own self which is a blending of body and mind. Hence all things are said to be contained in man. According to Maximus and Eriugena, man is the *officina omnium*, the container of all things.

> For man was created with a nature of so high a status that there is no creature, whether visible or intelligible, that cannot be found in him. For he is composed of the two universal parts of created nature by way of a wonderful union.
>
> *Periphyseon,* vol. 2, 531a-c[61]

Not only is man said to contain all things in this rather loose sense, but Eriugena actually believes that the seeds or principles of all things are contained in the human mind. We have already seen that Eriugena thinks of all things as present in God's wisdom (the Son). It is a short step from this to seeing all things as present in the human mind, because Christ is, Eriugena says, the perfect man.[62] Man not only operates with reason, he also contains the entire domain of the rational as one aspect of his higher intellectual self. Man, as it were, enfolds reason in himself.[63]

But how does Eriugena conceive of this human trait of "containing" all things? To answer this question, we need to look at Eriugena's theory of knowledge, his epistemology.

Eriugena understands knowing primarily as a comprehending or defining. Knowledge, for Eriugena, is not simply the scholastic adequation of thought with reality, but is rather the absorption or subsumption of reality into thought. As with the Neoplatonists, and later with the German idealists, knowledge can best be understood as possessing a certain kind of being in its own right, higher than the being of ordinary material reality.[64] To know something is to define its essence, that is, for Eriugena, to situate the object into one's conceptual or mental scheme. Since Eriugena held that to know is "higher" than to be known, the mind is placed higher than anything which can be known; but since it can know all things, it is thought to be able to define all things, to give them a place in the logical structure of the mind's knowledge:

> Do you see that place is simply the act of him who understands and by virtue of his understanding comprehends

those things which he can comprehend, whether they be
sensible or accessible only to intellect.

Periphyseon, vol. 1, 485d[65]

The mind which knows things gives them their place. This is true
idealism. Place, Eriugena says. is inseparable from time, and all things
in this world are subject to place and time, hence all things are *contained* in the mind. Place is nothing but the limit and definition of
every finite nature.[66] This limit is given by the mind's act of defining or knowing, and since the mind is incorporeal then place itself
must be incorporeal. By this circuitous route Eriugena has managed to
argue both that the mind contains and circumscribes the whole world
and that the spatio-temporal world is essentially immaterial and incorporeal. It is only a fantasy of sense which gives rise to the common
belief that the world is made up of corporeal matter.[67] Once this
fantasy has been recognised as an illusion, the mind is brought back
to recognise its true power and function in the world (it gives every
created essence in the cosmos its place and time), and it is freed from
the slavery of the body. It is then free to make the intellectual journey
back to God.

But comprehension or definition is not man's only mode of knowing. There exists also in man a kind of non-defining knowledge, a
knowledge which does not contain or dominate the known, but is
one with what is known.[68] This is the mode of knowledge by which
man grasps those beings which are either equal to or above his own
nature. Man cannot define himself or any other human or angel. Man
cannot define or comprehend God.

How then does man know himself, others, the angels or God?
According to Scottus, the mind has a direct knowledge of its own existence: it knows for certain *that* it exists even though it does not know
what it is, since knowing-what implies definition, and no mind can
define (that is, be the place of) itself.[69] Man's existential knowledge
that he exists is as it were a formless kind of knowing, which does
not seek to impose structure or limit or definition. It is akin in fact
to a form of ignorance.[70] Ignorance in this sense however is not a
defect but is rather an acknowledgement of the unlimited, infinite
nature of man. Man knows that he is unknowable and undefinable,
this knowledge in itself brings him near to God.

Hence Eriugena does offer a kind of definition of man's nature;
he says in volume 3 of the *Periphyseon* that "man is a certain intellectual idea formed eternally in the mind of God."[71] Man knows himself
only by defining himself in reference to God's unknowable infinite
nature. Eriugena is here expressing the true nature of human transcendence above the world — man's being can only be fully understood by invoking the concept of God. As Eriugena says elsewhere,
"man and God are paradigms of each other."[72]

Thus, just as it can be said of God that He is being *and* that He is the non-being above being, so also it can be said of man that he is a rational animal and that he is not a rational animal.[73] He is an intellectual being who comprehends all things in the created world, but he is also a being whose intellect is formless and "circles about" itself and about God. But more than that, Eriugena recognises that man's existence itself is the result of his self-knowledge in the higher sense (knowing-that). Not only does the human mind provide the essential definitions of all other things, but it may also be seen as self-creating:[74]

> If then the inner notion (*notio interior*) which is contained in the human mind constitutes the substance of those things of which it is the notion, it follows that the notion by which man knows himself may be considered his very substance.
>
> *Periphyseon,* vol. 4, 770a[75]

The mind knows itself, Eriugena concludes, as creative of itself (*causa sui*) because it knows that it is identical with the object of knowledge which is itself. When we define man in relation to God we see that man can be understood as one with God because man is an idea in God, and an idea in God according to Eriugena's thinking is a form of self-manifestation of God. When man comes to true self-knowledge, he learns of his proximity to God as the source of his being, and he actually comes to participate in the creative act by which he himself is made.[76] Thus by thinking back from the spatio-temporal world up through the various motions of the soul until we arrive at the highest self-knowledge, man makes the journey from the fallen embodied world, separated from God, to the *nous* or intellect which shares in God's creative process. The highest form of human self-knowledge turns out to be also a contemplation of God's infinite richness:

> And this is the greatest and perhaps the only step towards knowledge of the truth, namely, that human nature should first know and love itself and then refer the whole of its knowledge of itself and the whole of its love of itself to the glory and love and knowledge of the Creator. For if it did not know what is at work in itself, how can it desire to know the things that are above it?
>
> *Periphyseon,* vol. 2, 611a[77]

This is perhaps the highest expression in medieval philosophy of the need for self-knowledge as a means to gain access to true knowledge and love of God.

V
CONCLUSIONS

In this essay I have tried to show how Eriugena's ideas on man and world culminate in a complex and idealist metaphysical system, the main tenets of which are closer to the modern understanding of the self and the world than they are to our current understanding of the medieval world. Eriugena's system cannot be dismissed as of merely historical interest. The history of philosophy is not so much a history of dead facts and ideas, but is rather an index of possibilities. Eriugena's understanding of human nature as a kind of formless and boundless self-knowledge, which contains within itself infinite possibilities of growth and self-perfection leading ultimately to deification, has very real similarities with both Sartre's and Heidegger's modern conception of man as a "nothingness", an empty space for the revelation of Being. Who can say whether Eriugena's insight, based as it is on the synthesis of Greek and Latin philosophical traditions of a thousand years, may in the end prove more valuable than the insight of contemporary philosophers who have based themselves on less than two hundred years of post-Kantian and phenomenological philosophy? Either way, the contribution of Ireland's first thinker to European philosophy must now be recognised as both original and profound; it will surely be a well-spring of ideas for many generations of philosophers to come.

Harry Bracken

GEORGE BERKELEY, THE IRISH CARTESIAN

Berkeley is the most important Irish philosopher. Yet despite a number of original ideas and considerable influence, his portrait does not grace one of the new series of Irish bank notes (as does Eriugena's). Although the new library at Trinity College, Dublin, has recently been named in his memory, his name adorns more American than Irish institutions.

It is difficult to learn very much about the forces which moulded Berkeley's reputation in the eighteenth and nineteenth centuries, but it does seem clear that the reputation he acquired was not firmly based either on the philosophical principles which influenced him or the ideas he in fact articulated. For example, Berkeley's classification (along with John Locke and David Hume) as *British empiricist* helped, I suspect, to create the picture of him as an outsider to Irish intellectual currents. In what follows, it is urged that Berkeley's arguments ought to be taken more seriously in their own right, rather than be forced into a preconceived abstract framework. In short, I contend that one stands a better chance of understanding Berkeley if one reads him as an Irish Cartesian rather than as a "British empiricist".[1]

I

While there is little to suggest that Berkeley should be counted as an Irish nationalist, in several entries in the *Philosophical Commentaries* he counts himself as an Irishman: "There are men who Say there are insensible extensions, there are others who Say the Wall is not white, the fire is not hot &c We Irish men cannot attain to these truths" (entry 392). The *We Irish men* is repeated in entries 393, 394, and 398. In his note upon these entries, the great Berkeley scholar, A.A. Luce (from Trinity College, Dublin) writes that "we need not read a political reference into the words. Berkeley certainly always regarded himself as an Irishman, and Newton was, to him, 'a philosopher of a neighbouring nation' (Princ. 110, 1st ed.); but when he writes 'we

Irishmen' he simply means 'we ordinary folk, shrewd judges of fact and commonsense. . .'"2

I shall try to show that in several major respects Berkeley is not a Lockean empiricist but, rather, more of a rationalist with close affinities both to Descartes and to the most important philosopher in the Cartesian tradition, Malebranche.3

If we believe that in understanding a thinker we must take into account the varying cultural and intellectual traditions to which that thinker is heir, we should at least try to get those traditions right. To call Berkeley Cartesian is to claim that his philosophy contains several major features in common with Descartes. To call a philosopher Irish, British, or German is not to make a similar sort of claim about philosophical structures — unless one is already committed to a philosophical thesis about the role of a national culture. When Berkeley is called an "Irish" philosopher no more is intended than that he was born and educated, lived and worked, in Ireland.

It is thought that Berkeley was born near Kilkenny on March 12, 1685. On completing his studies at Kilkenny College he matriculated at Trinity in 1700, took the Bachelor of Arts degree in 1704, and was elected fellow in 1707. He held various college posts including college librarian and lecturer in Greek and Hebrew. Ordained priest in 1710, he was awarded the Bachelor of Divinity and Doctor of Divinity Degrees in 1721. With his appointment as Dean of Derry, his formal association with Trinity ends. He devoted some years to his project for a college in Bermuda, a project which brought him to Rhode Island in 1729 for almost three years. He was named Bishop of Cloyne in 1734 and seems to have remained there almost continuously. In 1753 he left to visit Oxford where he died six months later.

Berkeley travelled for eight years beginning in 1713. He visited London and was involved with Addison, Steele and Swift, among others. According to Luce[4] Berkeley probably met Malebranche in Paris in 1713. The greatest philosopher of the period, Malebranche's major work, *De la Recherche de la Verité* appeared in 1674-78.[5] Two English translations appeared in the 1690s. Malebranche's philosophy might briefly be described as "platonising"Descartes. Descartes, and later Malebranche, both reject the thesis that our senses correctly represent the way things "really" are in the world. They believe, for example, that since there is apparently no criterion for distinguishing dreams from waking experience, there is no assurance that abstracting knowledge from what may appear to be sensory data provides an adequate foundation for knowledge. After all, if we actually had a secure criterion for deciding what is a dream, we would never have nightmares! For this and other reasons, Descartes grounds knowledge on ideas innate in all humans. Malebranche, in turn, takes what is innate in Descartes and places it "in" God. Both Descartes and Malebranche take these ideas (mainly mathematical) to be what they are, totally independent of us. Our thoughts do not "make" these ideas; our knowing them does not affect them. As Luce shows, Berkeley tries to convert his own sensory ideas into the "tough substantial 'ideas' "[6] of Malebranche. It is a philosophically exciting move. It is also not what one would expect from a Lockean. Indeed, we now know that Locke took an extremely dim view of Malebranche's *ideas.*

One reason we are in an improved position to talk about influences on Berkeley is that just before publishing an edition of Berkeley's works in 1871, A.C. Fraser turned up some Berkeley notebooks in the British Museum. In 1944 Luce, with the help of some earlier scholarship, deciphered the abbreviations and published a *diplomatic* edition of the text. In 1976 George Thomas, using the latest scientific equipment to examine the manuscript, published a new edition (incorporating Luce's superb notes on the entries).[7] Dubbed by Luce the *Philosophical Commentaries*, these notebooks constitute a tremendous contribution to our understanding of Berkeley. They appear to have been written just before the *Theory of Vision* (1709) while he was in the process of working out the immaterialist option which he articulates in the *Principles*. In calling his own position *immaterialism,* Berkeley was placing himself close to Malebranche – so close, indeed, that he felt the need in the *Principles* to distance himself.[8]

When Berkeley published his *Principles* in 1710, the text was marked Part I. It was expected that Part II would deal with minds. But Berkeley tells us in a letter[9] that he lost the manuscript for Part II on his travels in Italy. The 1710 edition was, to Berkeley's dismay, greeted with mirth by the London wits. Hoping to correct misunderstanding and to anticipate in greater detail possible objections to his arguments on behalf of his thesis that *esse* is *percipi*, that the being of things consists either in perceiving or in being perceived, Berkeley published *Three Dialogues between Hylas and Philonous* in 1713. Thanks to the *Philosophical Commentaries* we are now in a position to see in detail the types of problems Berkeley seeks to solve as well as the solutions he favored prior to writing the *Principles* and *Three Dialogues*. For example, it was once thought that Berkeley had not realised that if he meant to say that the being of things consists solely in their being perceived then it would seem that since we have no ideas of minds or spirits (including God), they do not exist. It was thought that the emendations which Berkeley made in his 1734 editions of these works were afterthoughts. In fact, the *Philosophical Commentaries* provides ample evidence that Berkeley was fully aware of these problems—and had plausible answers—prior to writing the *Principles* and *Three Dialogues.*

In the light of the *Commentaries* we can now see that Locke, Malebranche and Bayle[10] were all major influences on Berkeley. It becomes easier to understand not only that Berkeley saw himself as an immaterialist, but even why a 1713 reviewer[11] (in *Mémoires de Trévoux*) could describe him as a "Malbranchiste de bonne foi". The fact is that Berkeley was extremely well-versed in a wide range of French thought − both Catholic from France and Protestant from the Netherlands. Access to this literature was available in the library which the Archbishop of Dublin, Narcissus Marsh, had only recently presented to Ireland. The library was built during the first decade of the eighteenth century. From a philosophical standpoint, it got off to a glorious start: the first librarian, in 1701, Dr Elias Bouhéreau, a Protestant refugee, contributed his own library, including a fine collection of Calvinist controversialist literature. Many of these theological debates concern the penetration by Cartesian ideas of what had, for much of the seventeenth century, remained a scholastic intellectual framework. Also, Marsh purchased the library of Edward Stillingfleet, late Bishop of Worcester, in 1705. If Stillingfleet's name is known to philosophers today, it is as the author of three book-length "letters" to John Locke. Indeed, the Locke-Stillingfleet correspondence (1697-99) marks the rare case when Locke felt compelled to respond publicly to criticism. The correspondence is now not much read. That is unfortunate. Stillingfleet is an able philosopher and he taxes Locke with a series of significant difficulties. Fortunately, Stillingfleet possessed a really first class library. It is rich in all aspects of Cartesianism. From the standpoint of a student of philosophy, few cities in Europe had better collections. As Muriel McCarthy observes in her scholarly study of Marsh's Library[12] there is no concrete evidence that Berkeley used Marsh's. However, the fact that he cites material[13] which is to be found in Marsh's but not in Trinity suggests that he made the short walk to this library.

II

If it is correct to claim that the influences upon Berkeley's philosophy owe much to the rationalism of Continental thinkers, it is still necessary to examine Berkeley's complex relation to British empiricism. There are four major and technically complex aspects in which Berkeley's thinking differs substantially from Lockean empiricism.

The Question of Qualities
Locke introduces a distinction between what he called the primary and the secondary qualities of things. According to Locke, certain qualities of material objects are "such as are utterly inseparable from the Body, in what estate soever it be. . ."[14] He adds: "divison . . . can never take away either Solidity, Extension, Figure, or Mobility from any Body." If the process of division continues below the threshold of sense, "the Mind finds [these qualities] inseparable from every particle of Matter." *Ideas* of primary qualities are said to resemble patterns which exist in material objects. As for secondary qualities, they are also capacities of material objects to produce in us certain ideas, but the

ideas of the secondary qualities do *not* resemble those qualities. "There is nothing like our *ideas,* existing in the Bodies themselves."[15] Throughout this chapter Locke employs the atomistic model first articulated two millennia before by Democritus. The real world of atoms can be specified in terms of a few, i.e. their primary qualities. This real world is, however, insensible. It is what gives rise to the world of sense, the world of appearance, but it cannot itself be sensed.

The interpretation of Berkeley as a British empiricist takes him to be extending the logic of Locke's "mentalisation" argument. That is, Locke is read as mentalising the secondary qualities. Berkeley is read as holding that consistency requires that we extend the "mentalisation" to the primary qualities. The trouble is that proponents of this tradition misinterpret both Locke and Berkeley. Berkeley *does* seek to show that a certain argument for mentalising the secondary qualities can be extended to the primary ones. He does seek to collapse the distinction as part of his general argument that the philosophers' doctrine of material substance is conceptually absurd. For example, if we admit that a relation of *likeness* does not hold between ideas and material qualities, then what can ideas tell us about those qualities? But if we do admit a likeness relation, how can we establish it? Either we compare ideas one with another, or we make a comparison with something unperceivable. That is impossible. So, if an idea can be like nothing but an idea, then our idea of something must be *like* an (idea) quality in the material thing. But *that* (idea) quality cannot exist in senseless matter; as an idea it must exist in a mind. In brief, the doctrine of "material substance" requires that we locate idea-like things (corresponding to our own ideas) in an *un*perceiving material substance! And this, Berkeley realises, is nonsensical.

In attacking the primary/secondary quality distinction, Berkeley attacks a distinction drawn via what the sceptics call "variations in sense experience." Berkeley demonstrates that the argument that warm and cold are not really in objects because they vary so widely, holds also for extension. Locke, however, draws *his* distinction by appealing to the atomistic framework. He has nothing but contempt for the sorts of sceptical arguments Berkeley seeks to exploit. Also, Berkeley's discussion is not directed primarily against the atomist model. Berkeley devotes his attention to *extension*. In fact, Berkeley's account of the primary/secondary quality distinction owes more to Pierre Bayle than to Locke. To repeat, Locke does not, like Berkeley, derive his version of the distinction from sceptical arguments about sense variations nor does he accord priority to extension.

The Question of Scepticism

Sensitivity to scepticism is an essential theme in Berkeley's argument.[16] In the simplest terms, one can say that Berkeley's most famous thesis, *esse* is *percipi,* is clearly intended by him to constitute the heart of his refutation of scepticism. He provides us with a diagnosis: "the very root of *scepticism*" is to suppose "a twofold existence of the objects of sense, the one *intelligible*, or in the mind, the other *real* and without the mind."[17] Solution: collapse the distinction between what appears and what is real. So long as any such distinction is drawn, the question arises of how we can decide which appearances are true appearances of the real. Some sort of decision procedure is required; some sort of criterion is called for. And that is precisely what the sceptical dialectic flourishes upon. Sextus Empiricus provides many arguments to show the difficulty in employing *any* criterion, since one needs a proof that the criterion is true, and a criterion for the proof, etc.

Berkeley tells us explicitly on the title-pages of the *Principles* and the *Three Dialogues* that he is attacking scepticism. In the *Commentaries* he makes frequent references to sceptical issues. For example, in the opening sections he develops his arguments against Zeno's paradoxes — paradoxes generated by treating space and time as either finitely or infinitely divisible. It is in this connection that Berkeley presents his doctrine of *minima sensibilia*. These sensory particulars are operationally defined. Hence, if one seeks further to divide a minimum it simply ceases to exist — in effect, by being below the threshold of visual acuity "it" ceases to be. Also, the question of knowledge of extension, or whether extension being in the mind means that the mind is extended, is a worry within the continental tradition of Cartesianism. As early as the *Philosophical Commentaries* Berkeley asserts "Extension a sensation, therefore not without the mind,"a point he makes in somewhat different form at *Principles* No. 49.[18]

The Question of Ideas
This question owes as much to Descartes as it does to Bayle. It purports to answer a question about the nature of ideas. Berkeley says that he chose the word *idea* "because a necessary relation to the mind is understood to be implied by that term."[19] In asserting that ideas stand in a *necessary* relation to minds Berkeley is making a radically non-Lockean move. Moreover, he must know that it is non-Lockean. Locke repeatedly claims that there is no necessary relation between, say, the idea of yellow and the idea of gold. He makes it clear that our talk about the essences of things, about species, etc., is based simply on descriptive tallies which we may choose to make.[20] More to the point, we cannot rule out as a "manifest contradiction" that gold might think.[21] Because of Locke's view about the opaqueness of our complex ideas of substance, there is neither physical nor logical *cement.*[22] Locke's account of mind or mental substance simply and firmly precludes the move which Berkeley makes. For Locke no such *necessary relation* to minds is "understood to be implied" by the term *idea.* This was not some arcane aspect of Locke's theory. Locke was denounced as a

Spinozist for blurring the mind/matter distinction so vigorously defended by Berkeley. He was attacked by Stillingfleet for having made the concepts of soul and person unintelligible. The point here is not to decide whether Berkeley or Locke is correct, but only to emphasise that it is hard to imagine a more decisive indication that Berkeley was pursuing a very different line from Locke.

Berkeley takes his discovery of immaterialism to be a truly astonishing philosophical break-through. At one and the same stroke he dissolves that appearance/reality dichotomy which had been the *root* of scepticism, affirms the existence of a substantial immaterial self, and proves the existence of God. Berkeley stands committed to a doctrine of substance. He believes that consciousness involves both a perceived (idea) and a perceiver (mind). Neither is reducible to the other. Minds cannot, however, be known via ideas. Ideas are passive, minds are active. We cannot have a passive idea of an active spirit.[23] Knowledge of minds or spirits requires *notions,* a non-ideational (conceptual) entity by means of which we are said to know spirits and mental acts. Berkeley's minds or spirits are also taken to be continuants. As with Descartes, there is no question about a theory of personal identity. Presumably Berkeley, like his contemporary, Joseph Butler, Bishop of Bristol, finds the effort to "construct" a self from remembered experiences (as Locke does) question-begging. To appeal to memory is to appeal to a substantial self which already "had" a series of experiences. I believe that it is because Berkeley opts at the very outset for a substantial self that we find no doctrine of personal identity. As for God, Berkeley again takes a line from Descartes: some ideas are independent of our wills. But they must depend on some other mind or spirit, i.e. that superior one we call God.

The Question of Abstraction
This *fourth* non-Lockean theme in Berkeley is his opposition to abstract ideas. This can in part be seen as an attack on the empiricist and scholastic accounts of concept formation. Berkeley is not committed to the thesis that "there is nothing in the intellect which was not first in the senses." He is not even hostile to innate ideas.[24] And as David Berman has pointed out,[25] Berkeley made a non-Lockean choice in selecting the term *Principles* for the title of his book. Locke is distincly averse to the term because he fears its innatist connotations. Berkeley's attack on Locke's theory of abstraction is an important part of the "Introduction" to the *Principles.* It also plays a role in the argument for *esse* is *percipi* since the separation of the being of things from their being perceived is held to be an unwarranted abstraction. Finally, anti-abstractionism marks Berkeley's profound difference from Locke and places him on the side of Descartes and Malebranche in opposition to abstractionist accounts of concept formation.

Thus there are "internal" reasons for questioning the Locke-

Berkeley-Hume British Empiricist picture.[26] In addition, the earliest critics did not take Berkeley to be a Lockean. Only much later in the eighteenth century do the affiliations begin to be talked about. Insofar as any of the early commentators linked Berkeley with other philosophers, it was to Malebranche, Bayle and the sceptics, and occasionally to Arthur Collier, an English philosopher whose *Clavis Universalis* appeared in 1713. None makes reference to Locke. A decade later, using a classification scheme devised by Christian Wolff, C.M. Pfaff labels Berkeley, on the basis of early reviews, a species of idealist, i.e. *egoist*.[27] Wolff calls Berkeley an "idealist" in his 1734 *Psychologia Rationalis,* and Leibniz, writing in the margin of his copy of the *Principles,* sees Berkeley as a kindred spirit.[28]

In brief, the arguments Berkeley provides for his case, and the reactions of his contemporaries, suggest that Berkeley ought not to count as operating with Lockean notions. Since on a range of major points Berkeley stands with Descartes or Malebranche or Bayle, rather than with Locke, then the label "British empiricist" is inaccurate; it is the sort of inaccuracy that constitutes a hindrance to our understanding of a thinker. If anything, as mentioned initially, Berkeley should be labelled an Irish Cartesian working along the paths of continental philosophy and contributing to his own original insights particularly on the question of immaterialism and scepticism.

III

And now to turn to some primarily non-philosophical aspects of Berkeley's writings – particularly those with an Irish dimension.

During his eighteen years in Cloyne, Berkeley appears to have coexisted well enough with his Catholic neighbours. So far as it has been possible to determine, aside from taking his seat in the House of Lords shortly after his consecration, he never returned to Dublin. Thus he was not involved in either the debates or the votes on legislation in the Irish parliament over those years (1730s and 1740s). In a diocese in which Catholics outnumbered Protestants eight to one[29], perhaps a certain measure of discretion was in order.

On political and social matters, Berkeley appears to have been conservative insofar as one is able to "locate" him within the attitudes of his time. For example, he published in 1712 three sermons given at the Trinity College chapel under the title "Passive Obedience" on the text from Romans, xiii, 2: "Whosoever resisteth the power, resisteth the ordinance of God."[30] As we know only too well, the task of providing reasonable criteria for determining when citizens can legitimately resist "lawful" authority is extraordinarily difficult. Berkeley offers what appears to be a Jacobite answer. He seeks to defend the notion that one has an obligation to obey *passively*. Thus if one is ordered to perform an act contrary to the dictates of one's conscience, one must submit oneself passively to the penalties imposed. Profoundly fearful of "anarchy" he is troubled by the use of private conscience to authorise rebellion, and indeed he argues that rebellion is a "breach of the law of nature."[31]

But Berkeley's commitment to conscience and innate moral structures is so great that he soon admits "that by virtue of the duty of non-resistance we are not obliged to submit the disposal of our lives and fortunes to the discretion either of madmen, or of all those who by craft or violence invade the supreme power; because the object of the submission enjoined subjects by the law of nature is, from the reason of the thing, manifestly limited so as to exclude both the one and the other."[33] Finally, *Passive Obedience* is not a Lockean or empiricist text: Berkeley rejects Locke's contract language, and his natural law comments are straightforwardly innatist and run directly counter to the position advanced by Locke in Book I of the *Essay concerning human understanding.*

> These propositions are called "laws of nature" because they are universal, and do not derive their obligation from any civil sanction, but immediately from the author of nature himself. They are said to be "stamped on the mind," to be "engraven on the tables of the heart,"[33] because they are well known to mankind, and suggested and inculcated by conscience. Lastly, they are termed "eternal rules of reason," because they necessarily result from the nature of things, and may be demonstrated by the infallible deductions of reason.[34]

The suspicion that Berkeley was a Jacobite delayed his advancement in the church, although "During the second rebellion (1745)," Luce writes, "besides publishing two letters against it, he raised and equipped a troop of horse."[35] It is interesting that Berkeley takes the view that the (English) glorious revolution of 1688 amounted simply to turning out a ministry.[36]

When Berkeley went to America, he settled in Rhode Island, a colony noted for its religious pluralism and tolerance. The experience did not, however, lead him on to challenge the institution of slavery. Berkeley urges that the reluctant colonial planters be encouraged to convert their black slaves to Christianity.[37] He argues that "their slaves would only become better slaves by being Christians."[38] A few years later, in *A Word to the Wise* (1749), he asks the Catholic clergy to conquer the "innate hereditary sloth"[39] of the native Irish. Berkeley recognises that people with no stake in the land have little encouragement to work. "There is small encouragement, say you, for them to build or plant upon another's land, wherein they have only a temporary interest. To which I answer that life itself is but temporary."[40]

In *The Querist*, first published in 1735, Berkeley takes a softer line. He offers a range of economic advice and analyses within the context of English colonial policy — a policy which, unlike Swift, he is not really prepared to challenge. Contrary to his 1749 opinion,[41] he asks, "Whether the suffering Roman Catholics to purchase forfeited lands would not be good policy, as tending to unite their interest with that of the government?" He proposes that Catholics be admitted, without the obligations to attend chapel, etc., to Trinity, "in imitation of the Jesuits at Paris, who admit Protestants to study in their colleges."[42] In the first edition he also writes: "Whether in granting toleration, we ought not to distinguish between doctrines purely religious, and such as affect the state?"[43] He also urges the use of the Irish language as perhaps "the most practicable means for converting the natives."[44] Much of *The Querist* is devoted to economic questions and in particular, to Berkeley's argument for a nationally owned national bank for Ireland. He clearly sees this as part of a long term cure for the basic ills of Ireland.

Siris (1744), Berkeley's last substantial work, is an odd mixture of philosophy and medicine. I believe that by and large it does not mark any major change in Berkeley's philosophical thought. That it once was viewed as something of a reversal seems to be mistaken — an interpretation which arises from reading the *Principles* and *Three Dialogues* as exemplars of an extreme empiricism. The medical side of the text concerns tar-water. Berkeley believes he has discovered a universal panacea. He propagandises on its behalf with almost religious fervour. He is convinced that it will cure the bodily ills of all the people of Ireland, and particularly improve the lot of the poor.

The book Berkeley wrote in America, the *Alciphron*, has not been mentioned. It is a defence of Christianity against deists and free-thinkers. Bernard Mandeville, author of *The Fable of the Bees, or Private Vices Public Benefits,* and the third Earl of Shaftesbury, whose appeal to taste in moral judgments, were attacked. But it is also something more profound. George Davie has written about *Alciphron* in the course of arguing that Berkeley and Francis Hutcheson set the stage for the classical period of Scottish philosophy. He contends that they did this by offering two very different ways out of the difficulties which western culture faced with the rise of commercialism and the new economics. That is, both philosophers had the "same aim of reconciling material advance with the intellectual principle."[45] Berkeley, writes Davie, "saw much promise in the atomistic reductionism and the egoistic utilitarianism of the free-thinking empiricism, provided that it was accompanied and offset, in a dualist way, by a revival of a metaphysically-minded rationalism modelled on Cartesianism."[46] He concludes:

> Hume's repudiation of system did not prevent the other
> Scottish philosophers from taking up the problem where
> he left it. In course after course of lectures, professor after
> professor — Reid, Stewart, Brown, Hamilton, Ferrier, and

Adam Smith, in some ways the greatest of them all – sought to overcome the tension between the common sense of Hutchinson and the paradoxes of Berkeley by producing a system that would harmonise the standpoint of the vulgar with the standpoint of the learned in a moderate philosophy of modern progress.[47]

IV
CONCLUSION

It is appropriate that our understanding and appreciation of Berkeley should vary and shift with our own interests and concerns.

First, we have his contribution to philosophic thought. For much of the time since the publication of the *Principles of Human Knowledge* (1710), Berkeley has been seen as a partner with Locke and Hume in something called "British empiricism." I have briefly tried to show that this is a mistaken picture. It is mistaken both in terms of our knowledge of Berkeley's sources and of his texts. It has been contended that Berkeley's philosophy is better understood as a product of Cartesianism. As noted, Berkeley sees *esse* is *percipi* as (i) dissolving the very distinction between the being of things and their being perceived which constitute the source of scepticism; (ii) yielding a substantial self in which ideas inhered, not a mere unfocused "cluster" of ideas derived from empirial sensations, and (iii) providing a solid basis for a simple awareness of God – who speaks to us in the language of our perceptions.

Second, if Berkeley failed to found a college in America, he did significantly further the American dream to be a divinely chosen nation. He argued vigorously on behalf of a national bank for Ireland and for new monetary policies. Apparently from the time of the South Sea Bubble economic collapse (1720) Berkeley was profoundly troubled by the direction in which he felt European society was moving and by the malaise which he believed afflicted it. On this as on other issues, Berkeley takes the long view. Davie is right in crediting Berkeley (and Hutcheson) with providing the sparks of insight which alerted Scottish philosophers (including David Hume, Adam Smith, and Thomas Reid) to the need for a new and deep analysis of the nature of social relations and economic forces in the light of the rise of commercialism.

Berkeley generally stands apart from the arena of immediate political problems in Ireland or elsewhere. He never exercises his right to engage actively in politics. He favors preaching in Irish – as a tool to facilitate conversions. He condemns the racist bigotry of American planters but even when given the opportunity, he does not oppose slavery. He hopes to convert the American Indians, but seems to have been prepared to recruit students for his college by kidnapping them.

Yet despite a conservative cast of mind on many matters, when we turn to what Berkeley obviously took to be *the* fundamental questions we find radical analyses and proposals. In his philosophical immaterialism, his American scheme, his probing of the Irish economic order and banking system, and his diagnosis of the sickness affecting Europe, he is fully prepared to recommend profound changes in our thinking and our policies. In these respects, Berkeley's original contribution to modern thought extends well beyond the pale of what is Irish and even what is British and Continental, to assume a universal significance.

6

David Berman

THE IRISH COUNTER-ENLIGHTENMENT

Whether there is an Irish tradition in philosophy is arguable. Certainly between the 1690s and the 1750s there flourished a line of Irish thinkers born with John Toland, growing with Peter Browne, William King, George Berkeley, and Francis Hutcheson, and dying with Robert Clayton and Edmund Burke. In this line were lesser men, too: Edward Synge (father and son), Thomas Emlyn, Henry Dodwell (the elder), Philip Skelton and John Ellis. In this essay I will trace their themes.

Their bent is theological: they grew up with deism and in the interplay of enlightenment with counter-enlightenment. Throughout those sixty years these Irishmen wrote originally and influentially; and Swift's writing records their popular diffusion.

* * *

John Locke's *Essay concerning Human Understanding* (1690), sometimes called the "Philosophers' Bible", was authoritative in Irish thought. William Molyneux had brought it to the attention of Dr. Ashe, Provost of Trinity College, Dublin, which became the first learned institution to appreciate its importance. Without Locke's *Essay* it is hard to imagine that there could have been a Berkeley, Browne, Hutcheson or Burke; yet, apart perhaps from Molyneux, no Irish thinker claimed to be Locke's disciple. Rather, the Irish criticised and reinterpreted Locke's standpoint. Following his lead, Irish thought turned primarily on epistemology; and within epistemology, on the nature of perception and on language.

Molyneux wrote no philosophical work, but an influential book on optics, *Dioptrica Nova* (1692) and on Irish political theory, *The Case of Ireland's Being Bound* (1698). His philosophical opinions he expressed in letters to Locke, later printed in *Some Familiar Letters* (1708). He formulated the most celebrated problem of Irish philosophy, justly named after him; and yet he remained in the background. So, too, did Robert Molesworth, who wrote the anti-clerical *Account of Denmark* (1694). Like Molyneux, he was a politician and practical man who influenced more through personal relations than through published work. The so-called Molesworth circle gathered around him in the Dublin of the 1720s. As Molyneux was the apostle of Locke, so was Molesworth of Shaftesbury, author of the *Characteristics* (1711), who was himself Locke's pupil.

The two main tendencies of philosophy in Ireland are the liberal and the traditional. Both tendencies drew on Locke, and the traditionalists more imaginatively. Locke stands to Irish philosophy in the eighteenth century as does Hegel to German philosophy in the nineteenth. In the interplay of enlightenment and counter-enlightenment there are left-wing Lockeans, such as Molesworth, Toland, Emlyn, Hutcheson and Clayton, and right-wing Lockeans, such as Browne, Dodwell, King, Skelton and Burke. The left-wingers favour natural religion, rationalism and toleration, while the right-wingers favour empiricism, fideism, and intolerance. There are exceptions: and Berkeley is most exceptional, for his thought comprises elements that are rationalistic and empiricistic; he favours neither fideism nor toleration. Our broad distinction is nonetheless useful, if only to emphasise the uniqueness of Berkeley's thought, which is the centrepiece of Irish philosophy.

* * *

Toland, the father of modern Irish philosophy, unites its heritage. Born a Roman Catholic in County Donegal, at fifteen he became a Dissenter, then left Ireland to become a protégé of Shaftesbury, Molesworth and Locke. His *Christianity not Mysterious* (1696) brought Irish philosophy into being and haunted it until its death in the late 1750s. Though the father of Irish philosophy, Toland was neither beloved nor gratefully acknowledged.

In *Christianity not Mysterious* Toland applied the Lockean theory of meaning to religious mysteries. He argued that since mysteries like the Trinity do not stand for distinct ideas, Christianity must either employ meaningless doctrines or else be non-mysterious. His subtitle declares his radicalism: "that there is nothing in the Gospel contrary to reason, nor above it". Toland is a rationalist: not, however, a metaphysical but an epistemological rationalist. It is not that the world has no cognitive dark spots, but that our understanding need have none. While we do not know all that can be known of what is, we can be sure of what we do perceive and conceive. So, although we do not know the real inner nature of bodies; we do know what we perceive of them – their nominal essence, as Locke called it. Hence we should not be sceptical, nor should we think that our understanding of the world is mysterious. We should give our assent to what we know, and regard what we do not know as meaningless – like "Blictri" – and of no concern. In this way Toland's epistemological rationalism vanquishes mysteries. Though based on Locke's epistemology, he draws a conclusion — that Christianity is not mysterious — which is distinctively his own. As Pope expressed it (and then suppressed it) in the *Essay on Man:*

> What partly pleases, totally will shock:
> I question much if Toland would be Locke.

The reaction to Toland's book was fierce, and nowhere more so than in Ireland. Much that is distinctive and valuable in the Irish counter-enlightenment can be seen as a reaction to "the great Oracle of the Anti-Christians" — as Swift described the Donegal heretic. In 1697 Toland returned to the land of his birth, and within a short time, as we are told by William Molyneux, he had "raised against him the clamour of all parties;" the clergy, especially, were "alarmed to a mighty degree against him." His book was burnt by the common hangman, and it was moved by someone in the Irish House of Commons "that Mr. *Toland* himself should be burnt". It was decided, however, that he should be prosecuted. Toland wisely fled to England where he published his *Apology in a Letter from Himself to a Member of the House of Commons in Ireland* (1697). It is not clear why Toland returned to Ireland. There is some evidence that he hoped for a political appointment. Possibly he also wished (notwithstanding his protests in the *Apology*,[1]) to encourage a return to the tolerant religion of the ancient Irish, "the Western Latitudinarians", as he described them in his *Nazarenus* (1718).

The next person to express views similar to Toland's was not permitted to escape so easily. This was Thomas Emlyn, a Dublin dissenting minister who was imprisoned for more than two years for his *Humble Inquiry into the Scripture Account of Jesus Christ* (1702). The proceedings against Emlyn — who made an unsuccessful attempt to escape to England — were "severe and cruel", so much so that — as Emlyn tells us — "My case seem'd so odious, that I found it hard to get counsel." Emlyn heard one person say that "he had never seen such a persecution since he had been at the bar." This "rage and violence", this "Dublin zeal"—as Emlyn expressed it—was connected with the Toland escapade. In short, Toland waved the red flag in 1697 and five years later poor Emlyn was gored. A rationalistic clergyman was not to be tolerated, even though his views were more Christian than Toland's. Emlyn is a moderate left-wing Lockean. This comes out in his rationalistic rejection of the Athanasian doctrine of the Trinity, and also in such statements as: "No man can believe explicitly what he does not understand, for faith is an act of the understanding."

*   *   *

I shall now consider the three most important replies to Toland's challenge from the right-wing Lockeans. In 1697 appeared *A Letter in*

Answer to. . .Christianity not Mysterious. As to all Those who Set up for Reason and Evidence in Opposition to Revelation and Mysteries by Peter Browne, who was to become the leader of the right-Lockeans. In the following years Edward Synge published an *Appendix* (1698) to his *Gentleman's Religion*; the *Appendix* criticises Toland from the viewpoint of the moderate right wing.

In responding to Toland's challenge that Christianity is not mysterious, both Synge and Browne employ a key illustration: a man born blind who is told about light and colours. About otherworldly objects we have, says Browne, "no more notion than a blind man hath of light. And now that I am fallen into this metaphor which seems well to explain the nature of the thing, let us pursue it a little . . ."[2] This he does, pointing out that the blind man must understand light in terms of some other sense; thus he might think that light is 'wonderous soft and smooth". For Browne, we must trust that such representations are answerable to the things they are supposed to represent, even though we know that the two are of totally different natures. The illustration is also central to Synge. In the 1698 *Appendix*, he tells us of a conversation he had with a blind man who at one time did not believe that there were colours and light. The blind man initially thought that those who spoke of colours were imposing on him, just as Toland held that priests were imposing their mysteries on the laity. But after certain experiments, Synge tells us, the blind man came to believe that other people could see light and colours. For example, he was put at a distance from someone, who was able to tell him, without the use of touch, what he was doing. In this way the blind man became convinced that there were indeed things existing of which he had no direct or proper ideas.

Synge and Browne have much in common in their use of the illustration. They both emphasise that it is reasonable to believe in things of which we have no direct ideas. They play on the fact that knowledge of colours is inaccessible to the blind man, although we know that colours do exist. Hence we feel that the blind man *should* assent to their existence. The difference in their deployment of the illustration is that, whereas Synge tries to provide rational justification for the blind man's assent, for Browne it is largely a matter of trust and authority. For Browne we have evidence *that* the mysterious doctrines of Christianity are divinely inspired, but we have no direct or literal knowledge of *what* the doctrines mean. Whereas for Synge, our knowing *that* they are divine does also seem to reveal some hint of *what* the mysteries are in themselves. This constitutes an important but subtle difference, because both men must retain a very delicate balance in their use of the metaphor. The blind must have no idea of colours as they actually are, because we have no understanding of religious mysteries. If we had, they would cease to be mysteries. But colours must *in some way* be knowable, for if they were not then colour words would be mere Blictris, nonsense.

The similitude of the blind man is more than a mere illustration. It is the root metaphor, as it were, of Irish philosophy. And it is hardly an accident that the Molyneux problem, with which it is clearly associated, was very much an Irish problem. It was the Irishman Molyneux who first asked whether a blind man made to see would recognise by sight alone a sphere and cube which he had formerly known only by touch. Molyneux answered no; and two of the earliest known affirmative answers were given also by Irishmen, namely, by Synge and Francis Hutcheson. But the most important (negative) answer is given in Berkeley's *New Theory of Vision* (1709) which makes extensive use of Molyneux's problem and *Dioptrica Nova*. Be that as it may, in his critical account of our knowledge of God (not however of God's mysterious nature) Berkeley uses the root metaphor as a touchstone. Plainly alluding to Browne (and perhaps to Synge) he asks those holding views like Browne's to

> return to speak of God and his attributes in the style of other Christians, allowing that knowledge and wisdom do, in the proper sense of the words, belong to God, and that we have some notion, though infinitely inadequate, of those divine attributes, yet still more than a man born blind from his birth can have of light and colours.[3]

In 1709 Archbishop William King preached a *Sermon on Predestination* in which he too employed the key similitude;[4] his *Sermon* must be seen, in part at least, as a delayed response to Toland's rationalist challenge and the more recent one of Emlyn. Thus in a revealing letter to Henry Dodwell, the elder, dated January 1710, King writes: "I did expect that the Deists and Socinians would be alarmed at the (1709) Sermon for it seemed to me to take away the foundations of their objections against the mysteries of religion. . ."[5] King's position is similar to that of Synge and Browne. Indeed, Browne called attention to this similarity, in order to rebuke King for not having given him credit for the first formulation in 1697. I have described their common theory as theological representationalism, and it will be necessary to dwell on it in some detail, since it is the most widespread, influential and central theory in Irish philosophy. From this theory issued—by reaction or extension many of the significant contributions of Hibernian philosophy.

*　　　*　　　*

Browne, Synge and King should be seen as presenting the traditional fideistic negative theology (which goes back to the Pseudo-Dionysius, whose work was translated by John Scotus Eriugena) through a theory of perception drawn from the new learning, namely, the representative theory of perception. This theory had been and was being developed by Descartes, Boyle and, most notably, Locke; and one of its main purposes was to explain how and why certain experiences of objects, e.g. pains, illusions and odours, do not adequately (or at all) reflect actual qualities of the objects; while accounting for how these experiences allow us, nonetheless, to deal successfully with physical objects.

Now the representative model supposes that our perception of the physical world involves three terms: (i) the mind, (ii) its immediate experiences, called ideas or perceptions and (iii) the physical object and its qualities. Furthermore, the mind's experiences of (ii) are caused by (iii). Perception is the effect of a physical cause. Hence, in experiencing the fire, e.g., as painful, we are not obliged to attribute pain to the object (iii) – the fire – but only to our immediate idea or experience (ii) – the pain. In a realist account, on the other hand, we seem obliged to locate pains, odours, colours in the object. But this was contrary to the theory of the physical world developed by Descartes, Newton and Boyle, which held that physical objects really only possessed quantitative qualities, such as extension, solidity, motion and weight. This is not to say that the non-quantitative qualities, sometimes called secondary qualities, are not connected with the physical world. According to this model the quantitative qualities, called primary qualities, cause in sentient beings ideas such as pains, colours and odours. And experiencing secondary qualities can help us to deal with the actual physical objects. For example, smelling gas will probably make one leave the room before the primary qualities of the gas produce changes in one's heart and lungs – thereby terminating life.

This, in short, is representationalism. I am not claiming that this composite outline captures the whole of the representative model. But the outline does, I believe, identify the new model of perception developed by Locke; and it is this model which King, Browne, and Synge use to explain the nature of man's knowledge of God. Like that of the physical representationalists, their theological theory has three terms: (i) the mind, (ii) what it knows of God's attributes, and (iii) God's attributes as they are in God. Like the physical representationalists, it supposes that (iii) is known through (ii), and that (ii) represents (iii); and it also tends to see a casual relationship between (iii) and (i), which is productive of (ii). Again, like physical representationalism, there is a problematic relationship, *qua* resemblance, between (ii) and (iii). But, nonetheless, our knowledge of (ii) can help us to deal with (iii). Browne, Synge and King all emphasise the problematic and tenuous relationship between the second and third terms: they cast doubt on whether there is any sort of resemblance between (ii), our conceptions of the divine attributes and (iii), the attributes in themselves. On the other hand, Synge and King magnify the utility of (ii) as a surrogate for (iii), suggesting also that such utility is sufficient.

In his 1709 *Sermon*, King uses this representative model with some ingenuity, and our ideas of secondary qualities provide him with a

Newton
Boyle

particularly fruitful way of explaining and justifying our knowledge of God. Our idea of colour, for example, is unlike colour as it is in an external body, but we nonetheless say that a body is coloured. In the same way, King maintains, it is permissible to use the term "wisdom" in speaking of the divine attribute; although our conception of it and the thing in itself are entirely different, we may say that God is wise or has foreknowledge:

> I think it is agreed by most Writers of *Natural Philosophy*, (says King) that *Light* and *Colours* are but the Effects of certain *Bodies* and *Motions* on our Sense of seeing, and that there are no such Things at all in Nature, but only in our Minds; (and) of this at least we may be sure, that *Light* in the *Sun* or *Air*, are very different Things from what they are in our Sensations of them, yet we call both by the same Names, and term what is only perhaps a *Motion* in the *Air*, *Light*, because it begets in us that conception (i.e. sensation) which is truly *Light*. But it would seem very strange to the Generality of Men, if we should tell them there is no *Light* in the *Sun*, or *Colours* in the *Rain-Bow:* And yet strictly speaking, it is certain, that which in the *Sun* causes the Conception of *Light* in us, is as truly different in Nature from the Representation we have of it in our Mind, as our *Fore-knowledge*, is from what we call so in God.[6]

[handwritten marginal note: 2ndary Qualities]

Because God's attributes are entirely different from what we can understand, our theological statements cannot be true in the sense of correspondency. This impossibility is, as we have seen, built on traditional negative theology and is illustrated or confirmed by a problematic or sceptical interpretation of representationalism. But if we cannot know that any of our theological statements is true, *qua* correspondence or cognitively, it does not follow that they are false, or in no sense true. There is just no point in talking about them as true (or false) in the cognitive sense. When we say that we have knowledge of God we mean, King holds, such "Knowledge (as) is sufficient to all (the) Intents and Purposes of Religion. The Design whereof is to lead us in the Way to eternal Happiness, and in Order thereunto, to teach and oblige us to conquer ... our Passions and Lusts, to make us beneficient and charitable to Men. . ."[7] If theological statements can effect these things, i.e. produce practical theism, then they are true. They are not cognitively, but pragmatically true – which is the valid sense of true for human beings in this life.

It is upon this basis that King argues that God has foreknowledge. It is not that we cognitively know this to be the case. We do not. But our faith that it is so generates the right sort of results. Believing that God does possess foreknowledge "at once stops our Mouths, and silences our Objections, obliges us to an absolute Submission and dependance . . .;[8] and "This is plainly the design and effect of this terrible Representation . . ." That is, the meaning of foreknowledge or predestination lies in its capacity to produce feelings and actions expressive of a complete dependence on God. It is in this way that King justifies apparent contraditions not only in Scripture but also in mysteries such as the Holy Trinity, and, of course in foreknowledge and free-will. Although divine foreknowledge and human free-will are not *logically* compatible, they are *pragmatically* compatible: and that is what matters. Our conceptions of the former "are not so much designed to give us Notions of God as he is in himself, as to make us sensible of our Duty to him, and to oblige us to perform it."[9] Again, "When we hear these Things (e.g. that God foreknows) we are not so much to enquire, whether this Representation exactly suits, with what really passeth in the Mind of God, as how we ought to behave ourselves in such a Case. . ."[10]

King's sensitivity to models appears also in his own use of them to justify his general thesis that our knowledge does not reflect the world but enables us to deal with it. So a map is different from the land it represents;[11] a line is used to represent time but is different from time;[12] we speak of the mind and its operations by means of sensible things, e.g. we say someone is bright, depressed, buoyant — but the mind is not sensible, i.e., it is not bright, depressable, etc.[13] Yet in all these cases the models are highly useful. King tries to put his readers into the state of mind of someone who is confronted with a representation that appears to him totally different from what it is supposed to represent. He wants us to appreciate that the incredulous person, who does not try to see the utility of the theological representation or model, is only standing in his own way. Thus King deserves credit for his pragmatic interpretation of the representationalist model of perception and for its application to theology and, to a lesser extent, science. And as an anticipator of pragmatism, King's claim is at least as strong as that of Locke, Berkeley or Hume.

*   *   *

Where King and Synge stressed the pragmatic aspect of our theological representations, Browne emphasises what he calls their "analogical" aspect and their unknown correspondence to the divine archetypes. It was for this reason that Browne accused King of transforming analogy into metaphor and Synge of changing the analogical into the literal and thereby assimilating faith to reason. Browne's main contribution, however, is his sensationalism. More than Locke, he deserves credit for being the first full-blooded sensationalist with regard to the mind and its acts. In the *Procedure*, he attempts to prove, by means of his sensationalism, that we have no direct, proper or literal knowledge of anything purely mental or spiritual. Synge and King largely take this for granted, that is, they assume the truth of negative theology — although there are some hints of sensationalism in the latter's *Sermon*.[14]

Browne argues that as all our ideas are derived from sensation, our ideas of the emotions and operations of our minds are not essentially different from our ideas of colours and odours. There are not, as Locke and others claimed, two original sources of experience—sensation and reflection—but only sensation. For Browne, anger is not something which we experience or know directly and distinctly from a source other than sensation — as Locke held; rather it is composed of sensations, such as a feeling of warmth, gritting of teeth, reddish face, increased pulse, etc. We conceive "sorrow by a down look and contraction of our features"[15] and these ideas are clearly "borrowed from sensation"[16] Also important for our idea of emotion is the "object which occasioned" the feeling.[17] Having provided what he considers to be an adequate account which does not resort to ideas of reflection, Browne challenges his (Lockean) opponents to produce or find a mental idea which is not sensational.[18] Having issued the empiricist challenge, Browne musters the following specific arguments.

He criticises the Lockean theory for postulating an unnecessary entity: we do not require both the mental acts and the ideas of these mental acts, particularly since we can never, by hypothesis, perceive the mental acts (or emotions) themselves. Occam's razor demands, therefore, that they be cut.[19]

But the theory is not just uneconomical, it is also incoherent, according to Browne, for it supposes that, "The same thing shall be an *idea*, and the *operation* of the mind upon the idea at the same time; and thus we have a new idea for another second operation, and so on *in infinitum.*"[20] That is, every time we are said to operate about an idea, there will be an idea of that operation, and an idea of that operation, and so on. The theory leads to an infinite multiplication of ideas and operations.

Browne also uses what might be called the familiarity argument against Locke: "Had we *simple original ideas* (of reflection) of other objects beyond that of sensation, we should all indifferently and readily acquiesce in our opinions about them; a peasant would have as *clear* and *distinct* ideas of them, of the intellect for instance . . . (as a psychologist)."[21] The mind is, therefore, incapable of any "such unnatural *squint*, or distorted *turn* upon itself."[22] "An *idea of reflection* is an empty sound, without any intelligible and determinate meaning."[23] "All the *ideas* we attempt to form of the manner of its (the mind's) acting, and the expressions we use for it, are borrowed from sensation."[24] And this applies also to the mind's knowledge of mind as such. For Browne, we have no idea of a purely mental mind in a corporeal body. He was one of the first philosophers to react against what Gilbert Ryle has called the dogma of the ghost in the machine. Thus he writes that, "Men commonly speak of (spirit) as of something *within* us, and not *of* us; as if it thought and reasoned *in* the body, and not together *with* any part of it; as if the body were a mere *box*, or *case*, or place of residence for it."[25] For Browne, it is the man, and not some immaterial substance, which thinks.[26]

Browne's concept of mind may well owe something to Henry Dodwell, the elder, who in 1706 issued his *Epistolary Discourse, Proving . . . that the Soul is a Principle Naturally Mortal*, in which he denied the natural immortality of the soul and inclined to a materialistic account of it. Both King and Browne were on friendly terms with the Irish born Dodwell, who was a student and fellow of Trinity College, Dublin. According to King, Dodwell had held the theory of conditional immortality for more than thirty years prior to publishing it (Dodwell was a scholar and theologian of considerable European stature in the early part of the eighteenth century.) The anti-dualistic accounts of mind offered by Dodwell and Browne are, in many respects, in advance of their time. Yet although the theories were progressive, their end or purpose was traditional, even reactionary. By arguing that the mind neither is nor can be known to be immaterial, or naturally immortal, they hoped to force theologians to return to scriptural and fideistic ideas of the afterlife.[27]

Thus Browne's sensationalism provides the philosophical justification for the negative side of theological representationalism — its denial that we can literally understand things divine and supernatural. In his *Sermon* King develops the pragmatic aspect of the representationalist model, as well as providing the most succinct and articulate statement of theological representationalism itself. Synge's contribution— the slightest of the three—is his collateral experiment which helps to knit together the approaches of Browne and King as well as a specific application of the model to the Trinity. In this way did the three prelates ingeniously argue, against Toland (and perhaps Emlyn), that Christianity was indeed mysterious, and that it was reasonable to hold that it was.

*   *   *

Berkeley opposed theological representationalism. He first wrote against it, in the form King had lent it, in a private letter of 1709, then publicly in *Alciphron, or the Minute Philosopher*.[28] Believing himself the butt of Berkley's criticism, Browne responded in the long, often harsh eighth chapter of *Things Divine and Supernatural Conceived by Analogy with Things Natural and Human* (1733), whereupon Berkeley addressed to him a firm, yet moderate, letter.[29]

Berkeley's *Principles of Human Knowledge* (1710) opposed representationalism in its materialistic form, on the same grounds as he opposed it in theology. Synge, Browne and King had placed God in the epistemological position to which Berkeley assigned matter. If these supposedly representative notions resemble their objects, then they afford us knowledge of God; and if they do not resemble their objects, then we can draw no analogy at all: there is no half-measure. In Berkeley's eyes King, Browne and Synge had defended God's mysterious nature by making him unintelligible — an "unknown subject of Attributes absolutely unknown."[30] Similarly in *Principles*[31] Berkeley had claimed against the materialists that matter is an "unknown support of unknown qualities".

Berkeley's response to the challenge that "Christianity is not mysterious" lies between the left-wing Lockeanism of Toland and Emlyn and the right-wing Lockeanism of Browne, King and Synge. Whereas the three prelates had made all knowledge of God representational, Toland and Emlyn had reduced religion to rational theology: Berkeley, of course, as a believing Christian agreed that Christianity was mysterious. In the Introduction to his *Principles*, Berkeley criticises the assumption that the cognitive is the only legitimate kind of meaning.[32] In *Alciphron* he returns to this, applying it to theology.[33] Religious mysteries, he says, are not cognitive, but emotive. Faith is not, as Emlyn had claimed, "an act of the understanding," but an emotional act. Thus talk of the Trinity is able to produce love, hope and gratitude; grace is likely to evoke piety; and original sin may well produce a salutory sense of one's unworthiness. Berkeley disagrees with Browne's view that God's wisdom is in itself unknowable, holding instead that we know it just as we know that other men are wise: by inferring analogically from their associated sensible effects. As orderly human effects imply a human mind, so the infinite orderliness of nature implies an infinite divine mind. So Berkeley responds to Toland by accepting in rational theology the rationalism of the left-wing Lockeans and in religious mysteries the pragmatism of the right wing.

*   *   *

After Emlyn's incarceration in 1704 there seems to have been little or no freethought in Ireland until the 1720s, when it revives with the Molesworth Circle. The most important joint production of this group, which included Francis Hutcheson, James Arbuckle, and Edward Synge the younger, is the collection of essays and letters originally published in the *Dublin Journal* in 1726, and reprinted by James Arbuckle in *A Collection of Letters and Essays* (1729), a work written in the Shaftesburian spirit and manner, reflecting his moderate anticlericalism and sympathy for natural religion and religious toleration — in short, enlightenment values.

Earlier in the 1720s, the leading figure of the group, Molesworth, issued a pamphlet *Some Considerations for the Promoting of Agriculture* (1723), which may be taken as representative of the views of the Circle. His sympathy for liberty and latitude in religion is apparent. He proposes schools for teaching agriculture, but notes that, "In these schools I would not have any precepts, differences or distinctions of religion taken notice of, and nothing taught, but only husbandry and good manners, and . . . the children should daily serve *God*, according to their own religions . . ."[34] Molesworth was a cautious man in print, and we are entitled, I think, to believe that this patron of Toland would have been happy to apply the principles of his agricultural school to society at large. The conversation of the Molesworth Circle is bound to have been more radical than its published utterances. Yet even these were warmly attacked, as we can see from the reception given to Edward Synge's 1725 sermon—*The Case of Toleration*—which advocated a very limited toleration. The orthodox reacted so violently against it that — apart from a *Vindication* published in the following year — Synge refrained from any further liberal pronouncements. Not surprisingly, his sermon was defended by a member of the Circle in the *Dublin Journal* of October 29, 1726. Synge's unexpressed views were very close to those of Francis Hutcheson, the most distinguished philosophical member of the Circle.[35] Hutcheson, a son of Irish philosophy who left Ireland around 1730 to become father of Scottish philosophy, wrote and published most of his important philosophical works while he was teaching in a Dissenting Academy in Dublin in the 1720s. He also published in Arbuckle's *Collection* three essays attacking Mandeville's *Fable of the Bees* as well as three essays on laughter.

Between the demise of the Molesworth Circle in the late 1720s and the last notable effort of Irish freethought with Clayton in the 1750s, there seems to have been almost no published freethought or left-wing Lockeanism in Ireland. There is, however, much rumour of extreme freethinkers, even of atheists. Thus in *An Essay on the Existence of God* (1730) by Wetenhall Wilkes we find an intriguing account of an alleged atheist, called J——h T——r, and his "dissolute associates", who are said to have been active in Dublin around 1729. Even more elusive is the so-called "impious society of Blasters," who created a stir in the late 1730s, and provoked Berkeley's one appearance in the Irish House of Lords as well as his reactionary *Discourse Addressed to the Magistrates* (1738). Irish freethinking was timid and slight when compared with that in England, Scotland and France; but there was plainly a continuing spectre of freethought which frightened Irish philosophers into producing some of the most inventive and weighty defences of religion published in the eighteenth century.

*   *   *

When Robert Clayton's *Essay on Spirit* (1750) was first published, he held one of the richest bishoprics in Ireland, that of Clogher, and he had been an Irish bishop for nearly thirty years. This may partly explain the furious reaction to the *Essay*, which advocated substantial changes in the Thirty-nine articles of subscription. In the *Essay* Clayton advances a curious theory of spirits. He accepts the dualism of active mind or spirit and passive body or matter. In his view every piece of matter has, united to it, a spirit, which governs and effects its movements. This follows because "*nothing can act where it is not,* (hence) that power whereby any body continues in (or resists) motion is . . . the effect of some concomitant spirit." The degree of intelligence and power of a spirit depends, it would seem, on the kind of material system to which it is united. It is even possible, Clayton thinks, that all the innumerable created spirits are "equally perfect". The difference in their actual degree of intellect and power may only be the result of the particular "formation of their bodily organs". But, although it is possible that the spirit associated with a speck of dust is as perfect as that of a man or angel, it is certain that not even God can "produce any being, equal in power to, or independent of, himself; because two all-powerfuls, two supremes, would imply a contradiction."[36]

I have called Clayton's system a pluralistic version of occasionalism, because he, like the occasionalist writers, makes much of our (supposed) ignorance of how our bodily organs move.[37] However, his imaginative metaphysical system was probably less important to him than his Arian conclusions and the plea for religious toleration made eloquently in the *Essay's* long dedication to the Primate of Ireland.

Irish left-wing Lockeanism culminates in Clayton, and in him there is much that is admirable – a broad range of interests, intellectual honesty, and (what may be called) ecumenism. Thus he wrote pamphlets in a tolerant, and reconciliatory spirit, not only to those of his own church, but to the Quakers, Jews, and Roman Catholics. But there is also much that is half-hearted and unoriginal in him. He embraces Toland's rationalism, Emlyn's Arianism, and the polished aestheticism and toleration of the Molesworth circle; yet he also clings to some of the weakest and most naive parts of revelation. With Clayton we have the impression (in more than one way) of history's repeating itself, and there is a sense (as Marx has put it) of tragi-comedy in such repetitions: the new Toland is no brilliant *enfant terrible* but a wealthy *bon vivant,* perhaps grown bored with comfort. The Clayton controversy strongly recalls the two earlier heresy hunts of Toland and of Emlyn. As the victims were becoming more respectable they were also suffering more acutely. Dublin zeal frightened Toland, imprisoned Emlyn and killed Clayton.[38]

Clayton's rationalism comes out in (i) his employment of an equivalent to Toland's "Blictri" and (ii) his stand against theological representationalism. (i) In his *Vindication of the Old and New Testament* Clayton introduced the nonsense word "Abodubenden", telling us that if an accredited angel informed us that there was an Abodubenden in Heaven, we should believe that the angel said it and that it is so, "but our belief cannot reach the mystery any more than our knowledge can."[39] Talk of mysteries above our reason, or of Abodubenden, is like talk of absolute secrets, Clayton acutely remarks. And "while anything continues to be an absolute secret, it is impossible for any one to believe anything about it."[40] (ii) One of Clayton's many critics was Thomas McDonnell, formerly a fellow of Trinity College (1737) and then Rector of Derryvullen (1744), a parish in Clayton's own diocese of Clogher. In two pamphlets McDonnell sought to defend the Athanasian doctrine of the Trinity against Clayton by means of theological representation. In *Some Remarks on McDonnell's Essay* . . . , published in the year of Berkeley's death, Clayton responded; and in some respect his criticisms are similar to those Berkeley levelled against theological representationalism in *Alciphron*. [41] But Berkeley by no means approved of his former associate in the Bermuda project; for in a letter to McDonnell (his last extant), he speaks of "the weakness and presumption" of the *Essay*.[42] Clayton attacked McDonnell's theological representationalism seeing it as a danger to reasonable religion. He also seems to have been aware that in the 1740s and 1750s a school of theological representationalism had developed which was inspired by Browne's sensationalism. In *Some Thoughts on Self-love* (1753), Clayton observes:

> . . . some late Writers* had asserted that we have no *ideas*
> but of sensible objects, which alone are capable of making
> any impressions on our minds . . .

*Brown on the *Procedure, Extent, and Limits of human Understanding*. And from him the Authors of the *Natural State of Man*; and of *Deism Revealed*.[43]

The author of An *Enquiry into the Natural State of Man* (1743), was William Thompsoñ, whose allegiance to Browne's theological representationalism is most noticeable in the introduction, which contains a number of sensationalist *dicta:* e.g. "All human knowledge is originally derived from sensation . . . " and "what, therefore, are usually called ideas of reflection, can only, if they mean anything, be reflex acts of the intellect upon ideas of sensation . . . " Of considerably more interest is Philip Skelton, the author of *Ophiomaches: or Deism Revealed* (1749), who, like McDonnell, held a living in the diocese of Clogher. Although he was not an original thinker, he was a vigorous writer, and, at the same time, somehow typical of the right-wing Irish philosopher. Skelton had not always been unreservedly partial to Browne. As a relatively young man, in 1733, he issued *A Letter to the Authors of Alciphron and Divine Analogy* in the guise of an old soldier, attempting to conciliate the dispute between Berkeley and Browne in the interests of Christian solidarity against the infidel enemy. When he wrote *Ophiomaches,* however, he had firmly committed himself to the author of the *Divine Analogy*. His endorsement of Browne's sensationalism and theological representationalism is typical of his confident and peremptory manner:

> It is vain to say we have any proper or immediate idea of spirit, and its operations, or that we have any other source of notions than sensation. If *Brown's Procedure and Extent of the understanding* had not clearly demonstrated this, the trials every man may make in his own mind would do it effectually. When we look into ourselves with a sharp and unprejudiced eye, we plainly perceive spirit represented there analogically by our idea of subtil matter, its operations by those of body . . . 44

In the British Library there is a copy of Skelton's collected works (1824), which were formerly owned by S.T. Coleridge. On the blank page opposite the title-page of volume one, Coleridge has written the following perceptive character sketch of Skelton (and perhaps of Irish right-wing Lockeanism in general): "By the bye, the Rev. Phil. Skelton is of the true Irish Breed – i.e. a *brave* fellow but a *Bit* of a *Bully*. 'E.g. by St. Patrick but I shall make cold mutton of you, Mister Arian.' "

Skelton employs theological representationalism in an interesting little pamphlet entitled *The Censor Censured* (1750), in which he defends his *Ophiomaches* against a critical review by the editor of *A Literary Journal* (1749), John Peter Droz, a moderate left-winger, who published the first limited edition of Clayton's *Essay* in 1750. On the whole, Skelton accepts theological representationalism without bothering to justify it; but he is blunter in his use of it, e.g. on the question of the immortality of the soul. Theologians such as Samuel Clarke and Berkeley had laboured to prove that because the soul is immaterial and indivisible, it is therefore impossible to conceive its dissolution. Skelton, on the other hand, uses theological representationalism to argue that the soul *may* (in some way inconceivable to us) dissolve. In this he is aligning himself with the earlier Dodwellian position; but he also comes dangerously close to the freethinking position of those like Anthony Collins and David Hume who effectively denied immortality altogether. Here extreme right-wing fideism meets extreme left-wing scepticism.

This is even more apparent in the case of John Ellis, a Dublin clergyman, who may be called the Irish fideistic Hume. In his *Knowledge of Divine Things from Revelation and not from Reason or Nature* (1743), Ellis pushes theological representationalism to its boldest and most logical conclusion. Like Browne, he is a rigorous sensationalist with regard to the mind:" . . . our senses . . . are the entire ground-work of our knowledge both human and divine".45 But his main influence is Locke, whom he takes to be the greatest philosophical authority. At the centre of Ellis's thought is a linguistic argument for the truth of revelation and the God of revelation. The argument moves as follows:

(i) There is no natural way in which we could come to a knowledge of God or things spiritual. Ellis carefully goes through such sources as (a) innate ideas – which he rejects on Lockean lines – (b) instinct, (c) sensation, (d) reflection and (e) reason. Because we have only sensationalist knowledge we could never naturally come to "a notion of an immaterial object".[46] Reason can or would never have suggested that the world was created, "because the intermediate relations between a created effect and a creative cause, are no way apparent or discernible by us . . .".[47] We cannot move from a creature to creator because they "are infinitely distant".

(ii) But it is plainly the case that we *do* know of God and things spiritual.

(iii) But if we could not have come by this knowledge naturally, then we must have derived it supernaturally, i.e. from revelation. Ellis ingeniously drives his point home with an (often) acute examination of the question of how man first learned language. He takes it that "we cannot think but by the help of language".[48] But without language, he maintains, we could not think. "It is by the help of words, at least in great measure, that we even reason and discourse within ourselves . . .".[49] Therefore language could not have developed naturally. Just as language is imparted to children by their parents, so man must have been taught language supernaturally at the beginning; and this is indeed confirmed by the book of Genesis, where we learn that God taught Adam and Eve the words for all things. Therefore the God of revelation exists.

This may appear a crude argument (and in some respect it is), but Ellis's keen grasp of the alternatives catapult him from the middle ages to the nineteenth century. For example, he writes:

> Man could not of himself have discovered the knowledge of fixing sounds to signify objects, ideas, or conceptions, so as to be signs . . . Or, if this were possible, . . . it must have been the work of many ages, during which time man had been neither an intelligent nor sociable creature, and so sent into the world to no purpose . . . [50]

Thus ". . . men without language would rather be a species of apes, than rational creatures . . .".[51]

There is a comparison to be drawn between Ellis's linguistic argument for the existence of God and that of Berkeley.[52] Both make use of language for a theological conclusion; both see God as talking, or having talked, to man; but whereas Berkeley's sophisticated optic-language argument depends on an appreciation of the wide range of meaning and language, Ellis's argument requires a narrow conception of language. The two philosophers are worlds apart in their method but united in their end. They are both anxious to justify belief in a God that is less distant and more personal than the God of deism.

There is almost total agreement between Ellis and Skelton, not merely in their commitment to theological representationalism, but on its application to such matters as our knowledge of immortality and the creation of the world. In addition to Skelton, Thompson, Ellis, and McDonnell there was an anonymous writer on Analogy in the Dublin Supplement to Chambers' *Cyclopaedia* (1753), who is sympathetic to King. And of the three original proponents, Synge (who became Archbishop of Tuam in 1716), was still alive and still defending his version of theological representationalism in 1734. The vigour and popularity of this representationalist school can be seen also in the statements of its critics. Thus a writer in the *Literary Journal* [53] speaks of "the dangers I apprehend to all religion, either natural or reveal'd, if the Bishop's (Browne's) system of analogy should be received, *and from the intelligence I have . . . it is by many industrious defended.*"

That there was in the 1740s and 1750s an Irish school of theological representationalists grounded on sensationalism is important both in itself and also for an appreciation of Burke's sensationalist aesthetics. Burke was a student at Trinity College in the 1740s and wrote his chief philosophical works in the late 1740s and early 1750s. His sympathy for theological representationalism shows in his *Reformer* (1747 and 1748). Thus he says that religion "exceeds all systems of philosophy. . . by fastening our thoughts on something indeed *past our comprehension, but not our hopes*".[54] Burke's commitment to the theological position of Browne, King, Ellis and Skelton is even more noticeable in his *Philosophical Enquiry into the Origin of our Ideas of the Sublime and Beautiful* (1757). Our understanding of God's attributes, writes Burke, is "stretched to a degree far exceeding the bounds of our comprehension . . . Thus when we contemplate the Deity, his attributes and their operation coming united on the mind, form a sort of sensible image, and as such are capable of affecting the imagination."[55]

Swift seemed to remain aloof from these theological speculations. He was interested more in the church than in religion. He did, however, use his own admirable skills against freethought in his vigorous satires, *An Argument against the Abolishing of Christianity* (1711) and in the less well-known though no less effective *Mr C–ns's Discourse of Freethinking, Put into Plain English, by Way of Abstract, for the use of the Poor* (1713). In *Mr C–ns's Discourse* – a work on which Burke may have modelled his satire on Bolingbroke's freethought, *A Vindication of Natural Society* (1756) – Swift ridicules Collins by converting his innuendos into pithy assertions. Compare, for example, Collins' suggestive catalogue of lost gospels [56] with Swift's half sentence: "Some books of scripture are said to be lost, and this utterly destroys the credit of those that are left . . . ".

Swift's lack of sympathy for theological representation may, perhaps, be gathered from his remarks on Browne and, even more, from his comments on what I have called the root metaphor of Irish philos-

ophy – the blind man trying to deal with visual shapes and colours.[57]
In *Gulliver's Travels* he ridicules the idea that a blind man can effectively deal with colours by means of touch or smell. "There was (in the
Academy of Lagado) a man born blind, who had several apprentices
in his own condition: their employment was to mix colours for painters, which their master taught them to distinguish by feeling and
smelling. It was indeed my misfortune to find them at that time not
very perfect in their lessons . . . ".[58] Similarly in the *Memoirs of
Martinus Scriblerus* the hero-pedant, Martinus, is said to have "first
found out the *Palpability* of *Colours;* and by the delicacy of his touch,
(he) could distinguish the different vibrations of the heterogeneous
Rays of Light."[59] If Swift followed Berkeley in regarding the colour
ability of a blind man as a touchstone for distinguishing the two opposed theological positions, then we may infer that he sided with him also
against King, Browne and Synge on our knowledge of God.[60] Towards
the end of his *Sermon on the Trinity,* however, Swift says that "there
is some kind of unity and distinction in the divine nature, which mankind cannot possible comprehend . . ."; hence, we must "believe a
fact that we cannot understand". While this is certainly in accord with
theological representationalism, he does not apply it to the more
crucial area of God's non-mysterious attributes, such as wisdom and
goodness. Nor is he prepared as Browne and King are to accept contradictions in mysteries: "If I were directly told in scripture that three
are one, and one is three, I could not conceive or believe it in the
natural common sense of that expression . . .". From this it seems
unlikely that he would be sympathic to Berkeley's emotive account of
mysteries, but there is some evidence in *Gulliver's Travels* that he
shared Berkeley's opposition to the restrictive referential theory of
meaning – that a word is essentially a name which stands for a particular idea, which is the full meaning of the word.[61] Thus another of
the absurd Lagado projects was the "leaving out of verbs and partic-
iples, because, in reality, all things imaginable are but nouns." A similar
but more radical project "was a scheme for entirely abolishing all words
whatever . . . since words are only names for things, it would be more
convenient for all men to carry about them such things as were necessary to express a particular they are to discourse on".[62] This referential,
noun theory of meaning was developed at length by Locke [63] and was
wholeheartedly accepted by nearly all theological representationalists, but it is rejected by Berkeley in his emotive theory of meaning, a
theory which Burke applied to aesthetics.[64]

* * *

Why was there such a unique flowering of Irish philosophy between
1696 - 1757? Why did it happen then, and not before or after? No
doubt this is a complex question, part of the answer to which will be

that extraordinary individuals, such as Toland, King, Browne, Berkeley and Burke, produce extraordinary results. But I should like to propose a deeper and less facile answer, which will at the same time add a final dimension to our study.

Let us first briefly consider the politicial and economic background. By 1691 the Glorious Revolution had been concluded. Irish Anglicans were thereby saved from the dominance of James II and their Roman Catholic countrymen. The previous fifty years had been stormy indeed. First the Irish Anglicans were buffeted by the Roman Catholics during the 1641 Rebellion, then by Cromwell and the Presbyterians, and then by the Roman Catholics under Tyrconnell and James II. There was now to be a period of political stability and calm, which would last for more than a century.

Initially, at least, the Irish Anglicans were in an insecure and precarious position. They were faced with a hostile dispossessed majority, and a Treaty that did not seem to go far enough in restricting the Catholic majority.[65] The Presbyterians also seemed a dangerous minority, as William III was known to favour them. Yet from this insecure position the Irish Anglicans developed a remarkably successful *modus operandi*, whose foundation was the Penal legislation against both Catholics and Presbyterians. This legislation, which came into being in the 1690s and 1700s, established the ascendancy, just as it repressed the two other religious classes politically, economically and socially.

Consider now the birth of Irish philosophy in Toland. He was christened Janus Junius, and appropriately enough, for his background posed a two-faced threat to the ascendancy: born a Roman Catholic, he became a Dissenter at fifteen. But Toland's most threatening face was shown in *Christianity Not Mysterious*. His attack on Christian mysteries and his defence of natural or deistic religion represented a fundamental challenge to the ascendancy establishment. For if there were no Christian mysteries then there could be nothing to separate the rival Christian religions or sects. And then there could be no basis for the Penal Code. The success of deism or natural religion would be fatal to the ascendancy. Deism's belief in a few fundamental religious doctrines and little or no ritual, and its emphasis on morality and toleration, could hardly fail to soften or erode the Penal Code. At any rate, historians have agreed that this is what did happen, but that it happened late in the eighteenth century in Ireland. "An attitude of scepticism was fatal to the Penal Code."[66] If we allow that Toland's deistic thinking represented a threat to the material well-being of the ascendancy, then we can explain not only the fury unleashed against him (and Emlyn and Clayton) but also the distinctively counter-enlightenment character of most of Irish philosophy.

The case of Archbishop King is especially instructive. Seven years before King delivered his 1709 *Sermon* he had published *De Origine Mali*, a work which earned him considerable reputation, as it was criticised by Leibniz and used by Pope for the *Essay on Man*. In his preface to the English translation (1739), Edmund Law published King's summary of the treatise.[67] Two of King's principles for explaining evil are of interest here:

(i) "An equality of perfection in the creatures is impossible . . .;"[68] therefore, even granting an all good and wise God, it is not possible that everyone or everything can be in a superior position. However, since there are a limited number of superior positions in the great chain of being, this does not cast doubt on God's justice or goodness.

(ii) If a man has lost a superior position, then it must have been lost through some folly of the agent. One's fall is not God's, but one's own, fault. God "is not to be blamed for suffering one to degrade himself by his own act . . . ".[69] Therefore "He that is in a less convenient situation has no room for complaint . . . ".[70] Consequently, to move from a superior to an inferior position implies that one has committed some folly. So King tried to justify the ways of God to man, that is, to explain the existence of apparent evil in a world said to be created by an all good and powerful God.

Now ten years earlier King had published another influential work — *State of the Protestants of Ireland* (1691). It, too, was a work of vindication. As King puts it in the conclusion:

> (What has) moved me to say what I have said (is) that I might vindicate ourselves (the Irish Anglicans) by speaking Truth in a matter that so nearly concern'd us both in Our temporal and eternal interest.[71]

That is, the Irish Anglicans were justified in rebelling against James II and justified, too, in trying to gain and then maintain a superior position over the Roman Catholics.

> Upon the whole, the *Irish* (Catholics) may justly blame themselves and their Idol, the Earl of *Tyrconnel*, as King *James* may them both, for whatever they have, or shall suffer in the issue of this Matter, since it is apparent that the necessity was brought about by them, that either they or we must be ruin'd.[71]

In the course of his work, King details the acts of folly committed by the Catholic supporters of James.

Either the Irish Catholics or the Irish Anglicans were going to occupy the dominant position in Ireland. It could not be both. Again, either James II or William III was to be king. This does not detract from God's justice. The fact that a monarch was deposed is a regrettable and an apparent evil, but it should not reflect on God or the Protestant church. And the fact that it is William III and the Irish Anglicans who are in the superior position implies that James and the Catholics have committed follies: they deserved to change places.

Thus the *Origin of Evil* provides the theoretical framework for the *State of the Protestants:* the justification for the justification of the Protestants.

As the *Origin* seeks to vindicate God's ways, so the *State* seeks to vindicate the ways of the Protestants. But as the *Origin* provides the basis for the *State,* it is difficult to resist the conclusion that *its* origin was also ideological. That is, it was prompted in part as a justification of the ruling élite in Ireland, of which King was to be such a prominent member. King was indeed a bulwark of the ascendancy.

The Christian mysteries were needed by the Irish Anglicans to divide, explain or (as some would say) mystify. I am not claiming, however, that the Irish philosophers were clearly aware of this, or that this genetic analysis *in any way* invalidates the truth of their philosophical writings. It merely reveals the underlying cause or occasion. Sometimes, in an impulsive writer like Skelton, the ideological motivation comes out in a most disarming manner. Arguing against Droz's liberal and tolerant Christian position, Skelton asks in the *Censor Censured:* "If your latitude is allowed of, why may not a Papist subscribe and take orders with us, as well as a Socinian?"[72] The unstated absurdity is: "Would not your sort of latitudinarianism destroy our privileged position?" I do not believe that Skelton actually thought, or clearly thought, in these terms; rather it was at the very back of his mind and that of the ascendancy.

Perhaps the most compelling evidence for my genetic thesis is to be found in *An Argument Against the Abolishing of Christianity* (1711), where Swift gives as his last reason that abolishing the Christian religion "will be the readiest course we can take to introduce Popery". Swift suggests that the freethinkers are really disguised "Popish missionaries". He mentions Matthew Tindal – who was for a time a convert to Catholicism, and, not surprisingly, Toland "the great Oracle of the Anti-Christians . . . an Irish priest, (and) the son of an Irish priest". Not only the biographies of freethinkers but also their "reasoning" shows that freethinking is bound to lead to Popery: "For supposing Christianity to be extinguished the people will never be at ease till they find out some other Method of worship; which will as infallibly produce superstition, as this will end in Popery".

It is difficult to say how seriously Swift took this conspiracy theory. But the inner meanings of it should be clear. Deism or freethought will, if it is successful, favour the Irish Catholics, by undermining the privileged position of the Protestant ascendancy. In accordance with the accepted idea of historical causation the freethinkers are seen as intending, or aiming at, a certain goal. But what goal? This perplexed Skelton, who also believed that the freethinkers were really disguised Catholic missionaries. In *Ophiomaches* he provides us with the most elaborate account of the conspiracy theory. Since the freethinkers do not seem to be aiming at any open end or purpose, their purpose must be hidden:

it must be conspiratorial. He then musters in detail various kinds of circumstantial evidence, and most ingeniously answers apparent difficulties in the theory.[73] This conspiracy theory is even presented by Berkeley [74] whose account is more detailed than Swift's but less so than that of Skelton. It is plain from verbal parallels that he was influenced by Swift. Thus, where Swift mentions "the constant practice of the Jesuits to send Emissaries, with instructions to personate themselves members of the several prevailing sects amongst us", Berkeley says that "The Emissaries of *Rome* are known to have personated several other sects, which from time to time have sprung up amongst us . . . " A slighter and less conspiratorial version also appeared in an anonymous Dublin pamphlet *A Protestant's Address to the Protestants of Ireland* (1757).[75] The earliest statement, curiously, is given in *An Apology for Mr Toland*. Here the writer (who is apparently not Toland) details the Irish campaign of vilification against Toland around the time of his visit to Dublin in 1697:

> At length comes from the North (of Ireland?) a finish'd master of such (slavish or devious) politics, and he doubts not but Mr *Toland* after all is a *Jesuit*. But his Book utterly destroys all the Principles of *Popery* and *Superstition*. That's nothing; for *Jesuits* to unsettle us will preach against their own Religion.[76]

The same writer also notes that "the last effort . . . to blast him (Toland), was to make him pass for a rigid *Nonconformist*".[77] Toland's deism or freethought was, in a sense, the reconciliation or cancellation of his being an "Irish Priest" and a "rigid Nonconformist". The Irish Anglicans could happily tolerate one or the other, but not both, and not deism. Hence it is understandable that Toland "was dreaded in Ireland as a . . . second Goliath",[78] as P. Des Maizeaux put it in his 1726 memoir of Toland. Whether or not Swift took his conspiracy theory from *An Apology for Mr Toland,* or from the northerner, or whether he himself was the northerner, is not known. What we have is a fantastic theory expressed at various times between 1698 and 1757 by at least three writers of repute — all suggesting that the purpose and drift of the writings of Toland and his followers was to advance the cause of the Roman Catholicism. My conclusion is that the conspiracy theory reveals as fantasy the very real fear of the ruling class that freethought, as a tolerant, enlightening and counter-divisive force, could insidiously undermine the priviliged status of the ascendancy.

* Portions of this essay originally appeared in the journal
Archiv für Geschichte der Philosophie.

PART III

7

Seamus Deane

EDMUND BURKE
AND
THE IDEOLOGY OF IRISH LIBERALISM

The modern tradition of liberal, even radical, thought in Ireland began in the 1690s with Robert Molesworth's *An Account of Denmark* (1694), John Toland's *Christianity not Mysterious* (1696) and William Molyneux's *Case of Ireland being Bound by Acts of Parliament in England Stated* (1699). Toland's pamphlet was probably the most influential of these three, although Molyneux's is much the best known to an Irish audience. In 1697 a senior fellow of Trinity College, Dublin wrote an angry reply to Toland's deistic tract in language which now seems oddly in tune with the writings of the last eight years of Edmund Burke's life, almost exactly a century afterwards. The Trinity don claimed that "persons of miscellaneous education ... are secretely forming themselves into clubs and caballs, and have their emissaries into all parts, which are supported by contributions, and I make little doubt that their design is at length to show us that all dominion as well as religion is founded on reason."[1] This is succinct. Authority and religion are to be subjected to reason, their sources discovered, submission to them withheld until there is shown to be a rational principle underlying their claims.

Although the group of Irish intellectuals of the late seventeenth and early eighteenth centuries was preoccupied, in the short term, with the dangerous compromises of the English settlement of 1688-89, the anxieties which dominate their works were derived from a philosophical interest in the fundamental questions of freedom and toleration. Along with the United Irishmen of the 1790s, the small band of Irish socialist thinkers of the nineteenth century and more isolated figures like James Connolly and Liam Mellowes in the twentieth century, they constitute the dominant liberal tradition in Irish political thought. Yet they remain largely unread. The influence of Edmund Burke is one of the factors which help to explain this.

In a famous passage in his *Reflections on the Revolution in France* (1790), Burke attacks the French philosophes, atheism, and the native tradition of freethinking.

I hear on all hands that a cabal, calling itself philosophic, receives the glory of many of the late proceedings; and that their opinions and systems are the true actuating spirit of the whole of them. I have heard of no party in England, literary or political, at any time, known by such a description. It is not with you composed of those men, is it? whom the vulgar, in their blunt, homely style, commonly call atheists and infidels? If it be, I admit that we too have had writers of that description, who made some noise in their day. At present they repose in lasting oblivion. Who, born within the last forty years, has read one word of Collins, and Toland, and Tindal, and Chubb, and Morgan, and that whole race who called themselves Freethinkers? Who now reads Bolingbroke? Who ever read him through? Ask the booksellers of London what is become of all these lights of the world. In as few years their few successors will go to the family vault of "all the Capulets". But whatever they were, or are, with us, they were and are wholly unconnected individuals. With us they kept the common nature of their kind, and were not gregarious. They never acted in corps, or were known as a faction in the state, nor presumed to influence in that name or character, or for the purposes of such a faction, on any of our public concerns. Whether they ought so to exist, and so to be permitted to act, is another question. As such cabals have not existed in England, so neither has the spirit of them had any influence in establishing the original frame of our constitution, or in any one of the several reparations and improvements it has undergone. The whole has been done under the auspices, and is confirmed by the sanctions, of religion and piety.[2]

It would be easy to reply that Burke himself, among those born in the previous forty years, had read Bolingbroke. *A Vindication of Natural Society* (1756), his first published work, is an ironic mimicry of Bolingbroke's style and ideas. Further, it might be said that Burke, in contrasting the defeat of the liberal and deistic tradition in English political thought with its triumph in France, is concerned, among other things, to show the ominous difference between the French and English situations – that is, the organised power of the intellectuals in France, their ineffective isolation in England. He is boasting of what he calls, a few lines later, "the simplicity of our national character", the "native plainness and directness of understanding" of English political leadership, very different from that of the French aristocracy which had cherished and supported the philosophic viper in its bosom. Yet even when we allow that much of what Burke says in the *Reflections* and in later writings is coloured by his belief in, or his exploitation of the idea of a conspiracy between various intellectuals of atheistic dispostion to bring down the old order of things, there is a more substantial and less eccentric objection to the intellectual temperament being lodged here. Whether he spoke of Bolingbroke or of Rousseau, "the great professor and founder of *the philosophy of vanity*",[3] or indeed of Dr Richard Price, Voltaire, Condorcet or any other writer of an "infidel" cast, Burke emphasised their natural tendency, as he described it, towards the spirit of innovation and the love of novelty on the one hand, and their alliance with the disaffected or the restless. So, in France, the new financial interests formed a close union with "the political men of letters."[4] The result was disastrous. It was the failure of any such alliance in England which, up to the time of the revolution, made the intellectual cabals ineffective. Part of the purpose of the *Reflections*, which is as concerned with English and Irish Jacobins, corresponding societies and the Society for Constitutional Information as it is with French *philosophes* or the *ancien régime*, was to ensure that this ineffectiveness would continue, by weaning away from the Dissenters and their friends the support and sympathy of the Whig lords and politicians who had welcomed the revolution.

This view of the relationship between the world of ideology and the world of politics is central to Burke's understanding of the Irish situation in particular. In general, it can be said that the liberal English tradition, including men as different as John Stuart Mill, Matthew Arnold and John Morley, read Burke correctly in relation to Irish affairs, although their reading of those affairs left a deal to be desired. They understood, that is to say, that large-scale disaffection and radical intellectualism formed an explosive mixture when combined together for any length of time. It was the aim and purpose of liberalism to avoid this, either by curing the disaffection, or by defusing the radical implications of the ideology, or by both.

Yet to restrict our view of liberalism to such a description would involve us in very serious misunderstandings. For liberalism, as Toland and Montesquieu and Burke knew it, was not simply a dilute form of radicalism. The term is protean and elusive, but its historical origins lie with those who opposed European despotism and the politics of the *raison d'état* with a vision of a form of government which was a reflection of the character of the nation rather than the preserve of a selfish elite or of a powerful individual. The English vision of the Commonwealth, and the Dutch and Venetian republican ideals provide us with that peculiar but distinct liberal ethos which distinguishes the works of Foscarini, Montesquieu, Rousseau and all the other defenders of the seventeenth and eighteenth centuries' republican model. While the distinction between Molesworth, Toland and Molyneux as a trio of republican liberals anxious to preserve the re-emergence of despotism in any form after 1688 and Burke, the defender of the *status quo* against revolution, may seem to be so pronounced that no conciliation between them is possible, there is in fact a continuity of interest which establishes them as members of the same liberal tradition.

Before 1790, the similarity would have been easily conceded, even though Burke had already made it clear that the British form of government was suited to the national character in its religious as well as in its civil institutions. Yet the important point is that the congruence between native habit and the political arrangements which evolved from that complex of habit and custom, was a liberal idea which had for long been used as a weapon against artificially imposed despotism. This is a view to which Burke faithfully adhered, even in the writings of his late years. It enabled him to attack the French revolutionaries and to defend the Irish Catholics, to attack British government policy in the thirteen colonies and to defend the Indians against the depredations of Warren Hastings and the East India Company. The difference which does indeed emerge in Burke's writings is initially one of emphasis; he finally put such weight on the importance of national character that it became central to all of his thought, even though it led him to an excessive admiration for what he considered to be the perfection of the British constitution.

The system of mixed government which had emerged in eighteenth century England was widely admired, particularly in France, as a model of the institutional means by which despotism could be resisted. In this sense, and not in the sense of its effectiveness as a representative institution, it was regarded as a liberal mode of government. Montesquieu's famous description of the British constitution as a beautifully organised system of checks and balances, based on the separation of the executive, legislative and judicial functions, has seemed to many commentators to express perfectly the liberal distrust of power. Although it has also been often pointed out that Montesquieu misread the British system, seeing separation of powers where they were in fact confounded, or, even worse, giving a description of the system which did not support his interpretation of it, that passage in the sixth chapter of the eleventh book of *L'Esprit des Lois* (1748), has become a classical instance of the liberal constitutional ideal, most particularly for anglophiles.[5] Burke's panegyric on Montesquieu in *An Appeal from the New to the Old Whigs* (1791), (although he had paid tribute to him as early as 1757 in his *Abridgement of English History)* may be taken as the acknowledgement of a debt as well as a polemical manoeuvre designed to show the difference between the scholarly care and labour of Montesquieu and the shallow *simplisme* of the other, more radical enlightenment thinkers.

It is important, though, to establish that Burke's view of the responsibility of the *philosophes* for the revolution is not also a repudiation of the enlightenment. For him, the enlightenment, as represented by Montesquieu, had been travestied by people like Helvétius and d'Holbach. He understood himself to be remaining faithful to the liberal tradition by resisting the revolution and the abstract theorising which had promoted it. For in the *Reflections*, Burke makes it perfectly clear that the disorder created by the revolution would lead to the restoration of order by a military dictator. In saying this, he was not forecasting the rise of Napoleon so much as he was remembering the despotism of Cromwell and of Louis XIV. His fear of the concentration of power in the hands of one person was of a piece with his hatred of the distribution of power among all. Anarchy, in his view, inevitably led to despotism.[6] As a liberal, he resisted both.

Nevertheless, it would seem that Burke's liberalism, however it may be said to have survived in his writings against the French Revolution, failed to survive the test of his own country's problems. The spirit of Molyneux, Molesworth and Toland may have survived in Swift, Lucas, Grattan and others and may have re-emerged in the revolutionary garb of the United Irishmen, but it did not, current opinion would have it, pass to Burke. Lord Acton, after much hesitation, came to see Burke as a renegade from his liberal faith, and thought that Ireland had made this clear. For Burke had failed to apply to Ireland the principles he applied to the American colonies (in particular, the principle of legislative independence.) Yet Acton seems to have ignored Burke's repeated description of the essential difference between the Irish and the English situations — that in Ireland there was general disaffection from the existing system of government, largely because of the operation of the Penal Code, and that measures needed to be taken there which were not necessary in England. Such measures would have as their central aim the reconciliation of the Irish Catholic majority to the Whig settlement. For Burke was one of the few who believed in pursuing the logic of the liberal position adopted by Montesquieu, the great Whigs and others. If the British constitution was indeed as close to the ideal as had been so far achieved, then the obvious benefits of living under it would be clear to those who were in a position to avail of them. The Irish Catholics were not. Were their situation to be sufficiently altered to allow them to see what the Whig Revolution meant, what liberty was, then they would become reconciled. Liberty, in his view, was a powerful healer. However, the improvement of the Catholic position and the stability this would lend to the British system and to British foreign policy were both prohibited by the sectarian prejudice of the Protestant ascendancy junta. Here was the crux of the problem.

As early as 1760-65, Burke was engaged on his *Tracts relative to the Laws against Popery in Ireland.* In this unfinished work, he chose to plead for justice and to claim that it should be practised irrespective of religious belief. However, in witnessing the spectacle of French Protestant victims of persecution fleeing to Ireland and being welcomed there by their co-religionists even while Irish Catholic victims of persecution were fleeing from Ireland, Burke believed that he was observing something more than hypocrisy, something more profound than an anomaly. He was witnessing a radical dislocation of natural feeling:

✳   But to transfer humanity from its natural basis, our legitimate and homebred connexions; to lose all feeling for those
who have grown up by our sides, in our eyes, of the benefits
of whose cares and labours we have partaken from our
birth, and meretriciously to hunt abroad after foreign
affections, is such a disarrangement of the whole system
of our duties, that I do not know whether benevolence so
displaced is not almost the same thing as destroyed, or what
effect bigotry could have produced that is more fatal to
society.[8]

Sectarianism, as Burke understands it, is the worst form of disaffection
in a society. It leads to division and injustice; that is inevitable and easy
to see. But it also corrupts even the most generous feelings by confining
them to persons of one's own persuasion and denying them to others.
Although he could then say that he believed there would still be men,
"who do not think that the names of Protestant and Papist can make
any change in the nature of essential justice," this is a feeling much
muted about twenty years later in his *Letter To A Peer of Ireland on
the Penal Laws Against Irish Catholics* (1782) where he seems to admit
the ineradicable force of essential injustice:

From what I have observed, it is pride, arrogance, and a
spirit of domination, and not a bigoted spirit of religion,
that has caused and kept up those oppressive statutes. I am
sure I have known those who have oppressed papists in
their civil rights, exceedingly indulgent to them in their
religious ceremonies, and who really wished them to continue Catholics, in order to furnish pretences for oppression.
These persons never saw a man (by converting) escape out
of their power, but with grudging and regret. I have known
men, to whom I am not uncharitable in saying, (though
they are dead,) that they would have become papists in
order to suppress Protestants; if, being Protestants, it was
not in their power to oppress papists. It is injustice, and not
a mistaken conscience, that has been the principle of persecution, at least as far as it has fallen under my observation.[9]

In 1792, writing to Sir Hercules Langrishe on the question of admitting
certain categories of Irish Catholics to the franchise, Burke further
defines the problem of the Protestant-Catholic relationship in Ireland,
although this particular recognition of the problem is more usually
associated with the Irish poets, O Bruadair and O Rathaille, who had
lived through the first painful phase of the Whig settlement in Ireland.

Burke sees that the political system in Ireland is oligarchical; but, it is an oligarchy without an aristocracy. The Protestants in Ireland are plebeian. And

> A plebeian oligarchy is a monster: and no people, not absolutely domestic or predial slaves, will long endure it. The Protestants of Ireland are not *alone* sufficiently the people to form a democracy; and they are *too numerous* to answer the ends and purposes of *an aristocracy*. Admiration, the first source of obedience, can be only the claim or the imposture of the few. I hold it to be absolutely impossible for two millions of plebeians, composing certainly a very clear and decided majority in that class, to become so far in love with six or seven hundred thousand of their fellow citizens, (to all outward appearance plebeians like themselves, and many of them tradesmen, servants, and otherwise inferior to some of them,) as to see with satisfaction, or even with patience, an exclusive power vested in them, by which *constitutionally* they become the absolute masters; and, by the *manners* derived from their circumstances, must be capable of exercising upon them, daily and hourly, an insulting and vexatious superiority.[10]

He might have added, for he must have known, that the Catholic Irish did still retain admiration for an aristocracy, but it was the Irish Catholic aristocracy in exile. The Protestant settlers who came in the wake of the Jacobite and Williamite wars made a sorry comparison indeed with what had gone before.

Only three years later, in his second letter of the period to Langrishe, Burke made his most savage and most comprehensive attack on Protestant ascendancy, linking it now with his crusades against the French revolutionaries and the impeachment proceedings against Warren Hastings:

> I think I can hardly overrate the malignancy of the principles of Protestant ascendency, as they affect Ireland; or of Indianism as they affect these countries, and as they affect Asia; or of Jacobinism, as they affect all Europe and the state of human society itself. The last is the greatest evil. But it really combines with the others, and flows from them. Whatever breeds discontent at this time, will produce that great master-mischief most infallibly. Whatever tends to persuade the people, that the *few*, called by whatever name you please, religious or political, are of opinion that their interest is not compatible with that of the *many*, is a great point gained to Jacobinism.[11]

The association of the Protestant ascendancy with the French Jacobins seems, from a later point of view, quite astonishing, since no more natural enemies could be imagined — especially considering that the rebellion of 1798, insofar as it had an ideology, had a Jacobin one. But Burke was unyielding on this point during the nineties. Unless the ascendancy was disabled, the Catholics would remain dangerously disaffected; "in a country of monopoly there *can* be no patriotism." Partial measures to relieve certain burdens from the Catholics were, in his view, insufficient in themselves and symptomatic of the illiberal cast of mind characteristic of the Dublin junta:

> But it will be said, in that country some people are free — why this is the very description of despotism. *Partial freedom is privilege and prerogative, and not liberty.* Liberty . . . is an honest, equitable, diffusive and impartial principle. It is a great and enlarged virtue, and not a sordid, selfish and illiberal vice. It is the portion of the mass of the citizens; and not the haughty licence of some potent individual, or some predominant faction.[12]

Thus a plebeian group masquerading as an aristocracy, a sectarian caste pretending to occasional liberality, a leadership without the led, can do no other than create a combustible situation in a country which is integral to the whole British scheme of things. More especially, though, the system of government in Ireland was, in his view, a one-party system; a system in which the whole machine of the state was designed to one exclusive end — the preservation of power for the few and the exclusion from it of the many. This seemed to him a characteristically modern development of which the new French state was the most extraordinary example. Furthermore, it ran against the grain of British experience and British political wisdom; for the system of mixed government, so well described by Montesquieu, was not devoted to one aim at the expense of others, but was instead concerned to cater to a multiplicity of interests, thereby serving many different needs and desires and reducing the areas of exclusion to the minimum. It was, in effect, an anti-monopolistic state. It therefore was capable of creating feelings of patriotic loyalty in a whole variety of groups and sects, not limiting itself to any one predominant and despotic faction. It was, in short, a liberal ideal. Power, not concentrated but dispersed; loyalty, not commanded but won; complexity conceded to, simplicity of system avoided. In the *Letters on a Regicide Peace* (1796) he speaks of the European Christian nations:

> In all these old countries, the state has been made to the people, and not the people conformed to the state . . . It is therefore no wonder, that, when these states are to be considered as machines to operate for some great end, this

dissipated and balanced force is not easily concentred, or
made to bear with the whole force of the nation upon one
point.

The British state is, without question, that which pursues
the greatest variety of ends, and is the least disposed to
sacrifice any one of them to another, or to the whole . . .
Personal liberty . . . in England, has been a direct object
of government.[13]

This could not be said either of France or of Ireland.

Burke feared the presence within the state of a highly organised
group which sought to gather the reins of power into its own hands.
Whether it was the King's friends, the philosophes, the cabal, the revolutionary club, the Dissenters' societies, the Protestant ascendancy
groups in the Irish parliament and in Dublin Castle, the East Indian
Nabobs or the Jacobins, they all seemed to him dangerously insulated
from the full range of complex interests which constituted the political
world. The idolatry of the state, the machine which was driven by the
dynamo of the party, demanded a species of fanaticism and single-
minded simplification which was the direct opposite of what he meant
by "liberal". Impelled by this conviction, Burke was drawn to distinguish between state and nation, favouring the latter as an entity which
was beyond the range of doctrinaire apprehension or definition but yet
was within the experience of all who formed part of its history. So he
could speak, in the years 1791-96, in *Thoughts on French Affairs*,
in *The Policy of the Allies* and in *Letters on a Regicide Peace*, of the
difference between two Frances — the new France which had been
taken over by the revolutionaries and appeared, in its spurious geometric administrative form, as the new country from which the old
France, in the form of the emigrés, the monarchy, the clergy and so
forth, had been expelled. Burke would not accept this.

Nation is a moral essence, not a geographical arrangement,
or a denomination of the nomenclator. France, though out
of her territorial possessions, exists; because the sole possible
claimant, I mean the proprietary, and the government to
which the proprietary adheres, exists and claims.[14]

Perhaps, though, the implications of the idea of nation as a moral
essence emerge more clearly in the earlier *Policy of the Allies* (1793):

The first question on the people is this, whether we are
to consider the individuals *now actually in France, numerically taken and arranged into Jacobin clubs*, as the body
politic, constituting the nation of France? or, whether
we are to consider the original individual proprietors of
lands, expelled since the revolution, and the states and
bodies politic, such as the colleges of justice called parle-

ments, the corporations noble and not noble of bailliages,
and towns, and cities, the bishops and the clergy, as the
true constituent parts of the nation, and forming the
legally organized parts of the people of France?[15]

This may be taken as nothing more than a Burkean ploy to gain diplomatic support, even recognition, for a French government-in-exile.
Whigs would naturally be readier to recognise a government-in-exile
that was anti-Jacobin than they would earlier have been to recognise an
exiled government which was pro-Jacobite. The analogy between the
two situations is not far fetched. For Ireland made it close.

   If the robbers had taken over the house, as Burke put it, if the
original proprietors in France had been thrown out and their goods
confiscated by the revolutionaries, then, in his view, it was right and
moral to continue to identify the moral essence of the nation with
these dispossessed people and to seek redress for the injustice done to
them. But if this was acceptable in the French situation, was it not
also acceptable in the Irish situation? There too existed a dispossessed
aristocracy, a disaffected people, religion abused, justice flouted, a
concentration of power in the hands of an organised party which
had a single and narrow-minded view of the State as an instrument
in the service of its own interests. In fact, the Irish situation was a
deal worse than the French, and Burke had been aware of the savagery
with which Ascendancy rule would assert itself when it felt threatened. The Sheehy case of 1766 was a case in point. He referred to
it on several occasions because of the deep and embittering influence of this particular execution on Irish Catholic feeling. Yet, it
may be that here Burke deserves Acton's reproach, although in modified form. He failed to apply to Ireland the principles he applied
to the France of the ancien regime. Burke, in his anxiety to establish
sympathy for the old European order, seems to have forgotten that
Gaelic Ireland belonged to it, not Whig Ireland. It was the newcomer.

   Nevertheless, Burke's authentically liberal stance in his last years
has been sadly warped by later history into a species of reactionary
conservatism which is far removed from the central convictions of his
thought. This has been especially true in Ireland. Apart from Lecky
(in *Leaders of Public Opinion in Ireland* (1861)) and Isaac Butt, few
paid him explicit attention. John Wilson Croker, one of nature's bigots,
degraded Burke's thought into a blind British chauvinism. In England,
Hazlitt carried on the radical quarrel with Burke which Paine and others
had begun in the nineties, while Coleridge tried to recover him for the
philosophical defence against the Revolution. Yet the strangest development of the Burkean inheritance was the manner in which it became
allied with a general defence of the principle of nationality in its conservative, not its revolutionary, form. The irony here consists in the
fact that, in Ireland, the leaders of that defence were, for the most

part, members of that ascendancy class which Burke had identified as being allies of the Jacobinism which they were at pains to defeat. All those elements which went to supply Burke's liberal theory of constitutional forms which would be a natural expression of national character—antiquity, "home-bred affection", complexity, nostalgia, mystery, and the spectacle of ruin—were all incorporated into the literature of Thomas Moore, Sir Samuel Ferguson and, in an etherealised version, of James Clarence Mangan, thereby leading to the promotion of a sense of Irish cultural identity which was thereafter to rejoin with the revolutionary republican tradition, with its concentration on the notion of a distinct Irish political identity.

Burke was not, of course, an Irish nationalist but he was the occasion of its emergence in others as a political faith. His political creed led him to place so much emphasis on the importance of manners, custom, prejudice, and their influence on the formation of national character that opposition to revolutionary thought became, through him, associated with a respect for history and for the manifold and subtle ways in which it conditioned temperament and the political institutions which reflected the peculiar genius of a group. A theory of nationalism founded on race was not remote from Burke's thought although it was distinct from it. Further, the view that the political radical was liable to be a person given to simplistic and ahistorical theories, stripped of the specific detail and intimate circumstances which coloured each political situation, also gained in popularity after Burke, although he was by no means the originator of such an idea. Goldsmith, for instance, had given a sketch of Lord Bolingbroke which is in accord with that notion.[16] What distinguishes him and Burke from those who had been of like mind earlier in the century was the intensity of the pathos with which they invested their portraits of old-style virtue and venerability threatened by the new barbarism. The sentimental movement in literature, by making virtue appear to be archaic and out of fashion in the new world, gave it an appeal, as of something rare and fine, which was now to be lost forever. It made vice itself lose "half its evil by losing all its grossness."

Still, it is true that much of the nostalgia and easy sentiment which is so prominent in Thomas Moore's poetry derives from a whole climate of feeling in the late eighteenth century, of which Burke is only one instance. Politically, Burke's reputation remained a matter of dispute between those who valued him as an articulator of conservative, anti-revolutionary thought and those who valued him for his conciliatory and principled liberalism, opposed to revolution of the extreme doctrinaire kind and to conservatism of the rigid, unyielding sort. Burke's direct relevance to Irish affairs is delayed until the last decades of the nineteenth century when Matthew Arnold attempts to reintroduce him as a textbook for British politicians who were, as usual, mishandling the Irish situation because they misunderstood it. That was Arnold's view. In June 1881, Arnold published his anthology of Burke's writings, *Letters, Speeches and Tracts on Irish Affairs*. In February 1882, his *Irish Essays* appeared. It is clear that Arnold did indeed grasp a good deal of what Burke had to say about the Irish situation and he was well equipped to do this since he, like Burke, could not bring himself to envisage any form of ultimate political separation between the two islands. Although his attempt to reintroduce Burke's influence had been anticipated by John Morley, whose *Burke, A Historical Study* appeared in 1867, Arnold's influence in this respect is much the greater of the two. For Arnold, in his crusade to improve "the bad civilisation of the English middle classes,"[17] helped to increase the contribution of Burke in a cultural as well as in a political sense. For his version of Burke, accurate as it is in respect of his perception of the role of the ascendancy, of English as well as of Irish religious bigotry, of the land question, of the failure in Ireland of the principle of aristocracy, and on other matters, is determined to an important degree by Arnold's conviction that there is a specifically Celtic and Saxon, that is to say, racial, element in the problem. This, of course, is simply not there in Burke. But Arnold gives it primacy.

Thus, while he pleads in Burkean fashion for the "healing measures" which will help to reconcile the Catholic majority to the British political system, he does so in a literary-cultural context very far removed from anything Burke would have been likely to invoke. Although the rebellion of 1798, the Act of Union, Catholic emancipation, the Famine, the Fenians and Young Ireland, not to mention the awesome figures of O'Connell and Parnell, had all intervened in the ninety odd years since Burke's death, Arnold's plea for a greater liberality of spirit towards the Catholics remains monotonously familiar. To adapt Wordsworth's phrase, disaster had not apparently opened the eyes of the English conscience. But Arnold's explanation for this failure, and for the Irish refusal to accept what was admirable in British civilisation, is that the spirit of Mr Murdstone stalks abroad in Ireland, particularly in the North. And this is not good enough:

> But the genuine, unmitigated Murdstone is the common middle-class Englishman, who has come forth from Salem House and Mr. Creakle. He is seen in full force, of course, in the Protestant north; but throughout Ireland he is a prominent figure of the English garrison. Him the Irish see, see him only too much and too often . . .
> The thing has no power of attraction. The Irish quick-wittedness, keen feeling for social life and manners, demand something which this hard and imperfect civilisation cannot give them. Its social form seems to them unpleasant, its energy and industry to lead to no happiness, its religion to be false and unhappy . . .

It is difficult to avoid the analogy in Arnold's writings between tne Hellenic and the Hebraic spirit on the one hand and the Celtic and Saxon spirit on the other. The Celts were to become the lost poetry of Saxon morality, a view with which Yeats would not have seriously disagreed. Yet, somehow, in the midst of all this chemical interaction between two racial types, Burke and his healing measures seems to have got lost or at least temporarily mislaid.

Yet this is not an aberration on Arnold's part. The liberal inheritance in English politics, insofar as it derived from Burke, was bound to place considerable emphasis on his ideas of cultural factors and the necessity of giving expression to them in political institutions, especially in relation to Ireland, where the experiment, although central to the British system, had never been tried. But when this cultural factor is intensified to the point where it becomes or gives grounds for the emergence of a racial factor, then Burkean liberalism begins to be transformed into a defence for Irish nationalism, even though this is very far from Arnold's (not to mention Burke's) intention. Arnold, in his efforts to Hellenise England, also helped Irishmen like Yeats and Pearse in their efforts to Celticise Ireland. In defining the deficiency of the English middle class civilisation, he gave the Irish the cultural distinction which they sought. Ever since his 1867 Oxford lecture on the Celtic element in literature (acknowledged by Yeats in his 1902 essay *The Celtic Element in Literature*), Arnold had been tending in this direction. But by the 1880s he had completed the transformation of Burkean liberalism into Irish Revival nationalism. It was a strange kind of intellectual death for Burkean liberal England.

It also spelt the end for the Irish liberal tradition, which writers like Lecky, Dowden and politicians like Dillon and Justin McCarthy were to attempt to rescue. Pearse, as usual, helps us to see the essential nature of the distinction between the liberal and the nationalist revolutionary when, in his essay *Ghosts*, he dismisses the tradition of Burke, Berkeley and Swift (which Yeats was to transform into such an illiberal, anti-modernist grouping), in favour of the revolutionary tradition of Tone, Davis, Lalor and Mitchel:

> I am seeking to find, not those who have thought most wisely about Ireland, but those who have thought most authentically for Ireland, the voices that have come out of the Irish struggle itself.   *—Pearse*

Authenticity had replaced wisdom. It is as though Rousseau's voice had triumphed over Burke's. Yet, Irish nationalism owes a great deal to Burke, the greatest of the Whigs. Burke's fear of the organised Jacobin group was perhaps justified in the emergence in Ireland of the Fenians and the Irish Republican Brotherhood; but it had also been realised in the appearance of those other more literary groups, like Young Ireland, and like the Abbey Theatre grouping, around whom so much that was culturally energetic came into contact with the major political forces of the moment. The relationship between these groups and conspiracies and the modern idea of the State is something Burke understood. Liberals after him failed to do so. In that failure, lay some of the reasons for the decline of liberalism from what had after all, been its initial impulse − to find escape, by political arrangements, from despotism.

*   *   *

There is another reason for the comparative failure of liberalism as a political creed in Ireland and Burke provides us with the key to it also. The resistance to the French Revolution, led by England, was based on a repudiation of radical social consequences which would follow upon the triumph of radical opinions. Liberalism was a creed of amelioration, not transformation. The long battle in Ireland over the land question showed how far amelioration could go. The land question was modified, but the political question remained untouched. The necessary link between them had always been recognised by radical nationalists. Social reformation and political revolution were more intimately associated in Ireland than in England, largely because the drastic need for the first of these in Ireland was constantly frustrated by the failure of the second. Liberalism was the English alternative to French radicalism. But if it was seen not to work in Ireland, then the radical alternative lay open. The odd fact was that English liberalism, based on the principles of tolerance and liberty of 1688, was always more effective in England than elsewhere. It suffered always from a certain provincialism in practice, despite its universalist claims. French radicalism, on the other hand, while founded even more assertively upon universalist principles, tended to become associated with nationalist feelings, since it supplied individual separatist movements with a universalist justification. Thus, in Ireland, two sets of principles, closely allied in many ways, became associated with two entirely opposed factions − liberals and radicals. The breaking point between them was always on the political question. But the form of the break almost always took the mould of class. Radicalism became more and more associated with the violent dislocation of the existing social arrangements by those most victimised by them; and, in Irish conditions, this inevitably became associated with nationalism. Liberals, seeing this, found that they were faced by a social revolution and a nationalist movement which had in common the feeling of revenge linked to the vocabulary of universal rights. The rise of socialism merely emphasised the strength of this linkage.

Thus the liberal suspects nationalism because it seems to be of its nature provincial; and he distrusts radicalism because it is, of its nature, too abstract. The alliance between the dispossessed and the intellectuals, feared by Burke in the 1790s, has been forged and broken, broken and forged, many times in Irish history since that date. When it is epitomised in a single individual, like Liam Mellowes, the result is a startling blend of unquenchable nationalist feeling expressed in the vocabulary of a radical and socialist. The execution of Mellows by the Free State Government indicated the limits of Irish nationalism when it is free of the radical tradition. It also indicates the limit beyond which liberalism will not go. After all, it was a British liberal government which executed the leaders of 1916. Liberalism, as Burke had indicated, is not incompatible with violence. The use of violence must, however, be based on the consent of those on whose behalf it is (ostensibly) exercised. Radical violence is not, from this same point of view, justifiable since it is exercised by a faction or party, which claims the right to use it even against the wishes of the majority of the people on whose behalf it nevertheless is ready to exercise it. More often, and especially in Ireland, that kind of violence has been used by those who claim the right to use it on ideological grounds which do not include the consent of the aberrant majority. So we have the violence of the state as against the violence of the party which has not yet become co-identical with the state. Criss-crossing both, there is the claim to represent the national interests of the people. Although in such conditions liberalism becomes almost indistinguishable from the pronouncedly illiberal and right-wing elements which it would normally oppose, there is a distinct ideological difference. From the radical's point of view, it is almost invisible. In the same way, Burke the liberal advocate of violence against the French revolutionaries was almost indistinguishable from the Younger Pitt, the Tory prime minister, who prosecuted the war against revolutionary France.

The career of Conor Cruise O'Brien is a contemporary illustration of the complexities of the situation here described. For a long time, he was a radical, a child of the enlightenment with a pronounced Marxist tinge. Then he became a Burkean liberal, although his vision of Burke has probably altered a good deal since his introduction to the Penguin edition of the *Reflections*. But between the publication of his brilliant study of *Camus* (1970) and his becoming Minister for Posts and Telegraphs (1973), he moved away from liberalism towards a harsh and unrelenting conservatism, largely because of his distaste for republican violence in Northern Ireland. The interesting fact about O'Brien's changing opinions, however, is his willingness to condone and support state violence in Northern Ireland and even, by omission, loyalist violence which is directed to the preservation of the state. This is not incompatible with liberalism. It is incompatible with nationalism. Tom Paulin has described him as a loyalist, as has John Hume. This is accurate, but it is not the outright condemnation of Dr O'Brien's past it is generally deemed to be. In the nature of things, a liberal is a loyalist when the chips are down and the preservation of the state is the issue. Of course, in Irish conditions, the preservation of the Orange state seems to be totally out of line with the preservation of even the mildest of liberal opinions. Yet, from his point of view, it is the preservation of the British, not the Orange state, that is at issue. Given the choice, O'Brien obviously feels that liberalism would flourish more readily in the British than in the present Irish or in any future all-Irish state. For nationalism, allied to radical terminologies, is still for him, as for most liberals, a deadlier enemy than any species of conservatism. The question, in the end, is one of authority. If authority derives from electorally expressed consent, then violence in defence of it is justified. If it derives from ideological convictions shared by a group or party within and opposed to the state, then it is not justified. Liberalism has its limits and almost all forms of nationalism and almost all forms of modern radical theory exceed them. Nationalism exposes the limits by virtue of its inwardness, its mystique, its exclusiveness; radical theory exposes them by virtue of its abstraction, its primacy for the party, its coercive utopianism. It is the Burkean battle being fought over again. The splendour of that first engagement may have disappeared, but the issues remain as fundamental and as recognisable as they were then. It seems appropriate that Dr O'Brien should be writing the great man's biography. In each of them, the exposed position of the Irish liberal has been, in different ways, revealed to us.

Liam de Paor

THE REBEL MIND:
REPUBLICAN AND LOYALIST

In looking back we see nothing on the one hand but savage
force succeeded by savage policy; on the other, an unfortunate nation 'scattered and peeled, meeted out and trodden
down'. We see a mutual intolerance and a common carnage
of the first moral emotions of the heart, which lead us to
esteem and place confidence in our fellow-creatures. We
see this, and are silent. But we gladly look forward to
brighter prospects—to a People united in the fellowship
of freedom—to a Parliament the express image of the
people—to a prosperity established on civil, political and
religious liberty—to a peace—not the gloomy and precarious stillness of men brooding over their wrongs, but
that stable tranquillity which rests on the rights of human
nature, and leans on the arms by which these rights are to
be maintained.[1]

There is little ratiocination but much rationalising in the verbal conflict
that accompanies the sporadic political violence of present-day Ireland.
It is a mutual snarling of hereditary factions, a flaunting of party shibbo-
leths, a reaching-out for ready-made ideas, whether Marxist or neo-
Darwinian (and usually romantic anyway) to be used as cudgels. Yet,
in two or three centuries, there has been some shaping of minds as well
as a shaping of attitudes. Prejudices and settled habits of hostility or
approbation derive in part from ideas, often distant. Keynes pointed
out that politicians, thinking themselves practical pragmatists, usually
base their policies, unknowingly, on the ideas of long-dead economists.
In our present discontents, on the contrary, purely local, *ad hoc* and
ad hominem, feuds and hatreds claim justification in the well-remembered
names of long-dead ideologues — whose ideas are forgotten. The people
who 'remember 1690' don't remember 1690; many of those who
honour—to the death—Wolfe Tone's memory don't appreciate that he
wasn't a Falls Road Catholic. ← catholic area in Belfast
    The tendrils of derivation cross and intertwine; sometimes they can

be traced back from opposite sides to a common root. Caught in all
the contradictions of compounded colonialism, Irish people throughout the modern age have suffered political frustrations whose irrita-
tion has stimulated thoughts to transcend the complacent traditionalism
that is the country's habit. As Burke put it in 1796:

> The Jacobinism which arises from penury and irritation,
> from scorned loyalty, and rejected allegiance, has much
> deeper roots. They take their nourishment from the bottom
> of human nature and the unalterable constitution of things,
> and not from the humour or caprice or the opinions of the
> day about privileges and liberties. These roots will be shot
> into the depths of Hell, and will at last raise up their proud
> tops to Heaven itself.[2]

But, rooted as they may have been in a particular history, the Jacobinism and other -isms of Ireland were not unaffected by the 'caprice
or the opinions of the day', or, in some cases, of the day before.

Republicanism is a case in point. Ireland's first experience of republican government was harsh. (It was also the first experience of union
with England.) The Cromwellian republicans had won a temporary
triumph in the conflicts of seventeenth-century England. They favoured
a kind of liberty which appealed to men of middling property, but they
had trodden down not only the absolutist pretensions of the blood
royal but also the democratic aspirations of various breeds of levellers.
In the time of the civil wars some of the levelling radicals had been
wholly ecumenical in their view of human rights and were willing that
the Irish should have the same freedoms that they sought for themselves. But most English republicans were not radicals, and most of
them, after the massacres of 1641, saw the Irish as virtually the enemies
of humanity and of God. The commonwealth was a godly law-and-order
republic enshrining the military authority of the state. Its polity was
alien to most of Ireland's traditions.

At that time and for long after, it would have been difficult to find a
shade of opinion originating within Ireland that wasn't royalist, aristocratic and traditional. Early modern Ireland was conservative. Its native
leaders, whether of pre-Norman or of post-Norman stock, took most
of their political concepts and precedents from the Middle Ages. Those
among them who felt at home in their own age and were open to some
kinds of change were in tune more with continental than with English
developments. They favoured the baroque devotionalism of the counter-
reformation and in their bones knew that 'divinity doth hedge a king'.
They were conquered in the wars of the sixteenth and seventeenth
centuries — men of property and power brought down largely by their
social inferiors who had risen in the turmoil of a more dynamic society.

The poor suffered too, but only because there was war, because
there was famine, because there was pestilence; not because liberty

triumphed over the absolute king or the absolute king over liberty. The people went on starving or scratching out a living, with merely a change of lords. The new masters were Protestant, spoke English, and in time came to enjoy 'the liberties of Englishmen' – which were as remote from the Irish people as the inscrutable ceremonies of Cathay or the silver apples of the moon.

Nonetheless the English revolution sowed a seed in Ireland as it did, about the same time, in America. The pulpits preached intolerant creeds but also asserted some freedom of conscience, even if at first only of a narrow and exclusive conscience. In the course of the fierce controversies before and during the English civil wars, some of the sectaries sought a fellowship of the lowly to replace the rule of the mighty. Some taught that rank and hierarchy, pomp and panoply, were the tawdry trappings of a corrupt society. These radicals however were defeated. Others offered an equality of the saved, God's elect, but preached a new dichotomy. This dichotomy was, in a way, a version of the old Platonic and Aristotelian division into the two moral natures of master and slave. It was to be the virtue of the inferior to do the will of the superior – a comfortable morality for application in the Massachusetts Bay colony, or on the confiscated lands of Ireland, or in the sugar plantations. The same comfort still serves as an opiate of the masses among the tin chapels of West Virginia, the backyard swimming-pools of Johannesburg and the brick barrios of Belfast.

This corrupting comfort of Election has been the worm in the bud of much British radicalism. The powerful and enduring influence of religious nonconformism on the left in Britain has given it a distinctive character and imposed a style which is poorly compatible with European radical ideologies and with traditions rooted in Roman Catholicism. It is, however, quite compatible with the traditions of Protestant Ulster, especially as these have developed since the industrial revolution.

In Ireland, the significant divide was religion. This, more than language or ethnic origin (although all three to an extent went together) sealed off master henceforth from servant. It gave great importance to the change of masters. The new lords felt themselves to be freed from superstitition, and looked with distaste—which sometimes ultimately yielded to paternalistic and amused indulgence—on their lackeys and tenants who were still enslaved in that subhuman bondage of darkened understanding.

The oppressed, on the other hand, knew that their new lords had no claims of antiquity in their lordship—they were common people newly rich—and no claim to virtue in their tenure of power—they were heretics, and damned. If we want to understand not only how the Protestant republic came to Catholic Ireland but why Ireland under the Union fared so differently from Scotland and Wales, this divide must command our attention.

The people had always suffered. After the seventeenth century they were taught to feel a deep communal humiliation as well as hardship:

> *Ní ins an ainnise is measa linn bheith síos go deó*
> *ach an tarcaisne a leanas sinn i ndiaidh na león. . .*[3]

The poets, retainers of the disinherited lords, gave plangent tongue to laments which bound all together, high and low, churl and Gaelic king, in the one terrible downfall. The Irish became, one and all, the disinherited of lost glory.

> If they call you 'Papishes'
> accept it gladly for a title.
> Patience, for the High King's sake.
> *Deo Gratias*, good the name!
>
> God Who art generous, O Prince of Blessings,
> behold the Gael, stripped of authority.
> Now as we journey Westward into Connacht
> old friends we'll leave behind us in their grief.[4]

This propaganda of the dispossessed created a fantasy world in which the return of the true prince would renew the truth and beauty of the Land of Youth. Landlords and rulers now in possession were lowborn usurpers and tyrants. The Irish people were Israelites in Egyptian bondage — all of them, God's chosen people. Like the unseated mighty in other times and places the old Irish ruling families expressed pity not only for themselves but also for those from whose neck their foot had been removed to be replaced by an alien foot. But this concept of universal dispossession made conservatism radical. Deprived of the rule of the ancient lords, and taught to hold the new lords in contempt, the people were released from ancient obligations of deference and loyalty — precisely at the moment in history when such obligations were widely coming to be questioned *in principle*.

It is important to grasp that, in its ideological history, modern Irish radicalism stems from an aristocratic ideology, an aristocratic grievance, an aristocratic rage. Although in course of time deeply coloured by the philosophy of the 'glorious revolution' and, more strongly, the philosophy of the American revolution (subtly different), Irish republicanism has even deeper roots, in Irish aristocratic reaction, formed initially when the second language of the native aristocracy was Spanish or French rather than English.

By the early eighteenth century some of the old Irish magnates contrived (although papist) to cling to a toehold in Ireland; many awaited in exile the restoration of their fortunes. They served and hoped to reinstate the Stuart dynasty. The time was to come, after the failure of Prince Charles Edward's invasion of England, when they tried to accommodate to the reality of Protestant Hanoverian permanence. But their own earlier teachings of the illegitimacy of the régime cut them off from bringing such new reality to the people, although one of them, O'Connell, was to come close to it (too late). Instead, among increasingly active sections of the population, the objective of undoing the Williamite usurpation gave way to the objective of undoing the conquest as a whole. When, round the turn of the century, the Catholic landlords were willing, and seemed to be offered the opportunity, to share power and leadership with their Protestant supplanters, they were overshadowed by democratic forces they had earlier, largely unwittingly, summoned to their aid. Jacobitism begot Jacobinism.

Liberty however had come to Ireland in Protestant guise, and 'liberty!' was to be the watchword of that age of democratic aspiration. True democrats had failed in the English conflicts of the seventeenth century, but they made claims which could neither be forgotten nor wholly evaded. They set in train a buzz of ideas. The movement of political thought was in the end to bring down much of the old order of society (perhaps not all *that* much) in a world turned upside down.

The British in the meantime had achieved a stable compromise, in that complex counter-revolution which culminated in the 'glorious revolution' of 1688, expelling James II and bringing in his son-in-law William of Orange. This was a palace revolution with a thousand precedents, but it proceeded successfully to justify itself, by a tremendous effort of propaganda, as an epoch in the history of humankind. The king was curbed, the mob was kennelled, and licence was given both to mighty aristocratic subjects and to turbulent entrepreneurs who dealt in wool, iron, sugar and slaves. The compromise proved to be remarkably successful in the sustenance of an overseas empire and a world-wide system of commerce.

The class which held Ireland for the empire had been established in power, property and privilege by the early years of the eighteenth century. The new class, staunch supporters of the Protestant constitution based on the 'glorious revolution', had control of the land, the law and the business of the country. Its members were English in origin and in language, and Protestant in religion; and loyalty to the British constitution was the core of the bargain by which they maintained English rule in Ireland, while British power maintained them in turn in enjoyment of their lands and privileges. They were landlords and magistrates, judges and administrators, politicians and soldiers. They formed a small world of their own, quite distinct from the more-or-less leaderless mass of the population, who were regarded as a people excluded both right of conquest and by lowly degree from any part in the life of politics or the civil or military affairs of the kingdom. The small world of the 'ascendancy' was extended through a middle and professional class of merchants, agents, lawyers, placemen and hangers-on of various kinds — the class which was literate, often discontented, ambitious and questioning in late-eighteenth-century Europe, the class which could produce a Clive, a Robespierre or a Tone.

At the end of the eighteenth century Ireland's population was growing fast (no one quite knows why, although the widespread use by that date of the easily-grown potato as a staple food had something to do with it) and was causing instability and social strain. Only three or four in every hundred of the five million or so inhabiting the country would have belonged, by family connection or otherwise, to the land-owning class which effectively had control of the country. A much larger number was involved in services, trade and manufacture — merchants, shopkeepers, shoemakers, saddlers, blacksmith, and so on. This was the class, under the popery laws, within which some Catholics could prosper, and even become rich. There were numerous cottiers, starting with the group described by Arthur Young as those who 'hold at will a small take of land, seldom more than an acre, and grass for a couple of cows, at an exorbitant rent which they work out at the small wages of four or five pence a day without diet'. There were also 'persons who have short leases or leases of uncertain tenure at high rents'. There were 'inhabitants of cottages in the neighbourhood of towns and small villages, who hold no land and are supported by daily labour'.[5]

Beyond and below the categories enumerated by Young were the destitute, the sick, the starving, the homeless. These lowest orders of society were Irish-speaking, illiterate, most without a knowledge of English. They were the first victims of the recurrent famines. The diet of the poorest classes was potatoes and sour milk for three-quarters of the year and potatoes and salt in springtime — if the potatoes lasted. They lived below any tolerable level of subsistence or consciousness, their nakedness barely covered by a rag or two, their physique undermined by hardship. According to one witness, their appearance contrasted with that of the 'middling class of people who live on potatoes, milk and butter and have a good healthy appearance'. They suffered commonly from scurvy and skin diseases. In parts of the west they probably amounted to close on half the population.

Virtually every visitor who comments on the scene in eighteenth-century Ireland refers to the abject destitution of these people, living with only the most exiguous clothing or shelter and giving an appalling character to parts of the countryside. Ireland in large areas looked as if it had suffered some fearful disaster. It had. The country in many parts had been fought over for a century, at intervals, conquered and exploited as a source of rents and pensions for a class whose essential purpose was to secure England's strategic security in the west. In England itself, a progressive, extravagant, arrogant, ruthless class was sweeping aside many immemorial customs along with the old common

lands, relentlessly changing the face of the countryside, causing unparalleled hardship to the rural poor, and in the process laying the
foundations for new and unprecedented industries and new and
vastly more efficient agriculture: making the modern world. In England
there was provision by law for the poor: at the very beginning of the
revolutionary process, in the sixteenth century, the parishes were
charged each with the maintenance of its own poor. There was no such
provision in Ireland. Here, starvation was legal and the more fortunate,
who avoided it, maintained their equanimity, like people in Calcutta or
New York today, by becoming blind to the sight of perpetual and
irremediable poverty and callous to the sufferings involved. It was the
visitors who received the shock. But the misery that underlay a certain
surface of elegance and even grandeur in late eighteenth-century Ireland
must have had its slow effect and must help to explain the appeal of
radical ideas as a way out of an intolerable predicament. It was a
desperate country, and modern Irish republicanism springs from a time
of desperation.

It does not however spring from the most desperate themselves.
The destitute, illiterate, monoglot Irish-speaking class of the late
eighteenth century and the early nineteenth century is, in historical
terms, a-political. This class, in so far as it became involved in politics
at all, was to provide not republicans but cannon-fodder for Trafalgar
or Waterloo; but mostly, like an endangered species, it was simply
doomed to extinction. Ireland in the nineteenth century was to provide
a paradigm for rural radicalism in deeply conservative societies in the
modern era (there are many parallels in China). Marx, in the *Communist Manifesto* got this important process understandably (for 1848)
but fundamentally wrong:

> The bourgeoisie has subjected the country to the rule of
> the towns. It has created enormous cities, has greatly in-
> creased the urban population as compared with the rural,
> and has thus rescued a considerable part of the population
> from the idiocy of rural life. Just as it has made the country
> dependent on the towns, so it has made barbarian and semi-
> barbarian countries dependent on the civilised ones, nations
> of peasants on nations of bourgeois, the East on the West.[6]

This may be broadly true in the long run. In the short or middle term
rural populations increased alongside urban in many parts of the world,
including Ireland. The fearful example of mass destitution, leading at
times to mass starvation and death from famine diseases, acted powerfully on those who were close to it and who felt threatened and resent-
ful. Agitations, often violent, against rents, against tithe, against the
whole threatening (and alien, as it was perceived) social super-structure,
provided the hotbed of radical politics among the numerous class which

was just above destitution, just sufficiently conscious and literate to escape, barely, the 'idiocy of rural life'.

Republicanism also of course springs from a seedbed of ideas, not planted in Ireland. Rationalising of what had gone on in seventeenth-century Britain produced writings in England and Scotland which stimulated and ran with ideas being put forward in France, Italy and other centres of the European Enlightenment. An opposition was found to the notion of a God-ordered world and a God-ordered social system. The universe was a piece of clockwork, wound up by a clockmaker who had then, for all we can tell, forgotten all about it. The social world was a sorry mess. It too should run like clockwork, but ancient corruption had seriously impaired the workings, introducing, like grit and dirt, ignorance, superstition, malevolence and the distortions of ecclesiastical and political hierarchies. Men, originally autonomous captains of themselves, had surrendered their liberty to the mutual advantage of a general will, through which the unified many would operate to the benefit of the individual ones. (Women appear somewhat uncertainly in this scheme of thought as a kind of auxiliary species.) If corruption were undone, a benevolent calculus was possible: the balance of a myriad of enlightened self-interests would produce the maximum of pleasure and the minimum of pain, in the smoothly running world of the 'public good'.

The philosophers refined their ideas. Their message came to the literate discontented in a very simplified form: the present scheme of things had no divine, or even human, sanction but was rotten and corrupt; it should be swept away and a new scheme devised. To the ambitious the message came in another simplified form: if all existing advantages are to be done away with, then there is opportunity for new people, previously overlooked in the dole of life to obtain what the old corrupt system had not given them. To the puritan the message came that virtue should and could be rewarded.

It is not surprising that, after the intensification of the eighteenth-century debate which was produced in the American revolution, Protestants, notably Presbyterians, of east Ulster should be specially drawn to liberal Enlightenment views. They had numerous connections in America; they drew on a pulpit culture similar to that which was perhaps as important as the writings of Locke or of the Scottish philosophers in laying the groundwork for the Declaration of Independence. Serious, moral, broad in their theology, formed in a tradition which believed in numeracy, literacy and self-sufficiency and in the exercise of private judgment, a section of the mercantile class of that part of the country belonged to the new modern species of humanity which was about to attempt the direction of the western world. They were surrounded in Ulster by people who had narrower and more traditonal views but who also had many grounds for the greatest dissatisfaction with things as they were.

'*Écrasez l'infâme!*', however, was hard doctrine in Ireland. True republicanism required the clockwinder God, or none. Its ground was not the mystical communion of saints but the benevolent brotherhood of freemasons. The deism of many eighteenth-century people of Anglican tradition; the rarefied monotheism, dissolving God into an aniconized Being, as in the Unitarianism towards which one small section of the Ulster Presbyterians was moving; these were the modes of thought which fostered the late eighteenth-century republic. It is difficult to find a true republican of the era who was also a true Roman Catholic believer.[7] Tridentine Catholicism had a long and hard struggle in Ireland to supplant the medieval religion (which in its popular forms was as syncretistic as Hinduism) but by the end of the century it was taking hold. The Enlightenment was its enemy. Its political, as distinct from religious, message to the people was to practise a farseeing prudence. After the abandonment of the Jacobite cause, this included coming to terms with Hanoverian legitimacy and the Protestant constitution. The Roman Catholics had the advantage of overwhelming and increasing numbers, but no political place. Long-term prudence required a quiet steady pressure for admission to the political nation; otherwise to wait patiently while the mills of God ground slowly. This, from the eighteenth century to the present day has been the main flow of the main current of articulate Catholic opinion and practice. The deeper swift current of republicanism has formed major eddies and carved more interesting channels, but it is not the main stream.

However, the French revolution, coming a short generation after the American but soon moving into the much more extreme and radical enterprise of making the world anew, appealed instantly both to benevolent idealism and to bitter discontent. It seemed possible to rid the world of kings, aristocrats and priests, and to found the new Enlightenment society. The movement of sympathy was very broad in the first year or two of the revolution, but when the terror began it narrowed down to those of committed and extreme views. Political corresponding societies were formed to make a network throughout Britain and Ireland to agree on the principles and prepare the politics of the dawning age. In Britain they remained isolated and ineffective. In Ireland they came to make contact, in the context of a much less stable polity, with already organised discontent. Rural discontent had been stirring in reaction to enclosure and 'improvement', to rents and tithes, and to the overcrowding due to a rising population that forced cut-throat competition for a bare subsistence and was driving many into destitution. Oathbound gangs and secret societies expressed the discontent through violence. It was urban clubs, however, that first preached the new political gospel: this was diffused to rural areas often in the form of a greatly simplified millennialism, in which one of the chief marks of the new age would be the end of rent.

The activity was greatest in the north, where some Presbyterian sentiments from the first favoured republicanism (although the Presbyterian tradition as a whole was abidingly royalist). The northerners indulged somewhat less in the framing and passing of resolutions than did those in the other main centre of the movement — Dublin. The train of ideas may be gathered from a few extracts from the paper, circulated in June 1791, proposing the founding of a political association in that city, the club which came into being in December as the Dublin Society of United Irishmen:

> It is proposed that at this conjuncture a Society shall be instituted in this City, having much of the secrecy, and somewhat of the ceremonial attached to Free-Masonry . . .
>
> . . . Our Provinces are perfectly ignorant of each other; — our Island is connected; we ourselves are insulated; and the distinctions of rank, of property, and of religious persuasion, have hitherto been not merely lines of difference, but brazen walls of separation. We are separate nations met and settled together, not mingled, but *convened;* an incoherent mass of dissimilar materials, uncemented, unconsolidated, like the image which Nebuchadnezar saw with a head of fine gold, legs of iron, and feet of clay, parts that do not cleave to one another . . .
>
> . . . For this Society is not to rest satisfied in drawing speculative plans to reform and improvement, but to be practically busied about the *means* of accomplishment. Were the hand of Locke to hold from Heaven a scheme of government most perfectly adapted to the nature and capabilities of the Irish Nation, it would drop to the ground a mere sounding scroll, were there no other means of giving it effect than its intrinsic excellence. All true Irishmen agree in *what* ought to be done, but how to get it done is the question. — This Society is likely to be a means the most powerful for the promotion of a great end — what END?

 The Rights of Man in Ireland, the greatest happiness of the greatest number in *this island,* the inherent and indefeasible claims of every free nation, to rest in the nation — the *will* and the power to be happy — to pursue the Common-Weal as an individual pursues his private welfare, and to stand in insulated independence, an imperatorial people. —. . .

> . . . The Greatest Happiness of the Greatest Number — On the rock of this principle let this Society rest; by this let it judge and determine every political question, and whatever is necessary for this end, let it not be accounted hazardous, but rather our interest, our duty, our glory, and our common religion. The rights of Man are the rights of God, and to

vindicate the one is to maintain the other. We must be free
in order to serve Him whose service is perfect freedom . . .
. . . On the 14th of July, the day which shall ever commem-
orate the French revolution, let this Society pour out their
first libation to European Liberty, eventually the Liberty of
of the World, and with their hands joined in each other,
and their eyes raised to Heaven, in his presence who breathed into them an ever-living soul, let them swear to maintain
the rights and prerogatives of their nature as men and the
right and prerogative of Ireland as an independent People.
– 'Dieu et *mon* Droit!' is the motto of kings. – 'Dieu et
la Liberté!' exclaimed Voltaire, when he first beheld
Franklin his Fellow-Citizen of the World. – 'Dieu et *nos*
Droits!' – Let Irishmen cry aloud to each other. – The
cry of Mercy – of Justice – and of Victory. [8]

The themes sounded here are unity (ever one of the most urgent notes
in the motif of the United Irishmen), liberty, equality – and nationalism. Liberty - the autonomous right of the individual - preserved
through the social contract, was to be expressed through the common
will of the *nation,* to produce the greatest good of the greatest number.
Into the utilitarian equation there has been slipped the factor of the
'general will', a common gloss on the social contract, but one which
conceals a logical contradiction. The general will requires an entity in
which the will is embodied – hence the nation.

Here we come to a point which is important in the history of
republicanism everywhere – in America (not only in respect of the war
of the revolution but, even more interestingly, in respect of the later
war between the states), in France, and, in a very special way, in
Ireland. The republican tradition, quite early in the nineteenth century,
under the powerful influence of romantic nationalism, was diverted
onto a switch-line: liberty became a matter not so much for individuals
as for *nations,* to which the individuals were subordinated. The aspiration of the nations was to become *states;* not, however, the 'artificial'
nation-states (like the United Kingdom) presided over by early modern
monarchs, but 'natural' nation-states defined by religion, language,
culture – 'ethnicity'. Here the contradiction shows harshly.

In its very origins, Irish republicanism tried to create a new non-
ethnic nation. The second paragraph quoted above from the 1791
manifesto shows that the republican founders were aware that 'we
are separate nations met and settled together, not mingled, but *conven-
ed',* and their aim was to abolish these separate nations in favour of a
new Irish nation whose basis must - or it could have no basis - be
secular, tolerant and benevolent.

The people who were responsible for beginning this movement were
mostly middle-class people. They included some of the more impatient

Catholics (although the example of Tom Moore's dallying with republicanism as a Trinity student, of his quick prudent withdrawal, and of
his later guiltily sentimental regret, provides an instructive paradigm)
but were mainly drawn from the two sections which had thought of
themselves as occupying Ireland as conquerors and holding by that
right. One section, the Anglican Protestants, had thought of themselves
as representatives of England, or at least of what was coming to be
called 'the British empire', in Ireland; [9] the other section, the Presbyterians, with a more complex response to the position of the ascendancy, had thought of themselves as a people of exodus.

These groups now proposed equality — the recognition of the
conquered as part of the body politic, part of the *nation:* but what
nation? They tried to define it through rhetoric:

> The code of penal laws against the Catholics reduced
> oppression into a system: The action and pressure of this
> system, continually accumulating without any re-action on
> the part of the sufferers, sunk in the lethargy of servitude,
> have confirmed the governing portion of the people in a
> habit of domination. This *Habit*, mixing with the anti-
> pathies of past times, and the irritations of the moment, has
> impressed a strange persuasion, that the rights of the
> plurality are Protestant *property*, and that the birth-right of
> millions, born and to be born, continue the spoils of war
> and booty of conquest. The perversion of the understand-
> ing perverts the heart, and this Protestant ascendancy, as it
> calls itself, uniting power with passion, and hating the
> Catholics because it has injured them, on a bare inquisitor-
> ial suspicion, insufficient to incriminate an individual,
> would erase a whole people from the roll of citizenship,
> and for the sins (if they were sins) of remote ancestors
> would attaint their remotest posterity . . . [10]

> . . . It was not till very lately that the part of the nation
> which is truly colonial, reflected that though their ancestors
> had been victorious, they themselves were now included in
> the general subjection; subduing only to be subdued, and
> trampled upon by Britain as a servile dependency. When
> therefore the Protestants began to suffer what the Catholics
> had suffered and were suffering; when from serving as the
> instruments they were made themselves the objects of
> foreign domination, then they became conscious they had
> a country; and then they felt — an Ireland. They resisted
> British dominion, renounced colonial subserviency, and
> following the example of a Catholic Parliament just a
> century before, they asserted the exclusive jurisdiction
> and legislative competency of this Island. A sudden light
> from America shone through our prison. Our Volunteers

arose. The chains fell from our hands. We followed Grattan, the angel of our deliverance, and in 1782 Ireland ceased to be a province and became a nation. [11]

. . . By Liberty we never understood unlimited freedom, nor by Equality the levelling of property, or the destruction of subordination . . . This is a calumny invented by that faction or that gang which misrepresents the King to the People, and the People to the King, traduces one half of the nation to cajole the other, and by keeping up distrust and division, wishes to continue the proud arbitrators of the fortune and fate of Ireland. . . . Liberty is the exercise of all our rights natural and political, secured to us and our posterity by a real representation of the people . . . and equality is the extension of the constituent, to the fullest dimensions of the constitution, of the elective franchise to the whole body of the people, to the end that government which is collective power, may be guided by collective will, and that legislation may originate from public reason, keep peace with public improvement, and terminate in public happiness. [12]

The nation to be created was a new nation, compounded of the distinct cultural and political elements which existed in Ireland; but these were thought of chiefly in terms of religious persuasion. Only by the creation of such a nation could the chief aim of the movement be achieved — separation from England so that the Irish social contract could be fulfilled. There is implicit the assumption that religious antagonisms would fade away (perhaps with religion) and that the culture of the new nation would be that of the Enlightenment — Tone's 'strum strum, and be hanged!' was an Enlightenment comment on the native harpists' festival which was one of the celebrations of July 12 in Belfast in 1792. The early republic was universalist. It recognised nations indeed, but they were to be remarkably similar to one another, and joined together in a universal freemasonry of benevolence — after they had separated from the old political systems of the kings and emperors. Tone's most famous words are often slightly misinterpreted. He distinguished between means and ends: his end was the separation of Ireland from England; his means the 'common name of Irishman' in place of the designations Catholic, Protestant, dissenter. This, not wholly representative of his own movement, has been since then a mark of Irish republicanism.

How did these somewhat mutually inconclusive objectives work out in practice? The Protestant northerners, the part of the movement most alarming to the government of the time, were social and political reformers, committed to the nation, it would seem, not so much for its own sake as in support of these aims. The northern radical paper, the *Union Star,* gives the radical tone:

Let the indignation of man be raised against the impious
wretch who prophanely assumes the title of reigning by the
grace of God, and impudently tells the world he *can do no
wrong.* — Irishmen! is granting a patent and offering prem-
iums to murderers to depopulate your country, and take
your properties, no wrong? . . .
Insurrection and revenge, however described or discounten-
anced by the abettors of tyranny, should always be
respected by a people, as they have operated powerfully
towards the preservation of liberty and the distribution
of justice. As revolutions in every age and country, were
acts contrary to laws then in existence, they consequently
were insurrections. The thing called in England a revolution
in 1688, justifies the assertion; and in the declaration of
rights, the men who drew it up, and the people who read it,
defended and admired the virtue and necessity of resistance
to oppression. The revolutions of France and America were
founded on insurrection; and before them the Portuguese
and Dutch revolutions. Antiquity furnishes many splendid
insurrections; amongst others, the celebrated one of the
Roman people retreating to the Mons Sacer, and defending
themselves by wholesome regulations from the privileged
patricians, — the Luttrells, Fitzgibbons and Scotts of the
day. History ornaments her page with the bold struggles, as
honourable, edifying, and worthy of imitation by suffering
humanity. Revenge! glorious revenge! Your name is as
sweet as liberty; as Paine says, 'He that would not punish
cruelty offers a premium to vice', or, as Ganganelli
expresses it, 'Mercy to the wicked, is cruelty to the
worthy'. — The Irishman who would not expiate the
burning of his cabbin, by the burning of a tyrant's palace,
is accessory to his neighbour's destruction . . . [13]

The formidable northern movement was smashed by repressive
measures, largely in 1797, since it was treated by the government as the
most dangerous. The uprisings in Antrim and Down in 1798 were only
a shadow of those that would have happened had the government not
acted first. More important, perhaps, after the crushing of the rebellion,
the British government to some extent conciliated. The Act of Union, for
example, embodied, so far as Irish parliamentary representation was
concerned, a large part of the electoral reform which the United Irishmen had initially demanded. It was not until about 1830 that the com-
plexion of British politics began to change generally, however, in a
liberal direction. When it did, Ulster politics changed too.

In other parts of Ireland, the republican idealists trapped themselves
in a fatal compromise. They appealed to grievances which were not
wholly relevant to their own purposes. The grievance against tithes, for

example, was one which could perfectly respectably be given a republican cast; but it was already, of its very nature, set in a sectarian mould. The rural organisations already in being in the nineties were in the pattern of the many rural secret societies of the eighteenth century. The Defenders, whom the United Irishmen used as a quick means to a countrywide federation of effective bodies opposed to government, were a Catholic organisation whose tactics were not always as defensive as their title might suggest. By the very condition of Ireland, the war of the poor against the rich, the war of the citizens against the king's men, was to become in large part the war of the Catholics against the Protestants. United Ireland, as the United Irishmen had known from the beginning of their enterprise, did not exist to start with. But wishing for the union of orange and green didn't bring it about: on the contrary, the bloody violence of 1798, on all sides, widened divisions in the long run.

The division ran through the '98 uprisings themselves, contrary to the mythological history of republicanism, which looks back to that year as a golden time of Protestant-Catholic unity. Part of the explanation of the failure to unite is that the United Irish societies were not numerous enough in their proper membership and didn't command enough outside support to organise insurrection as they stood. They looked to other groups which were attracted by the glamour of French ideas but were essentially local and limited in their aims.

> The Defenders [writes Marianne Elliott] inaugurated a new era in the history of the Irish secret society. With them the traditional attacks on tithes, rents, hearth-tax, county-cess or church dues became identified with vague ideas of revolution, and it was the Defenders and their offspring, the Ribbonmen, who sustained the notion of foreign-assisted revolution during the long interval between the collapse of the United Irishmen and the reappearance of organized republicanism with Fenianism. . .
>
> . . . But what distinguished Defenderism most from previous secret societies was its distinct revolutionary tone, and its rapid progress after 1792 is a classic example of how catholic consciousness had been aroused by the campaign of upper-class reformers. Their oaths were a hotchpotch of biblical imagery and other religious references, but they had also absorbed much of the language of the advanced reformers. One handbill spoke of restoring their laws to their 'primitive purity'; another claimed that "All men were born equal; we will have no king but the Almighty'. Most Defenders were encouraged to expect some startling improvement in their material situation and this was closely associated with the old idea that the protestants must be ousted before the catholics could prosper. 'I expected that I would get what

livings you and the likes of you have, for myself', one
former Defender told Counsellor Curran in the Louth
trials of 1794, and he agreed that they had planned 'to
knock the Protestants on the head, and. . . take their
places'.[14]

This exemplifies one persistant tendency in later nationalism, and it is
hardly necessary even to enter the qualification *'mutatis mutandis'* to
equate the Defenders, whom the United Irishmen took as allies, with
the twentieth-century Provisionals. The signficance of such societies
in the nationalist tradition has recently been examined in some detail
by Thomas Garvin.

But generalisation about political attitudes in the eighteenth and
early nineteenth centuries cannot be unqualified. There was much
variation, by locality, class and religion—and language. For a great many
people—in a rural population—the strongest sense of communal identity
centred on the townland, the parish, the barony. How much, beyond
this, it meant at the beginning of the nineteenth century to be Irish
rather than English probably varied hugely. We know we are European,
not Asian, but the intensive indoctrination of one or two centuries has
produced a much more acutely felt 'national' identity. In early nineteenth-century Ireland many were alienated from, and resented, local
petty tyrants—who often formally represented, in one way or another,
the distant king—but they acquiesced in a tepid and vague allegiance
to the remote monarch; unless and until they were taught to associate
him with the immediate oppression. For the lowest orders of rural
society the king could be a potential benefactor, offering the possibility of manumission from bondage to the small farmer:

> Oh, I wish the Queen of England
> Would write to me a line,
> And place me in a regiment
> All in my youth and prime;
> I'd fight for England's glory
> From the clear daylight of dawn,
> And I never would return again
> To plough the rocks of Bawn.

But, on a slightly higher social level, the tenant farmer's son was
often taught a kind of radicalism. The 'hedge-schoolmasters' in their
humble way at the turn of the century trained this class for survival
in a new, English-speaking, English-dominated world, and they taught
a kind of radical resistance, a tradition in which loyalty to the old
aristocratic Catholic Gaelic world had been transmuted into refusal
to yield wholly to the Protestant English ascendancy that had succeeded
it. Irish-speaking schoolmasters taught English grammar — and Irish
values, often garbled, often borrowing, with bizarre metamorphosis,

from the outer world. The conjunction of this native tradition with the vogueish romantic nationalism, as taught, for example, in the *Nation*, fostered a find of radical dissent.

However confused it was in its immediate outcome, the republicanism of the end of the eighteenth century left a heritage. The Union, and the reforming spirit and measures of the nineteenth century met, to a large extent, the grievances of the Ulster Protestants, who came to find the freedoms they sought within the framework of the enlarged British nation-state. Most Catholics went with them in this direction, but more sluggishly. Tardiness in meeting Catholic grievances—especially in the passing of emancipation—led to impatience, and to the growing demand for a repeal of the Union so that the great Catholic masses could be looked after (within the British imperial system) by those who understood them. The remnants of the Catholic landowning class were found wanting in the practice of genteel and deferential politics to this end; O'Connell's demagoguery, successful in achieving Emancipation, aroused hopes of the millennial utopia whose prospect sustained the secret societies, and then dashed them.

Catholic democratic movements were frightening, because Catholic numbers in Ireland were overwhelming, and in democratic systems numbers count. Therefore, in the demand for equality, it was the *Catholics* who came in the long run to lay the greatest emphasis on the 'common rname of Irishman'. With this formula they couldn't lose. For very similar reasons, England at about the same time espoused the cause of free trade. But the Catholics also began to insist on the pure, Celtic, Gaelic, ancient Irish nation (which had preceded the advent of planters and Presbyterian settlers).

After the frightfulness of '98 and the easy suppression of Emmet's rebellion, republicanism, as such, faded for a while. Reaction reigned in England and had triumphed in Ireland. The utilitarian aspirations of the United Irishmen persisted for a time on parallel courses, in Ulster whiggery and in the campaign of O'Connell. But by the time republicanism began to revive, fitfully and uncertainly, under the aegis of the romantic nationalism of the forties, the paths had already diverged. The romantic cultural nationalism of Davis, however noble its aims, was extremely confused. He preached, almost in the same breath, the restoration of the ancient Gaelic nation (about which he was no better informed than his contemporaries although he did his best to seek the information) and the acknowledgement of the new nation in which Saxon, Norman, Dane and Gael were representatives of traditions equally acceptable. He was not a republican, but some of his contemporaries were — not quite on the same grounds as the United Irishmen who looked to Voltaire, to Locke, to Hampden, but on the grounds that the only feasible true separation from England was one which would cut off not only the English crown but any notion of a crown.

The second phase of republicanism, after the Famine, saw a movement addressed to one purpose of the United Irishmen, which was not strictly republican: breaking the connection with England. It was separatist, nationalist, and, in a sense, democratic, aiming at 'government of the people by the people', rejecting the 'deferential' constitution that Bagehot was expounding, rejecting along with the landlord, the judge, the bailiff, and the wielders of the battering-rams that levelled the house of the poor, the whole connection with England, and implying a Lincolnian concept of a new democratic national union. America rather than France inspired the Irish republicans of the later nineteenth century.

However much they were to be acknowledged afterwards in ballads, in the enshrining of 'Speeches from the Dock' on farmhouse shelves, in the oral tradition of country politics, it was not the drawing-room nationalists of the romantic movement who made the reality of the nineteenth-century tradition but, as in the eighteenth century, the organisations of the countryside, with what must often be regarded as their offshoots in the towns.

The rise of democracy in eighteenth-century Europe is a subject as yet little studied or understood, but it is likely that it was much more of a business of the grass roots than has been appreciated in the past. No doubt some large part was played by the 'enclosing' and other movements which broke up the medieval patterns of the countrysides, and some other large part by the general increase in population (whatever may have caused *that*). Organisations of young men are to observed all over rural Europe, exercising a measure of social control in peasant societies, expressing the growing political consciousness of the time. The part played by the ideologists and theoreticians of towns and universities—the *philosophes* and their likes—in the development of political revolution is more evident than the less articulate, or at least less literate, groundswell of the villages. But one didn't have to be a philosopher expounding the social contract to ask the simple question:

> When Adam delved and Eve span,
> Who then was the gentleman?

And many did ask it. In Ireland, for example, the tavern poets responded to such events as the American revolution in simple, basic, but apposite ways:

> Washington relentlessly
> Consigns Cornwallis to the devil.

> Oh bright the day in Inis Fáil:
> God's friars will soon be in their churches,
> Art and learning free from law;
> And Irish in the foreign houses.[15]

That is from a poem by Ó Míocháin of Ennis. The passion of envious hunger in the lines of the Limerick poet William Ó Lionáin celebrates the deprivations of the English in Boston in 1776:

> As they are roaring for lack of the meat
> That without limit the bastards used eat.[16]

There is not much of Locke in the doggerel and squibs of these voices of quite a considerable section of the people. Washington is spoken of as ruling his kingdom, and King Louis is envisaged as the future ruler of North America. But it was this section of the people— small tenant farmers, schoolmasters, some artisans and craftsmen, shop-boys and others who were neither among the more comfortable elements of the population nor among the poverty-stricken— that was to provide the ground for later developments of republicanism. This was not, for most of the nineteenth century, a doctrinaire republicanism – even among the Fenians, almost all of whose leaders at one time or another indicated that they were not wholly opposed on principle to monarchy.[17]

They were, however, radical opponents of the existing system on the ground. This they shared with the movement of the eighteenth century. They lacked the secular outlook of many of the men of that period, but as they frequently still formed oath-bound secret organisations, whether for the redress of local grievances or for wider purposes, they came into conflict with the church and devised their own limited anti-clericalism and rationalising moral theology. The conflict came to a head with the Fenians and is well traced in some of the novels of Canon Sheehan, notably *The Graves at Kilmorna*. In their attitudes many of the Fenians resembled sections of the American eighteenth-century revolutionaries—not the Virginia gentlemen but the New England artisans.

> Mechanics are, as a rule, in my opinion [wrote John O'Leary] more intelligent, and even often more cultured, than any, save the professional and professedly cultured class; that is, such portions of the middle or upper class as in some shape or other devote themselves to the acquisition of knowledge, either for its own sake, or for the material gain to be got out of it. The middle class, I believe, in Ireland and elsewhere, to be distinctly the lowest class morally – that is, the class influenced by the lowest motives. The prudential virtues it has in abundance; but a regard for your own stomach and skin, or even for the stomachs and skins of your relatives and immediate surroundings, though, no doubt, a more or less commendable thing in itself, is not the stuff out of which patriots are made. Your average *bourgeois* may make a very good sort of agitator, for here

he can be shown, or at least convinced, that his mere
material interests are concerned, and that he may serve
them little or no material risk. A rebel, however, you can
rarely make him, for here the risk is certain and immediate,
and the advantage, if material advantage there should be,
doubtful and distant. As for the upper classes in Ireland,
as all the world over, you can find models of all the virtues
or of all the vices among them. Better in my limited and
perhaps mistaken sense—by goodness I may be roughly
said to mean altruism—than the middle classes they may
be considered to be, as also worse. It is our misfortune,
however, that in Ireland our upper class are only Irish in a
more or less limited and imperfect sense. . .[18]

This is a passage of great interest, because it exemplifies the basic
attitude of mind of modern Irish republicanism: it is separatist, anti-
bourgeois, and hankers for aristocracy while rejecting the existing
Anglo-Irish aristocracy: it epitomises conservative radicalism driven
to espouse egalitarianism for want of an acceptable social hierarchy.

Irish republicanism in the later nineteenth century was essentially
separatism, but it was extreme, root and stock separatism, and therefore—since there was no Irish heir presumptive waiting in the wings to
replace the British monarch after separation—it took the form and
subscribed to the ideology of republicanism. It was also in general
tendency violent, even if only intermittently so in practice.

Since Ireland was in some measure ungovernable through most of
the nineteenth century, this core of directed as distinct from random
physical force had an importance greater than its actual strength
(which was often quite small) might suggest. The background threat
of republican force was specially significant when there was a dis-
ciplined Irish party making Ireland's nationalist case in the House of
Commons under Parnell's leadership. This tradition was so strong
that the physical force became, as it were, part of the concept of the
Irish Republic. There were two views of the winning of Irish freedom.
The 'constitutional' view was that freedom would be won by agitation
and through parliament. It would, in other words, be granted by
England and was in England's gift. The 'physical force' view was that
Irish freedom was not in England's gift, that the conquest had never
been and should never be accepted, and that freedom was only freedom when it was independently asserted: it must be seized, not accepted. Republicanism was revolutionary separatism.

As it turned out, it was the mass violence of the Great War that
provided the background for the startling assertion of freedom by
force in 1916, after the constitutional approach had seemed to triumph,
and then had seemed to fail. For the Fenians—since England's right to
rule in Ireland was not acknowledged at all—the republic already existed,
and they swore allegiance to the 'Irish Republic virtually established'.

In 1916 the republic was openly proclaimed, and from that point on it became almost impossible for nationalists of any colour to slip back fully into the constitutional negotiation for a grant of independence. By the time of the twentieth-century upheaval, the republicans were attempting to reconstruct an ideology. Both Pearse and Connolly attempted to set their separatist aspirations in a framework of general theories of society, and they weren't alone. Pearse indeed attempted to define the republican tradition itself, somewhat eccentrically, pronouncing the true succession to be traced through Tone, Davis, Mitchel and Lalor. But the emphasis in this succession was on breaking 'the connection with England' and the transmission of a creed, not so much of republicanism as of revolutionary nationalism.

Connolly's teaching, while drawing on a somewhat similar radical tradition, diverged from what has usually been labelled 'republican', without qualification, in twentieth-century Ireland. Pearse remained in the main stream of it, all the more since he came to political revolutionary activity late in his short career, from a long involvement in cultural nationalism. While he examines and analyses with approval the writings of Tone and the programme of the United Irishmen, while he endorses their aim—'the rights of man in Ireland'—his emphasis is different.

> National independence [he wrote in his pamphlet *The Sovereign People*] involves national sovereignty. National sovereignty is twofold in its nature. It is both internal and external. It implies the sovereignty of the nation over all its parts, over all men and things within the nation; and it implies the sovereignty of the nation as against all other nations. Nationality is a spiritual fact; but nationhood includes physical freedom, and physical power in order to the maintenance of physical freedom, as well as the spiritual fact of nationality. . .
>
> . . .But the nation is under a moral obligation so to exercise its public right as to secure strictly equal rights and liberties to every man and woman within the nation. The whole is entitled to pursue the happiness and prosperity of the whole, but this is to be pursued exactly for the end that each of the individuals composing the whole may enjoy happiness and prosperity, the maximum amount of happiness and prosperity consistent with the happiness and prosperity of all the rest.[19]

Pearse professed not only such broad principles, but also the intention of giving shape to a particular vision of Ireland—'not free merely but Gaelic as well'—the nationalist aim which wasn't wholly consistent with pure republicanism, since it sought to prescribe for the free citizens a particular ethos. This characterised the 'Irish Ireland' nationalism of the early part of this century, which wasn't always republican but which by its anti-*bourgeois* and anti-modern bias tended towards a kind of Jeffersonian model, compatible (in so far as anything can be compatible with a contradiction) with separatist ethnic republicanism.

The model might be described as a nostalgic utopia, and can be illustrated by two similar passages, one of them well known.

In the Irish-speaking districts [wrote William Rooney in *The United Irishman*], as well as insisting on Irish being taught in the schools from the first stage up to the fourth or fifth to the complete ignoring of English, we must restore reverence for the seanachuidhe, who is still with us in the Gaelic places. We must reorganise the fireside college, and make the songs and poems of the district once again popular. Nay, more, we must have an evening Irish class in every village and town, Irish-speaking or otherwise, where, as well as calling into service the seanachuidhe, the scribe shall again become an institution to set down and prepare for the permanency of print the stories, histories, songs and ballads that are even yet being produced in every part of Gaelic Ireland.[20]

That Ireland which we dreamed of [said Éamon de Valéra in a radio broadcast in 1943 for the fiftieth anniversary of the foundation of the Gaelic League] would be the home of a people who valued material wealth only as the basis of right living, of a people who were satisfied with frugal comfort and devoted their leisure to the things of the spirit – a land whose countryside would be bright with cosy homesteads, whose fields and villages would be joyous with the sounds of industry, with the romping of sturdy children, the contests of athletic youth and the laughter of comely maidens, whose firesides would be forums for the wisdom of serene old age. It would, in a word, be the home of a people living the life that God desires that man should live.[21]

This model, not too far removed from some late-eighteenth-century ideals and fancies, coloured the mind of twentieth-century Irish republicanism. But that republicanism had a much harder edge to it: to be 'republican' meant to be committed to the extreme policy, to achieve complete separation from England by revolutionary force.

Like other revolutionaries, twentieth-century Irish republicans were often fanatical and often puritanical. The ideology emerged most clearly in the Dáil debate on the Treaty. It has often been remarked, as an oddity, that this debate was hardly concerned at all with a great matter of substance—partition—but was passionately engaged with a matter of form—the Crown. This may be odd, but it is a matter of great importance for modern Ireland. The larger part of the country became a republic, not by a chance of history but through the passionate assertion of a priority. The priority was the rejection of the English *system*, which came before national unity. Unity at that stage was unobtainable anyway, and the debaters may have known this in their bones, if not in their heads. But they did debate what *kind* of state they were establishing, and this is by no means as silly as it has sometimes been made to seem.

Partition was, however, to be the reality that shaped republican attitudes after 1922. Often it further distorted the basic republican outlook into mere irredentism or *revanche*. In particular it brought into the foreground a conflict whose menace in the wings had always tended to overshadow the central engagements on the stage of nineteenth-century Ireland. In Ulster, both the Catholics and the Protestants were different.

The first society of United Irishmen was founded in Belfast, although with Dublin participation (Wolfe Tone was there), and it was to become one of the aphorisms of republicanism that, in the words of the title of Eoin MacNeill's famous article in *An Claidheamh Soluis* (October 1913), 'The North Began'. There was much Ulster Presbyterian involvement, in particular, in the spread of the United Irish organisations and in the uprisings of Antrim and Down in 1798. It was they, principally, who proclaimed the 'rights of man in Ireland'. But their alliance with the Catholics was fragile at best. Many of them never overcame a distrust of Catholics which was founded both on a kind of religious horror at Catholic belief and practice and on an abiding suspicion of the political rôle and ambitions of the Roman Catholic church. Their republican idealism led them to condemn and to endeavour and hope to overcome the inter-denominational strife which was already taking place in parts of Ireland (mainly in Ulster and principally in Armagh) where there was competition for land and weavers' wages and where a growing population and a fairly even balance of numbers between Catholics and Protestants had led to bloody friction. The Orange order was founded in 1795 at the Diamond not long after the United Irish organisation had been founded in Belfast and Dublin.

The terrible events of '98 gave a check to the revolutionary collaboration of Catholic and Presbyterian. Even in the north there were difficulties in the collaboration. In Wexford and Wicklow some of the insurgent peasants found liberty in turning on their immediate oppressors whom they identified as Protestants, and the burning of Protestants at Scullabogue, the piking of Protestants on the bridge of Wexford, spread dismay, alarm and anger through the Protestant population of Ireland, not least in the north. Besides, the rebellions were bloody in the extreme, their suppression terrible. Some of the United men of the north became Orangemen and supporters of the government within a short space of time.

The Orange order, however, in its early years, drew its personnel largely from rural labourers and artisans attached to the established church. The majority of Presbyterians had not been associated with the republican uprising and only a small minority of Presbyterian clergy had taken part. Among the 'new light' Presbyterians, centred on Belfast, a sturdy liberalism continued for many years, but the radical extreme of republicanism quickly faded. Protestant Ulster was then, as it is now, complex, and many distinctions must be made — of class, of location, of shades of theological and political opinion. Two major changes took place at the turn of the century: the Act of Union which, among other things, did away with the political independence of Ireland's Protestant ascendancy, and an evangelical movement which acted as a powerful counter-force to theological liberalism and was to have far-reaching effects on political opinions too. Catholic emancipation was to have come with the Union but was blocked by royal and British parliamentary resistance. The ensuing campaign for its achievement, which started respectably enough with genteél lobbying, developed into a democratic mass movement (led by O'Connell) of a character unprecedented not only in British but in any politics. As this movement was organised and locally led by priests and as at this time the numbers of Catholics, especially the numbers of destitute or near-destitute, in the country were increasing in a population explosion, there was growing concern, turning to alarm, among Protestants.

Other very important demographic and economic changes were taking place in Ulster. The 'industrial revolution', centred on north-west England and south-west Scotland, included east Ulster. The home weavers in the densely populated countryside went through a generation of increasingly crushing hardship before yielding to the new concentration of textile manufacture in mills clustered around the Lagan. Linen gave way to cotton, then cotton to linen again, when technical invention made the machine production of linen possible. The small mercantile city of Belfast (with about 20,000 people at the end of the eighteenth century) became the focus of an industrial urban landscape. East Ulster, because of different settlement history and different landholding customs, had already shown a contrast to the rest of Ireland: this now became greatly sharpened. The rest of Ireland, especially after the war-stimulated boom in agriculture ended in 1815, was economically stagnant, with many unprofitable landed estates, overpopulation (still growing fast) and appalling widespread poverty.

Catholic emancipation was won in 1829. O'Connell's mass movement, its organisation still largely staffed by priests, was directed into agitations for repeal of the Union (although it is probable that O'Connell would have accepted in lieu, within the Union, such drastic socio-political changes as were wholly unacceptable to all the ruling and entrenched groups of the time). The later campaigns involved enormous mass meetings which aroused upper- and middle-class fears of the mob, and Protestant fears of Catholics. The repeal movement collapsed, but the mob, in a way, became even more menacing when so many of its members died of starvation and disease in the great calamity of the forties — the famine, among many, which is still known as *the* Famine.

Parts of Ulster, meantime, prospered. There was much movement of population. Belfast grew, in the course of the nineteenth century, from a city of about 20,000 people to one of about 350,000, drawing in skilled mechanics and supervisors from the industrial north of Britain, labourers and 'hands' from the Protestant and Catholic townlands and baronies of rural Ulster, absorbing sudden floods of refugees from the famine in west Ulster, creating new industries (such as shipbuilding and heavy engineering in the later part of the century) on its industrial base, being swept from time to time by evangelical and revival movements. By 1900 it matched Dublin in size but resembled it in little else. Dublin, the elegant eighteenth-century capital of the ascendancy (one of the chief cities of Europe at that time), now still the administrative centre of the British executive in Ireland, had also absorbed some overflow from the countryside, but not into an industrial dynamic. In 1900 it was somewhat larger than it had been in 1800, but was decayed, with acres of the worst slums in western Europe, and with a social life centred on a provincial court, a large military garrison, and a feeble comprador economy — a 'centre of paralysis', as James Joyce called it. The revival of republicanism and radical nationalism round the turn of the century is partly attributable to sheer, shamed hatred of this shoddy provincialism.

In the north, to understand the formation of loyalism we have to take into account the great local variation in Ulster and the many changes brought about by the nineteenth century. The liberal and enlightened merchants of Belfast were in large part replaced by much coarser-grained industrial capitalists, while their city's population was swelled with clerks and mill-girls, mechanics and draymen, with illiterate Protestant labourers from Armagh and Derry, fundamentalist Presbyterian farmers' sons, poor Catholics from west Ulster, Glaswegian and Mancunian experts, graduates from the theological academies of Scotland, and many more. In the broad band of country extending from Dundalk bay to Sligo, marked by swarms of little drumlin hills that hem in claustrophobic valleys, the masses of rural Catholic Ireland impinged on the frontiers of Ulster's rural Protestant settlement, and bigotries festered in the overlap zone. In the plantation lands of mid-Ulster and Donegal, a Protestant ascendancy—like the gentry of most of Ireland, but with a distinctly sterner and more emphatically military cast of mind—commanded in the broad valleys a Protestant tenantry in ancestral style and viewed with an ancient arrogance the Catholic farmers on the poorer hillsides. In parts of coastal Antrim and Down unreconstructed Calvinists led lives without Catholic, urban or liberal neighbours on lands which had been deserted when their ancestors colonised them, while not too far away (as in the Glens of Antrim) sharply contrasting, but also largely homogeneous, communities lived in old Irish Catholic style. In other places the potent symbols of a modern mythology dominated, as where Protestant Derry's walls looked down on the extramural settlement of Catholics on the bog-side to the west of the city.

In stages through the nineteenth century, the overwhelming majority of the remarkably varied Protestant population of Ulster was brought together on one issue, and on one issue only: the rejection of dominance by Catholic Ireland.

Protestants—Presbyterians in particular—continued to oppose government policy very vigorously on many other issues throughout this period (on the whole broad range of educational policy, for example). A vigorous liberalism flourished and there were always many Ulster Protestants who strongly opposed the religious intolerance of the time (just as there were pamphleteering place-holders and rabble-rousing preachers who fostered it). But O'Connell's misjudgment and failure in his attempt to bring the repeal agitation to Belfast in 1843 marked the real beginning of a process of consolidation of Ulster Protestant resistance to what was increasingly seen as a threat both to civil and religious liberty and to the prosperity of the north-east: the threat of resurgent Catholic Ireland. The chief safeguard seemed to be the Union, within which Catholics were safely in a comparatively small minority, the Protestant Irish executive could temper the effects of the widening franchise and maintain the principles of the Protestant constitution (and it is the constitution of 1688-89 to which Protestants who felt threatened by Catholics politically looked), and had unrestricted access to British markets both in Britain and overseas. What Ulster protestants feared was not theoretical republicanism, but virtually its opposite: a Roman Catholic Theocracy. In the time of Pius IX and the first Vatican council such fears weren't wholly irrational.

Gladstone's introduction of the first home rule bill, which closely followed on his disestablishment of the Church of Ireland, brought about the most important stage of the consolidation of Protestant Ulster's resistance. Home rule cut across differences of opinion which were at the time being pursued vociferously. In the circumstances, the leadership of resistance to home rule was Tory (to be joined by liberal unionists and imperalists) but the Tory leadership was able to gather behind it both liberals and those rebellious radicals who had never ceased to be an element in Ulster Protestantism. This was a reactive movement, a laagering in emergency. It couldn't develop a radical ideology. Instead it aligned itself with the 'new imperialism' and with neo-Darwinian racism. It produced its own mythology to counter the romantic nationalism of Catholic Ireland, and it gradually began to discard the round towers and shamrocks which had been shared emblems of Irishness.

At the time of the first home rule debate, J.B. Woodburn wrote a series of articles in *The Scotsman*, later published as a book:

1914

mind of ulsterman

> What are the characteristics of the type of man who has made Ulster what she is today? Her history has shown that he is brave and courageous in the midst of bitter oppression and great hardship, and fights best when he fights great odds; he is determined to the verge of stubbornness and will accept no compromise; stern, dogged, and strong of purpose; independent, self-contained, and self-reliant, able to stand on his own feet, and intensely proud of the fact. He has the passion, alertness, and quickness of the Celt in addition to the adventurous spirit of the Norseman. He is steadfast and industrious beyond most races. In his uncultivated state he is blunt of speech and intolerant of shams, and lacks the attractiveness of manner of the Southerner. But perhaps the most outstanding fact about him is his power to command. Call to mind the fearless soldiers, and wise and far-seeing statesmen of Ulster. Think of the Lawrences and Lord Dufferin whom she gave to India, and the numerous Presidents of the United States of America with Ulster blood in their veins. . .
>
> . . .The religion of the North is one that inculcates freedom of life and conscience, and must produce a more robust race of men than the South with its traditional and enervating Catholicism. Take the words of the calm, philosophical, and judicious historian Lecky, who speaks of Catholicism as follows – 'It is on the whole a lower type of religion than Protestantism, and it is peculiarly unsuited to a nation struggling with great difficulties. It is exceedingly unfavourable to independence of intellect and to independence of character, which are the first conditions of rational progress. It softens, but it also weakens the character, and it produces habits of thought and life not favourable to industrial activity, and extremely opposed to political freedom.'[22]

In this phase of its development, the Ulster ideology opposed liberty to democracy, was suspicious of parliament and even of king, and fell back on the rights of superior race and superior character and on the rock of the settlement of 1688. Hence the rejection of any authority which was seen as "ephemeral and specious." As one of the shrewdest observers of this, David Miller, has put it: *fleeting & superficial*

> Loyalty is a moral principle translated from the realm of personal relationships into politics; it ought to override any

pleas of nationality. It carries the connotations of lawful-
ness, which Protestants understood to be what distinguished
them from their Catholic fellow-countrymen. Obviously
there was a problem in sustaining the self-image of lawful-
ness when the community undertook preparations for the
massive defiance of a statute, and this is why these preparations were organised, both in 1892 and in the 1912-14
agitation, with such obsessive regard to discipline, order and
solemnity. Law meant less the actual statutes which lawyers
contest in the courts, than the public order which they are
intended to maintain. . .

* . . .'Loyalty' defined an external relationship to the British
state, not a wholehearted sense of incorporation into the
British nation.[23]

To this it might be added that the kind of strained legalism involved
is shared with modern Irish republicans.

Having organised and armed in 1913-14 to defy and if necessary to
fight the British rather than yield to Dublin home rule, the Ulster loya-
lists fought *for* the British in the Great War. The bulk of their Ulster
Volunteer Force, reformed into the Ulster Division, was part of the
Kitchener volunteer army which went into action on the Somme in
1916. It suffered extremely heavy casualties in futile attacks, adding
both to the Ulstermen's pride in their own people and to their sus-
picions of the British.

Partition gave home rule to Northern Ireland (six of Ulster's nine
counties), but this could be sustained only so long as the Protestants
presented themselves as a monolith, since there was a large and dissi-
dent Catholic minority waiting to see the territory brought in with
independent Catholic Ireland. The many divergent tendencies in Ulster
Protestantism were locked into a pose of rigid and perpetual unani-
mity, and great tensions built up. With the breakdown of Ulster home
rule between 1968 and 1972 these tensions were released in an explosion which matched that of the Catholic forces that had initiated the
collapse. There were, as it were, multilateral declarations of independence, and expression of long-felt rage and frustration was, for a while,
free. To take one example more or less at random, the paper *Loyalist
News* printed this in April 1973:

> The illegal administration of Mr William Whitelaw the day
> to day running of which is left almost entirely to the staff
> officers of the English Army, so that Ulster is governed, in
> matter of fact terms, by a Military Junta — goes to great
> lengths and much expense (ours) to brainwash the Ulster
> People into believing that without the maternal beneficence
> of Westminster, that bitch of Parliaments, our society would

flounder. Faceless, pinstriped English Civil Servants are noted for lengthy 'Wrath of God' speeches which they write for their political puppet-masters to mouth on this subject. This side of the water, too, those strange beings whose one ambition in life seems to be that they be taken for members of the English County élite, while shrugging off their Ulster birth as one of those things which a gentleman must bear with a stiff upper lip, are to be found, almost daily, prostrate before the altar Westminster, urging the rest of us (poor, ignorant peasants, of course) to do likewise. . .

In the Irish Free State, which came into being in 1922, a similar disintegration occurred. In the few years immediately after 1916, republicanism became, for the first time, the dominant and, briefly, the accepted ideology of Catholic Ireland. Perhaps this was partly because—probably more by political instinct than by conscious intent—the institutional Roman Catholic church, disappointed in Redmond's failure to deliver the home rule state it aimed at, abandoned his parliamentary party suddenly and gave radicalism its head for a year or two. It was within this short period that republicans, duly elected, formed an independent parliament and, under some socialist influence and after careful deliberation and editing, declared themselves:

> We declare that we desire our country to be ruled in accordance with the principles of Liberty, Equality, and Justice for all, which alone can secure permanence of Government in the willing adhesion of the people.
>
> We affirm the duty of every man and woman to give allegiance and service to the Commonwealth, and declare it is the duty of the Nation to assure that every citizen shall have opportunity to spend his or her strength and faculties in the service of the people. In return for willing service, we, in the name of the Republic, declare the right of every citizen to an adequate share of the produce of the Nation's labour.
>
> It shall be the first duty of the Government of the Republic to make provision for the physical, mental and spiritual well-being of the children, to secure that no child shall suffer hunger or cold from lack of food, clothing or shelter, but that all shall be provided with the means and facilities requisite for their proper education and training as Citizens of a Free and Gaelic Ireland.[24]

Within three years the country was partitioned and the republic at an end. After several splits, five chief bodies of political opinion could be discerned in the Irish Free State: the government, which accepted the Treaty and the Crown, was supported by the Roman

Catholic church, promoted the Irish language, replaced Protestant government with Catholic government and otherwise, by and large, left things unchanged; the main opposition, led by Éamon de Valéra, who founded the Fianna Fáil party in 1926 and promoted a moderate republican nationalism based on economic self-sufficiency; the labour opposition; the unionists, a dwindling force; and the radical republicans, defeated in civil war, who bided their time but were determined that, in a slogan of the time, 'We will rise again'.

They in turn had a tendency to divide. One section believed in radical transformation of the country by social and socialist (if necessary violent) means. Another believed in 'freeing' Ireland from England first, by military means. This included ending partition. There were differences about the emphasis which should be placed on, for example, cultural policies – especially in respect of the Irish language. Like all radical movements outside any political power system, the republican movement split and split again. The factions had in common a belief in the use of force and a structure in which the military leaders directed political policy. The broad and persistent division was between the socialists (Marxists for the most part) and the nationalists (Catholics by conviction as well as origin for the most part). The splits are repetitive, but one of the most striking cases of recent times was the split of December 1969, when a large group, mainly of northerners, separated from the 'official' I.R.A. and set up a 'provisional' army council.

Republicanism, like its loyalist counterpart (the radical groups which stand separate from official unionism), remains anti-bourgeois. Even the members of the Fianna Fáil party whose republican origins are now fairly remote, would appear in their social aspirations to aim at becoming kulaks of great wealth rather than aiming, like their Fine Gael opposite numbers, at becoming true bourgeois. But socialism and Irish republicanism, as it has come down by tradition, seem strangely incompatible, in spite of many efforts to match the two.

The special character of republicanism in Northern Ireland derives from its being not merely separatist and committed to physical force, but strongly coloured by anti-Protestant resentments. In the North, the traditions of the Ancient Order of Hibernians are to the I.R.A. as the traditions of the Defenders were to the United Irishmen. The Provisionals' aim is a united Ireland, but the model offered (as in the policy document Éire Nua) is perfunctory, resembling old and failed political programmes such as that of Fianna Fáil in the 1930s and '40s, and offered seemingly as an afterthought to their real business, which is the 'war'. Their other publications usually refer to the existing Irish state and government with dislike and contempt. Their legalism doesn't recognise existing states in their present form, neither the United Kingdom nor the twenty-six-county republic. Their organisation is, like so many radical organisations in the world, a sect –

exclusive, millennialist, unworldly, ultimately anarchic, self-obsessed and self-sufficient, dedicated not so much to an imagined future as to an imagined past.

But, the greater part of Ireland is, contrary to what might have been expected, a republic of sorts. And, the northern Provisionals apart, there has long been a body of people in the country, a smallish minority, who stand half aloof from the mainstream of compromising nationalism, from church and state, from mass entertainment and aspirations to affluence — the political puritans, whose eighteenth-century virtue is (they know in their hearts) the righteousness of the fifty just men by which the city will be saved.

> Hearts with one purpose alone
> Through summer and winter seem
> Enchanted to a stone
> To trouble the living stream.[25]

Desmond Fennell

IRISH SOCIALIST THOUGHT

In his historical preface to the English translation of Anton Menger's *Right to the Whole Produce of Labour* (1899), Prof. H.S. Foxwell of University College, London wrote that "Socialist propaganda has been mainly carried on by men of Celtic or Semitic blood."* When he used the word Celtic, he was thinking primarily of the Welshman Robert Owen and Irishmen such as William Thompson, John Doherty, Feargus O'Connor and James Bronterre O'Brien.

The leading thinker of that group, and the first Irish socialist, was William Thompson, born in Cork in 1775. His father, Alderman John Thompson, a prosperous Cork merchant and member of the Protestant ascendancy, had a 1,500-acre estate at Roscarbery, forty miles west of the city. As a young man, William Thompson travelled on the continent and spent some time in France and the Netherlands. He read Saint-Simon, Sismondi and similar French thinkers who believed (as he later wrote) that the "tendency of civilisation and of manufacturing improvements was to deteriorate the situation of the industrious classes as compared with that of the idle classes." Back in Ireland he was a supporter of Catholic emancipation. When he inherited the family property in 1814, he went to live in Roscarbery and became an improving landlord. Besides giving leases on generous terms and seeing that his tenants were well housed and properly equipped, he instructed them in the latest agricultural methods and put his knowledge of chemistry and medicine at their disposal. His personal kindness made them tolerant of his atheism and anticlericalism, and of his "utilitarian" carping about the number of church holidays.

Thompson was a humorous, idealistic man of penetrating mind and frugal habits: he neither smoked nor drank and, in the latter part of his life, was a vegetarian. As a member of the local Philosophical, Scientific and Literary Society, and as one of the proprietors of the Cork Institution—founded to provide education cheaply for middle-class children—he took a prominent part in the intellectual life of Cork. He was obsessed by a sense of guilt about living on rent, "the produce of the effort of others", and he sought redemption by devot-

The quotations used in this chapter are taken from the books listed in the short bibliography at the end.

ing himself to the welfare of others. He hoped thereby to "raise himself to an equality of usefulness with the productive classes." As the word "usefulness" there might indicate, and as has already been suggested, he was a utilitarian and a follower of Jeremy Bentham. Finding that the Cork Institution was not fulfilling its functions properly, and having failed to make headway with his co-proprietors, he addressed himself to the public in a pamphlet called *Practical Education for the South of Ireland*. While working on this, he had some correspondence with Bentham. They became friends and Bentham invited him to visit him in London.

Essentially, Thompson was a humanist. His basic concern was that men and women might live together contentedly, free from anxiety, and as human beings ought to live – morally, generously, and in relationships of mutual trust, respect and help. Believing that the "excessively unequal" distribution of wealth prevented this, he wanted to work out a science of society which would show the wrongness of this inequality and of the production relationships based on it, and justify the creation of a different system favourable to man. This was the purpose he had in mind when, in 1822, he accepted Bentham's invitation and went to study the problem in the capital of modern capitalism.

In London, first in Bentham's house and later living near him, he got to know the leading English utilitarians. He also met Robert Owen and studied his ideas on cooperative communities. From the first, he disagreed with Owen's belief that such communities could be brought into being by the enlightened action of the rich or with funds supplied by capitalists. He wrote:

> The rich, as a class, like all other classes in every community, must obey the influences of the peculiar circumstances in which they are placed, must acquire the inclinations and the characters, good or bad, which spring out of the state of things surrounding them from their birth.

Only "a few individuals" may rise above the impulses of their class and view impartially matters closely related to them. However, Thompson became convinced that cooperative communities, created by the "industrious classes" themselves, were the right way to organise society.

In 1824 he published his first major work, *An Inquiry into the Principles of Distribution of Wealth most Conducive to Human Happiness; Applied to the Newly-Proposed System of Voluntary Equality of Wealth*. That last phrase referred to the Owenite communitarian programme. The central argument of this book is that the distribution of wealth should be reorganised on the principles of equality and of the labourer retaining the full product of his labour. The existing, unequal distribution of wealth stood condemned because it was not conducive to the greatest happiness of the greatest number and to virtuous living but to their opposites, and because it involved the robbery and exploitation of the majority who possessed no capital by the minority who did.

Building on Ricardo's thesis that the value of a commodity was equal to the value of the labour which produced it, Thompson argued that labour was the source of value. Capital was "that portion of the product of labour which, whether of a permanent nature or not, is capable of being made the instrument of profit." In natural justice, the labourer was entitled to the full value which his labour had provided, less depreciation of the capital employed. However, "as long as the accumulated capital of society remains in one set of hands, and the productive power of creating wealth in another, the accumulated capital will be made use of to counteract the natural laws of distribution, and to deprive the producers of the use of what their labour has produced." The "surplus value", that is, the product value over and above the lowest wage payable, will be appropriated by the capitalists. They had the power to do this, not only because they possessed, in their capital, the available means of production, but also because they managed, directly or indirectly, to control the state power, the judiciary and the priesthood. "As long as a class of mere capitalists exists...", they "must be always law-makers." "The whole system of human regulations" was "little more than a tissue of restraints of one class over another."

Distribution of Wealth had much to say about the "competitive" nature of modern capitalism (Thompson was the first to use this word to describe it, as he was the first to use "industrial" in its modern sense.) In measured, passionate language, he described how the enforced competition between individuals, rich and poor, corrupted human relationships and caused widespread apathy, fury, and spiritual suffering.

Cooperative communities, Thompson argued, would eliminate competitiveness and allow both the equal distribution of wealth and the retention by the labourers of the full product of their labour. Productivity, far from decreasing (as some suggested) because the whiplash of fear and insecurity had been removed, would increase greatly through the release of the creative forces of the individual workers. The more widespread affluence would not, as Malthus argued, lead inevitably to an excessive increase in population. On the one hand, the tendency to improvident multiplication decreased with affluence; on the other hand, people could be educated in methods of birth control. Then, with sexual intercourse made independent of childbearing, women equal with men, and divorce easily available, each community could make rational regulations for sexual intercourse and pursue a prudent population policy. Thompson predicted that, under communism, the state and religion would wither away. "Almost all the occasions for the exercise of the ordinary functions of government would have ceased." Public opinion would replace coercive laws. With spreading enlightenment and growing affluence, "the trade of religion, like the trade of law" would gradually cease.

With the publication of *Distribution of Wealth*, Thompson became, at one and the same time, the founder of "scientific" socialism and the leading theoretician of Owenite "utopian" socialism. At home again in Cork, he worked on a book entitled *Labour Rewarded – the Claims of Labour and Capital Conciliated; or, How to Secure to Labour the Whole Products of its Exertions.* This appeared in 1827 and contained more of Thompson's theory of the state as well as his recommendations for labour politics and trade unionism. No positive furtherance of cooperation, he argued, was to be expected from the existing state which was merely "the aristocratic law-making committee of the idle classes." He criticised its over-centralisation as both tyrannous and inefficient. The most important immediate reform which labour should seek was the democratisation of parliament, because a parliament representing the workers would be certain to facilitate the building of a cooperative commonwealth. At the same time, the people should create a decentralised political system based on self-governing communes and provinces. Trade unions had an important role to play. They could not, under the existing system, secure just wages for the workers, but they could prevent individual competition among workers. To do this, effectively, they must establish a "central union of all the general unions of all the trades of the country." They should also establish producer cooperatives which would develop into cooperative communities.

In Bentham's circle in London, Thompson had met Anna Wheeler, daughter of a Church of Ireland archbishop, who had fled from an unhappy marriage in County Limerick. An intellectual and a socialist, she was well acquainted with contemporary French socialism, had encouraged Charles Fourier during his early years in Paris, and was active in the English cooperative movement. She and Thompson became close friends and, in collaboration with her, he wrote *An Appeal of One Half of the Human Race, Women, Against the Pretensions of the Other Half, Men, to Restrain Them in Political and Thence in Civil and Domestic Slavery.* The immediate occasion of the book was an article by the utilitarian James Mill, which argued that it was unnecessary for women to take part in public life or politics. The *Appeal* criticised the legal "rightlessness" of women and argued for their full participation in politics and law-making. It was a more comprehensive statement of the feminist case than Mary Wollstonecraft's *Vindication of the Rights of Women* (1792) and the first book to deal directly with female suffrage. In the dedication, to Anna Wheeler, Thompson summed up most of his programme:

> You look forward, as do I, to a state of society very different from that which now exists, in which the effort of all is to outwit, supplant and snatch from each other; where

interest is systematically opposed to duty, where the so-
called system of morals is little more than a mass of hypocrisy preached by knaves but unpractised by them, to keep
their slaves, male as well as female, in blind uninquiring
obedience; and where the whole motley fabric is kept together by fear and blood. You look forward to a better
state of society, where the principle of benevolence shall
supersede that of fear; where restless and anxious individual
competition shall give place to mutual cooperation and
joint possession; where individuals, in large numbers male
and female, forming voluntary associations, shall become a
mutual guarantee to each other for the supply of all useful
wants, and form an unsalaried insurance company where
perfect freedom of opinion and perfect equality will reign,
and where the children of all will be equally educated and
provided for by the whole.

In 1830 Thompson published his last book, *Practical Directions for the
Speedy and Economic Establishment of Communities, on the Principles
of Mutual Cooperation, United Possessions, Equality of Exertions and
of the Means of Enjoyment.* This was a minutely detailed guide to the
establishment and running of cooperative communities, more or less on
the lines of the early Israeli kibbutz or the Maoist commune. Thompson argued against any notion of a return to the social or technological
conditions preceding the industrial revolution, and for the full use of
the new technology. The communities he envisaged, whether agricultural or industrial or mixed, would replace both the "village" and
the "town", combining elements of rural and urban life in a new
synthesis.

Thompson played an active part in the first three cooperative congresses in England in 1831-2. *Practical Directions* was adopted as the
guiding model of the Owenite cooperative movement in preference to
Owen's own ideas. Thompson visited the cooperative community in
Ralahine, County Clare and presented a copy of the book to its manager, E.T. Craig. He had drawn up plans for a community on his own
estate, and had some of the buildings erected. But his poor health,
which had dogged him throughout his life, culminated in a fatal illness
and he died in Roscarbery in May 1833. He bequeathed his body to
science and most of his property to the cooperative movement. But the
latter bequest was contested in the courts and frittered away there.

The Ralahine commune, established by the landlord John Scott
Vandeleur, was one of the few Owenite communities which actually
got off the ground. Vandeleur had heard Owen lecturing in Dublin in
1823 and was converted to his ideas. After visits to Owen in England
and correspondence with him, he decided to establish a cooperative
village on his untenanted 600-acre estate at Ralahine, near Bunratty,

peopling it with tenants from his other estate. He built comfortable stone cottages, dormitories for single men and single women, a store, a school, a large dining-room and a meeting room. In 1831 having persuaded Edward Thomas Craig, editor of the *Lancashire Cooperator*, to be the manager − if his tenants approved − he assembled the tenants and had them elect fifty-two persons to form the Ralahine Agricultural and Manufacturing Cooperative Association. Vandeleur, the Association's self-appointed president, rented the land to it and lent it livestock and farm implements, at six per cent annual interest, until it would have made enough money to buy them. Rules were agreed, wages and prices fixed. There was a currency of labour notes, acceptable for internal purchases and changeable into money for spending outside. Various labour-saving machines were introduced. The community prospered for two years until, in October 1833, Vandeleur lost all he owned at gambling and left suddenly for America. The Vandeleur family resumed direct possession of Ralahine and evicted the community without compensation.

* * *

William Thompson's thought had no influence or sequel in Ireland and his analysis of competitive capitalism did not become a significant part of Irish working-class ideology until the end of the century, and then by way of Marxism. Irish politics and the Irish economy differed sharply from those of England and the rest of Britain. Unprotected against cheap British imports, manufacturing industry had been declining rather than expanding, except in the northeast. The main political feature of the 1820s had been O'Connell's campaign for Catholic emancipation, and the early 1830s were marked by the tithe war − the violent rebellion of the rural tenantry against the payment of tithes to the Church of Ireland. In England, however, Thompson's *Distribution of Wealth* exerted a strong influence on neo-Ricardian economic thought and on working-class ideology. His *Labour Rewarded* encouraged the growth of trade unionism and inspired the demand for the democratisation of parliament which issued, from 1838 onwards, in the Chartist movement.

Many trade unions established consumer or producer cooperatives to gather capital for the founding of cooperative communities. John Doherty, a cotton spinner from Buncrana, County Donegal, was the outstanding trade union organiser of the time. Rather than the local unions which were the norm, he wanted unions spanning the entire state and organised on the lines of O'Connell's Catholic Association. In 1829 he founded the Grand General Union of Operative Spinners of Great Britain and Ireland, based on Manchester, and, in 1830, the National Association of United Trades for the Protection of Labour. This "central" union, which soon embraced one hundred and fifty unions and had its own, widely-read newspaper, *The Voice of the People*, was an early precursor of the British Trades Union Congress (TUC). Like Thompson, with whom he worked on committees of the cooperative congresses, he regarded trade unions as dual-purpose agencies: for worker protection in the short term, and for the creation of the co-operative commonwealth in the long term.

As a mass movement of the lower classes under a middle-class leader, Chartism was the British parallel of the Irish Repeal movement. Feargus O'Connor, the Chartist leader, had begun his political career as a parliamentary colleague of O'Connell; he was elected for County Cork in 1833 and 1834, but was deprived of his seat on the grounds that he lacked the necessary property qualification. He went into working-class politics in the north of England and, from the power base which he created there, hijacked Chartism from its London founders. They and many other Chartists were socialists, but O'Connor cannot be so described. He hated industrialism and what it was doing to people, and wanted to re-settle the unemployed on the land in non-collectivist colonies, as peasant proprietors. He believed this would have the added beneficial effect of raising the wages of the urban workers by reducing competition for employment.

Among the socialists in the Chartist leadership was James Bronterre O'Brien from Granard, County Longford. A graduate in law of Trinity College, Dublin, he had worked under Thompson in the cooperative movement. He was the chief intellectual of Chartism — O'Connor nick-named him "the schoolmaster". Most of O'Brien's ideas were drawn from French socialism, especially Babeuf, Blanqui and Saint-Simon, and his writing was mainly in periodicals. He was the first to use the term "social democrat" in English. In the early 1850s, as a founder and leader of the National Reform League, he formulated an evolutionary socialist programme which envisaged the conquest and use of the existing state, rather than its replacement. In this general respect, and in some of its particulars, the National Reform League programme foreshadowed the Independent Labour party's policies in the 1890s.

While the Chartist movement and its successor groups ran their course, another Irish socialist, Hugh Doherty, refrained from political activity because he believed, as Owen had, that it was pointless. Doherty was the principal exponent in Britain of the doctrines of Charles Fourier about the immutability of human nature and the construction, in place of the existing state, of a system of social "solidarity" based on communities called "phalansteries." In these same years, Christian socialism emerged in Britain, as various socialist and social movements based on Christianity had already emerged, or were now appearing, on the continent. Interestingly, and indicative of the ingrained secularism and individualism of modern Irish Christianity, neither in this period nor later did any Irish Christian find inspiration in his religion for thought or action of a socialist kind.

One of the aims of O'Brien's National Reform League was the gradual nationalisation of land and the use of the resulting rent or tax on land use to cover all state expenditure. In Ireland, a couple of years previously, Fintan Lalor had described the landlords as usurpers of the nation's ownership of the land and advocated the payment of all land rents to the nation "for public purposes". Lalor, who was championing the cause of the tenant-farmers and plot-holders, was on the left wing of Young Ireland with Devin Reilly and John Mitchel. They were not socialists, but they preached social revolution; Reilly had written in *The Nation* about the French socialist Louis Blanc, and both he and Mitchel, in *The Irish Felon,* used socialist rhetoric in writing about the workers' revolt in Paris in 1848.

* * *

In Ireland in the second half of the nineteenth century, revolutionary fervour among the poorer classes took the forms of republican national-ism (mainly Fenianism), or the struggle for the land, or a combination of both. The National Land League, founded in 1879, was the out-standing instance of both causes combined. Its founder and chief organiser, Michael Davitt, also united both causes in himself, while at the same time being deeply committed to the industrial workers' struggle, particularly in England. The son of an evicted Mayo tenant-farmer who had moved with his family to Lancashire, Davitt had worked in a factory as a child, lost an arm in an industrial accident, become a Fenian and spent seven years in jail for his activities on behalf of the brotherhood. He was released in 1877. By the time he was returned to jail in 1881 — together with Parnell and other leaders of the Land League — he had moved, ideologically, to a socialist posi-tion. In his book *Leaves from a Prison Journal,* which he sketched out during his fifteen months' imprisonment, Davitt argued for land nationalisation, cooperative production, state "regulation and organi-sation of labour", and a labour party in the House of Commons.

His arguments for land nationalisation, and a tax on land use which would fund state expenditure, were probably derived from Henry George, whòm he had met in America in 1878 and whom he invited to visit Ireland. But George did not propose the nationalisation of the land — he advocated merely the "single tax" aspect and later called his scheme by that name — and he believed in a *laissez-faire* economy free from state interference.

Davitt began by arguing that the real relations between labour and land, and between land monopoly and poverty, could best be discerned in Ireland where there was no abundance of industry to obscure the matter. Land and labour "are absolutely essential to one another." "Land is valueless without labour" and labour, which creates value, "cannot exert itself without land". When the ownership of land is monopolised by a special class, they can and do determine access to land, and consequently, both the amount of wealth produced and its distribution. They exclude many people from access to land, and when they permit access, it is on terms which deprive their tenants of most of the value they produce and allow them mere subsistence. Moreover, the land monopolists receive, as an extra bonus, the unearned increment which accrues to land by virtue of the growth of population and the spread of towns and industry. This unjust state of affairs can be righted, and the productive capacity of land and labour fully realised, only by taking all land, including mines and minerals, into public ownership and "taxing it, exclusive of improvements, up to its full value". "By the term improvements," Davitt continued, "I mean such erections or qualities as can be clearly shown to be the results of the labour of those now in the occupation or enjoyment of the land or their predecessors." Thus land would be available to all, "and every individual worker would be in a position to command exactly that share of the wealth produced which he had by his labour created; while the community at large would be put in possession of that part of the wealth produced of which it was the sole creator."

Davitt was strongly opposed to peasant proprietorship as a remedy of the land problem. "Increasing the number of those holding private property in land" would not remedy "the evils of land monopoly". Peasant proprietorship is "simply landlordism in another form". "A million proprietors, or petty landlords, would act together as cordially as the present landlord party in the three kingdoms." To increase that party "and particularly with public money" (by buying out the landlords), would be "suicidal" for "popular liberty". Moreover, peasant proprietorship "excludes the (agricultural) labourers from all hope of being able to elevate themselves from their present degraded condition."

With regard to the industrial workers, Davitt believed that his land nationalisation scheme would benefit them both by increasing the amount of productive enterprise and by making land available to the poor. In both ways, the competition among workers for jobs would be reduced, and employers would have to compete for labour. However, if the industrial workers were to receive the full value of their labour, more was needed. Industry must be cooperatively organised, "on the basis of joint ownership of capital and absolute control on the part of the worker". But that was "a thing of the future". It could be hoped for only as a result of educating the workers and creating successful examples of cooperative industry which would inspire them "to look in this direction for their emancipation from their present state of dependence". In the meantime, and in preparation for that eventuality, "social reformers would do well to exert themselves to extend state regulation of the relation between labour and capital, and governmental control and ownership of enterprises similar in character to those which are already subject to such supervision or ownership." This "state" and "governmental" action should occur at the local as well as the central level. In a chapter on Irish self-government — which he no longer envisaged in a republican form but on the Canadian or dominion model — he advocated elective county boards with wide powers, including control of the police; each county would be "as far as practicable, a self-governing community". (The thought occurs that, if the Home Rule proposal had included county self-government on these lines — or if such a measure had been implemented, say, in the 1890s — Home Rule would not have seemed so threatening to the northeastern capitalists.)

Leaves from a Prison Journal provides the only comprehensive statement of Davitt's socialist beliefs. In the years after his release from prison, he often spoke in favour of land nationalisation; but apart from Bishop Nulty of Meath and Archbishop Walsh of Dublin — who supported the idea in principle — few in Ireland would hear of it, least of all the tenant-farmers or the growing numbers of peasant proprietors. His views on this matter got a better reception in Britain and America. In his career as a member of parliament in the Irish Home Rule party, Davitt was a Labour-Nationalist (or Lib-Lab) favouring "state socialism" — in effect, a reforming state paternalism. He became well-known, and acquired considerable influence in the English and Irish labour movements. Chiefly he worked to create two unions of interest: on the one hand, between the Irish agricultural labourers, urban workers and tenant-farmers, on the other (as Feargus O'Connor had attempted before him) between the Irish national movement and the British working class. In 1890–91 he initiated the process which led, three years later, to the foundation of the Irish Trade Union Congress. Shortly before his death in 1906, he had the satisfaction of forging an electoral alliance between the Irish parliamentary nationalists and Keir Hardie's Independent Labour party, and of fighting the general election on that basis.

* * *

In the second half of the nineteenth century, the cooperative movement in Britain shed its socialism. It became a movement consisting of consumer cooperative societies — engaged in retail and wholesale trading — and, to a lesser extent, producer cooperatives, with no end in view beyond the successful operation of these enterprises and the benefits, material and moral, to be derived therefrom. Its guiding principles were those of the Rochdale cooperative society in Lancashire, founded in 1844; interest was paid on share capital, and dividends on members' purchases. Legislation in the 1850s and 1860s gave binding force to the societies' rules and limited the liability of members to their shares. In Ireland there were very few co-ops until the 1890s, when, under the leadership of Horace Plunkett, Robin Anderson, Father Tom Finlay and others, a major cooperative movement got under way. For

Plunkett, who was a wealthy, patriotic Unionist and the main driving force, the overriding purpose of the movement was to rebuild the "character" of the Irish people by encouraging self-reliance, care and enterprise.

Most of the new co-ops were engaged in agricultural business of one kind or another, and especially dairying. The Irish Agricultural Organisation Society was founded to provide overall servicing and direction, and by 1913 it had 985 affiliated societies. To a considerable degree, the movement was inspired by the advanced state of agricultural cooperation in Denmark — Ireland's principal competitor on the British market — but organisational models were derived from other continental countries also, notably France and Germany. Looking back to the Ralahine venture, Plunkett praised E.T. Craig as "the author of the most advanced experiment in the realisation of cooperative ideals", but doubted whether joint ownership of land, except for common grazing, was practicable.

Father Finlay, in 1913, expressed tentative hopes that the cooperative movement would lead to a "cooperative commonwealth" which would remove the exploitative element from capitalism. The notion of a cooperative commonwealth had become separated from the notion of "socialism", largely because the latter term was now associated primarily with the urban context, industrial workers, and state or municipal ownership or control. However, this did not prevent cooperativist thinking from assuming *de facto* socialist or near-socialist forms. and this was the case with George Russell (AE), particularly in his book *The National Being* (1917). Russell, who was primarily a poet and mystical philosopher, had been brought into the cooperative movement by Plunkett in 1897 and trained as an organiser. Later he became the editor of the movement's journal, *The Irish Homestead,* and both there and in other writings such as *Cooperation and Nationality* (1912), he moved towards the notion of a cooperatively organised Ireland. He regarded Ralahine as an inspiring forerunner and a pointer towards the Ireland of the future.

In *The National Being,* Russell writes:

> It is not enough to organise farmers in a district for one purpose only — in a credit society, a dairying society, a fruit society, a bacon factory, or in a cooperative store. All these may be and must be beginnings; but if they do not develop and absorb all rural business into their organisation, they will have little effect on character. The specialised society only develops economic efficiency. The evolution of humanity beyond its present level depends absolutely on its power to unite and create true social organisms.

Moreover, cooperation must extend into towns and factories. "I desire to unite countrymen and townsmen in one movement, and to make the cooperative principle the basis of a national civilisation." The industrial workers should begin by acquiring cooperative control of the distributive trade. Then, working from that base, their trade unions could gradually "transform themselves into cooperative guilds of producers". At the same time, scope must always remain both for individual business enterprise and for other kinds of collective ownership. "By degrees it will be discovered what enterprises are best directed by the state, by municipalities, by groups, by individuals." But the cooperative economy would be the "spinal column" of the national body, setting the tone for every other form of economic activity. Voluntary initiative and effort was the way to bring it into being.

Russell was as sceptical as Thompson before him of any really transforming action by the capitalist state. "Governments in great nation-states, even representative governments, are not malleable by the general will." They are controlled and manipulated by "the holders of economic power." Similarly with the press, which does not reflect public opinion, but rather, "capitalistically controlled creates public opinion". Russell noted that, in the institutions of self-government proposed for Irish Home Rule, "the signature of the Irish mind is not apparent anywhere." It seemed that the English system of self-government, with all its inefficient, oppressive and antiquated features, was to be imported into Ireland. "I fear the importers of this machinery will desire to make it do things it can only do badly, and will set to work with the ferocity of the new broom, and make it an obstruction" which will prevent the genius of the Irish people from expressing itself and "enchain us for centuries to come." If Irish self-government were really to be government by and for the Irish people, then the "national assembly concerned with general interests" must be accompanied by "councils, representative of classes and special interests, controlling the policy and administration of the state departments concerned with their work." Speaking with the cooperative movement's experience of the Irish Department of Agriculture in mind, Russell says that "the continuous efficiency of state departments can only be maintained when they are controlled in respect of policy . . . by the class or industry which the state institution was created to serve."

*   *   *

While the land had been the main social issue in the late nineteenth century, urban trade unions had been slowly growing, and there were groups of socialists in some cities. The First International, based on London and under the virtual leadership of Karl Marx, had a substantial Irish membership. James Stephens, John O'Mahoney, John Devoy and other leading Fenians belonged to it, and it had branches in Dublin and Cork and among the Irish in England. A manifesto of the Irish section in 1871 stated that the establishment of these branches had helped to end "the national antagonism between English and Irish working men in England" which had been "one of the main impediments in the way of every attempted movement for the emancipation of the working class, and therefore one of the main stays of class domination in England as well as in Ireland." After the disintegration of the International, the small groups of socialists in Dublin and Cork attached themselves, like the Irish trade union movement of the time, to British organisations. This situation began to change in 1894 with the foundation of the Irish Trades Union Congress. Two years later it changed further when the Dublin Socialist Club, learning that James Connolly in Edinburgh was in dire need of work, offered him a job as organiser at one pound a week. Connolly, who was then twenty-seven years old, came to Dublin and, within a couple of weeks, had persuaded his new comrades to found the Irish Republican Socialist Party with himself as secretary.

The importance of this event lay not so much in itself as in what it signified, namely, Connolly's determination to create a socialist theory and practice which would be rooted in Irish history, persuasively related to Irish circumstances, and grafted onto both the revolutionary nationalist movement and the broader movement of national humanism of which it was the core and concentrating force. This humanist movement, in its various manifestations, sought to heal the broken humanity of the Irish people — to restore them to personal integrity, self-possession and self-reliance. Already by 1896 it included enterprises as diverse as the nationalist Gaelic Athletic Association, the non-political Gaelic language movement, the rural cooperative movement, and the nascent literary revival. To these would be added, in the following few years, Arthur Griffith's Sinn Féin, D.P. Moran's *Leader* and Yeats's Abbey Theatre, and finally, after another few years, the "redemption by blood" project of Pearse and the other poets of the Easter Rising. From all of these, successively and collectively, the nationalist revolution drew its force.

Connolly was a humanist by instinct who believed "there is nothing on earth more sacred than humanity." The Irish nationalism he had imbibed as a boy in the slums of Edinburgh, and the Marxist socialism he had learned in the same city in the 1890s, combined to focus his humanist zeal on the Irish working class, and to convince him that the only way it could recover its lost humanity was through a national and social revolution which would liberate its nation and put it in control of the nation's material resources. In the meantime, its struggle towards that goal was a humanising process. "Every victory for labour," he wrote, "helps to straighten the cramped soul of the Irish labourer." Jim Larkin's new, militant trade union, the Irish Transport and General Workers' Union (ITGWU) was to be praised because "it found the workers of Ireland on their knees, and has striven to raise them to the erect position of manhood; it found them with all the vices of slavery in their souls, and it strove to eradicate these vices and replace them with some of the virtues of free men." Moreover, like Thompson, Connolly made clear that the humanity he was concerned about was female equally with male. "The worker," he wrote, "is the slave of capitalist society, the female worker is the slave of that slave . . . Down from the landlord to the tenant and peasant proprietor, from the monopolist to the small businessman eager to be a monopolist, and from all above to all below, filtered the beliefs, customs, ideas, establishing a slave morality which enforces the subjection of women as the standard morality of the country." But "in Ireland the women's cause is felt by all labour men and women as their cause; the labour cause has no more earnest and wholehearted supporters than the militant women."

The necessity in Ireland for national liberation and social emancipation was the core of Connolly's doctrine. Many of its other points arose either from his effort to present this core persuasively to Irish workers, socialists and revolutionaries, or from his defence of one or other aspect of the resulting corpus against criticisms by other socialists.

From the start, he maintained that primitive communism had existed in Ireland under the Gaelic clan system until the seventeenth century, and that an Irish socialist republic would therefore be a restoration, in contemporary terms, of this native Irish principle. Searching for a forerunner in the Irish revolutionary tradition, he fastened at first on Fintan Lalor — his social revolutionary zeal, his hatred of landlordism, and his clear contention that the ownership of the land was vested by right in the nation. Later, in *Labour in Irish History* (1910), Connolly re-wrote Irish history since the seventeenth century from a labour standpoint, dwelling on Thompson, Ralahine, the Irish socialists in England, and the social and labour dimensions of Young Ireland and Fenianism. With regard to Ralahine, he said that an independent Ireland "must seek the happiness of her people in the extension on a national basis of the social arrangements of Ralahine".

Facing the Ireland of his day, he maintained that the Workers' Republic would be "the application to agriculture and industry . . . of the republican ideal" to which the Irish revolution had committed itself. At the same time, it would be a "cooperative commonwealth", and therefore a goal which the rural cooperative movement and urban labour could collaborate to achieve (Connolly noted, with praise and appreciation, George Russell's progress towards a junction with the urban labour movement.) Labour was the "natural ally" of the language revival movement: both had in capitalism a common enemy and both were aiming to restore self-respect in Irish people. Repeatedly Connolly attacked the "middle-class" and "gombeen" nationalists who hoped to achieve, through Home Rule, a self-governing, capitalist Ireland. That, he argued, would mean continued economic subservience to London and no real change in circumstance for the majority of Irish people. He described the northern Protestant workers as "slaves in spirit" who accepted enslavement by their "pastors and masters" because they had beneath them, in the Catholics, people who were even more oppressed. Socialism demanded, he told them, that the people of Ireland should rule and own Ireland, but on the day that Home Rule went through, the socialists would "go into opposition."

While seldom referring to Marx and never calling himself a Marxist, Connolly used Marxism, selectively, as a method of social and historical analysis, modifying it or adding to it as he saw fit. His belief in the socialist necessity of Irish national liberation was in accordance with Marx's express teaching, but he went further than Marx in denouncing the subjection of any nation by another nation and in defining socialist internationalism as "a free federation of free peoples". This definition occurred in the course of his controversy with William Walker, the Belfast "gas and water" socialist, who maintained that the aim of Irish independence ran counter to the internationalism required of workers within the United Kingdom. For Walker, as for many socialists of the time, internationalism meant collaboration between the workers of different nations regardless of whether some of these nations were subject to others. Connolly remarked that such "internationalism" was "scarcely distinguishable from imperialism". (Lenin, several years later, developed a doctrine on the rights of nations which was close to Connolly's without going quite so far.)

Again, Connolly differed from Marx and many other socialists in maintaining that socialism was not an all-encompassing philosophy with views on everything. The socialist movement, he wrote, had been "hampered by the presence in its ranks of faddists and cranks, who were in the movement, not for the cause of socialism, but because they thought they saw in it a means of airing their theories on such questions as sex, religion, vaccination, vegetarianism, etc." whereas socialists "as a body were concerned only with the question of political and economic freedom for our class" and "were not repositories of all truth." In particular, socialism had been harmed by those socialists who mixed anticlericalism and hostility to religion with their socialist propaganda. Anticlericalism was a survival from the eighteenth-century freethinkers, and a product of capitalist individualism which had no place in socialism. Nor was religion part of socialism's concern: the socialist creed had to do with secular and human matters only, and could therefore co-exist with any religion, and particularly with Christianity. In *Labour, Nationality and Religion* (1910), written in reply to criticisms of socialism by an Irish Catholic priest, Connolly corrected the critic's misrepresentations of socialism, cited passages in the scriptures, church fathers and Christian philosophers which seemed to point to socialist principles, and predicted that the church would adapt, ultimately, to socialism as it had adapted to a variety of social systems in the past.

This was typical of Connolly's relationships with Christian clergy, whether hostile or friendly: unyielding on principles and insistent on clarifying the facts, he persistently claimed identity of purpose and welcomed collaboration when it occurred.

As to the means of social emancipation–given national independence–Connolly wrote in 1899 that it would be achieved through the "ownership by the state of all the land and materials for labour, combined with the cooperative control by the workers of such land and materials". Resources and enterprises should be made "the property of the government" only "in proportion as the workers are ready to make the government their property". At this stage, Connolly envisaged the workers' political party as playing the leading role by winning control of the government. But already, as can be seen from the above, he was aware of the simultaneous need for the growth of direct control of production by the workers, as distinct from the state, bureaucracy or party. Later, this awareness crystallised in the synthetic syndicalism which he adopted from the American socialist Daniel De Leon – a combination of Marxist analysis with a syndicalist praxis deriving ultimately from Marx's opponent, Proudhon. Craft unions must give way to "industrial unions" spanning each entire industry; and these, combined in one big union, would build up the "working-class administration" – the "industrial republic"–to the point where, with the help of direct political assault through the ballot-box, and possibly with armed force, it could take over and replace the bureaucratic, capitalist state. Connolly gave his fullest exposition of this syndicalist programme in *Socialism Made Easy*, published in Chicago (1908) during his period in the United States. Later, in *The Reconquest of Ireland* (Dublin, 1915), he reaffirmed it, in combination with cooperativism, in a manner reminiscent of Thompson in *Labour Rewarded* and close to Russell in *The National Being*: the industrial unions were to be the means of establishing, in place of the existing state, a cooperative commonwealth administered by the unions.

In the years 1912-14, Connolly played a leading part in persuading the Irish Trade Union Congress to establish a Labour party which would serve as its political agent. But his main work in these final years was with the Irish Transport and General Workers' Union, an "industrial union" founded by Jim Larkin which had become the largest affiliate of the Irish Trades Union Congress. Larkin, the son of Irish emigrants to Liverpool, had come to Ireland in 1907 as an organiser for a British union. A syndicalist and an Irish republican, his great gifts as a labour leader lay in his oratory, personal magnetism and fighting spirit. He founded a very successful paper, *The Irish Worker*, as the organ of the Irish Transport and General Worker's Union. In the Great Lock-out of 1913, Larkin, seconded by Connolly, led the union against the Dublin employers. When he left for America in 1914, Connolly took over as acting general secretary of the union, editor of *The Irish Worker*, and commander of the Irish Citizen Army. This small workers' army—the world's first "Red Guard"—had been set up to protect workers during the great lock-out, and then, subsequently, reconstituted "to enforce and defend" the principle that "the ownership of Ireland, moral and material, is vested in the people of Ireland."

In the period leading up to the Easter Rising, Connolly wrote about guerilla warfare and drew close to Pearse. It was in this context that he made his final theoretical adaptation to the national revolution. Over twenty years previously he had stopped practising his religion and he subsequently ceased to be a Christian believer. Pearse, on the other hand, was a deeply religious man who saw the coming rising as an act which would redeem the Irish people, morally, in a manner analogous to Christ's self-sacrificing death. Connolly, responding to this notion, remembered the words of a French socialist he had known in Edinburgh and made them his own in the *Workers' Republic:* (Feb. 5, 1916): "Without the slightest trace of irreverence, but in all due humility and awe, we recognise that of us, as of mankind before Calvary, it may be truly said 'Without the shedding of blood there is no redemption.'" In prison, after the rising, he received the sacraments again, and his last words, spoken to the chaplain as he faced the firing squad, were "Father, forgive them for they know not what they do."

*   *   *

Pearse, in his turn, was influenced by Connolly. Already, Lalor and the 1913 lock-out had been radicalising his views on property; Connolly, in those last months, made him a socialist. In Pearse's final political essay, *The Sovereign People* (March, 1916), he wrote that "the nation's sovereignty extends . . . to all the material possessions of the nation, the nation's soil and all its resources, all wealth and all wealth-producing processes within the nation." "No right to property is good against the public right of the nation." Furthermore, "right to the control of the material resources of a nation . . . resides in the whole people and can be lawfully exercised only by those to whom it is delegated by the whole people, and in the manner in which the whole people ordain." It was against the background of this basic agreement on the social question between Pearse and Connolly that the Proclamation of the Irish Republic declared "the right of the people of Ireland to the ownership of Ireland."

When the First Dáil met in January 1919, one of the fundamental texts read and assented to was the famous "Democratic Programme". It began by re-stating that phrase from the proclamation and some of the key passages on sovereignty and property from Pearse's *The Sovereign People*. Then it committed the republic to policies of social welfare, declared "the right of every citizen to an adequate share of the produce of the nation's labour", and stated that the republic would ensure that industries were "developed on . . . progressive cooperative industrial lines." This broadly socialist declaration had been drafted, at the Dáil's request, by Thomas Johnson, treasurer of the Irish Trades Union Congress and Labour Party (which had not participated in the general election leading to the establishment of the Dáil.) The more extreme and explicit socialism of Johnson's original draft was modified before the document was put to the Dáil and passed in a mood of thoughtless euphoria. Both the new Irish republic and the labour movement were sympathetic to the new soviet regime in Russia. The Soviet Union government recognised the republic, and the Dáil authorised the establishment of diplomatic relations.

*   *   *

After Connolly's death, and with Larkin still in America, the labour movement was left under the leadership of cautious functionaries. The most talented of the Irish Citizen Army men died in the 1916 Rising or shortly afterwards, and the army, under ineffective leadership and virtually disowned by the Irish Trades Union Congress/Labour Party, went on to play a passive and undistinguished role in the War of Independence. The new acting secretary of the Irish Transport and General Workers' Union, William O'Brien, was a syndicalist who regarded the achievement of national freedom as a matter for Sinn Féin and the Irish Republican Army. O'Brien and Johnson—an Englishman who had come to Ireland in 1892 and lived for many years in Belfast—were the leading figures in the congress/party during the revolutionary years and afterwards. Both were dedicated trade unionists who believed that the winning of economic power through the growing trade union movement was the direct road to the socialist society. They called that society the "cooperative commonwealth" or "workers' republic", and Johnson said that the Labour party's constitution (1918) was based on the teachings of James Connolly and George Russell. While the urban trade unionists and unemployed, the small farmers and landless labourers, became increasingly involved in the republican struggle, the congress/party held to the neutral line on Irish nationalism which it had pursued since before the 1916 Rising. A practical reason for this was the fact that many Irish Trades Union Congress members were northern unionists. At the same time, in indirect and informal ways, the labour movement helped the nationalist cause: most notably, by the general strike against conscription into the British army, by winning recognition for Ireland at international labour conferences, and by local or transport strikes directed against the British during the War of Independence.

These were years of great growth for the trade unions, and particularly for the Irish Transport and General Workers' Union. The labour leadership seems to have believed that this growth would lead, inevitably and without violence, to the cooperative commonwealth. Nominally, the congress/party executive was committed to promoting cooperative societies, but it took no steps to do so, and the only cooperatives sponsored by trade unions were long-established ones in Belfast and a clothing factory set up in Dublin by the Irish Transport and General Workers' Union. Moreover, on those occasions, during the War of Independence, Truce and Civil War, when groups of country people seized land or groups of workers seized factories and set up "soviets", the congress/party leadership gave no encouragement and evaded the issue.

When Labour, in 1922, at last contested a general election to the Dáil (winning seventeen seats out of one hundred and twenty-eight), it did so on a purely reformist programme. This set the tone for Labour thenceforth. It became, in the Dáil, a reformist, economist party, advocating state paternalism on the British model (including a degree of public ownership and state industrial enterprise.) Just as the Bolshevik leadership in Russia stopped short at the state despotism which, in its own theory, was to be the prelude to the communist society, so the Irish labour leadership confined itself to advocating and supporting a state paternalism which, in its own theory, was at best a holding position on the way to the cooperative commonwealth. In effect, therefore, the cooperative commonwealth was tacitly shelved. Nor was this state of affairs altered by the various socialist flurries of the 1920s: Larkin's return, his splitting of the Irish Transport and General Workers' Union and founding of the Irish Workers' League as the Irish affiliate of the Comintern; Roddy Connolly's Communist Party of Ireland; the socialist rhetoric of Liam Mellows, Peadar O'Donnell and others on the left wing of the outlawed Irish Republican Army. All of these were impotent in face of the double-edged fact that the mass of the labour movement and its formal leadership were committed to state paternalism and that Fianna Fáil was on the way to making this the socio-economic orthodoxy of the state.

Labour described itself as the party of Connolly and called for the implementation of the Democratic Programme. De Valera, speaking for Fianna Fáil, proclaimed his allegiance to the Democratic Programme and his adherence to Connolly's social vision. Both parties, in practice, offered state paternalism, but Fianna Fáil, as the left wing of the national revolution—as that which Connolly had wanted the Labour party to be— was uniquely able to offer it in combination with militant nationalism. By doing this, Fianna Fáil came to power, ruled the country for sixteen years, and outdid contemporary social democratic governments in the degree of state paternalism which it practised – particularly in its expansion of the state sector of the economy. After that—whether governed by Fianna Fáil or by coalitions of Fine Gael, Labour *et al.*—the republic was set in the pattern of state paternalism which has characterised all liberal democracies in the twentieth century. The trade union organisation, now called the Irish Congress of Trade Unions and devoted primarily to wage-bargaining, became a leading institution of the state, and its officials wielded considerable influence. The Labour party struggled on, fell under the sway of middle-class liberals, and survived on the electoral crumbs left over by the two big parties.

*   *   *

In these circumstances, socialism, whether as a fervour or a theme, has become as marginal to Irish life as it has been, say, to American life since the First World War. It has been an issue, sporadically, in the trade union movement, and has rumbled, occasionally, in the Labour party and the republican movement, giving rise to splits or splinterings. In the late 1940s, the Irish Transport and General Workers' Union, in a bout of power politics, alleged communist infiltration of congress and party, and for a time set up a rival organisation. In the last twenty years, "socialist trouble" in the Labour party has arisen from left-wing caucuses rebelling against the party's lack of socialism. On one occasion, in the late 1960s, the party took the bull by the horns, declared that the "seventies will be socialist", presented an election programme with some socialist features – and fell back from twenty-one to seventeen seats in a Dáil of one hundred and forty-four seats.

In the republican movement, veerings towards socialism have occurred as reactions to the failure, or poor prospects, of physical force. In 1933, with de Valera triumphant, the left wing of the Irish Republican Army, led by Peadar O'Donnell and George Gilmore, split from the Irish Republican Army to form the Republican Congress with the Communist party and other left-wing groups. This lasted until 1936, when the chief militants went off to fight on the republican side in the Spanish Civil War. Again, in the 1960s, after the failure of the Irish Republican Army's campaign in Northern Ireland, Sinn Féin under Tomás Mac Giolla, turned to social issues and cooperative-building. Roy Johnston and Cathal Goulding tried to remodel the movement on Marxist principles. This contributed to the split in 1970, when the Provisional Irish Republican Army emerged. During the 1970s they refounded traditional republicanism as a military movement fighting for British withdrawal from Northern Ireland, and a political movement aiming at a democratic, socialist, federal Ireland. Their programme, which envisaged four federated provinces based on self-governing district units, cooperative production and distribution, and national ownership of the chief resources, was the most explicit revolutionary programme published for decades. But the movement's commitment to federalism and to radical decentralisation was never more than nominal, and the federalism was effectively rejected at the Sinn Féin Ardfheis of 1981.

While socialist activism has been confined to the margins of recent Irish life, socialist thought has been virtually non-existent. Connolly, whether nominally or really, is still the chief reference-source of Irish socialism, with no other Irish thinker intervening in the past sixty years. Notable socialist writing has been confined to historical works such as Rayner Lysaght's *The Republic of Ireland* (1970), Michael Farrell's *The Orange State* (1976) and the historical essays published by the Irish Communist Organisation.

However, this cessation of creative socialist thought must be seen in context. From the end of the 1930s until recently, there was hardly any Irish theoretical writing about society or the state, apart from Jeremiah Newman's erudite books on political morality. A slight revival has occurred in the last fifteen years. In *The Distasteful Challenge* (1968), Charles McCarthy, an ex-president of the Irish Congress of Trade Unions, argued for decentralised government, participatory democracy, and worker-management. Subsequently, Thomas Barrington, in a succession of publications—notably, *From Big Government to Local Government* (1975) and *The Irish Administrative System* (1980)—made a profound critique of Irish governmental structures and argued for radical decentralisation. But these are very unusual books for contemporary Irishmen to write, and they have been virtually ignored. In short, the absence of socialist theory in contemporary Ireland has been part of a general decay, leading to an extreme scarcity, of social or political thought.

PART IV

10

John Jordan

SHAW, WILDE, SYNGE AND YEATS:
IDEAS, EPIGRAMS, BLACKBERRIES
AND CHASSIS

With certain notable exceptions Irish drama is not distinguished by its
originality of thought. It may of course be properly argued that it is
not the business of the drama in any case to embody originality of
thought, philosophical, metaphysical, ethical or otherwise, that the
theatre of Jean-Paul Sartre is diminished rather than enriched in its
effectiveness by the overtones of his philosophy and that the same
holds true of the Christian existentialist Gabriel Marcel and his theatre.
There are some who would argue that the theatre of Bernard Shaw is
vitiated by "ideas", that for example, the "Don Juan in hell" section of
Act III of *Man and Superman* is a violation of the play's comedic
structure.[1] There are also some artless or fatuous enough to believe
that Yeats's penultimate play *Purgatory* (1938) perhaps his most perfect, could have been written had he eschewed his notions about reincarnation and the memories of the dead.[2] Quite rightly, critics,
academic and otherwise, have hailed three Irishmen, George Farquhar,
Oliver Goldsmith, and Richard Brinsley Sheridan, as the chief ornaments of eighteenth century stage comedy.[3] But it is not possible
to speak about the philosophical background of these brilliant men,
for it does not exist. And they wrote almost exclusively for the London
stage. In that context, they may be said to have a common mentality;
the émigré mentality not at all to be confused with the casts of mind
that led Joyce first to Paris in 1902 and later to Trieste in 1904 and
Beckett finally to Paris in 1938. Even in pre-Union days London was
Mecca. After the Union, it was not only Mecca but Moscow (in the
Chekovian sense) for gifted young Irish dramatists-to-be, like Oscar
Wilde and his junior by two years, Bernard Shaw, neither of them
particularly concerned with Irish woes.[4]

Almost everywhere we turn during the first decade of the "Irish
dramatic movement" (to use Una Ellis-Fermor's terminology)[5] we run
into the monitory intellectual shade of Henrik Ibsen. It was of course
Shaw, through his criticism, and William Archer through his translations, that brought the name of Ibsen before the public in these
islands. In 1891 Shaw published a small book called *The Quintessence*

of Ibsenism.[6] It was a fruit of his association with the Fabian Society which he had joined immediately after its foundation in 1884.[7] In the spring of 1890, the society planned a series of papers "under the general heading of 'Socialism in Contemporary Literature'." Shaw consented to "take Ibsen". By his own account his lecture might have lain fallow were it not for the "frantic newspaper controversy" which followed upon the first London performances of successively, *Rosmersholm/Ghosts* and *Hedda Gabler*. Shaw stepped in to clear the air with his little book. Thus before ever any play of his was staged, Shaw was identified with his own coinage: Ibsenism.[8] His first play produced was *Widowers' Houses* in 1892. He tells us in the preface to the *First Volume of Plays: Pleasant and Unpleasant* (1898) how it came to be written. Originally he and William Archer had set out in 1885, to write a play in collaboration. But their aims diverged and Shaw was left with two acts of an unfinished play which he set aside, only to complete seven years later, when a native work was required for J.T. Grein's Independent Theatre, founded specifically for the purpose of proclaiming the New Theatre. *Widowers' Houses* may seem tame nowadays, but, irrefutably, it has an Ibsenite theme: the stripping of illusion and self-deception, in this case those of the young doctor, Harry Trench. But in the original preface to *Widowers' Houses* (1893) Shaw was careful to point out that there were respectable native sources for many of the ideas in his play that critics detected as Norwegian importations.[9] We must of course always be careful about the absolute truth of Shaw's disavowals. In this connection the preface to *Major Barbara* (1905) is of crucial importance and merits extensive quotation, if only because of the light that it throws on a slightly earlier play *Man and Superman* written between 1901 and 1903. "Schopenhauer wrote a splenetic essay which, as it is neither polite nor profound, was probably intended to knock this nonsense on the head." (The "nonsense" was all aspects of the male romantic convention about women). "A sentence—denouncing the idolised form as ugly has been largely quoted" (Schopenhauer in the essay "On Women" in *Parega*, (1851), referred to them as "that undersized, narrow-shouldered, broad-hipped, and short-legged race" and "the number two of the human race".)[10] Shaw goes on: "The English critics have read that sentence, and I must here affirm with as much gentleness as the implication will bear, that it has yet to be proved that they have dipped any deeper. At all events, whenever an English playwright presents a young and marriageable woman as being anything but a romantic heroine, he is disposed of without further thought, as an echo of Schopenhauer." In what for Shaw is something uncharacteristically close to a *cri du coeur*, he complains, "My own case is a specially hard one, because, when I implore the critics who are obsessed with the Schopenhauerian formula to remember that playwrights, like sculptors, study their figures from life, not from philosophic essays, they reply passionately that I am not a playwright and that my stage figures do not live." And he tells us that long before he ever read a word of Shopenhauer, the socialist revival of the 1880s had brought him into contact with Ernest Belfort Bax, an English socialist and philosophic essayist, "whose handling of modern feminism would provoke romantic protests from Schopenhauer himself, or even Strindberg."[11]

In the same preface, Shaw disavows the direct influence of Nietzsche in *Man and Superman*. Here some of his statements are harder to take than his disavowal of Schopenhauer in favour of Ernest Belfort Bax. "I first heard the name of Nietzsche from a German mathematician, Miss Borchardt, who had read my 'Quintessence of Ibsen', and told me that she saw what I had been reading: namely, Nietzsche's *Jenseits von Gut und Bose* (*Beyond Good and Evil*, 1886). Which I protest I had never seen, and could not have read with any comfort, for want of the necessary German, if I had seen it."[12]

Shaw may here be pulling our legs. A modern philosopher, R.J. Hollingdale, tells us that by the end of 1889, Nietzsche's philosophy was "available to anyone who could read and reach a bookshop".[13]

Shaw, however, cannot deny that he has borrowed the word *Ubermensch* (Superman) from Nietzsche, but in relation to *Major Barbara* is constrained to deny that Nietzsche was the first to put forward the "objection to Christianity as a pernicious slave-morality". Just as he claims to have been made familiar with Schopenhauerian notions before he had ever heard of that philosopher, so the Nietzschean view of Christianity "was familiar to me, before I ever heard of Nietzsche". And he cites a Captain Wilson, inventor of the term "Crosstianity", to distinguish the retrograde element in Christendom, and the Scottish philosophic historian Stuart-Glennie, both of whom he had encountered thirty years earlier, shortly after he arrived in London.[14]

But one must turn now to *Man and Superman* which Professor Turco has described as "the first of Shaw's efforts to bear the unmistakeable stamp, of a major work by a major writer."[15]

It is in this play that Shaw coined the expression "the life force" as a motive power behind the universe. Critics of an earlier period may be forgiven for equating this with the *élan vital* of Henri Bergson, who used it in his *Creative Evolution*. But Bergson's book was published in 1907, four years after *Man and Superman*.[16]

In his glittering "Epistle Dedicatory" to A.B. Walkley, Shaw, as perhaps nowhere else, gives us an account of his personal predilections in literature (and painting and music) "Bunyan, Blake, Hogarth and Turner (these four apart and above all the English classics) Goethe, Shelley, Schopenhauer, Wagner, Ibsen, Morris, Tolstoy, and Nietzsche are among the writers whose peculiar sense of the world I recognise as more or less akin to my own."[17]

And he arrives at an outrageous synthesis: "Bunyan's perception that Righteousness is filthy rags, his scorn for Mr Legality in the village of Morality, his defiance of the Church as the supplanter of religion, his insistence on courage as the virtue of virtues, his estimate of the career of the conventionally respectable and sensible Worldly Wiseman as no better at bottom than the life and death of Mr Badman: all this expressed by Bunyan in terms of a tinker's theology, is what Nietzsche has expressed in terms of post-Darwin, post-Schopenhauer philosophy; Wagner in terms of polytheistic mythology; and Ibsen in terms of mid-nineteenth century Parisian dramaturgy;"[18] One does not think, usually, of Bunyan as a man of "ideas": yet perhaps there is a touch of him in the silenced priest Keegan in Shaw's only full-length play set entirely in Ireland: *John Bull's Other Island* (1904). "For four wicked centuries the world has dreamed this foolish dream of efficiency; and the end is not yet, but the end will come."[19] Many years later in the preface to *Back to Methusaleh* (1921) Shaw was to return to the importance in his mental world of John Bunyan: when he first began to write for the stage, "Nietzsche . . . was supposed to have been the first man to whom it had occurred that mere morality and legality and urbanity lead nowhere, as if Bunyan had never written Badman. Schopenhauer was credited with the distinction between the Covenant of Grace and the Covenant of Works . . ."[20]

In this brief discussion of Shaw's ideas, I have come only as far as 1905 and I have not touched upon English influences like Samuel Butler, author of the Victorian classic *The Way of All Flesh* and *Erewhon*. It will have been seen that Shaw, while admitting to intense admiration for Schopenhauer, Nietzsche and Ibsen, was at pains to stress that he came to them intellectually prepared, in a mental state of grace, so to speak. It so happens that the present writer does not believe that knowledge of Shaw's intellectual background is a prerequisite to the enjoyment of his plays in the theatre. And in print we have always the assistance of those cogent and ebullient prefaces . . . Perhaps the last words may be left to an unlikely advocate, Jorge Luis Borges:

> The collective and civic problems of his early works will lose their interest, or have lost it already; the jokes in the Pleasant Plays (*sic*) run the risk of becoming, some day, no less uncomfortable than those of Shakespeare . . . the ideas declared in his prologues (prefaces?) and his eloquent tirades will be found in Schopenhauer and Samuel Butler; but Lavinia, Blanco Posnet, Keegan, Shotover, Richard Dudgeon and, above all, Julius Caesar, surpass any character imagined by the art of our time. If we think of (Paul Valéry's) Monsieur Teste alongside them or Nietzsche's histrionic Zarathrustra, we can only perceive with astonishment and even outrage the primacy of Shaw . . . The

biography of Bernard Shaw by Frank Harris contains
an admirable letter by the former . . . "I understand everything and everyone and I am nothing and no one." From
this nothingness (so comparable to that of God before
creating the world, so comparable to that primordial divinity
which another Irishman, Johannes Scottus Eriugena, called
Nihil) Bernard Shaw educed almost innumerable persons or
dramatis personae: the most ephemeral of these is, I suspect, that G.B.S. who represented him in public and who
lavished in the newspaper columns so many facile witti-
cisms . . . The work of Shaw . . . leaves one with a flavour
of liberation, the flavour of the stoic doctrines and the
flavour of the sagas.

And to his references to Schopenhauer and Butler, Borges appends a
dazzling footnote: "In *Man and Superman* we read that hell is not a
penal establishment bur rather a state dead sinners elect for reasons
of intimate affinity, just as the blessed do with heaven; the treatise,
De Coelo et Inferno, by Swedenborg published in 1758, expounds
the same doctrine."[21] The encyclopaedic Borges has given us a formidable conspectus of the "Irish mind:" from Eriugena to Shaw.

II

Earlier in the year that Shaw inaugurated a native Ibsenite drama with
Widowers' Houses (1892), Oscar Wilde had his first great London
success on the stage with *Lady Windermere's Fan*. There will be more
to say about this and Wilde's other comedies later in this essay, but it
is first necessary to go back a decade and investigate what ideologies,
if any, preoccupied the younger Wilde. His mother, of course, had been
"Speranza" of *The Nation*, author of the inflammatory article in 1848
which led to the suppression of the magazine.[22] Such nationalist feeling as Wilde possessed came from her. The only substantial evidence
of attachment to nationalism as such is to be found in records of his
American lecture tour in 1882, just a decade before the three glorious
years that preceded the debacle of 1895. For instance in Chicago on
February 10, 1882 he is reported as saying: "Ireland is the Niobe
among nations. The noblest of materials for a great nation were there
wrecked by the folly of England."[23] More important is the lecture
he gave in San Francisco on April 5, on "The Irish Poets of '48" part of
which has been included by Mr Montgomery Hyde. "As regards the
men of '48, I look on their work with peculiar reverence and love, for
I was indeed trained by my mother to love and reverence them as a
Catholic child is the saints of the calendar." Whether this be sincere or
no, one cannot help noting the familiarity of the sentiments, which
might have come from any humble Catholic nationalist: the equation

of patriotism and religious fervour is an excessively common Irish trope. He goes on to pay tribute to William Smith O'Brien, John Mitchel and Charles Gavan Duffy, and of course to his mother. And he certainly knew his Irish-American audience when he came out with this splendid fustian:

> Indeed the poetic genius of the Celtic race never flags or wearies. It is as sweet by the groves of California as by the groves of Ireland, as strong in foreign lands as in the land which gave it birth. And indeed I do not know anything more wonderful, or more characteristic of the Celtic genius, than the quick artistic spirit in which we adapted outselves to the English tongue. The Saxon took our lands from us and left them desolate — we took their language and added new beauties to it.[24]

And while Wilde was spouting these callow nationalist sentiments for a fat fee, we may remember his junior by two years plunging into his twelve year career as a socialist orator for no fees at all, just about the same time.[25]

The juxtaposition may be fruitful since it high-lights two Dublin genuises at the inception of their careers, and reminds us that while Wilde's rhetorical nationalism blossomed and wilted very quickly, Shaw's, after the turn of the century, was to manifest itself in many modes, not least in *John Bull's Other Island*, both play and preface, albeit of a kind the natives did not know.

In 1880 Wilde had written his first play: *Vera* or *The Nihilists*. The American actor-manageress Marie Prescott put it on in New York in August 1883 and it was a total failure. But of interest is Wilde's own attitude to what was currently the red-hot subject of nihilism. He wrote to Marie Prescott:

> . . . I have tried to express within the limits of art that Titan cry of the peoples for liberty, which in the Europe of our day is threatening thrones, and making governments unstable from Spain to Russia and from north to southern seas. It deals with no theories of government, but with men and women simply; and modern nihilistic Russia . . . is merely the fiery and fervent background in front of which the persons of my dream live and love.[26]

Vera must be set aside as a work of art: but it has a curiosity value as evidence of Wilde's interest, in his twenties, in political heterodoxy, going hand in hand with his rebellion against artistic orthodoxy. We may even see in this interest in nihilism (or anarchy) a pointer towards the remarkable essay he was to publish in February 1891, "The Soul of Man Under Socialism". This is the text, some fourteen thousand words, which entitles Wilde to consideration as a serious political thinker. whether it be in the context of socialism, anarchy, or individualism. At time of publication, the Tory *Spectator* commentated: "The article, if serious, would be thoroughly unhealthy, but it leaves on us the impression of being written merely to startle and to excite talk." According to Robert Ross it was suggested by a lecture on Fabian socialism given some months before by Bernard Shaw at which Wilde spoke.[27] Possibly because of the unlikely authorship it was to attain widespread circulation: when in 1908 Robert Ross was honoured at a dinner on the occasion of the first collected edition of Wilde's writings, he could inform the audience that there were Chinese and Russian translations of *The Soul of man Under Socialism*, on sale in the bazaars of Nijni Novgorad.[28] Eight years later, in the course of defending Wilde against an attack by Alfred Douglas in his *Oscar Wilde and Myself* (1914) the German critic Ernst Bendz wrote: "I fancy there is just a chance that, when all the un-exhilarating lucubrations of a hundred well-meaning Sidney Webbs are long dead and forgotten, '*The Soul of Man*' will still be remembered and read, not for its magic of words only, but because, after another century or two has completed its course, poor incorrigible humanity will still be as hopefully yearning for and struggling towards those fortunate shores that Wilde has presented to us with intuitive and ideal truth."[29] This, I believe, has been so far the best formulated emotional reaction to *The Soul of Man*. A doctrinaire socialist reaction may be found in a letter written by the inferior American novelist Upton Sinclair to Frank Harris about the latter's biography of Wilde: "There is an essay of Wilde's which is extensively circulated in pamphlet form — *The Soul of Man under Socialism*. You do not mention it. We ought to know about it. Was it a youthful aberration? It is so utterly out of key with the rest of his early work. I, of course, would like to believe that it was an expression of his true self, before leisure-class society corrupted him."[30] This seems to me a cogent testimony to the conviction communicated in Wilde's essay, its fundamental gravity.

But *The Soul of Man under Socialism* may be viewed at its most significant from the points of view of both aesthetics and politics when we consider its importance for another great Dubliner, James Joyce, an importance carefully documented by Dominic Manganiello.[31] "If the only indication Joyce ever gave of a political outlook was with reference to Tucker,[32] he found the most complete expression of the anarchistic ideal for artists in Oscar Wilde's *The Soul of Man under Socialism*."[33] In 1909 Joyce considered Wilde's essay sufficiently important to warrant translation into Italian.[34] As Professor Manganiello suggests, "It may be argued that Wilde is speaking of socialism, not anarchism, but as Hesketh Pearson points out, Wilde's whole trend of thought was antagonistic to the Webb-Shavian, deification of the State."[35] Wilde is recorded as having in the 1890s in Paris declared himself to be an anarchist.[36] There is then the famous passage in *De Profundis*: "I hope to live long enough, and to produce work of such a character that I will be able at the end of my days to say 'Yes. This is just where the artistic life leads a man.' Two of the most perfect lives I have come across in my own experience are the lives of Verlaine and of Prince Kropotkin: both of them men who passed years in prison; the first, the one Christian poet since Dante; the other a man with the soul of the beautiful white Christ that seems coming out of Russia."[37] Wilde certainly had known Verlaine,[38] and "in my own experience" suggests that he had known Kropotkin, possibly through William Morris, who may even have introduced Kropotkin into *News from Nowhere* which was published in 1890, just before *The Soul of Man under Socialism*,[39] Kropotkin was to praise Morris's book as "perhaps the most thoroughly and deeply Anarchistic conception of future society that has ever been written."[40] But "Kropotkin viewed anarchism as a species of socialism and he, along with Bakunin and Proudhon, considered himself a socialist."[41] The fact that Wilde's essay followed so closely after Morris's book does not mean that we need entertain the possibility, given striking similarities in content, that Wilde dashed off his essay post-haste; almost certainly he would have read Morris's fantasy when it appeared earlier in serial form in *The Commonweal*, the weekly journal of the Socialist League which Morris had helped to found in 1884 after leaving the Social Democratic Foundations.[42] But if there are similarities in thought between *News from Nowhere* and Wilde's essay, it must not be forgotten that Morris's book is a utopian romance in form, while Wilde encapsules his reflections on socialism in the essay form as he had himself individualised it: conversational though elaborately mannered, epigrammatic and ironic. A few instances will suffice to illustrate Wilde's method. Having considered the evils of the system as it stands and the efforts by humanitarians to alleviate them, he concludes, "Charity creates a multitude of sins."[43] In a catherine-wheel of pseudo paradoxes he demolishes received opinion of the unprivileged:

> The virtues of the poor may be readily admitted and are much to be regretted . . . the best among the poor are never grateful. They are ungrateful, discontented, disobedient and rebellious. They are quite right to be so . . . Disobedience, in the eyes of anyone who has read history, is man's original virtue . . . As for the virtuous poor, one can pity them, of course, but one cannot possibly admire them.[44]

And so in a tone of voice easily recognisable as the tone used by Lord Henry Wotton in *The Picture of Dorian Gray* just about the same time, and to be used in the next four years by Lord Darlington in *Lady Windermere's Fan*, by Lord Illingworth in *A Woman of no Importance*, by Lord Goring in *An Ideal Husband* and by Algernon Moncrieff in

The Importance of Being Earnest, Wilde arrives at his devastating conclusion about the "virtuous" poor:

> They have made private terms with the enemy and sold their birthright for very bad pottage. They must also be extraordinarily stupid. I can quite understand a man accepting laws that protect private property, and admit of its accumulation, as long as he himself is able under these conditions to realize some form of beautiful and harmonious life. But it is almost incredible to me how a man whose life is marred and made hideous by such laws can possibly acquiesce in their continuance.[45]

Wilde is working up, enlisting on the way the precepts of Christ, often perhaps interpreted idiosyncratically, towards his notion of individualism. And it is to be attained through socialism. "As a natural result the State must give up all idea of government."[46] Wilde's description of the forms of despotism and his general exposition of the necessity for non-government probably influenced Joyce.[47] Wilde distinguished three kinds of "despot": "the prince" who tyrannises over the body, "the Pope" who tyrannises over soul, and "the People," that tyrannises over body and soul alike. "Wilde made explicit what is only implicit in Joyce."[48]

Wilde's essay concludes with a utopian vision:

> The new individualism, for whose service socialism, whether it wills or not, is working, will be perfect harmony. It will be what the Greeks sought for, but could not except in thought, realise completely because they had slaves, and fed them; it will be what the Renaissance sought for, but could not realise completely except in Art, because they had slaves and starved them. It will be complete, and through it each man will attain to his perfection. The new Individualism is the new Hellenism.[49]

The Soul of Man under Socialism was not, of course the "youthful aberration" supposed by Upton Sinclair: Wilde was just past thirty-six when he wrote it. But it does seem initially an unlikely work coming from him. It is only when reading passages such as those quoted above about the "virtuous" poor, "anarchic" statements even today, in the west or anywhere else, that one realises how much of the wit in the four West End comedies is "anarchic:" Those exquisite young noblemen (all of course projections of Wilde himself) do represent a threat to the *status quo*: they are anarchists in that laughingly they postulate overturning the values of the polite society in which they move.

In February 1893 *Salome* appeared, simultaneously in Wilde's original French and in the English version by Lord Alfred Douglas. This "Tragedy in One Act" is written, as Professor Kevin Sullivan has pointed

out, in "that curious jewelled style, vivid and obscure at once, full of
argot and archaisms . . ." which characterised the "poisonous book"
(the *A Rebours* of J.K. Huysmans) that so fascinated Dorian Gray.[50]
The importance of *Salome*, apart from the fact that it was to provide
a libretto for an opera by Richard Strauss (in 1905), may have been
sociological rather than literary or dramatic: the Lord Chamberlain
refused it a performing licence and further highlighted the absurdity of
British theatrical censorship.[51] It can only have been coincidence
that fourteen years later another Dublin dramatist, John Millington
Synge, should have spoken so disparagingly about Huysmans.

III

For their first season in May 1899 the Irish Literary Theatre gave
W.B. Yeats's *The Countess Cathleen* and Edward Martyn's *The Heather
Field*. By a curious coincidence, in Ireland at that stage, only the Catho-
lic landowner Martyn (1859-1924) and the Catholic undergraduate
James Joyce, who would publish an article the following year on Ibsen's
last play *When We Dead Awake* in the prestigious *Fortnightly Review*,
were declared Ibsenites. In October 1901 on the occasion of the Irish
Literary Theatre's third and last season which presented Yeats's and
George Moore's *Diarmuid and Grania* and Douglas Hyde's one-act
Casadh an tSúgáin, Joyce wrote an article, published in pamphlet
form, *The Day of the Rabblement*, in which he denounced the Irish
Literary Theatre as "the property of the rabblement of the most be-
lated race in Europe."[52] He considered the programme a surrender to
"the trolls" almost a direct insult "to the old master who is dying in
Christiania".[53] The three giants of the Abbey Theatre's first quarter
century, Yeats, Synge, and O'Casey were to be unaffected in their
practice by "the old master".[54] Synge indeed, is openly hostile to
Ibsen. This is on the evidence of two prefaces, the first to *The Playboy
of the Western World* dated January 21, 1907 (just before the play's
first production) and the second to *The Tinker's Wedding*, dated
December 2, 1907. (This play was however written originally "about
the time I was working at *Riders to the Sea* and *In the Shadow of the
Glen*" which would be circa 1902-3.[55] The preface to *The Playboy*
scarcely needs quoting . . . But it may be possible to gloss some of its
contents with rather a different emphasis than usual. In itself the preface is a fine, resonant, piece of prose, characterised though by those
noble, almost hieratic generalisations to be found unlimitedly in Yeats.
The sombre rhythms of the prose may lull the sympathetic reader
into acceptance of beautiful half-truths. "It is probable that when
the Elizabethan dramatist took his ink-horn and sat down to his work
he used many phrases that he had just heard, as he sat down at dinner,
from his mother or his children."[56] This romanticised picture of the

Elizabethan dramatist at work is not convincing: a working dramatist like Shakespeare or Ben Jonson, not to mention roisterers like Marlowe or Greene, are unlikely to have worked in the circumstances of easy domesticity evoked by Synge. Even if they did, there is no valid analogy with what Synge goes on to tell us. "In Ireland those of us who know the people have the same privilege. When I was writing *The Shadow of the ·Glen*, some years ago, I got more aid than any learning could have given me from a chink in the floor of the old Wicklow house where I was staying, that let me hear what was being said by the servant girls in the kitchen."[57] This reader has no inclination to sneer at the inevitable image of Synge on his hunkers with his ear to the ground. But there is a world of difference between the putative Elizabethan after-dinner playwright and the turn of the nineteenth century eavesdropper. His next point is valid in a limited way: "in countries where the imagination of the people, and the language they use, is rich and living, it is possible for a writer to be rich and copious in his words, and at the same time to give the reality, which is the root of all poetry, in a comprehensive and natural form."[58] But its validity is sapped when he goes on: "In the modern literature of towns, however, richness is found only in sonnets, or in one or two elaborate books that are far away from the profound and common interests of life. We have, on one side, Mallarme and Huysmans producing this literature; and on the other, Ibsen and Zola dealing with reality in joyless and pallid works."[59] That imposing phrase "the profound and common interests of life" means virtually nothing unless Synge is proposing the intolerable doctrine that only among peasants with a rich folk-speech can the texture of the human condition be found in its authenticity, and that there is no way in which the artist can render that texture by subtle, oblique, or glancing means. By reducing Mallarme (the most esoteric instance in modern European poetry he could find) he is reducing the whole symbolist movement in poetry, which of course embraced the work of his friend, mentor and senior by only six years, W.B. Yeats. Further generalisations, however high sounding, are quite as vulnerable. "On the stage one must have reality, and one must have joy; and that is why the modern intellectual drama has failed." One is reluctant to say it but only a strangely provincial or obsessed mind could conceive of Ibsen, Chekov, Strindberg, or indeed Shaw as early as 1907, as having "failed". "In a good play every speech should be as fully flavoured as a nut or an apple..."[61] To which some critics might reply that if that indisputable masterpiece *The Playboy* has a weakness it is in its "over-flavouring", its surplus of nuts and apples.

In the preface to *The Tinker's Wedding*, dated some ten months later, Synge is even more intransigent about "the intellectual modern drama". "We should not go to the theatre," he pronounces, "as we go to a chemist's or a dram-shop but as we go to a dinner where the food we need is taken with pleasure and excitement. This was nearly always so in Spain, England and France when the drama was at its richest – the infancy and decay of the drama tend to be didactic – but in these days the playhouse is too often stocked with the drugs of many seedy problems."[62] The alert reader must ask what the problems of Hamlet or the Phèdre of Racine or the Cipriano of Calderon in *El Magico Prodigioso* are, if not "seedy", if "seedy" implies issues of good and evil and delving into "the foul rag-and-bone shop of the heart". He may also ask whether *Oedipus Rex* represents "the decay" of Greek drama and if it be "didactic" or not. Just how short-sighted Synge could be may be seen in a further passage: "The drama, like the symphony, does not teach or prove anything. Analysts with their problems, and teachers with their systems, are soon as old-fashioned as the pharmocopoeia of Galen – look at Ibsen and the Germans – but the best plays of Ben Jonson and Moliere can no more go out of fashion, than the blackberries on the hedges."[63] Even as I write the Abbey Theatre is preparing a productions of Ibsen. As Mícheál Ó hAodha has pointed out, Nora in *In* Ibsen had achieved what was in effect the true glory of Ibsenism, "the writing of a major serious play in simple prose, employing characters who were not kings and princesses, nor even Capulets and Montagues, but ordinary people called Mr and Mrs such as might live next door."[64]

The curious anomaly in Synge's attitude towards Ibsen is that his own plays should have provoked initially audience and journalistic reactions not dissimilar from those provoked by the first London productions of Ibsen. As Mícheál Ó hAodha has pointed out, Nora in *In The Shadow of the Glen* (which outraged nationalists, including Arthur Griffith, widely read enough to know better, and Maud Gonne, who outside Ireland had clearly been sexually emancipated in the fullest sense) "is a more modern woman than Ibsen's Nora in *A Doll's House.'*[65] One could go further and say that if we clear our minds of nuts, apples, blackberries and the like, Pegeen Mike in *The Playboy* is in respects as Ibsenite (or even Schopenhauerian!) as Ann Whitefield in *Man and Superman,* which preceded Synge's play by a few years. There is no question but that she makes the running, initially, in the relationship with Christy Mahon. In her father's house she is the dominant figure, and in so far as she can be in her particular circumstances, she is an emancipated woman, scorning male strictures and subservience to clerical ordinance. And in the splendid assertiveness of Synge's Deirdre (in the unfinished *Deirdre of the Sorrows)* we may find traces (they are to be found of course in the Irish original of the tale) of, of all possible heroines, Ibsen's Hedda Gabler.

"The drama, like the symphony does not teach or prove anything." In so far as Synge's theatre is conspicuously apolitical this statement holds true. At a time when nationalism, in varying shades of green, some dashed with socialistic red and some with ecclesiastical purple, was very much on display in the market-place and the dram-shops, in numerous short-lived periodicals and the activities of the Gaelic Athletic

Association founded in 1884 and the Gaelic League founded in 1893, Synge held aloof. So far as he was concerned, Yeats's *Cathleen Ni Houlihan* might never have been staged in 1902, the year before his own first play *In the Shadow of the Glen* ruffled nationalist susceptibilities.

IV

"The old master" does crop up in relation to Sean O'Casey: still, arguably, the greatest of the dramatists cradled by the Abbey after Synge, but, in complete contrast to him, one who did not stand aloof from contemporary movements in politics. But the acknowledgement of Ibsen occurs only when Boyle the self-styled "Captain" of *Juno and the Paycock* (1924) comes upon a volume of Ibsen being read by his daughter Mary: "three stories, *The Doll's House, Ghosts,* an' *The Wild Duck* – buks only fit for chiselurs!" This Ibsen reference makes for more than an ironic joke: it is significant that Ibsen should be considered an essential part of the self-education of an ardent girl trade unionist from the slums of the Dublin 1920s.[66] There is more than ample documentation in the six volumes of his *Autobiography* (1939-54) and the two volumes so far published of his *Letters* to establish, outside the texts of his plays, that O'Casey from an early stage was a socialist-communist.[67] Jack Lindsay has singled out his resignation in October 1914 from the secretaryship of the Irish Citizen Army as a turning-point: the subsequent alliance of the Army with the Irish Volunteers O'Casey clearly foresaw. He was committed to the working-class cause but not willing to take part in what was essentially a middle-class revolution, the Rising of Easter 1916.[68] O'Casey's first three major plays *The Shadow of a Gunman* (1923), *Juno and the Paycock* (1924) and *The Plough and the Stars* (1926) were written extraordinarily close to the periods they imaginatively portray. Even in Ireland these periods tend to be confused in the minds of younger generations. The first deals with an episode during the Black and Tan stage of the War of Independence (1919-21), the second with events during the Civil War (1922-23) and the third, going furthest backward in time, with the events of Easter Week 1916. The title of this last play refers to the flag of the Irish Citizen Army, the labour leader James Connolly's relatively tiny army of workers. Sean O'Faolain has described O'Casey's early plays as "an exactly true statement of the Irish revolution whose flag should be, not tricolour, but the plough and the stars of the labouring classes." But, he continues, a labouring class did not come to power. It was in the event, as O'Casey recognised, a petit bourgeois revolution, and as Sean O'Faolain put it, "The upshot of it was the holy alliance between church, the new businessman, and the politicians."[69] Whereas for O'Casey, "My sympathies were always with the rags and tatters that sheltered the tenement – living temples of the Holy Ghost."[70]

There is no overt socialist critique in *The Shadow:* beyond perhaps the implication of moral inadequacy in the poet Donal Davoren, who quotes Shelley and paraphrases Shaw, but whose conduct in the face of arrest and possible death is no better or worse than that of the pedlar Seamus Shields (who quotes Shakespeare readily: perhaps poet and pedlar are aspects of two kinds of Irishman. Davoren is a sentimental socialist, Shields a superstitious and reactionary Catholic, for all his drollery). *Juno,* we can see now, quite clearly embodies a critique of economic conditions and their consequences for the dignity of human beings. The heroism of "Juno" Boyle is patent. She is the eternal slum mother, compounded of Erda and Anna Livia. Less patent are the incorrigible selfishness and moral coarseness of her "Paycock" husband, for the eminently good reason that he makes us laugh. The characters in *Juno* are not of course ever aware that they are actors on a world scene. But Boyle's famous curtain line, "I'm telling you ...Joxer... th' whole worl's... in a terr...ible state o'...chassis," must be seen as more than the cliche lamentation of a drunk. Given what has gone before, the revelation of Mary Boyle's pregnancy and the puritanical reaction of Boyle (and of her brother Johnny), Johnny's abduction by Irregulars (anti-Treatyites) with the appalling inquiry as a prelude to murder, "Have you your beads?" (This, so far as I know, never disturbs Irish audiences, long conditioned to the conjunction of violence and religious devotion), and the general disintegration of the Boyle family, that last line stands out as a ferocious indictment of a world where human dignity counts for nothing.

The comedic characters in *The Plough* are perhaps more salvageable than those in *Juno.* But the play is as much a depiction of chaos, of "chassis". Act II, set in a pub, perhaps gives us the fullest index to maelstrom. Wonderful and desperately human wrangling goes on while outside, a speaker gives us extracts from Pearse's oration at the grave of O'Donovan Rossa and also from an article he published in *Spark,* December 1915, called "Peace and the Gael". O'Casey culled from it the passage in which Pearse declares, "The old heart of the earth needed to be warmed with the red blood of the battle fields... Such august homage was never offered to God as this: the homage of millions of lives given gladly for love of country."[71] That statement, since it explicitly equates death in war "for love of country" with "homage" to the Almighty, is perhaps more crucial to Act II's overall significance than the passages from the Rossa speech. The Speaker's rhetoric and the several mini-wars of words in the pub (including that between the half-baked Marxist, the Young Covey, and the old-style nationalist Uncle Peter) make for an ironic counterpoint: dialogue and situation constitute O'Casey's first major pacifist statement. With hindsight we can see that it was on the cards that O'Casey would write an out-and-out anti-war play: which he did with *The Silver Tassie* (1928). While some of the characters in *The Plough* exhibit a kind of flawed nobility under stress — Fluther Good, Bessie Burgess — there is no nobility evident in *The Tassie* where even maternal, let alone conjugal love, is unmasked in the fairy light of separation allowances. Part of the harsh sadness of the physical and consequent spiritual mutilation of the hero Harry Heegan arises from the fact that he has confronted the actuality of war and returned to a society "in which civilians, in whom the springs of imaginative imagination have long since dried, if ever they existed, are now cocooned in their private fantasies, locked in themselves, and so, by the ethic of O'Casey, humanly half-dead, less alive in fact than Harry; who is paralysed from the waist down."[72] Although O'Casey in *The Silver Tassie* has broadened his expositional technique (by way, of the expressionistic Act II which employs chant, repetition of catch lines, and other devices of the period) he maintains the method of the earlier so-called "naturalistic plays", achieving his effects by the juxtaposition of the grave and the farcical, the clownish and the heroic. And in all four mentioned the message is clearly pacifist: war, of any kind, entails the destruction of the innocent and the possible corruption of the living, and as much moral poltroonery and spiritual meanness as it does occasional grandeur of conduct.

It is not until *The Star Turns Red* (1940) that we find O'Casey as explicitly a propagandist of Marxist revolution. This is one of the more difficult of the later plays since, inevitably, its reception will be coloured by the political orientations of audience, or reader. In it O'Casey strives to create a massive allegory which embraces his thinking on the Dublin strike of 1913, the 1917 Russian Revolution and the Spanish Civil War. While at times the play is cumbersome, even jejeune, its cumulative effect is powerful, leading up to the apocalyptic climax when the star of Bethlehem turns, literally, red, and the revolution begins just as the fatuous lord mayor and his wife are preparing for a Christmas Eve reception for the local notabilities, while somewhere off stage the poor are being entertained to tea (dispensed from a giant watering can, with another such can "of beautiful boiling water... to stretch out the lovely tea").[73] Although *The Star Turns Red* is as close as any Irish dramatist ever came to an explicitly communist play, the very fact that it is set during the last hours of Christmas Eve has immense qualificatory significance. Clearly O'Casey has a vision, however muddled, of a synthesis between communism and Christianity. His position might be summed-up as follows: basically communism is more Christian than institutional Christianity and the message of pristine Christianity is revolutionary. The expansion of the International is the expansion of the kingdom of God on earth: a naive concept, perhaps, but so far as I know O'Casey is the only dramatist in the English-speaking theatre to explore its theatrical possibilities.

I have touched on only about a third of O'Casey's dramatic output: *Red Roses for Me* (1942) for instance might be examined as a socialist play, as indeed might *Within the Gates* (1933). But no sane reading of

O'Casey can gainsay that he is of an ideological piece, while contriving to remain always different in his successive attempts to strip the comic mask he has himself imposed on apathy and the petrifaction of true feeling. Like all the greatest Irish dramatists he is concerned with the authenticity of feeling: like Shaw who had so much heart (as may be seen in *Heartbreak House* and *Saint Joan* for instance) for all that his mind might be crackling with Schopenhauer's *The World as Will and Understanding* and Nietzsche's *Thus Spake Zarathustra*, like Synge, caught up in his stark yet fantastic isolationist dream, like Wilde even, of whom it might be argued that the spangled epigrams were his defensive ammunition against the kind of world he rejected in *The Soul of Man Under Socialism*.

The two most famous Irish dramatists since the Second World War, indeed since O'Casey, have been Samuel Beckett and Brendan Behan, two very dissimilar manifestations of the Irish mind in the theatre. Beckett's *Waiting for Godot* appeared first in French in 1953 and has been followed by a numerous string of pieces for stage and radio, in both French and English originals. He who was once a nine-days' wonder, according to some is now a classic: probing ever more minutely into the feeling of *being*, and paring away ever more scrupulously at his findings. When we grow impatient with the more extreme instances of Beckett's investigation of being, let us remember how much he has given us of pity, if not of terror, by way of plangent, almost Virgilian shorthand dialogue, if not of the rhetorics which are the especial glory of Shaw, Synge and O'Casey. Shaw of course was scarcely palatable sustenance in a country that has managed only two internationally recognised philosophers, with some thousand years between them, the old Eriugena on our five-pound notes, and George Berkeley. His only heirs as a disputative dramatist have been Denis Johnston (born 1901), Conor Cruise O'Brien (born 1917) and Brian Friel (born 1929).[74] Synge's only heir of platinum quality has been the Kerry folk dramatist, George Fitzmaurice (1877–1963).[75] Fitzmaurice, though, is no trailer after Synge. His folk idiom is unmistakably his own and his imagination giddy and acerb. Brendan Behan (1923–64) must stand or fall on the strength of *The Quare Fellow* (1954) and *The Hostage* (1958). He may be said to have been influenced by O'Casey in his commingling of clownery and pathos: both owe much to the tradition of Dion Boucicault (as indeed does Shaw in such a play as *The Devil's Disciple*). For all their palpable faults, Behan's two plays are almost frantically alive, beakers of the tears and vomit and guffaws of an outsize personality with a just barely shielded soft centre.

It is worth noting that in the living theatre, as distinct from the study and the lecture-hall, Irish dramatists may survive this century on the strength of a comparatively small body of work, if we reckon from the 1890s: *The Importance of Being Earnest* from Wilde, *The Playboy* from Synge (and *Riders to the Sea), Purgatory* and *The Words Upon*

The Windowpane from Yeats, two or three pieces from O'Casey, *Waiting for Godot*... A respectable enough collection. But if put beside the *Collected Poems* of Yeats and the *Ulysses* of Joyce and a body of fiction embracing the best of O'Flaherty, O'Faolain, and Stuart and Flann O'Brien . . . Dare it be questioned that it is in the theatre that the Irish mind best expresses itself? Is it a preposterous notion to consider how our theatre might have developed had Swift written for the stage?... And it may well be that the Irish are a race of actors, producing instant theatre in the process of stravaiging from the cradle to the grave.

Elizabeth Cullingford

THE UNKNOWN THOUGHT
OF W.B. YEATS

As long as we stay at home we are usually unconscious of our national identity: the experience of exile is the beginning of cultural self-consciousness. To Yeats this experience came early, for he spent much of his adolescence in England, and was "called names for being Irish".[1] The insensitivity of his schoolmates aroused in the young poet a defensive patriotism that expressed itself in a longing for the hills and lakes of his beloved Sligo, and was initially unconnected with Irish political grievances. No matter where Yeats later made his home, the ideal Ireland of his imagination was always the west. Dublin, scene of his most memorable conflicts, the "unmannerly town"[2] of journalists, politicians, and bigoted Catholic priests, was the intellectual irritant that produced many a pearl, but never a spiritual home. Yeats hoped to find his audience in Sligo: an ideal audience embodied in the fisherman wearing "grey Connemara cloth"[3] and climbing a lonely hill at dawn.

Connacht must therefore be the starting point for any exploration of Yeat's beliefs. His dislike of the modern world was born in the process of comparison between rural Sligo and "this hateful London",[4] where his alienation was so acute that "I longed for a sod of earth from some field I knew, something of Sligo to hold in my hand."[5] London epitomised modern industrial and technological progress: it was soullessly ugly. Nature in Connacht, on the other hand, was not merely beautiful: it was divine. Discussing "On the Study of Celtic Literature" Yeats redefined Arnold's terms: the "natural magic" which Arnold thought distinctively Celtic was simply "the ancient religion of the world, the ancient worship of Nature . . . that certainty of all beautiful places being haunted."[6] Yeats saw the peasantry of Sligo, uncorrupted by modern civilisation, as inheritors of this primitive animistic religion. Nature for him was never "landscape" or "scenery": it was a mysterious source of ecstasy, pregnant with symbols. This romantic apprehension of his surroundings predisposed him to reject any view of the natural world as inert, dead matter governed by inexorable mechanical laws.

The fairy stories of the west, which Yeats heard in his childhood and collected as a young man, were to determine the course of his intellectual development. Belief in the apparitions of folk tales sent him to mediums in Soho and Indian swamis, to miraculous Catholic oleographs and to automatic writing. He read Swedenborg's *Spiritual Diary* and compared its account of the world of spirits with Irish peasant stories and with his own experiences in the seance room. During these researches, he .wrote, "I was discovering a philosophy".[7] All his life Yeats continued to search for a system of thought which might accommodate his early belief in a supernatural world, while satisfying the demands of his powerful, even sceptical mind.

Yeats's scepticism was perhaps inherited from his father, J.B. Yeats, a militant atheist who always disapproved of his son's mysticism. His father's influence, combined with his own early and shortlived passion for Darwinian natural history, deprived the young poet of traditional religious belief. He soon grew to hate science "with a monkish hate"[8] and determined to construct a new religion, yet he retained a lifelong tendency to demand scientific proof of the authenticity of spiritual or psychic manifestations. "Am I a mystic?" he asked Ethel Mannin in 1938, "no, I am a practical man. I have seen the raising of Lazarus and the loaves and fishes and have made the usual measurements, plummet line, spirit-level and have taken the temperature by pure mathematic."[9] Yeats was at once the most credulous of sceptics and the most sceptical of believers.

His attitude towards the intellect itself was similarly paradoxical. His early education, dominated by his father and disrupted by frequent moves, was extremely patchy and unsystematic. It left Yeats with a conviction of his own mental inferiority, and an intense ambivalence about intellectual matters. He was naturally drawn towards philosophy, but ashamed of the predilection: he was "full of thought, often very abstract thought, longing all the while to be full of images, because I had gone to the art schools instead of a university."[10] So sternly did he repress his tendency to abstraction that his early poetry was, he later felt, spoilt by sentimentality "through my refusal to permit it any share of an intellect which I considered impure."[11] This clash between his delight in speculation and his commitment to immediate sensations was only one of the conflicts out of which his later philosophy was to emerge.

His reaction to the influence of J.B. Yeats, for example, was also divided. As a young man he rebelled against his father's atheism by absorbing himself in magic, yet he could later acknowledge "how fully my philosophy of life has been inherited from you."[12] When J.B. Yeats read poetry aloud to his son he denounced intellect and praised emotion, choosing only intense and dramatic passages. He did not "care at all for poetry where there was generalization or abstraction" nor "even for a fine lyric passage unless he felt some actual man behind its elaboration of beauty."[13] His emphasis upon the particular and the individual, in life as in poetry, issued in his son's cult of personality. W.B.

Yeats even went so far as to conclude that "all sound philosphy is but biography"[14] and that history is a "human drama".[15] Abstractions like "philosophy" and "history" were vivified for Yeats only as they revealed the thoughts and actions of particular men. In "The Municipal Gallery Revisited" he invites his readers to

> . . . come to this hallowed place
> Where my friends' portraits hang and look thereon;
> Ireland's history in their lineaments trace.[16]

J.B. Yeats's emphasis upon individuality, intensity, and the superiority of feeling over reason, prepared his son to accept the premises of romanticism. Yeats's own passion for Shelley and Blake did the rest. The philosophical basis of the romantic movement can be traced at least partly to its opposition to the assumptions of mechanistic science. Against the Newtonian universe of dead matter in perpetual motion, determined by natural laws and inhospitable to the concept of free will, the Romantics set an organic universe. "Romantic philosophy sought to explain all phenomena, including so-called dead matter, by freedom, by conscious or unconscious mental processes, and by the analogy of organisms."[17] The romantic poets offered Yeats a world in which nature was alive with divine significance, in which mental events were as important as physical ones, and where truth belonged to the symbolic imagination, not to logicians or mathematicians. Romantic subjectivity exalted the freedom of the individual soul, and one of Yeats's overriding passions was the passion for liberty.

Yeats's romanticism, therefore, harmonised perfectly with his nationalism. Irish liberty became, after his meeting with the old Fenian John O'Leary and his study of Thomas Davis, one of his major intellectual preoccupations. Late in life he remembered how he had sought to unify his three most important interests: literature, nationalism, and philosophy. A declaration published in 1888 suggests that they were always inter-linked:

> To the greater poets everything they see has its relation to the national life, and through that to the universal and divine life . . . But to this universalism . . . you can only attain through what is near you, your nation, or, if you be no traveller, your village and the cobwebs on your walls. You can no more have the greater poetry without a nation than religion without symbols. One can only reach out to the universe with a gloved hand — that glove is one's nation, the only thing one knows even a little of.[18]

Yeats's appeal to particular Irish experience as the basis of his knowledge of divinity demonstrates the philosophical foundation of his nationalism. It also reveals his preference for inductive procedures. The *a priori* truths of logic and mathematics seemed to him cold abstractions which denied the uniqueness of the individual. "Two and two must make four," he wrote in disgust, "though no two things are alike."[19] Logic, often symbolised in his verse as a hawk, is clearly inferior to intuition, for

> . . . wisdom is a butterfly
> And not a gloomy bird of prey.[20]

The romantic nature of Yeats's nationalism is revealed in his conception of the Irish character: one which is in keeping with the idealised pastoral landscape of his own early verse and with the myths engendered by a long and bitter political history. Arnold's epigraph, "They went forth to the war but they always fell," became Yeats's proof of Irish nobility. In the light of Ireland's history before 1922 it might be said that Yeats was making a virtue of necessity, but a more important reason for his emphasis upon defeat and tragedy can be found in his association of intellectual, scientific, and political success with Ireland's oppressor, England. This success was not one which Yeats wished Ireland to share. The revolt against the "despotism of fact" which Arnold thought characteristic of the Irish imagination was, for Yeats, also a revolt against the despotism of English materialism and the despotism of English rule in Ireland. He therefore emphasised all those Celtic qualities which contrasted most strongly with the stolid, unimaginative, logical, prosaic character of the Anglo-Saxons. Ireland is "poetic, passionate, remembering, idyllic, fanciful, and always patriotic."[21] The Irish are described as intense, reckless, violent, energetic, and irresponsible, and also as dreamy, spiritual, solitary, and imaginative, for "in Ireland this world and the other are not widely sundered."[22] Yeats was aware that this characterisation failed to include a large proportion of his countrymen, but he argued that the Irish adoption of the spirit of "the Great Comedian"[23] Daniel O'Connell—bluff good humour, compromise, practicality—was an aberration. Under the shadow of the tragic Parnell Ireland would return to her true identity, and Yeats would make her a holy city in the imagination.

Yeats's early experiences and affinities were all important in the development of his mature philosophy, but his convictions were not absolute, or consistently expressed. His father thought that a poet should be free to believe in marriage in the morning and to reject that belief in the evening, and Yeats found within his own complex character ample evidence for a philosophy of life based upon paradox and conflict. The influence of Blake was seminal, and Blake taught him that "without contraries is no progression". "Propositions," Yeats wrote, "which set all the truth upon one side can only enter rich minds to dislocate and strain, if they can enter at all, and sooner or later the mind expels them by instinct."[24] The romantic proposition that the intellect is always inferior to the emotions was no exception to this rule. As he matured, Yeats discovered that he could become a metaphysician without sacrificing his grasp of concrete, sensuous experience, and that he must express the whole man, emotion and intellect combined.

His metaphysics, however, had as their object not the discovery of new truths, but the philosophical confirmation of old ones, for Yeats was convinced that "our intellects at twenty contain all the truths we shall ever find."[25] In his twenties Yeats was a romantic, a nationalist, an occultist, and an anti-materialist. His intellectual development consisted largely in his discovery of authorities, Irish, European, and Indian, who reinforced his first intuitions and helped him to understand and systematise them. "We do not," he wrote in 1930, "seek truth in argument or in books but clarification of what we already believe."[26] The concept of disinterested inquiry was foreign to Yeats's nature: his own experience had provided him with certain evidence, and he set out to discover an explanatory theory. T. Sturge Moore wrote to the poet in some exasperation: "I think you misunderstand my brother [G.E. Moore] . . . because you are interested in finding an imagined hypothesis which will reconcile certain strange facts."[27] Contempt for the "strange facts"—the supernatural manifestations of seances and peasant tales—has led many of Yeats's critics to dismiss his hypotheses as nonsense. Yet Yeats's philosophy represents the response of a powerful, complex, and subtle Irish mind to the problems of the modern world.

Yeats's interest in the fairy and folk tales of Connacht, for example, seemed merely silly to W.H. Auden.[28] Yeats, however, transformed childhood superstition into an object of serious research when in 1899 he began collecting and transcribing peasant stories. The publication of Frazer's *Golden Bough* in 1890 stimulated widespread curiosity about primitive myth: Yeats had read Frazer, and had long been familiar with the heroic sagas of ancient Ireland. The difference between Yeats and Frazer, it may be argued, is that Frazer writes as a critical investigator, while Yeats takes his Irish material literally. Yet both Yeats and Frazer are searching for the universal patterns which can be discerned in magical practices and marvellous tales: attempting to separate the myth from the trivia. Yeats had learned from Blake that "All Religions are One," and it was at the mythical level that such a statement might be demonstrably true.

Yeats therefore constructed his own religion out of

> a fardel of stories, and of personages, and of emotions, inseparable from their first expression, passed on from generation to generation by poets and painters with some help from philosophers and theologians. . . I had even created a dogma: "Because those imaginary people are created out of the deepest instinct of man, to be his measure and his norm, whatever I can imagine those mouths speaking may be the nearest I can go to truth."[29]

He was seeking in myth, folktale, and literature a truth which belongs to instinctive emotion, rather than to rational intellect, and which is valid for all men at all moments in history. Literature expresses and preserves these truths of the mythical imagination: "norm" and "measure" are found in the personalities of story, drama, and poem, not among the abstractions of conventional philosophy or mathematics. When Yeats listened to what these imaginary personalities had to say, "they seemed always to speak of one thing only: they, their loves, every incident of their lives, were steeped in the supernatural."[30]

Yeats's absorption in the supernatural, like his interest in the primitive, was widely shared. In the last half of the nineteenth century the decay of traditional religion and the dominance of the scientific world view led to a reactive upsurge of interest in psychical research. In 1887 Yeats attached himself to one of this movement's most dubious leaders, the Theosophist Madame Blavatsky. His attitude to this extraordinary lady, however, was coolly sensible. He admired her forceful personality, her dislike of both abstract idealism and scientific materialism, and her encyclopaedic knowledge of world religion; but he remained sceptical about her "manifestations". He took from Theosophy an introduction to the occult tradition, but kept himself aloof from the cranks who swarmed around its high priestess.

Madame Blavatsky, like Blake, believed that all religions are one; her book, *The Secret Doctrine*, revealed their ancient common foundation. She taught that existence is cyclical, and that life consists of opposites in conflict. Like Yeats's Indian friend, the Brahmin Mohini Chatterji, she believed in reincarnation. Her God was omnipresent and eternal, but completely unknowable.[31] As a symbolist poet Yeats was attracted by the doctrine of correspondences elaborated by the Esoteric Section of the Theosophical Society: "The seven principles which made the human soul and body corresponded to the seven colours and the planets and the notes of the musical scale."[32] Although it may vary in its details the idea of correspondences is prominent in most occult schools of thought, including astrology, alchemy, and the Kabbalah. Apparently disparate objects and emotions are organically linked: the world is pattern, not chaos, and the pattern is apprehended through symbols. Yeats, however, was not content with the "abstraction of what were called 'esoteric teachings'."[33] "I was always longing for evidence", he wrote;[34] and began a series of practical experiments. As a result of some charming attempts to evoke the spirits of burnt flowers, he was expelled from the Esoteric Section of the Theosophical Society. It was not to be the last time that his desire for scientific proof was to collide with the susceptibilities of true believers.

After leaving the Theosophists Yeats joined the Hermetic Order of the Golden Dawn, to which he belonged from 1890 to 1922. This order, which Yeats took intensely seriously, combined ideas and rituals drawn from Kabbalism, Rosicrucianism, and Christianity.[35] One of its founders, MacGregor Mathers, taught Yeats "a form of meditation that has perhaps been the intellectual chief influence on my life up to perhaps my fortieth year."[36] Fixing his attention upon a coloured geometric symbol Yeats would pass into a state of reverie during which certain correspondent images would arise in the mind's eye. From these experiences Yeats evolved a "magical philosophy" with three central doctrines, which he laid out in his 1903 essay, "Magic":

> 1. That the borders of our minds are ever shifting, and that many minds can flow into one another, as it were, and create or reveal a single mind, a single energy.
> 2. That the borders of our memories are as shifting, and that our memories are a part of one great memory, the memory of Nature herself.
> 3. That this great mind and great memory can be evoked by symbols.[37]

Yeats used this theory of the great mind and great memory to explain events as disparate as telepathy, the appearance of ghosts, and the nestbuilding instincts of canaries. Against the Lockean *tabula rasa*, the isolated infant mind clean as a blank sheet of paper, Yeats sets the mind shaped by, and still in contact with, the accumulated experience of the generations. Pre-natal memory, like Plato's assertion that all knowledge is recollection, also supports the doctrine of reincarnation. The *Anima Mundi* is not a reality outside of, or transcending, man; it is the sum of human wisdom, to which the individual gains access through the symbols of dream and reverie, or through deliberate magical invocation. We are thus organically linked to each other, to the dead, and to our former and future selves: the history of the world is a stream of souls, not a catalogue of facts. Yeats's doctrines were designed to challenge the prevailing scientific undervaluation of consciousness. According to the mechanical theory, the body functions like an engine, and its movements are produced by the natural laws which govern material things. Consciousness, accordingly, is no more than Ryle's "ghost in the machine". Yeats set out to reverse this assumption. If scientific materialism views consciousness as a sort of accidental by-product of physical events, Yeats elevates it into the determining principle of existence. The ghost takes over the machine. In 1903 he was not yet ready to assert that the ghost creates the machine, or that the machine does not exist, but his speculations on the *Anima Mundi* were leading him in that direction.

If Yeats's interest in the mythical content of folklore links him with Frazer, his belief in the *Anima Mundi* offers a striking parallel with Jung's concept of the collective unconscious. Although the mutual influence between poet and psychologist was non-existent, both posited the existence of a myth-creating substratum of the mind which finds expression through archetypal symbolism. Like Yeats, Jung was receptive to supernatural experience, worked with mediums, and investigated eastern philosophies. He too saw life as a conflict of opposites, viewing sexuality as the union of opposing principles, and therefore as a symbol of wholeness. His theory of the persona reflects Yeats's concept of the mask. Mandalas resemble the coloured geometric patterns upon which Yeats meditated, as well as some of the diagrams from *A Vision*. Jung's interest in alchemy led him to the tradition of "heterodox mysticism" which began with Plato's *Timaeus* and with the neo-Platonists. James Olney attributes the remarkable similarity between the world views of Yeats and Jung to the fact that they were both students of this tradition.[38]

If Yeats's relation to Jung was a question of affinity rather than influence, he was more directly affected by the writings of the German philosopher Friedrich Nietzsche, whom he first read in 1902. His enthusiasm for the "strong enchanter"[39] was immense, but he welcomed Nietzsche more as confirmation than as revelation. He "completes Blake and has the same roots".[40] His thought "flows always, though with an even more violent current, in the bed Blake's thought has worn."[41] Despite these statements, Denis Donoghue argues that the influence of Blake is "questionable",[42] while "the crucial figure in Yeats's poetic life, if any single figure may be named, is Nietzsche, and . . . the definition of Yeats's mind in theatrical terms was achieved mainly under Nietzsche's auspices."[43] He overemphasises this "single figure": it might, for example, be reasonable to suppose that the definition of Yeats's mind in theatrical terms had something to do with his long career as playwright and director of the Abbey Theatre. He also dismisses Blake too swiftly, and in the teeth of Yeats's own testimony. The idea that consciousness is dramatic conflict came to Yeats from many sources besides Nietzsche.

Without overstressing Nietzsche's importance, however, we may recognise how congenial Yeats found his thought. Cursed by a natural timidity and awkwardness, the poet spent much of his youth attempting to create a personality that would be powerful, self-confident, and self-controlled. He was "one that ruffled in a manly pose/For all his timid heart,"[44] forcing himself to make political speeches and to seek out testing social occasions. Yeats found philosophical justification for this role-playing, this attempt to become his opposite, in the paradoxes of his friend Oscar Wilde, whose sanctification of the "pose" had impressed him before he read the German philosopher. Acquaintance with Nietzsche confirmed his preference for a life lived heroically, in defiance of the given facts of character and environment. The creation of a mask is evidence of a Nietzschean "will to power" – the conquest, however, is primarily the conquest of self. The will chooses, according to Yeats, "whatever whim's most difficult/ Among whims not impossible",[45] because only the greatest obstacle that can be envisaged without despair rouses a man to full intensity. The transformation of the self, goal alike of the alchemists and of Jungian psychoanalysis, is such a Herculean labour.

Yeats was undoubtedly also interested in political power, and adopted in some measure Nietzsche's admiration of the hero and dislike of men in the mass. Annotations to a volume of selections, however, show Yeats modifying Nietzsche's harshness. He stresses that the "self must give to the selfless and weak or itself perish or suffer diminution."[46] He insists that "In the last analysis the 'noble' man will serve . . . the weak as much as the 'good' man."[47] Yeats was still too near to the social idealism of his early mentor William Morris to dispense altogether with concern for those who are not heroes.

Yeats was closest to Nietzsche as the prophet of eternal recurrence and the advocate of tragic gaiety in the face of ruin. According to Nietzsche, Greek tragedy expresses a will to life which transcends the pain it depicts. It does not purge the onlooker of pity and terror, but forces him to realise in himself the joy of eternal becoming, which includes the joy of destruction. This emotion is possible because destruction implies new birth: existence is cyclical and all events recur an infinite number of times. As Yeats put it:

> All things fall and are built again,
> And those that build them again are gay.[48]

The doctrine of eternal recurrence was not new to Yeats, but Nietzsche's heroic, tragic gaiety was different from the glummer speculations of the Theosophists. When Yeats writes, "We begin to live when we have conceived life as tragedy,"[49] we may trace the tone of proud jubilation directly to Nietzsche.

Yeats's interest in the occult tradition, his opposition to science, and his views on Irish and European history, were eventually synthesised in *A Vision*, which occupied him continually from its inception in 1917 until the publication of the second edition in 1937. Debate upon its peculiar genesis is fruitless: the spirits, if spirits they were, addressed Yeats in a language with which he was already profoundly familiar. The automatic writing offered him an opportunity of organising and classifying the contents of his own mind. How far Yeats accorded to his system literal belief remains uncertain, for while he occasionally regarded it as divine revelation he more often accepted it as symbol. In *A Packet for Ezra Pound* he wrote: "I will never think any thoughts but these, or some modification or extension of these; when I write prose or verse they must be somewhere present though not it may be in the words; they must affect my judgement of friends and of events; but then there are many symbolisms and none exactly resembles mine."[50]

A Vision may infuriate Yeats's commentators, but its importance

cannot be denied. The act of gathering together into a reasonably coherent pattern the various philosophical, psychological, and historical
theories of a lifetime was his propitiation of the abstract intellect:
that intellect which attracted, tormented, and repelled him. *A Vision*
is, with the exception of a few passages, a monumentally abstract
work. Paradoxically, Yeats uses abstraction to glorify concrete, sensuous experience, and to celebrate not God, not transcendence, not
even wisdom, but life itself, in all its ignorance and passion.

The symbolism of *A Vision* is founded upon the opposition between
what Yeats describes as primary and antithetical impulses: an opposition
which manifests itself in the psychology of the individual, in history and
politics, and in religion and philosophy. "Primary" signifies the Christian,
objective, scientific, democratic, and realistic tendencies; "antithetical"
describes the pagan, subjective, aesthetic, aristocratic, and idealistic
impulse. One individual passing through many incarnations, or a civilisation which rises and falls, is essentially cyclical. Yeats symbolises this cycle
which rises and falls, is essentially cyclical. Yeats symbolises this cycle
in his quasi-astrological phases of the moon. An individual or a civilisation begins in the primary phases one to eight, reaches maturity in the
subjective phases eight to twenty-two, and sinks back again into the
primary darkness of the cycle's end. This great wheel, however, being
one-dimensional, is inadequate to express the complexity of Yeats's
conception. Nothing human is ever completely primary or completely
antithetical: the two impulses are constantly at war. Yeats therefore
transforms the wheel into a gyre or spiral, and adds a second, opposing gyre with its point in the base of the first. As subjectivity increases
objectivity declines; then the process is reversed. There is no end,
no dialectical synthesis, only the constant whirling of antinomial impulses. "The anguish of birth and that of death cry out in the same
instant. Life is no series of emanations from divine reason such as the
Cabalists imagine, but an irrational bitterness, no orderly descent from
level to level, no waterfall but a whirlpool, a gyre."[51]

Yeats traces his gyres back to the *Timaeus*. He contrasts them with
Plato's "circle of the fixed stars which . . . confers upon us the knowledge of Universals."[52] This transcendent circle Yeats translates into a
sphere, which he calls ultimate reality, or God. In human experience
this ultimate reality falls into a series of antinomies, so nothing can be
known of it by ordinary men. Only the saint may escape from endless
recurrence into the phaseless reality of the sphere. All primary men,
however, desire the One, or the Good: their lives are God-centred. Antithetical man is not attracted by the sphere: his aim is freedom and self-
realisation. The conflict is dramatised in the poem "A Dialogue of Self
and Soul," in which the way of the saint is rejected in favour of life, no
matter how sordid or painful it may be. Yeats himself, a subjective man
of phase seventeen, is able to recognise both the primary and the antithetical impulses, but prefers the latter:

I think that two conceptions, that of reality as a congeries of beings, that of reality as a single being, alternate in our emotion and in history, and must always remain something that human reason, because subject always to one or the other, cannot reconcile. I am always, in all I do, driven to a moment which is the realisation of myself as unique and free, or to a moment which is the surrender to God of all that I am. I think that there are historical cycles wherein one or the other predominates, and that a cycle approaches where all shall be as particular and concrete as human intensity permits. **Again and again I have tried to sing that approach . . . Again and again with remorse, a sense of defeat, I have failed when I would write of God,** written coldly and conventionally. Could these two impulses, one as much a part of truth as the other, be reconciled, or if one or the other could prevail, all life would cease.[53]

When Yeats rejects Plato, therefore, as he often does, he is not denying the validity of Plato's supra-sensible world of ideal forms: he is simply expressing his own vehement preference for a subjective man-centred philosophy. Both impulses—towards unity and God or towards multiplicity and the individual—must be recognised as true, even though they are irreconcilable by human reason. Yeats is committed to the "particular and concrete" truth, and to the expression of himself as "unique and free", but is able to embrace his own philosophy in the clear knowledge that there exists another which is equally true but completely contrary to his own. The last two sections of the poem "Vacillation" show Yeats debating the attractions of simplicity and transcendent sanctity: he rejects them in favour of Homer and original sin, but treats the Christian mystic Von Hügel with humorous gentleness: "So get you gone, Von Hügel, though with blessings on your head."[54] Yeats is able to combine the detachment of the historian of ideas with the zeal of the devotee. This remarkable feat is partly an inheritance from Blake, who taught him that "there is a place at the bottom of the graves where contraries are equally true,"[55] and partly the result of his acquaintance with the ideas of Immanuel Kant.

Before completing the first version of *A Vision* Yeats knew some Plato, all of Blake, and a good deal of Swedenborg and Boehme: the instructors forbade him to read any more philosophy while their revelations were in progress. The arrival of the proof sheets lifted the ban, and from 1925 onwards Yeats embarked upon a massive course of philosophical reading: more Plato, Plotinus, Berkeley, Croce, Gentile, Hegel, Bertrand Russell, and others. Included on his list was Kant's *Prolegomena*. Yeats, like most people, found Kant extremely difficult, but Berkeley had prepared him for the idea that objects of sense experience are merely appearances, and he accepted eagerly the notion that space and time are forms of human perception.[56] He also seized upon Kant's antinomies as confirmation of the structure of *A Vision*. Because of the nature of perception and because of our ignorance of the noumenal world, Kant says, life appears as a series of irreconcilable contradictions. Eager as he was for respectable authorities, Yeats nevertheless modified them boldly. Kant's noumenal world (a world of "things-in-themselves" which really existed and were the cause of sense impressions, though they could never be known by the human intellect) struck Yeats, as it had struck the German successors of Kant, as too Platonic. Yeats followed Hegel in abolishing it: "**Hegel set free the human soul when he declared ('the thing [in] itself**' this theological echo had just been proved unnecessary) that 'there is nothing that is not accessible to intellect.'"[57] If the noumena are disposed of, Kant's antinomies cease to be merely appearances, they become reality itself:

> I found myself upon the third antinomy of Immanuel Kant, thesis: freedom; antithesis: necessity; but I restate it. Every action of man declares the soul's ultimate, particular freedom, and the soul's disappearance in God; declares that reality is a congeries of beings and a single being; nor is this antinomy an appearance imposed upon us by the form of thought but life itself which turns, now here, now there, a whirling and a bitterness.[58]

Yeats was prepared to agree with Kant that time and space are only "forms of thought": the antinomy, however, is not an appearance but reality, "life itself".

Exigencies of space necessitate the simplification of Yeats's ideas, which are more complex and more inconsistent than I have been able to indicate. Even within the limits of the previous paragraphs, however, a logical problem presents itself. God, or the sphere, is first shown as the ultimate reality which transcends the gyres, and then is apparently demoted into one term of the antinomy. The only way out of this impasse is via Yeats's own terminology: we may regard his vision of transcendent reality as a primary insight, while the conflict between immanence and transcendence belongs to his antithetical self. His system, after all, was constructed to accommodate just such paradoxes.

The conflict between immanence and transcendence is prominent in three magnificent poems written just after Yeats had taken up the serious study of philosophy. "Sailing to Byzantium", "The Tower", and "Among School Children" surely bear out Yeats's contention that this study improved his verse. The poems help to chart Yeats's love-hate relationship with Plato and Plotinus, who were among the first philosophers he read or re-read when *A Vision* was complete.

Plato, according to Yeats, is a primary man, the "first Christian", because he "thinks all things into unity".[59] His world of ideal forms, a reality beside which human life is no more than an illusion, seemed deathly to Yeats, "for when he separates the Eternal Ideas from Nature and shows them self-sustained he prepares the Christian desert and the Stoic suicide."[60] Platonic dualism leads to a terrible contempt for life, and especially for the life of the flesh. In "Among School Children" Yeats mocks Plato's abstractions:

> Plato thought nature but a spume that plays
> Upon a ghostly paradigm of things.[61]

Yet he demonstrates the cruel power of the self-sustained ideal images, the "self-born mockers of man's enterprise", to break human hearts. The last stanza is a challenge both to them and to Plato: a rejection of asceticism and an affirmation of spontaneous life. The ideal is in nature, not beyond it: "How can we know the dancer from the dance?"[62]

An ageing man, however, is by definition no longer a dancer. In certain moods Yeats turns towards abstraction and transcendence because the life of the flesh is failing him: his own life cycle has entered its primary phases. In "Sailing to Byzantium" he declares, punningly, that he himself will become an eternal form:

> Once out of nature I shall never take
> My bodily form from my natural thing.[63]

The rhetoric of "Sailing to Byzantium" is, of course, mined with ironies which suggest the inadequacy of the world of being and Yeats's nostalgia for the world of becoming. In Bertrand Russell's *The Problems of Philosophy*, which Yeats was reading just before he wrote the poem, there is a lucid contrast between the world of universals and that of existence, which suggests the philosophical framework of both "Sailing to Byzantium" and the later "Byzantium":

> The world of being is unchangeable, rigid, exact, delightful to the mathematician, the logician, the builder of metaphysical systems, and all who love perfection more than life. The world of existence is fleeting, vague, without sharp boundaries, without any clear plan or arrangement, but it contains all thoughts and feelings, all the data of sense, and all physical objects, everything that can do either good or harm, everything that makes any difference to the value of life and the world.[64]

The golden bird scorns the world of sexuality and war, the complexities of mire and blood, but the transcendent purifying flames are impotent in the world of sense, they cannot singe a sleeve.

More directly than "Sailing to Byzantium", "The Tower" states that the pursuit of Platonic perfection is only second-best; in fact it entails the abandonment of art:

> It seems that I must bid the Muse go pack,
> Choose Plato and Plotinus for a friend
> Until imagination, ear and eye,
> Can be content with argument and deal
> In abstract things.[65]

This cowardly proposition, however, is offered only to be dramatically cast aside:

> And I declare my faith:
> I mock Plotinus' thought
> And cry in Plato's teeth,
> Death and life were not
> Till man made up the whole,
> Made lock, stock and barrel
> Out of his bitter soul,
> Aye, sun and moon and star, all,
> And further add to that
> That being dead, we rise,
> Dream and so create
> Translunar Paradise.[66]

In a footnote Yeats apologises to Plato and Plotinus, because "it is something in our own eyes that makes us see them as all transcendence," and he quotes Plotinus' assertion that the "soul is the author of all living things."[67] Yeats's early emphasis upon the individual consciousness rather than the external world was flowering into a strange version of idealist philosophy, which rejected Platonic transcendentalism and scientific materialism alike, because both reduce the human mind to a mirror, drive it "into the quicksilver".[68] To Yeats the mind was not a reflector of divine ideas nor of physical objects, but their creator. "Plotinus . . . was the first to establish as sole source the timeless individuality or daimon instead of the Platonic idea, to prefer Socrates to his thought."[69] By this, Yeats means that the source of all being is not external to man, but is indeed man himself, a timeless spirit undergoing successive incarnations.

Yeats's romantic insistence upon the creative and imaginative instead of the reflective functions of consciousness received confirmation in the work of the Irishman George Berkeley, who argued that things exist only when they are perceived. Yet as the passage from "The Tower" reveals, Yeats went further than Berkeley, who escaped from the radical implications of his own argument by concluding that things exist continuously because they are all ideas in the mind of God. Yeats scorned such a compromise. "The essential sentence is of course 'things only exist in being perceived,' and I can only call that perception God's when I add Blake's 'God only exists or is in existing beings or men.'"[70] For Yeats, everything that exists is created by the mind; and every creation of the mind is equally real. Dreams and apparitions, tables and chairs: all exist in being perceived. Here is philosophical justification for acceptance of psychic phenomena. In his famous debate with T. Sturge Moore about Ruskin's phantom cat, Yeats accepts no theory that fails to recognise the phantom cat and the house cat as equally real. His own definition of reality is a strange mixture of Berkeley, Blake, Kant, and the daimons of Plotinus:

> I. Reality is a timeless and spaceless community of Spirits which perceive each other. Each Spirit is determined by and determines those it perceives, and each Spirit is unique.
> II. When these Spirits reflect themselves in time and space they still determine each other, and each Spirit sees the other as thoughts, images, objects of sense. Time and Space are unreal.[71]

Yeats's assertion that man "made lock, stock and barrel/ Out of his bitter soul" is therefore no mere piece of extravagance. It is his philosophical credo.

The writing of *A Vision* and the enormous extension of his philosophical knowledge gave Yeats a new confidence in his old positions, and made him into a polemical historian of ideas. His cyclical theories seemed to show that the end of the primary Christian era was near. In poems, prose writings, and the historical parts of *A Vision*, Yeats analysed the causes of modern civilisation's exhaustion and foretold its demise. "All our scientific, democratic, fact-accumulating, heterogenous civilization belongs to the outward gyre and prepares . . . the revelation . . . of the civilization that must slowly take its place."[72] The Great War, the Troubles in Ireland, and the Bolshevik Revolution seemed the beginning of the end. Yeats was not, of course, an objective observer: *A Vision* allowed him to systematise and document previously unfocused scientific and political antipathies. The battle between primary and antithetical became a new formulation of the old struggle between materialism and idealism, between England and Ireland.

While Yeats was working on *A Vision*, the establishment of the Irish Free State revived his old dream of making his native land a holy city in the imagination. Civil war checked but did not extinguish his hopes for the new nation, which he now saw as the young antithetical opponent of decadent primary England, and potential site and source of the coming subjective revelation. Using historical analysis for blatantly political ends, Yeats set out to show the Irish that they had always been antithetical idealists. He attacked the scientific revolution, demonstrated its social and political consequences, and then reminded his countrymen that numerous great Irishmen had attacked it before him.

His main targets were three Englishmen, Bacon, Newton, and Locke, whom Blake had long ago taught him to dislike. Now, however, he had a formidable Irish ally in Berkeley, and a philosophical position of his own. He challenged the very basis of science: the concept of objective reality, the sense-datum which exists apart from and independent of the perceiver. "I turn away from all attempts to make philosophy support science by starting with some form of 'fact' or 'datum'."[73] Here, in a more sophisticated form, is Arnold's Celtic revolt against the "despotism of fact": a revolt which Yeats carried as far as any Irishman has ever done. He quoted with nationalistic pride the passage from the *Commonplace Book* in which, after defining the positions of Newton and Locke, Berkeley wrote: "We Irish do not hold with this." According to Yeats, "This was the birth of the national intellect and it caused the defeat in Berkeley's philosophical secret society of English materialism, the Irish Salamis."[74] The birth of the national intellect, then, occurred when Berkeley challenged Locke's separation of the primary from the secondary qualities.

In declaring that bodies really possess mass, extension, shape, motion, and number (primary qualities), while they only appear to have colour, smell, and sound (secondary qualities), Locke conceived the idea that the world consists only of matter in motion. According to both Berkeley and Yeats, belief in a world of objects "separated from taste, smell, sound, from all the mathematician could not measure,"[75] led to a denial of everything unique, individual, and beautiful. Yeats thought that the nature created by man's perception exists only because of its secondary qualities, because it "shines and sounds". Newton and Locke, therefore, "took away the world and gave us its excrement instead." Berkeley, however, "restored the world"[76] by proving that primary qualities are also dependent upon the perceiver: shape is no less subjective than colour. Despite the cogency of Berkeley's argument, wrote Yeats, Locke's theory "remained the assumption of science, the groundwork of every text-book. It worked, and the mechancial inventions of the next age, its symbols that seemed its confirmation, worked even better, and it worked best of all in England."[77] In "Fragments" Yeats wittily expressed his vision of Locke as father of the English industrial revolution; he took the more pleasure in his image because Southern Ireland had never had an industrial revolution:

> Locke sank into a swoon;
> The Garden died;
> God took the spinning-jenny
> Out of his side.[78]

Science, for Yeats, was always political science. He saw the consequences of Locke's world view as "that dialectical materialism the Socialist Prince Mirsky calls 'the firm foundation-rock of European socialism'."[79] The political outcome of a scientific emphasis upon the measurable

as opposed to the beautiful was "mathematical" democracy: government by numbers. "Instead of hierarchical society, where all men are
different, came democracy; instead of a science which had rediscovered
Anima Mundi . . . came materialism."[80] In his quarrel with democracy
Yeats enlisted Swift and Burke: two great Irishmen who were, like
Berkeley, antithetical without knowing it. He frequently quoted
Swift's endorsement of hierarchical society, in which the one, the few,
and the many are held in perfect balance. He used Burke's organic
arguments against the abstract, theoretical ideals of the French Revolution to support his own dislike of the Bolshevik Revolution, which
he saw both as the culmination of the primary impulse and as an
immediate threat to Ireland. A capitulation to Marxism would jeopar-
dise her antithetical purity, so Yeats was anxious to prevent Ireland
from adopting "Marxian revolution or Marxist definitions of value in
any form. I consider the Marxian criterion of values as in this age the
spear-head of materialism and leading to inevitable murder."[81]

Yeats disliked the scientific antecedents of Marxism; about Marx's
philosophical forebear Hegel he had mixed feelings. Hegel had offered
to solve Kant's antinomies, and he saw history as proceeding dialecti-
cally towards an ideal final state. Each age was described as the negation of its predecessor: a concept which, Yeats thought, could be used
to justify the massacre of the superseded class. He therefore rejected
"Hegel's all containing, all sustaining, all satisfying final wakefulness. I
reject Marxian Socialism, in so far as it is derived from him."[82] In "A
Genealogical Tree of Revolution" Yeats demonstrates that Hegel's
solution of the antinomies led not to one but two political philosophies
which propose ideal final ends: communism and the victory of the
proletariat, fascism and the absolute state. Yeats dismisses both because
"the antinomies cannot be solved"[83] and there is no end to cyclical
conflict.[84]

Yeats's mind is commonly supposed to have been enveloped in mists
of occultist idiosyncrasy. Yet his pursuit of a spiritual world led him in
the same direction as some of the foremost thinkers of his time. Even
in the field of science he found what he most longed for: scientific
backing for his assault on materialism. In 1926 he read and heavily
annotated Alfred North Whitehead's *Science and the Modern World*.
Whitehead outlines the history of mechanistic science, and then describes the twentieth-century revolution effected by the work of Einstein and the quantum theory. The new physics, according to Whitehead, demands a new philosophy; and he propounds a theory of organism.
Yeats was delighted and impressed by the fact that science itself had
abolished the "objective" reality of matter, space, and time: modern
physics appeared to be offering justification for his own beliefs. Now
that he had the latest authorities behind him he could say, with an air
of careless condescension, "No educated man to-day accepts the objective matter and space of popular science."[85] Bertrand Russell,

whose *Outline of Philosophy* Yeats read with care, twice describes modern conceptions of matter as "ghostly": we are dealing not with objects but with events.[86] Yeats accepted with ease the most daring speculations of the physicists: he had, after all, always believed in ghosts. What began among the fairies in Sligo came to maturity in a world where, as Yeats expressed it, "Matter is the source of all energy,"[87] or, to put it another way, $e = mc^2$.

If, however, Yeats believed that "Einstein has done away with materialism,"[88] he also knew that Einstein's thought would have little effect on the popular mind. To the end of his life, therefore, he maintained his polemically antimaterialist stance, constantly reminding Ireland that her national intellect is rooted in subjectivity and idealism. He opens his "Private Thoughts" from *On the Boiler* (1939) with the declaration: "I am philosophical, not scientific, which means that observed facts do not mean much until I can make them part of my experience,"[89] and continues with a last condemnation of Locke, mathematics, and democracy, and a last blessing upon the unique Irish soul. When he has once again praised Swift and Berkeley, affirmed the mediumistic wisdom of the Irish peasantry, and expounded his theory of historical cycles, "Private Thoughts" appears as a summary of his major philosophical concerns. Yet there is a difference. Mario Rossi tells us that Yeats "did not feel philosophy as an abstruse speculation nor was he attracted to it by its technical difficulties. He wanted to solve his problems. He wanted to understand clearly his own mind."[90] As death approached it became clear to Yeats that philosophy had not solved his problems, nor even given him the key to himself. In "The Man and the Echo" he asks despairingly:

> Shall we in that great night rejoice?
> What do we know but that we face
> One another in this place?[91]

Knowledge is necessarily limited; the truth remains shrouded in mystery. "Of late," writes Yeats in *On the Boiler*, "I have tried to understand in its practical details the falsehood that is in all knowledge, science more false than philosophy, but that too false."[92] Yet he will not reject philosophy, for if we do not master knowledge, it will master us. Searching for a final statement of this paradox, he wrote to Lady Elizabeth Pelham on January 4, 1939, "Man can embody truth but he cannot know it."[93] Yeats's words remind us that, while a study of his philosophy contributes considerably to our intellectual appreciation of his work, for embodied truth we must return to the poems themselves.

Mark Patrick Hederman

THE "MIND" OF JOYCE:
FROM PATERNALISM TO PATERNITY

If Joyce is to be examined as a "thinker" it must be on his own terms. There is no question of his being deferential towards, or daunted by the philosophic habit. Stephen Dedalus, when asked if he wanted to be famous enough to become part of Ireland's history, replied that Ireland would be made famous because she was part of him. Joyce might have made a similar reply to the question about his place in the history of philosophy.

"At the very least," Denis Donoghue tells us,[1] "James Joyce was an amateur student of the philosophers. But his work shows little of that love of wisdom which constitutes the philosophic habit." This division between "amateur" and "professional" thinker, between "the love of wisdom" which "constitutes the philosophic habit" and the "work" of an author like Joyce could very well be an anachronistic prejudice which Joyce himself has helped to dispel.

Joyce's mind was at all times engaged in the search for truth. He could have been a professional philosopher if he had wanted to, but the truth to which he was committed required a more widespread panorama than that provided by the narrowly defined academic philosophy of his day. The truth which he felt himself called to express forced him to invent his own philosophic mode and habit. It caused him to break down the conventional barriers between art and philosophy and it forces us, who come after him, to undertake an unprecedented dialogue between art and philosophy if we are to understand the full import of his work. This dialogue is not a translation from the language of one medium into the language of the other; it is original in the sense that it creates something other than either of these disciplines would have been capable of achieving on its own.

I.

Joyce could also have become a Jesuit, a doctor of medicine, a scientist or a musician. He chose to become a writer because he felt that this was the only way in which he could express himself fully. He thought of himself primarily as a poet, but found that he could never become a great one.[2] He tried his hand at drama, which he regarded as the purest form of art, and finally became a novelist *faute de mieux*. His novels seem to have served as the necessary therapeutic exorcism which freed him from the emotional paralysis preventing his true genius from burgeoning. They allowed him eventually to undertake his most powerful and idiosyncratic work: *Finnegans Wake*.

Joyce's problem as an artist might well be described in the terms used by T.S. Eliot to assess the phenomenon of Shakespeare's *Hamlet*.[3] Eliot sees *Hamlet* as an artistic failure because the medium of drama, as an artistic form, was inadequate as an objective correlative wherewith to circumscribe the enormity of the project which Shakespeare intended to express. However great the end result may be, it is still a failure because the screen upon which the artist tried to project his nerves in patterns was too exiguous to act as adequate recipient. Similarly, the only objective correlative which was capable of expressing the artistic project of James Joyce was the one which he invented for himself, and was capable of inventing only during the last eighteen years of his life. He saw his other works as stepping-stones towards *Finnegans Wake*. Each one contributed to the process of releasing him for his final project, which was to be his unparalleled contribution to the history of human self-expression.

Finnegans Wake is a work of art, but, as such, it contravenes the boundaries of literary art as these had been demarcated up to its emergence. It is neither poetry nor prose. It is not a novel, not a play nor a poem. It includes within its scope literature, philosophy, philology, mythology, anthropology, science and most areas of human endeavour worthy of mention. It is a work of art which demands a reappraisal of that very term which we use to define it. To understand the achievement of Joyce the artist we have to readjust our attitudes to the phenomenon of art, and by extension, to philosophy as the quest for and the expression of truth.

II.

When trying to establish the status of Joyce the intellectual, the temptation is to make an inventory of those philosophers who might have influenced his work; to provide an exhaustive list of his reading material, culled from his own writings, his collected letters and the various biographies; and then to examine the way he adapted this philosophical material to suit his own purposes. Such a process is doomed to failure. Joyce was an unusually isolated explorer. He had great confidence in his own resources and ability to find his way. He did read widely and voraciously but, mostly, to find support for his own intuitions, information to illustrate his findings and, above all, stimulation for his imagination. There is little direct connection between the sources which act as input and the creative works which emerge as output. The strange chemistry of his mind was affected by outside stimuli and, in turn, appropriated such influences in a way that precludes the possibility of examining their interaction in terms of cause and effect. The reasons why certain people captured his imagination and the way he allowed such people to influence his work are often disconcertingly oblique. His intellectual heroes or mentors were often chosen for the most unscientific reasons and were used for his own purposes with unscrupulous abandon. Joyce was no man's intellectual disciple and no fellow worker, of whatever age or importance, was granted the deference or the homage due to a superior.

This point can be illustrated by Joyce's use of Vico and Bruno, the famous philosophical pair who provided much of the sustenance at *Finnegans Wake*. Their influence can be described as structural and paradigmatic. In the first case this means that he built his last work on a plan provided by the Italian philosopher Vico who divided history into recurring cycles of theocratic, aristocratic and democratic ages, each inaugurated by a thunder clap. The fact that the book begins halfway through the sentence on which it ends is also an imitation of Vico's *ricorso* or return to the beginning. Joyce was influenced by Vico's use of etymology and mythology to uncover the significance of events as if these were only superficial manifestations of underlying energies.[4] However, the use which Joyce made of these germinal ideas is entirely original, albeit eclectic. They fired his imagination in a way which bears little resemblance to the intentions of the author of *La Scienza Nuova*. Joyce was aware of this discrepancy when he wrote to Harriet Shaw Weaver: "I would not pay overmuch attention to these theories beyond using them for all they are worth, but they have gradually forced themselves on me through circumstances of my own life."

This last remark explains what is meant by paradigmatic. Joyce frequently identified himself with such philosophers simply because he found significant parallels between his life and theirs. He adopted Giordano Bruno of Nola, another Italian thinker, from his early undergraduate days because the latter had been burnt as a heretic by the Roman Catholic church and because he had sought to awaken his contemporaries from their theological stagnation by setting forth his own personal metaphysics in the guise of a commentary on the works of Thomas Aquinas. Some have claimed that Joyce built the story of his own martyrdom to the cause of art in *A Portrait of the Artist as a Young Man* as a parallel to the life story of Bruno. The fact that Bruno of Nola becomes, in *Finnegans Wake* the Dublin bookshop Browne and Nolan is an amusing metamorphosis which illustrates the kind of iconoclastic expatriation which all such philosophical influences were required to undergo in the mind of this unpredictable author. At this paradigmatic level also, it is clear that Joyce's sympathy for Vico was as much inspired by the fact that both of them suffered from an almost pathological fear of thunderstorms as it was by the various theories of history which were ushered in by each thunderclap in *Finnegans Wake.*

It is difficult to see how such influences can be studied in any serious attempt to trace Joyce's intellectual pedigree. However, it will be seen in the course of this essay that, in the context of the new kind of "thought" which Joyce was attempting to introduce, such apparently arbitrary connections assume a cardinal importance.

III.

There are other influences on Joyce's thought which are more direct and recognisable. Of these the most interesting and prototypical would be Thomas Aquinas on the one hand and Freud and Jung on the other.

Joyce's aesthetic was far nearer to that of Thomas Aquinas than is generally allowed by most commentators. This is not because the words he uses are directly borrowed from "the bulldog of Aquin",[5] but because the context in which he uses them implies a similar pre-occupation. It must be remembered that Joyce's acquaintance with Thomistic theories would not have been based entirely upon the texts of St Thomas himself, "whose gorbellied works" Stephen tells us in *Ulysses*, "I enjoy reading in the original."[6] He would also have had access to the contemporary *Revue Néo-Scolastique* in which scholars such as de Wulf and Mercier were applying Thomistic theories to aesthetics and sowing the seeds of the later Neo-Thomist Scholastic revival at Louvain.[7] William T. Noon in his excellent study of *Joyce and Aquinas*[8] has shown how closely the aesthetic theories which Joyce puts into the mouth of Stephen Dedalus echo ideas outlined in these contemporary works.

The famous definition of beauty in terms of *integritas, claritas* and *consonantia*, which was removed by later Neo-Thomists, such as Eric Gill and Jacques Maritain, from its original context and developed into a supposedly Thomistic aesthetic, was never in fact intended as such. St Thomas would have been surprised to find this particular detail of his thought transformed into the cornerstone of an aesthetic philosophy which hardly concerned him at all.

> The point which Aquinas seeks to establish is a theological one: an image or *similitudo* is beautiful if it perfectly represents another thing ... The Son in a very special sense must be conceived of in our minds as having a special, if not exclusive, title to the divine name: *beauty*. . . . To apply this text to works of art, like symphonies or poems

. . . would seem to be reading into the text an aesthetic
relevance much beyond what Aquinas could have had in
mind.[9]

The remarks of Aquinas on beauty occur in the middle of his argument for the suitability of applying to the person of the Son in the
uncreate Trinity a particular attribute or name which should be available to all three persons.[10] In other words, his preoccupation is with
creativity as a metaphysics of paternity rather than as aesthetics.

When we turn to Joyce's use of Aquinas we can, at a superficial
reading, imagine that his use of this particular source was derived
from the contemporary concern to apply Thomistic theories to the
world of art and the metaphysics of aesthetic creativity. However,
at a more poignant and important level, it can be seen that Joyce's
interest in Aquinas was derived from a shared preoccupation with the
fundamental problem of "paternity".

In 1949 Louis Gillet, a friend and contemporary of Joyce, wrote
an article in which he states that "the problem of paternity . . . is the
essential basis of the Joyce problem, the one that explains in *Ulysses*
. . . the long meditation of Stephen and Mulligan on the subject of
Hamlet. In fact this fragment is the key to the book."[11] Paternity, for
Joyce, means not only the relationship between father and son but also
the relationship between an artist and his work. Such a relationship
finds its aesthetic prototype in Shakespeare's *Hamlet* and its supreme
analogy in the word of an allpowerful creator. Thomas Aquinas combines the two strands of art and fatherhood in his theological presentation of the mysterious relationship which pertains between the
Father and the Son as uncreated principle and consubstantial word.

Both Joyce and Aquinas were aware of the many heresies which
threatened the subtlety of so delicately balanced a mystery. Of these,
the two most representative are Arianism and Sabellianism, both of
which feature constantly in Stephen's thoughts in both *A Portrait of
the Artist* and *Ulysses*. Arianism denies the possibility of fatherhood
in God. The Son is similar and "of like substance" (*homoiousios*) but
not "consubstantial" (*homoousios*) with the Father. This implied,
from Joyce's point of view, that any word, or creation, of his own
could never be the perfect form of himself. He was, therefore, more
attracted to "the subtle African heresiarch Sabellius who held that the
Father was Himself his own Son."[12] This heresy, sometimes called
modalism or monarchianism (that to preserve the prerogatives of
divine monarchy, it is necessary to present the son as no more than a
ghost, or a modality, of the Father) is dramatised in Shakespeare's
Hamlet:

— A father, Stephen said, battling against hopelessness,
is a necessary evil. (Shakespeare) wrote the play in the
months that followed his father's death . . . The corpse

of John Shakespeare does not walk the night . . . He rests
disarmed of fatherhood, having devised that mystical estate
upon his son. Boccaccio's Calandrino was the first and
last man who felt himself with child. Fatherhood, in the
sense of conscious begetting, is unknown to man. It is a
mystical estate, an apostolic succession, from only begetter
to only begotten . . . Well: if the father who has not a son
be not a father can the son who has not a father be a son?
When Rutlandbaconsouthamptonshakespeare or another
poet of the same name in a comedy of errors wrote *Hamlet*
he was not the father of his own son merely but, being
no more a son, he was and felt himself the father of all his
race . . .

That Joyce's obsessive preoccupation was the notion of "paternity"
is also suggested by his last and best poem, written on the occasion
of the death of his father and the birth of his grandson. The poem
elaborates three dimensions of paternity: the theological and trinitarian in the title (*Ecce Puer*) and the biblical tone of the last line:
"O, father forsaken/Forgive your son!"; the sexual and generative in
both the substance and the occasion of the poem; the aesthetic and
artistic in the structure and form of the poem itself.

However, this was only a makeshift and passing expression of the
problem. Joyce sent the poem to Gillet with the deprecatory note:
"Je suis papa mais pas poète." Poetry, he felt, could not be the adequate medium for expressing his obsessive preoccupation.

IV

If Milton felt called to explain the ways of God to men, Joyce seems
to have felt obliged to explain the ways of men to God. Having rejected the orthodoxy of the Roman Catholic church, he embraced with
passion and rigour the orthodoxy of humanity. He believed that there
was more to man than Jesuit philosophy had ever dreamt of and he
was determined to explore that dream. In this he was the spiritual
contemporary of Freud and Jung and, indeed, all those who sensed
new dimensions of consciousness opening up to humanity. Not that
he was in any way appreciative of such contemporaries. He despised
most of them and referred to Freud and Jung as Tweedledum and
Tweedledee.

"James Joyce," says Lionel Trilling, "with his interest in the numerous states of receding consciousness, with his use of words which point
to more than one thing, with his pervading sense of the interrelation
and interpenetration of all things, and, not least important, his treatment of familial themes, has perhaps most thoroughly and consciously
exploited Freud's ideas."[13] This is not to imply that he was directly

influenced by Freud's writings. As Lionel Trilling again puts it: "We must see that particular influences cannot be in question here but that what we must deal with is nothing less than a whole *Zeitgeist*, a direction of thought."[14] When Freud was hailed, on the occasion of his seventieth birthday, in 1926, as "the discoverer of the unconscious", he corrected the speaker and refused the title. "The poets and philosophers before me discovered the unconscious. What I discovered was the scientific method by which the unconscious can be studied."[15]

Joyce was not interested in the scientific method by which the unconscious can be studied. He dismissed psychoanalysis because its symbolism was mechanical[16] and is quoted as saying:[17] "Why all this fuss and bother about the mystery of the unconscious, what about the mystery of the conscious? What do they know about that?" But this reaction is, perhaps, correctly assessed by Ellmann as caused by the fact that Joyce was so close to the new psychoanalysis that he always disavowed any interest in it.[18] He was, in fact, working along the same lines himself at an artistic level and was disdainful of the plodding scientists who were tapping the same resources in a less direct and exciting way. Art, for Joyce, was the only appropriate medium for expressing this reality. Medicine and science were half measures which were even less satisfactory than the religion which he had rejected.

What was it that these thinkers were exploring? The answer is an inner continent, the discovery of which had perhaps greater significance and repercussions than the discovery of the "new world" in the fifteenth century. The difference between Joyce and the psychoanalysts was that he was discovering as an artist who sought to *express* this reality in all its originality, subtlety and polyvalence, whereas they, as scientists, sought to conquer it by reducing it to the machinery available to their limited fields of competence. "In *Ulysses*," Joyce is reported as saying, "I have recorded, simultaneously, what a man says, sees, thinks, and what such saying, seeing and thinking does to what you Freudians call the subconscious — but as for psychoanalysis, it's neither more nor less than blackmail."[19]

His search was, therefore, in a similar direction and dimension to that of the scientists who were investigating the inner world of dreams, of sexuality, of the subconscious. What he disliked about the scientists was their methodology. When asked by the Danish writer Tom Kristensen to provide some help in the interpretation of his *Work in Progress*, Joyce referred him to Vico. Kristensen asked him if he believed in the *Scienza Nuova*,[20] to which Joyce made a very significant reply: "I don't believe in any science, but my imagination grows when I read Vico as it doesn't when I read Freud or Jung."[20]

This remark stresses the distinction between the scientific and the artistic approach to discovery. The first has its identifiable and identifying equipment with which to harness the new dimensions of consciousness. This equipment is an immovable third term between the scientist and the object of research. The precast forms into which the new reality is required to mould itself have the effect of sterilising it and of preserving the scientist from any radical transformation in his contact with the newness which confronts him. The artist, by contrast, has no preconceived forms or approaches. He gives himself totally to the new reality which he senses and then has to invent those forms which alone can give adequate expression to this reality. In this sense Joyce was indeed something of a prophet. Jung was probably the first person to refer to Joyce as a prophet.[21] "There are major and minor prophets," he says, "and history will decide to which of them Joyce belongs. Like every true prophet, the artist is the unwitting mouth-piece of the psychic secrets of his time, and is often as unconscious as a sleepwalker. He supposes that it is he who speaks, but the spirit of the age is his prompter, and whatever this spirit says is proved true by its effects."

V

The way to penetrate the mystery of Joyce's "mind" is not the centripetal one of examining external sources and following them to a focus which would then be composed of the confluence of such extrinsic influences; it is rather the centrifugal one of finding first the central internal obsession which coloured the whole of Joyce's existence and dyed all his undertakings, and thence flowed out to embrace a whole plethora of external landmarks. This central obsession was, I suggest, the notion of paternity.

The fact that Joyce's real father was "the silliest man I ever knew",[22] a man who had "an extraordinary affection" for him and for whom he, too, had an enormous affection, even to the point of liking all his faults, only added fuel to his obsession. "I got from him" he wrote to Harriet Shaw Weaver after his father's death, "an extravagant licentious disposition (out of which, however, the greatest part of any talent I may have springs) but, apart from these, something else I cannot define. But if an observer thought of my father and myself and my son too physically, though we are all very different, he could perhaps define it."[23] This "something" which Joyce himself could not define, but which he sensed, provides a clue to an understanding of his fundamental creative energy.

Joyce's father, who supplied "hundreds of pages and scores of characters in my books"[24] also supplied the "licentious disposition" which amongst other things, may well have prevented Joyce from becoming a Jesuit and forced him into a psychic situation which Jung described as schizophrenic. This description, which Jung also applied to Picasso, caused such a furore that he was forced to explain himself in the following way: "By this I do not mean . . . a diagnosis of the mental illness schizophrenia . . . but a disposition or habitus on the basis of which a serious psychological disturbance could produce schizophrenia. Hence I regard neither Picasso nor Joyce as psychotics."[25]

If Joyce had not had such a father he might have been a very ordinary Irish citizen, embracing all the usual commitments to family, creed and nation. As it was, Joyce was aware that his mother died from his father's ill-treatment,[26] and that she died a victim to a system which made both herself and her husband what they were. Joyce cursed that system.[27] Within the narrow confines of a bourgeois puritanical society, John Joyce was something of a monster. He was hated and despised by most of his children except James, who was the only one, he felt, who understood him. Joyce did recognise his father's talent and wit and he sympathised with and inherited his "licentious disposition". He saw his father, too, as the victim of a society which condemned all his most endearing and promising aspects. His drunkenness and irresponsibility were the effects rather than the causes of his essential alienation from the society in which he lived. His father was cynical, anti-clerical and emasculated by the very powers he despised. His legacy to his son was the negative one of making it difficult for him to assume the conventional lifestyle of a child of his country, and compelling him to create a new idiom of being in exile.

The extraordinary affection which Joyce had for his father was also an affection for that part of himself inherited from him. The struggle between John Joyce and his society became internalised within the psyche of his son to the point of becoming schizophrenia. That this state was accurately diagnosed by Jung can, perhaps, be shown by the fact that Joyce's daughter, Lucia, was diagnosed on May 29, 1931 as suffering from hebephrenic psychosis which is a form of schizophrenia. As the etymology of this term suggests, this state is caused by a certain cleavage of the mind and a disconnection between thoughts, feelings and actions. In Lucia's case it was characterised by hallucinations, absurd delusions, silly mannerisms and other kinds of deteriorisation.

Joyce refused to accept that there was anything really wrong with his daughter, declaring that if she were insane then so was he. However, his attitude towards medicine and psychoanalysis changed somewhat when he was faced with the spectacle of his demented daughter. He even agreed to put her under the care of Jung and came to realise that the "night-world" which he himself was exploring was too harsh for many to face, and that the therapeutic and scientific approaches to it, which he had once disdained, were perhaps the only means of access to it for the majority of people. Jung wrote his considered opinion of Joyce and Lucia in a letter as follows:[28]

> If you know anything of my Anima theory, Joyce and his
> daughter are a classical example of it. She was definitely
> his "femme inspiratrice", which explains his obstinate

reluctance to have her certified. His own Anima, i.e. unconscious psyche, was so solidly identified with her, that
to have her certified would have been as much as an admission that he himself had a latent psychosis. It is therefore understandable that he could not give in. His "psychological" style is definitely schizophrenic, with the difference,
however, that the ordinary patient cannot help himself
talking and thinking in such a way, while Joyce willed it
and moreover developed it with all his creative forces,
which incidentally explains why he himself did not go over
the border. But his daughter did, because she was no genius
like her father, but merely a victim of her disease. In any
other time of the past Joyce's work would never have
reached the printer, but in our blessed twentieth century
it is a message, though not yet understood.

The powerful sexual disposition which Joyce inherited from his father
provided a striking contrast with the lofty spiritual aspirations and
almost prudish attitude which defined him at other times, especially in
public. These two aspects of himself made up the warring partners within
his schizophrenic temperament. Joyce's creative energies were galvanis-
ed into the task of finding some vindication for the disposition inherited
from his father and some way in which the various aspects of himself
could be united in an all-embracing principle. This principle is not
paternity in the limited sense of the relationship between this particular
father and his particular son. It is a new and alternative notion of
paternity, a spiritual fatherhood, quite in contrast to the paternalism
which surrounded and oppressed him. The new notion of paternity, as
opposed to paternalism, is a unifying and all-inclusive creative principle
from which the totality of manhood and sonship would derive and in
which both would find a satisfactory meaning and consummation. The
several antagonistic forces which Joyce found within himself and which
the oppressive paternalism of the Irish society of his time tended to
deal with by the annihilation of the "lower" forces by the higher,
should not, he felt, be sacrificed to some spurious God who would be
Father to only half of them. Even if these conflicting aspects produced
a psychological state of schizophrenia, Joyce was determined to seek
out the perspective within which such supposedly contradictory opposites would no longer be such. The creation of such a perspective meant
the destruction of the "normal" view and the substitution of a new
order of paternity, which is what Joyce eventually achieved in *Finnegans Wake*.

VI

Dissatisfied with the limitations of religion and science, Joyce turned
to literature which provided the possibility of creating new forms of

expression and experience. However, in the conventions of literature he found prejudices and weaknesses similar to those he had detected in the other two. He revolutionised the form of the novel[29] and exploited this medium to expose the paralysis which enveloped not only life in Ireland, but also the traditional conventions of literature itself.

The major weakness of the novel was, Joyce believed, that it had turned itself into a kind of science, governed by that same paternalistic hegemony which Joyce sought to usurp and replace by a new order of paternity. The text had become a highly controlled narrative which both writer and reader were able to dominate. The form which imposes this pattern of dominance from beginning to end is the narrative discourse. Through it the reader is aware that the author is telling the story and this allows the reader to submit to his overriding *auctoritas*. The text is the predictable third term between the reader and the writer, which is governed by a series of conventions preventing any unnecessary straying on the part of the reader. Obviously, the author does introduce voices other than his own into the text. But these are cordoned off between inverted commas, which Joyce calls "perverted commas", that remove any strangeness or threat in these discourses, quoted merely as illustrations of the narrative text. This domination of the author is the tyranny of the paternalistic father-figure which precludes any active participation of the reader beyond the carefully controlled manipulation of the narrative. It reduces the reader to a dull passivity and deprives language of its own specific life while it allows the author to use both as lifeless robots.

The revolution of the word which Joyce achieved was the liberation of language and the reader through his renunciation of the paternalistic dominance and his assumption of a new kind of paternity as the author of the text. It has been argued, for instance, that "the general strategy of *Dubliners* is the refusal of the production of a privileged discourse against which to read off the other languages of the text. This refusal forces the reader to experience the discourse of the characters as articulation rather than representation; in short to experience language."[30]

In *Ulysses* Joyce goes even further in his attempt to disrupt the conventional relationship between the author and the reader. The confident "I" of the first is silenced to allow something else to speak. This something else is the mystery of language itself.

This revolution of the word was not undertaken just for its own sake. It was arguably necessary for Joyce himself. As author he had no unified self-confident self which could act as privileged narrator of his text. Allowing language its freedom opened for him the possibility of finding his own voice. In fact, as we have seen, there were several voices in him, all of which achieve articulation in the deconstructed narrative which now becomes a tapestry of interlocking discourses. His project was not to record but to express himself and thus to effectuate the exorcism which would allow him to grow towards that fulfilment which the text prefigures. Joyce produces the text so that the text, in turn, can articulate Joyce.

Ulysses was originally meant to be another story in *Dubliners*. The much more extended work which it eventually became is to some extent both the result and the recording of the exorcism which *A Portrait of the Artist as a Young Man* achieved in Joyce. The central character of *A Portrait of the Artist*, Stephen Dedalus, becomes one point in the triangle of *Ulysses*. Each of these points, represented by Bloom, Stephen and Molly, is a different voice in the schizophrenic repertoire.

The first three episodes of *Ulysses* could almost be read as a continuation of *A Portrait of the Artist*. After these comes the real odyssey for both writer and reader. From here on each episode is apportioned a specific part of the body as its presiding symbolic organ. The first three episodes, which deal specifically with Stephen, have none. This emphasises the disembodied state of his character. He wanders through the world as a disconnected spirit which cannot adhere to anything and cannot release itself from itself.

There is an ironic retrospective glance at the Stephen, who, on the last page of *A Portrait of the Artist*, goes forth "to encounter for the millionth time the reality of experience and to forge in the smithy of my soul the uncreated conscience of my race." The last line of *A Portrait of the Artist* reads: "Old father, old artificer, stand me now and ever in good stead." In *Ulysses* it becomes clear that, as far as Stephen is concerned, this has not happened. "Fabulous artificer, the hawklike man. You flew. Whereto? New-Haven-Dieppe, steerage passenger. Paris and back. Lapwing. Icarus. *Pater, ait*. Seabedabbled, fallen, weltering. Lapwing you are. Lapwing he."[31] In this quotation Stephen has become identified with both the father (Daedalus) and the son (Icarus). Like the Cretan Daedalus, after whom he is named, he is confined to his own tortuous labyrinth. Joyce is presenting Stephen as the Sabellian-idealist artist disembodied and locked in his own cocoon. As the original Daedalus escaped from the labyrinth only when his own son came from the outside and released him, so Stephen, the hawklike man in search of a father, in a reversal of the original myth, will have to be released by the totally alien and unprepossessing figure of Leopold Bloom.

The discovery of Bloom by Stephen and Stephen by Bloom will force both of them to continue their odyssey towards the other world of *Finnegans Wake*, because, in fact, *Ulysses* is a forgery which provides no adequate solution to the problem of paternity. It is a series of false trails which achieve the destruction of the paternalistic mould of the novel but which fall short of leading us to Joyce's new order of paternity. There can be no question here of identifying Joyce with either Stephen or Bloom. The schizophrenic Joyce "creates Stephen and Bloom, juxtaposes them and defines their positions as widely and rigorously separated in order to dramatise a conflict within himself and within humanity which he is unable to reconcile."[32]

At the heart of *Ulysses* is a distinction which is similar to the one which Jung makes in his *Psychological Types*, written almost contemporaneously. The two types are incarnated in Stephen and Bloom and the structure of the novel, at one level, is directed towards the meeting of these two opposites and their final return to Ithaca, where they are confronted by the third term of the triangle, Molly-Penelope, the earth-mother, the *Gea Tellus*.[33] However, this final reconciliation, as we shall see, is also a false trail, which forces us to retrace our steps through the labyrinth and seek out another more potent source of reconciliation.

VII

When the Danish writer Tom Kristensen asked Joyce whether he had been correct in surmising in a review he wrote of *Ulysses* that Bloom was God, Stephen Jesus, and Molly Earth, Joyce would not confirm or deny but only said "Perhaps".[34] The incident is important because it opens up the possibility that what Joyce's "work" is providing us with is what Herman Broch described in 1949 as "the germ of a new religious organisation of humanity".[35] In other words, it implies that Joyce's obsession with the notion of paternity had not just literary, sexual, biographical, psychological and philosophical implications, but theological ones as well. The search for a unifying principle which would successfully recapitulate the several antagonistic realities which Joyce insisted upon investing with their heteronomous identity, demanded a new definition of paternity which would abdicate the totalitarian hegemony invested in the father-figure by western civilisation at every level of its cultural world.

At every level of human existence the idiom of domination by one tyrannical principle instigated a unification of all the rest which amounted to total uniformity. Joyce's search for a father was one which implied the substitution of the idiom of vulnerability for that of domination. It was this search which led him to study the intricate analyses of St Thomas Aquinas who set himself the task of describing among the three persons of the trinity a principle of fatherhood which would in no way lesson the independent and heteronomous identity of the other two persons. His interest in Giordano Bruno also derives from the latter's almost unique attempt to prescribe for the possible unity of contradictory opposites.

The description of Joyce as "schizophrenic" is no more than a translation of this same problem into psychological terms within his own particular psyche. On the one hand you have the rational and "spiritual" elements of his make-up; on the other you have the irrational and "subconscious" impulses. In the idiom of domination the first are required to conquer and subdue the second. Joyce was determined to find or create a source of unity which would preserve the autonomy, the identity and the dignity of both. The two most prominent cultural methodologies for undertaking such a programme were religion and science. Both of these were impregnated with the prevailing idiom of conquest.

Philosophy had not, at that time, released itself from the western paternalistic bias. If Joyce had been aware of the current trends in philosophical thinking, he might have taken more interest in this domain. There are remarkable similarities between the artistic project of Joyce and the philosophies of "deconstruction" which Husserl, Heidegger, Levinas, Merleau-Ponty and Derrida have since developed. These philosophers attempt to recuperate the meaning of "alterity" which western metaphysics had consigned to oblivion, by proposing the destruction of "representation" which reduces all the essential "strangeness" of Being to its unifying principles of "non-contradiction" and causality.

As it was, the only cultural medium open to Joyce was that of literature. Within the confines of this art-form he tried to enunciate the new order which would liberate the western world from the paralysing grasp of paternalism. The process of this liberation is described in his struggle with the conventional form of the novel in *Ulysses*; the achievement of his goal is finally articulated in *Finnegans Wake*.

In terms of Joyce's own personal psychology, the struggle was to find the adequate third term which would achieve the appropriate unification of the two antagonistic aspects of his make up which effected in him a schizophrenic opposition. These two terms are personified in *Ulysses* by the characters of Stephen Dedalus and Leopold Bloom. Stephen, in this dramatisation of the struggle, takes the place of the son, who, in the idiom of the novel, is in search of a father. Bloom, in his turn, is presented as the image of the father. He takes the place of that unifying principle which the western world has always looked to for the solution of its quest for order and unity. As such, however, he cuts a very inadequate figure. His impotence is the kernal of the novel's originality. The whole impetus of the novel is towards a meeting between these two principles. Their final confluence is such a deliberate anti-climax that we are forced to look elsewhere for a satisfying dénouement. This third term of the trinity, far from being supplied by the figure of Molly Bloom, is, in fact, supplied by the novel itself. We are forced to retrace our steps and examine the whole process of the novel form, wherein we discover the secret of Joyce's solution to the problem. A solution which will not achieve its final articulation until the anti-novel which is *Finnegans Wake*.

VIII

To understand this self-defeating excursus into the art form of the novel, which is *Ulysses*, it is necessary to examine in some detail the episode which Louis Gillet held to be the key to the book: the "Scylla and Charybdis" episode. It takes place in the library and contains the famous discussion about Hamlet. It is the last episode in which we meet the Stephen of *A Portrait of the Artist*. Now that we have entered the body of the novel proper, each episode must be presided over by some bodily organ. It is significant that the brain is the one chosen for this particular episode. Materially it deals almost entirely with Shakespearean criticism and is peopled by a group of very thinly disguised Dublin literati of the time. It records a long Platonic dialogue on the personality of Hamlet and the creative presence of Shakespeare in this play between Stephen Dedalus, Mr Best, John Eglington, George Russell (AE) and "Quakerlyster" (the librarian). It includes some lyrics, a short passage in blank verse and another in dramatic form, thus encompassing the three forms of literature defined by Stephen in *A Portrait of the Artist*. However, all this is simply the decoy of the lapwing (a bird which leads you away from its nest by bluffing you and leading you on) luring us away from the real significance of the episode which, as the title of the novel suggests, concerns the odyssey of the twentieth century Ulysses, Leopold Bloom.

In the original Odyssey of the mythological Ulysses, the hero had to choose between one of two perilous routes on his way back to Ithaca. He was advised by Circe not to attempt the passage through the "wandering rocks" but to take the less dangerous of the two, the journey between the sheer steadfast rock of Scylla and the whirlpool of Charybdis (the title of this spisode).

In Joyce's version of the twentieth century odyssey, these two dangers are symbolically present: "the beautiful ineffectual dreamer who comes to grief against the hard facts"[36] (Stephen), the rock of dogma and of Aristotle, and the whirlpool of mysticism and Platonism (AE). The real action of the novel in this episode is the breathless passing through of Ulysses-Bloom: "A man passed out between them, bowing, greeting."[37] The twentieth century Ulysses passes out from the dark gloom of the library into "a shattering daylight of no thoughts."[38] His actual presence in this episode takes up no more than a few throwaway lines. But each time this presence is felt it builds up the structural momentum of the novel.

Just at the moment when the solipsistic Stephen, influenced by both Berkeleian idealism and Sabellian modalism, is propounding a theory of art and literature which is totally dependent upon the author as dominating narrator, leaving no leeway to the heteronomous causality of chance, the novel itself takes over and language disrupts the flow of the episode.[39]

— Bosh! Stephen said rudely. A man of genius makes no mistakes. His errors are volitional and are the portals of discovery.

Portals of discovery opened to let in the quaker librarian, softcreakfooted, bald, eared and assiduous.

This chance external event heralds in the later arrival of Bloom through thesé same portals of discovery, disrupting Stephen's attempt to compromise the autonomous movement of the novel itself, the odyssey proper.

The most important dislocation of the narrative in this epidode occurs when we discover that Stephen's whole theory about Shakespeare is really not a description of Shakespeare at all but rather, in the idiom of the novel itself, as opposed to the "narrative" supposedly within Stephen's control, a prefiguring of the essential characteristics of the novel's "father-figure" Leopold Bloom.

This becomes textually irrefutable in the following way. Firstly, it becomes clear throughout the novel that all the characteristics which Stephen, in his narrative, applies to Shakespeare, are an exact description of Leopold Bloom, the father-figure for whom Stephen is unconsciously searching. Both Shakespeare and Bloom are "overborne" by a dominating female and are forced into marriage by an unforseen pregnancy. Both are unsuccessful lovers who forego sexual contact with their wives after the birth of their second child. Both have a daughter and lose a son. Both lose their fathers. Both are cuckolds who wilfully foster this state of affairs and both are Jews. Secondly, the way in which Anne Hathaway is described as overwhelming Shakespeare, mirrors exactly the key scene of Bloom's courtship with Molly on Howth Hill where she "got him to propose" and where Bloom was "ravished" by her.[40] Thirdly, Stephen uses the following unusual words and images to describe Shakespeare in this episode: "In a rosery of Fetter Lane of Gerard, herbalist, he walks greyedauburn. An azured harebell like her veins. Lids of Juno's eyes, violets. He walks. One life is all. One body. Do. But do."[41] This all takes place inside Stephen's mind as an interior monologue. But, as if to show the correspondence between Bloom and Shakespeare, the novel itself makes the connection by repeating, this time within the very different discourse of Bloom's interior monologue, almost the same words and in a Shakespearean context. In the Siren's episode, Bloom is musing to himself about Shakespeare: "Music hath charms Shakespeare said. Quotations every day of the year. To be or not to be. Wisdom while you wait." And immediately after this reference to Shakespeare, he repeats Stephen's words: "In Gerard's rosery of Fetter Lane he walks, greyedauburn. One life is all. One body. Do. But do."[42]

The fact that Stephen's words reappear almost verbatim in one of Bloom's monologues is not careless oversight. It is a deliberate destruction of the conventional structure of the novel. In the conventional narrative such an interchange of discourses would destroy the identity of character and upset the causal time sequence. Such a destruction is precisely what Joyce has in mind. The normal conventions which establish a predetermined relationahip between the author and the reader are disrupted for the very purpose of dislocating all three and creating an alien idiom in which all three are required to reestablish their bearings. The real odyssey of *Ulysses* takes place in a time-space continuum which is quite alien to the normal time-space sequences of the conventional novel.

The third term which acts as the unifying principle within this dislocated universe is the language of the novel itself. The language of the novel, disrupting as it does the narrative causality, the identity of character and the idiom of rational discourse, imposes upon both writer and reader a new idiom which derives its meaning from an entirely new order of things and events. It was this new order which Joyce saw as necessary for the establishment of the connecting principle which would provide the unity for which he was searching.

In an interview with Samuel Beckett in 1957, Richard Ellmann gleaned the following interpretation of Joyce's interest in this regard.

> To Joyce, reality was a paradigm, an illustration of a possibly unstateable rule. Yet perhaps the rule can be surmised. It is not a perception of order or of love; more humble than either of these, it is a perception of coincidence . . . a notion of the world where unexpected simultaneities are the rule. The characters pass through sequences of situations and thoughts of other living and dead men . . . Do Bloom and Stephen coincidentally think the same thoughts at the same time? Do they wander and fly like Ulysses and Daedalus? They are examples of a universal process. In all his books up to *Finnegans Wake* Joyce sought to reveal the coincidence of the past and the present. Only in *Finnegans Wake* was he to carry his conviction to its furthest reaches, by implying that there is no present and no past, that there are no dates, that time − and language which is time's expression − is a series of coincidences which are general all over humanity. Words move into words, people into people, incidents into incidents like the ambiguities of a pun, or a dream.[43]

IX

The obsession with paternity which led Joyce to reorder the universe and redefine the commonly accepted idioms of causality, space and time, so as to provide a more comprehensive understanding of the movement of reality, brings him close to a similar discovery which Jung was making almost contemporaneously and which he described in his paper on "Synchronicity: an acausal connecting principle." Here Jung defines this term as "the parallelism of time and meaning between psychic and psychophysiçal events, which scientific knowledge so far has been unable to reduce to a common principle. The term explains nothing, it simply formulates the occurrence of meaningful coincidences which, in themselves, are chance happenings, but are so improbable that we must assume them to be based on some kind of principle, or on some property of the empirical world. No reciprocal causal connection can be shown to obtain between parallel events, which is just what gives them their chance character. The only recognisable and demonstrable link between them is a common meaning or equivalence."[44]

This notion of the world, a new order of meaning, was one of Joyce's major preoccupations. It can be illustrated by the almost absurd fact that the picture of Cork which he had in his flat was surrounded by a cork frame and that he placed a certain paradigmatic significance in this correspondence.[45] It also emphasises the new idiom with which we are now forced to interpret the various "paradigmatic" influences upon his own work outlined at the beginning of this essay.

In this perspective it can be seen that the Scylla and Charybdis of *Ulysses,* which is presided over by the organ of the brain, is constantly being removed from the surface level of the narrative causality (and all causality, it must be remembered, is essentially the idiom of the brain) to another level of synchronicity which introduces a dimension beyond the space-time continuum of causality proper to the conventional novel. This other continuum of thinking and perceiving is hinted at by Jung although he never develops it in the way that Joyce was later to do in *Finnegans Wake.* "We must ask ourselves whether there is some other nervous substrate in us, apart from the cerebrum, that can think and perceive, or whether the psychic processes that go on in us during loss of consciousness are synchronistic phenomena, i.e. events that have no causal connection with organic processes." After a lengthy argument Jung concludes " that a nervous substrate like the sympathetic system, which is absolutely different from the cerebrospinal system in point of origin and function can evidently produce thoughts and perceptions just as easily as the latter."[46]

If such a substrate were to exist and if someone should set himself the task of expressing himself in such an idiom, it would, according to Jung, "produce a picture of the world so irrepresentable as to be completely baffling."[47] The dimension from which such a communication would have to be made would correspond to what Jung refers to as "a twilight state".[48] In such a state, Jung wonders whether "the normal state of unconsciousness in sleep, and the potentially conscious dreams it contains . . . are produced not so much by the activity of the sleeping cortex, as by the unsleeping sympathetic system, and are therefore of a transcerebral nature."[49] Such expression would require "a new conceptual language — a 'neutral language' ", a modality without a cause which Jung refers to as "acausal orderedness". Such communication implies a new kind of thought which Jung describes as "visceral thinking" or "a conversation in and with one's intestines" which in turn implies "an almost universal 'restratification' of modern man, who is in the process of shaking off a world that has become obsolete."[50]

The schizophrenic state of Joyce's psyche, caused by the opposition between his visceral sympathetic system, on the one hand, and his cerebral consciousness, on the other, forced him to discover, in his search for a satisfying principle of unity, a transcerebral continuum which would give expression to these two dimensions. The independent third term which supplied the matrix for such a combination was the reality of language. In his final work, *Finnegans Wake*, language becomes the main character of the novel. In *Ulysses* it had acted as the disrupting and dislocating factor which served to undermine the conventional idioms of character, space and time. In his final work it assumes its role as incubator of the meaning of man. *Ulysses* is a novel, but, as such, it is used as its mythological predecessor used the wooden horse, to enter and destroy the city. "What do you think Vulgariano did but study with stolen fruit how cutely to copy all their various styles of signature so as one day to utter an epical forged cheque on the public for his own private use."[51]

The "private use" for which the "epical forged cheque" of *Ulysses* was fashioned was the destruction of the language of the novel and the discovery of language as that psychic dimension which partipates in the acausal motor-force of reality. Language at this level springs from a substratum which includes, but does not derive from, our mental activities. It is the third term which unites the cerebrospinal and the sympathetic systems, whose apparent opposition had for so long created a schizophrenic cleavage in Joyce's personality. Language here is "a nameform that whets the wits that convey contacts that sweeten sensation that drives desire . . . that entails the ensuance of existentiality. But with a rush out of his navel reaching the reredos of Ramasbatham."[52]

The ordinary perspective which governs our world in terms of latitude and longtitude, outer and inner, conscious and unconscious, past, present and future, dream and reality, is one which was fashioned by man as cerebral spectator to the universe. *Cogito ergo sum* is the ultimate expression of such a distancing of the "I" from the "ensuance of existentiality". The "I" of *Finnegans Wake* is, in the words of Hermon Broch,[53] "at once the *sum* and the *cogito,* at once the logos and life, reunited; a simultaneity in whose unity may be seen the glow of the religious *per se.* "[54] The particular gifts of Joyce allowed him to situate himself quite "naturally" at another place within himself, from which place the language of *Finnegans Wake* quite naturally flows. It isn't as if Joyce were "consciously" trying the write in a deliberately exotic way. "I write like that because it comes naturally to me to do so," Joyce told John Eglington.[55]

Language here is the key to the work. Just as Joyce had turned on its head the triangle composed of the reader, the writer and the text, in the forged novel of *Ulysses*, causing language to assume the paternal role of generating a meaningful principle, so, in *Finnegans Wake* the triangle of mind, instincts and language has also been transfigured to allow the third term to assume the paternal role which will ultimately permit the unification and recapitulation of the other two.

X

In Part I vii of *Finnegans Wake*, where Joyce gives a portrait of himself as Shem the Penman and provides an apologia for his use of language in the *Wake*, a description can be found of the new kind of thinking which is language as the principle of paternity.

In this section there is a retrospective account of all Joyce's writings up to *Finnegans Wake: A Portrait of the Artist* is described as a "wetbed confession", all the stories in *Dubliners* are denigratingly mentioned by name,[56] and *Ulysses* is described as a forgery. This renunciation of his style of writing in the past as "pseudostylic shamiana . . . piously forged palimpsests . . . from his pelagiarist pen,"[7] is a prelude to the description of his new kind of writing in *Finnegans Wake*. "In writing of the night", he says in a letter,[58] "I really could not, I felt I could not, use words in their ordinary relations and connections. Used that way they do not express how things are in the night, in the different stages — conscious, then semi-conscious, then unconscious. I found that it could not be done with words in their ordinary relations and connections." *Finnegans Wake* is written "to suit the esthetic of the dream, where the forms prolong and multiply themselves, where the visions pass from the trivial to the apocalyptic, where the brain uses the roots of vocables to make others from them which will be capable of naming its phantasms, its allegories, its allusions."[59]

This attempt to express the "dark night of the soul" was "a long, very long, a dark, very dark, an allburt unend, scarce endurable, and we could add mostly quite various and somenwhat stumbletumbling night."[60] In this "Jungfraud's Messongebook"[61] we are never quite sure whether the language is "d'anglas landadge or . . . are you sprakin sea Djoytsch? "[62] Here "the war is in words and the wood is the world."[63] Joyce struggles with language to twist it into shapes ("Imeffible tries at speech unasyllabled") and to crush it into forms ("quashed quotatoes") so that "the silent cock shall crow at last"[64] and a hidden silent world ooze into speech.

Such a use of language allows Joyce to "psing a psalm of psexpeans, apocryphul of rhyme"[65] which exploits every aspect of the syllables which compose the words, "for to concentrate solely on the literal sense or even the psychological content of any document to the sore neglect of the enveloping facts themselves circumstantiating it is just as hurtful to sound sense . . ."[66] This is not a scientific use of language which would translate reality into clearcut and unambiguous terms. It is a surpassing of the principle of non-contradiction by a supralogical use of words, each one containing at least "two thinks at a time".[67] The pun, in Tindall's phrase, is mightier than the word because it uses the referential medium of sound to spark off correspondences simultaneously tangential to those suggested by the shapes. The artist of such a language does not fly in a cerebral fashion over the forest of language, he situates himself in the thick of the jungle and hacks away at the roots of vocables until he reaches that "root language" which holds "the keys of me heart".[68]

The difference between Stephen and Shem is in their attitude to and their use of language. Both are "selfexiled in upon his ego" and "writing the mystery of himsel in furniture". But Shem has found the way out of the solipsistic cocoon back beyond the confines of his own consciousness. He has learnt to produce "nichtthemerically" (a word that combines the ideas of "nighttime', "nonthematic" and "numerically") "from his unheavenly body" what Stephen is trying to unfold thematically from his heavenly body, disconnected from the material world.

It is the same Joyce who creates the two protagonists. As he says himself, "there is no body here present which was not there before. Only order is othered."[69] The order of being has been othered by the installation of language into the paternal role. Language is the main character in *Finnegans Wake*. Starting with the very particular European city of Dublin and the particular life of an individual author, the generative power of language leads the artist into an underworld of the universal subconscious, much as the entry into any particular subway station will lead down to that network of underground correspondences which connect with every other one.

The *Wake* of this universal dimension requires the sleep of the ordinary language and the daytime logic of the cerebrospinal cortex. The "stomach language" of this "prepronominal *funferal*, engraved and retouched and edgewiped and puddenpadded, very like a whale's egg farced with pemmican" makes no easy reading. Each sentence has to be "nuzzled over a full trillion times . . . by that ideal reader suffering from an ideal insomnia"[70] who has to forget the way he was taught to read, and allow language to become the "aural eyeness"[71] which will provide the "keys to dreamland".[72]

The image which Joyce uses to describe the source and the production of this new language is the sepia ink secreted by a squid. The house of Shem the Penman is described as "the Haunted Inkbottle", wherein "this double dye" is "brought to blood heat through the bowels of his misery." Just as the ink of an octopus is part of its being, so language is "the squidself which he had squirtscreened from the crystalline world;" it is not a translation, it is the reality itself. It comes from his reflecting upon "his own individual life unlivable" and his processing of the various "scalds and burns and blisters, impetiginous sores and pustules" through "the slow fires of consciousness". Its effect is not just an individualistic web of the artist's own making, a predictable, orderly and impotent ego trip. This language creates "a dividual chaos, perilous, potent, common to allflesh'."

The element in it which creates this escape route is its "antimonian manganese limolitmious nature", whose "corrosive sublimation" works itself back through the artist's individual consciousness until it reaches "one continuous present tense integument" which slowly unfolds "all marryvoising moodmoulded cyclewheeling history".[73]

It is in this sense that language, as the generating third term in the triangles of literature and psychology, becomes the father for whom Joyce was searching. As a corrosive river it can journey back into the deep recesses of the psyche to provide a meeting-place for those antagonistic principles which manifested a conscious state of schizophrenia. In terms of literature, it objectifies a "general omnibus character",[74] inclusive of all the elements of "homogenius" humanity, in the shape of a new kind of father-figure, "the Great Sommbody within the Omniboss"[75] or "someone imparticular who will somewherise for the whole".[76]

The "some where" which will summarise the whole of "cyclewheeling history" is the city of Dublin. The "general omnibus character" who personifies this totality of manhood is the Earwicker family. Although there seem to be several members of the family and several variations of each member, each one characterises one aspect of the integrated human omnibus. It is also difficult to distinguish them from the topography of the "anywhere" of Dublin. H.C.E., the original father-figure, is identified with the hill of Howth, Chapelizod and Phoenix Park. He is the masculine principle whose initials spell out his universality in their variation as "Here Comes Everybody". His wife A.L.P., identified with the river Liffey which runs through the city, is the feminine principle, "annyma" (anima), called Anna Livia Plurabelle. His daughter Issy is-a-belle who can represent any and every kind of girl, while his sons, Shem and Shaun, are those familiar, age-old, warring twins, equal and opposite, who inhabit each one of us in varying combinations. They are the rivals who compose the banks (rivae) of the river.

The structure within which their family history is unfolded is provided by Vico and Bruno. The coincidence that Dublin does have "a Vico road" which "goes round and round to meet where terms begin",[77] and a bookshop called Browne and Nolan, act as proof of the universal principle which Joyce understood to be a paradigm of reality. Both literature and life were one "grand continuum overlorded by fate and interlarded with accidence".[78]

Language, as an alluvial deposit, is both the source and the texture of this grand continuum. "In the buginning is the woid"[79] is Joyce's variation on the opening to St John's Gospel. Language, as father, replaces the monarchical autonomous principle by an anarchical and heteronomous one. The void of the word (woid) is constitutive of language. Although a "thing-of-words". language is not a "thing-in-itself" because words, however autonomous they may appear, are always referential, their being is to relate to something else. Language is the fluid principle of continuity between the "squidself" of the artist-father and the "squirtscreened" image of his consubstantial son at every level of creation from theology to literature. Far from being an invention of human consciousness to act as mere communication between men, language is an aboriginal source of meaning which flows through history and humanity, by whose shores the artist, as an alert and zealous beachcomber, is called to read "the signatures of all things".

Richard Kearney

BECKETT:
THE DEMYTHOLOGISING INTELLECT

The separation of philosophy from literary study has not
worked to the benefit of either. Without the pressure of
philosophy on literary texts or the reciprocal pressure of
literary analysis on philosophical writing, each discipline
becomes impoverished. If there is a danger of the confusion of realms, it is a danger worth experiencing.

Geoffrey Hartman, *Deconstruction and Criticism*

Beckett's attitude to philosophy, as to almost everything else which
obsesses him, is ambivalent. Malone epitomises the Beckettian intellectual when he concludes some fifty pages of clever metaphysical reflection by dismissing it as "ballsaching poppycock about life and
death" — only to begin all over again. Beckett's personal pronouncements on the subject are equally paradoxical. In his early essays, he
warns against the neat identifications of the "analogymongers"[1] and
declares that "allegory . . . must always *fail* in the hands of a poet."[2]
Yet Beckett's own works are replete with analogies and allegories and
he himself is the first to admit that his writing is a "fidelity to *failure*."[3]
Similarly, while he affirms in one interview that he "never read philosophers" and "wouldn't have had any reason to write novels if (he)
could have expressed their subject in philosophic terms,"[4] in another
he candidly admits that if he were a critic writing on his works he
would begin with the metaphysical quotations from Geulincx and
Democritus which recur in his novels.[5] Indeed, there is scarcely a work
of Beckett's that does not mischievously tease out the questions of
some great thinker — Aristotle, Augustine, Descartes, Berkeley, Malebranche, Leibniz, Schopenhauer or Eckhart, not to mention Geulincx
and Democritus. The fundamental ambiguity of Beckett's appraisal
of philosophy may be understood in terms of Oscar Wilde's maxim
that "a truth in art is that whose contradictory is also true."[6] So that
despite his prevarications, Beckett, perhaps more than any other

contemporary writer has succeeded in making philosophy literary and literature philosophical.

*   *   *

It was at *l'Ecole Normale Superieure* in Paris in 1928 that Beckett discovered Rimbaud's revolutionary plea to abandon inherited certainties and "become absolutely modern".[7] This meant for Beckett that modern art must become "pure interrogation".[8] It can be said that Beckett himself is absolutely modern to the extent that he compels literature to reflect upon itself, to question the conditions of its own possibility. Modern thought differs from its traditional antecedents in that it no longer assumes the world to be some assured reality to which the self could faithfully conform or correspond. The self becomes the sole critic of existence, putting everything in question, including itself! Beckett argues, accordingly, that the modern writer becomes a critical explorer of that "rupture of the lines of communication . . . between him and the world of objects".[9] Such critical explorations bring Beckett to the threshold of modern philosophy.

Beckett's writings demythologise some of the oldest and most revered traditions of intellectual identity. They playfully yet pointedly challenge two fundamental philosophical concepts of western culture: the idealist concept of a supreme substance or being (derived from Greek metaphysics) and the theological concept of a divine creator or first cause (derived from a rationalist interpretation of the Judeo-Christian tradition). Beckett's challenge to the former metaphysical tradition takes the form of a parody of idealist thinkers, particularly Descartes and his disciples Geulincx, Leibniz and Berkeley. His challenge to the theological conceptions of God concentrates on the dogmatic definitions of scholasticism as well as simplistic versions of biblical eschatology and mysticism. These major aspects of Beckettian demythologisation shall be dealt with in the first two sections of this essay. In a third section we shall comment on some similarities between Beckett's literary demythologisation and the contemporary continental critques of existence and language.

*   *   *

It is worth noting from the outset, however, that if Beckett attempted to demystify some of the key philosophical 'myths' which underwrote western man's sense of identity, he was never motivated to secure an alternative tenure in some indigenous Celtic tradition. A Celtic dogmatism of self-identity was considered by Beckett to be no less mythic or mystificatory than its Hellenic and Hebraic counterparts.

Beckett had no time for the native nostalgia of the Celtic twilight and found here a further fetish for his demythologising intellect. In his 1936 essay "Recent Irish Poetry", Beckett contrasts the "altitudinous complacency of the Victorian Gael", promoted by the "antiquarian" writers of the Irish Revival, with "other" Irish writers such as Joyce (and presumably Brian Coffey, Denis Devlin, Thomas McGreevy and of course himself) who took their cue from the European literary models of critical interrogation. Yeats, Clarke and Corkery represent the former "antiquarian" category. Beckett was singularly harsh on W.B. Yeats whom he accuses of a "flight from self-awareness". In the Yeatsian universe of Celtic myth and lore, the "self is either most happily obliterated or else so improved and enlarged as to be mistaken for the décor".[10] In pointed contrast, Beckett places the work of Jack Yeats—W.B.'s brother—in the "other" category of Irish artists and compliments him for his exploration of *"le plus secret de l'esprit"* as follows: "The artist who plays his being is from *nowhere*. And he has no brothers".[11] Furthermore, Beckett is prepared to give O'Casey the benefit of the doubt in his shifting attitudes to Irish identity. He was particularly sympathetic to O'Casey's anti-nationalism in *Juno and the Paycock*, judging it to be his finest work in so far as it communicates the "dramatic dehiscence" of insular identity: "mind and world come asunder in irreparable dissociation — 'chassis'."[12]

In his first novel *Murphy* (1938), Beckett continues his critical exposure of the Irish Revival pretensions and particularly its claim to a fixed national identity. He lampoons the patriotic efforts of Austin Clarke to found a literature on a national Hibernian heritage. He calls him "Austin Ticklepenny", the "pot poet from the county of Dublin" and derides the "class of pentametre that Ticklepenny felt it his duty to Erin to compose . . . bulging with as many minor beauties from the Gaelic prosodoturfy as could be sucked out of a mug of Beamish's porter."[13] In an equally mischievous vein, Beckett's portrayal of Neary's Cork chauvinism "mocks the narrow literary nationalism emanating from Munster and upheld by Daniel Corkery."[14] Of course Beckett did not hesitate to use Irish material for his own literary needs. *More Pricks than Kicks, Murphy* and *Molloy* are peppered with local allusions and the majority of Beckettian characters bear conspicuously Irish names. But his fondness for home-made material is largely to facilitate his parody of self-righteous or sentimental claims to a native literary identity. If contemporary European culture was undergoing a crisis of modernity typified by its art of "pure interrogation", the Celtic hinterlands were not to be sought after as an alternative. Such an Ireland, Beckett believed, could offer no legitimate refuge from the "filthy modern tide" of alienation. That is why he followed Joyce and McGreevy to Paris, preferring "France in war to Ireland in peace".[15]

I.

METAPHYSICAL IDEALISM

In 1926, while still a student in Trinity College Dublin, Beckett discovered the philosophy of René Descartes. This was his first real encounter with the western tradition of metaphysical idealism. Beckett read Descartes voraciously and filled three notebooks with his own reflections as well as commentaries by biographers and critics. In 1929, as an instructor at *l'Ecole Normale*, he resumed his reading of France's most original thinker. After months of almost total immersion in the life and thought of Descartes, Beckett transmuted his scattered notes into an esoteric ninety-eight line poem entitled *Whoroscope*. The poem was awarded a ten pound prize by the Hours press and was published in Paris in 1930. "This long poem, mysterious, obscure in parts," declared Nancy Cunard who judged the competition, "was clearly by someone very intellectual . . ."[16]

Whoroscope was a turning point in Beckett's career, not only because it was his first published work, but also because it succeeded in transforming intellectual obsession into literary creation. The punning title alludes to the Greek word for "hour" – *horo* (the Hours Press prize was for poems about time) and to Descartes' superstitious withholding of his date of birth to prevent astrologers from predicting his death (hence the concluding line – "starless inscrutable hour"). Curiously, Beckett himself has obscured the question of his own date of birth. Though his birth certificate gives the date as May 13, 1906, Beckett has always insisted that he was born on Good Friday, April 13, of the same year.

Beckett was fascinated by the Cartesian project to free the thinking self from all external constraints – symbolised in *Whoroscope* by the determining cycle of the stars and the revolting intrusions of our physical existence. The Cartesian self exists because it thinks–*cogito ergo sum*–and seeks to remain an autonomous substance entirely independent of material reality. The *cogito* aspires to the condition of an eternal and self-sufficient being far removed from corporeal and temporal decay. But the disturbing irony here, as elsewhere in Beckett's work, is that the idealist vision of spiritual freedom is forever confounded by the fact that we are born with bodies. Descartes conjured up all sorts of ways in which the soul might control the body without becoming contaminated by it, eventually concluding that the pineal gland (at the base of the brain) was the secret connection! But if such problems were a source of insufferable metaphysical anguish for Descartes, Beckett seizes upon them as a choice occasion for literary parody. Already in *Whoroscope*, Beckett mockingly juxtaposes Descartes' aspiration for intellectual autonomy with the gross infelicities of his personal biography. Closely following Adrien Baillet's *Life of Descartes*, which he was reading at the time, Beckett ridicules the French philosopher's attempts to transcend his biological ailments in order to achieve a pure spiritual liberty. Hence the ironic pseudo-philosophical question which opens the poem: "What's that? An Egg?" (referring to Descartes' daily breakfast of ten-day old "stinking" eggs). The rest of the poem traces Descartes' biographical itinerary from one episode of physical revulsion to the next. Apart from the titular allusion to whores, there are lurid references to "stagnant murky blood", "lashed ovaries with prostisciutto", "grey flayed epidermis and scarlet tonsils", "milled sweat" and "double-breasted turds". The poem concludes with Descartes' visit to the Swedish court of Queen Christina—"the murdering matinal pope-confessed amazon, Christina the ripper"—where he perished from lack of sleep and from cold weather. As Beckett explains in his irreverent notes to the poem: "At Stockholm, in November, (Christina) required Descartes, who had remained in bed till midday all his life, to be with her at five in the morning."[17]

Whoroscope is mined with countless other mock-heroic metaphysical allusions. There is a reference to the "Brothers' Boot" whose refutation of Aristotle occurred in Dublin in 1640; a pseudo-scholastic send-up of Descartes' "eucharistic sophistry" when responding to Arnauld's challenge "to reconcile his doctrine of matter with the doctrine of transubstantiation" – "So we drink Him and eat Him/ And the watery Beaune and the stale cubes of Hovis etc."; an allusion to Descartes' "sophistry concerning the movement of the earth" in his contemptuous rejection of Galileo; and a saucy mention of St Augustine's "revelation in the shrubbery" which culminated in his quasi-Cartesian proof of existence: *fallor ergo sum* (I err therefore I am).

In *Murphy*, his most explicitly philosophical novel, Beckett develops the Cartesian parody adumbrated in *Whoroscope*. Though his name is Irish, Murphy lives in London and is of indeterminate origin. He seeks the ideal Cartesian state of spiritual freedom beyond the material limitations of time, place, movement and death. The inner chamber of the cogito must accordingly be liberated from the ephemeral outer world: "Murphy's mind pictured itself as a large hollow sphere, hermetically closed to the universe without."[18] "The nature of outer reality," he affirms, "remained obscure." Murphy's favourite occupation is to strap himself to his rocking chair in mimicry of the scholastic definition of the supreme being as an unmoved mover: "it appeased his body" and "set him free in his mind . . . it was not until his body was appeased that he could come alive in his mind." Beckett is manifestly obsessed with this Cartesian rupture between mind (*res cogitans*) and body (*res extensa*). Throughout the novel, the coveted liberty of mind is threatened by interferences from the physical world. Murphy's irrepressible lust for Celia, "the part of him that he hated craved for Celia"[19] – as well as the astronomical determinations of place and time which govern Murphy's every action, suggest that his free volition is in fact a physically conditioned necessity.[20] Even Murphy's final will that his remains be flushed down a toilet bowl in the Abbey Theatre (a mockery of both Yeatsian nationalism and the Cartesian vortex) is ultimately denied him. The cremated ashes are, instead, ignobly scattered over the floor of a pub: "By closing time, the body, mind and soul of Murphy were freely distributed over the floor of the saloon; and before another dayspring greyened the earth, had been swept away with the sand, the beer, the butts, the glass, the matches, the spits, the vomit."[21]

Another idealist metaphysician who held a profound fascination for Beckett was the Belgian disciple of Descartes, Arnold Geulincx (1624-69). Beckett first became acquainted with Geulincx's thought in Dublin in the late 1920s. He was particularly impressed by his theory that since man can only secure freedom in the mind one should renounce the will's attempts to master or alter the external world of objects — which includes of course our own body. Murphy refers to "the beautiful Belgo-Latin of Arnold Geulincx" and enthusiastically cites his quietistic plea for independence from physical volition or desire: *Ubi nihil vales, ibi nihil velis* (where you are worth nothing, will nothing).[22]

Geulincx extrapolates Descartes' idea of the "freedom of indifference" arguing that the only reasonable approach to one's physical passions is to ignore them, thereby attaining a state of dispassionate neutrality. This notion of passive indifference beyond the determining cycles of cause and effect, birth and death etc. was to become a key theme not only of *Murphy* — which extols the virtues of "the freedom of indifference, the indifference of freedom"—but also of the *Proust* essay (1931) where Beckett sees a suspension of the active will (what he calls voluntary memory) as prerequisite to an authentic encounter with the "suffering of Being" (what he calls involuntary memory). But this metaphysical model of inaction freed from movement and desire, while devoutly to be wished, is usually portrayed by Beckett as a comic impossibility.

Beckett was well aware that the metaphysical ideal of immobility was derived from Parmenidean rationalism. Parmenides, the first of the Greek philosophers to invoke reason and logic to explain reality, held that true being was identical with thought. "It is the same thing to think and to be" runs his celebrated maxim. Rational being was considered to exist beyond the sensible and temporal world of becoming. Parmenides' most ingenious disciple, Zeno, employed the reductive arguments of logic to demonstrate that movement was impossible. Beckett refers to Zeno as the "old Greek" in *Endgame* and makes explicit allusion to his famous *reductio ad absurdum* example of the little heap of millet. This example, which recurs in several of Beckett's other works,[23] runs as follows: If I pour half of a finite quantity of millet grain into a heap and then pour half of the remaining quantity and so on *ad infinitum*, the heap will never be completed, for the remaining quantity, however reduced on each pouring, is infinitely divisible. Similarly, the hare can never overtake the tortoise because the original gap between them, no matter how many times it is halved by the approaching hare, can always be halved yet again. Thus Zeno shows that movement is logically impossible, a mere illusion of the senses. Aristotelian metaphysics refined the Parmenidean position in arguing that only the divine being (*telos*) or reason (*nous*) possessed the qualities of atemporality and immobility and that mortal beings were condemned, by virtue of their materiality, to time, movement and desire.[24] The only possible escape from mortality was to practise rational contemplation until one participated in the divine condition of the "self-thinking-thought" (*noeisis tes noeseos*). Aristotle's definition of the divine as a self-thinking-thought was later translated into the Augustinian and scholastic definition of God as a "self-loving-love" (*Amor quo Deus se ipsum amat*).[25] Beckett pointedly rebukes Murphy's pretensions to divine self-sufficiency by prefacing the Cartesian description of "Murphy's Mind" with the fake epithet: "*Amor intellectualis quo Murphy se ipsum amat*."

In the Beckettian universe, no man can shuffle off his mortal coil. We are beings who exist in time; death is inescapable. The "post-mortem" condition of "Belacqua bliss" sought by the characters of *More Pricks than Kicks*, *Murphy* and the later novels, is perpetually frustrated or deferred. And Beckett's *dramatis personae* are no less unfortunate. "Have you not done tormenting me with your accursed time?" cried Pozzo in *Waiting for Godot*. "We are born astride of a grave, the light gleams for an instant then it is night once more." But it is perhaps in his *Proust* essay, that Beckett first articulates man's failure to transcend his mortality. Affirming our enslavement to "that double-headed monster of salvation and damnation-time", Beckett concludes that "there is no escape from the hours and the days. Neither from tomorrow nor from yesterday."[26] It is equally impossible for the self to transcend desire; for we have to desire not to desire and so are invariably tied to the corporeal cycle of existence. As Arsène points out in *Watt*: "It is impossible not to seek, not to want, for when you cease to seek you start to find, and when you cease to want, then life begins to ram her fish and chips down your gullet until you puke, and then the puke down your gullet until you puke the puke and then the puked puke until you begin to like it."[27]

But it is surely in *Murphy* that the Cartesian construction of an immaterial cogito is most pitilessly undone. To Miss Counihan's (a former lover of Murphy) assertion that "there is a mind and there is a body" the Newtonian Neary replies: "Kick her arse!" Murphy's own version of dualism is also reduced to comic ridicule: "Thus Murphy felt himself split in two, a body and a mind. They had intercourse apparently, otherwise he could not have known that they had anything in common. But he felt his mind to be bodytight and did not understand through what channel the intercourse was effected nor how the two experiences came to overlap. He was satisfied that neither followed from the other. He neither thought a kick because he felt one nor felt a kick because he thought one."[28] And so Murphy persists in promoting the idealist fictions of his predecessor Belacqua, "scoffing at the idea of a sequitur from his body to his mind", content to reside in his "little internus homo, in the self-sufficiency he never wearied of arrogating to himself."[29]

While Descartes sought to explain the interrelationship of mind and matter by appealing to a pineal gland and a "divine guarantee", Geulincx formulated the equally implausible, if logically consistent, theory of occasionalism. This theory, espoused by several Beckettian characters from Murphy to Malone, stated that what really happens when the soul and body *seem* to interact is that the movement of one's body and the thought of that movement, as two entirely independent actions, are simultaneously willed by God. In other words, God in his goodness wills us to move at the same time as we desire to move. God's will is the true cause, man's will a merely illusory or "occasional" cause. To clinch the matter, Geulincx provides us with his notorious notion of the mind and body as two parallel clocks whose timing has been perfectly synchronised by a divine clockmaker! The human *cogito* is thus free to the extent that it conforms to the divine will and does not try to interfere with the workings of the material world.[30]

Murphy tries out the dualist theories of Descartes and Geulincx, before finally hitting upon the "monadological" solution of yet another Cartesian rationalist, Gottfried Leibniz. In his padded cell in the Magdalene Mercyseat asylum, Murphy believes he inhabits a self-contained monad: "The compartment was windowless like a monad . . . within the narrow limits of domestic architecture he had never been able to imagine a more creditable representation of what he kept calling, indefatigably, the little world." Leibniz held that every *cogito* is an isolated monadic soul ("little world") with no dependence on sensory perception: "*La monade est sans fenêtre*", as he puts it in *Nouveaux essais sur l'entendement humain*. To enable this monadology to comply with his theory that we live in "the best of all possible worlds," Leibniz introduced the notion of a "pre-established harmony" (or "pre-established arbitrary" as Watt mockingly calls it). By means of such harmonisation, God would assure an exact correspondence between the spiritual movement or *conatus* (which Lucky misnames "conation" during his "think" in *Godot*) of each monad and the physical movement of the outward universe.[31]

But Beckettian idealists differ from their Cartesian prototypes in that they can have no recourse to a divine Guarantor, Clockmaker or

Harmoniser. They can take no solace in a supreme will which might validate their self-thinking thoughts. If there is some pre-established correspondence between Murphy's mind and the astral movements of the universe there is no divine meaning in this correspondence: "They were *his* stars . . . it was *his* meaning."[32] Murphy is a Cartesian idealist bereft of God, a self alone (*solus ipse*), a solipsistic victim of his own "precious ipsumossity". Art, as Beckett affirmed in *Proust*, is the "apotheosis of solitude . . . There is no communication because no vehicles of communication."[33] Murphy can find no equivalence in the real world for the fictions of his own mind. The mind's desire is not translatable into correlative objective action. Thus Beckett follows the Cartesian procedure of universal doubt without ever founding the existence of the *cogito* on the existence of God. He takes the doubt and leaves the proof. The Beckettian self is at the mercy of the *malin génie*; he is a sceptic without salvation.

*   *   *

But of all the Cartesian idealists that haunted Beckett, it was perhaps with the Irish philosopher Bishop George Berkeley that he most identified. Born in County Kilkenny in 1685, Berkeley received his B.A. from Trinity College, Dublin, some two hundred years before Beckett. Interestingly, the definitive edition of Berkeley's works was brought out by Beckett's tutor at Trinity, A.A. Luce. Berkeley has been described as an Irish Cartesian since he subscribes to the metaphysical idealism of Descartes and Malebranche.[34] As Professor Harry Bracken argues: "Berkeley is neither British nor empiricist. If he must be labelled, he might more accurately be called an Irish Cartesian."[35] Beckett's reference to Berkeley's "*idealist* tar" (Berkeley's *Siris* is about tar water) in *Murphy* would suggest that he shares Bracken's position. The following are the principle Cartesian characteristics of Berkeley's thought: i) meaning derives from subjective consciousness rather than the objective world; ii) consciousness is fundamentally dual, divided into perceiver (*percipere*) and perceived (*percipi*); iii) the conscious mind is a free and immortal spirit irreducible to materialistic models of explanation.

In contradistinction to the empiricists who held that genuine knowledge comes from our empirical sensations, Berkeley is a thorough-going immaterialist. He sought to justify a speculative and spiritual vision of the world beyond the limits of the materialistic sciences (which he qualified as "minute philosophies"). Only a religious sensibility, Berkeley believed, could transcend sensory experience and intuit the supernatural causes of things. The error of the physical sciences is to argue from the visible universe (*visibilia*) to invisible principles of explanation (*invisibilia*), while maintaining that all rests on empirico-metric grounds. Berkeley exposed this error and retorted that it is only when we recognise the strictly material limits of the empirical sciences that we can acknowledge the existence of a higher and irreducible order of spiritual vision.

The material world is the visible world; it *is* because it is *seen.* While the being of matter is to be perceived, the being of mind is to perceive. Or as our Kilkenny luminary put it: *Esse est percipi aut percipere* (To be is to be perceived or to perceive). The table, for example, exists only because I see it existing. But since the world evidently possesses a permanence independent of man's finite and occasional perception of it, it follows for Berkeley that the infinite mind of God must assure its continued existence by perpetually perceiving it. God is the generous and ever-vigilant *percipere* who sustains all things in being. But Berkeley will allow that we can ultimately transcend our passive sensation of the material universe and participate in the active and creative *percipere* of God. It is only by the spiritual vision of our minds, attuned to God's supreme vision, that we may apprehend the secret cause of things. The spiritual "eye of the mind" transcends the subservient "eye of matter." And God's infinite mind is the transcendent cause of both the finite world and our own finite minds.

Beckett's Murphy is Berkeleyian in several important respects. The most unequivocal reference to Berkeley comes when Murphy, through a process of intense mental concentration in a chess game with the mad Mr Endon, mystically surpasses the condition of a material body that is *seen*, towards a quasi-divine *seeing*. In short, he goes beyond empirical sensation (colour, taste, sound etc.) towards an unadulterated spiritual vision: "Murphy began to see nothing, that colourlessness which is such a rare post-natal treat, being the absence (to use a nice distinction) not of *percipere* but of *percipi*. His other senses also found themselves at peace, an unexpected pleasure."[36] Furthermore, Mr Kelly's contemplative efforts to "determine the point at which seen and unseen meet" by sitting like Murphy in a chair for long periods, is surely an allusion to Berkeley's argument that only a suprasensible vision can apprehend the divine correlation between the *visibilia* of *percipi* and the *invisibilia* of *percipere*.[37]

But it is in Beckett's *Film*, that Berkeley's *esse est percipi* argument is pushed to its most extreme conclusion. In the general summary of the script Beckett writes: "*Esse est percipi.* All extraneous perception suppressed, animal, human, divine, self-perception maintains in being. Search of non-being in flight from extraneous perception breaking down in inescapability of self-perception."[38]

Film shows the muffled figure of Buster Keaton scuttling through laneways and corridors, desperately trying to escape the mortal condition of being seen. In the crowded streets, "all persons are shown in some way perceiving one another, an object, a shop window, a poster etc., i.e., all contentedly in *percipere* and *percipi*."[39] And so the one-eyed protagonist, fleeing from the uncritical complacency of the madding crowd, dashes through a narrow street and shuts himself away in a bare room. He takes every possible precaution to avoid being perceived: he drives out his pet animals, covers the bird cage, the gold-fish bowl, a portrait of "God the Father looking severely at him," the mirror, the windows etc. and finally settles down to sleep in a Murphyes-que rocking chair. But he cannot escape the awareness that, in spite of all his precautions, he is *still* not unperceived. The eye of the camera sees the victim even as he flees from all other eyes. And in the end this eye is seen by the horrified protagonist who realises he can never escape perception of himself self-perceived. The eye of the camera which opens in full close-up on the eye of the protagonist cannot be suppressed. We are condemned to be (*esse*) and to be perceived (*per-cipi*).

Only God could enjoy the privilege of perceiving without being per-ceived. We mortals, by contrast, can find no refuge from the perceiving other. Hence Beckett's frequent references to Job, Jonah and Moses as witnesses of the Unseen God who sees all. "Do you think God sees me?" says Estragon to Vladimir in *Godot*. There is, of course, no way of knowing. But what Estragon can be sure of is that Vladimir always sees him. In Beckett's universe the ideal freedom of invisibility inevit-ably collides with the slavery of visibility, for we can never dispel the presence of the other. Similarly, the ideal of silence is assailed by "other" voices, be they the voices of conscience and memory (as in *Krapps' Last Tape, Eh Joy, Footfalls* or *Not I*), the voices of the dead (as in *Embers* and *Godot*), the voices of some unnamable other who will not leave us be (*The Unnamable, Texts for Nothing* etc.), or simply the voices of other all-too-human human beings (as in *Endgame* or *Play*). "Accusative I exist," confesses the culpable author of *Texts for Nothing* who cannot avoid being seen and summoned. Always accused, always an accusative object of another's sentence, man cannot be God. Yet he is satisfied with nothing less.

II. NEGATIVE THEOLOGY

Beckett's demythologisation of enlightenment idealism also expresses itself as a resistance to all attempts to simplify the biblical notion of God in terms of a rationalistic theology. He opposes the conventional reduction of the "God of Abraham, Isaac and the Prophets" (as Pascal put it) to the "God of the philosophers". The transcendent God of Judeo-Christian faith is betrayed once it is translated into metaphysical definitions of a self-thinking-thought or self-sufficient-being (*ens causa sui, ens perfectissimum et realissimum* etc.). The God of the Bible is, for Beckett, a God of paradox and apocalypse, a *Deus Absconditus* who sends mysterious messengers, perhaps even his son, but never comes Himself. Beckett's Godot is an eschatological possibility of the future, a risk and a promise, someone we await in fear and trembling; His existence remains forever in question, in doubt. If Beckett is a sceptic in metaphysics, in theology he is an agnostic. Neither an atheist nor a theist. Hence his refusal to qualify his attitude to God and man as optimistic or pessimistic: "That would be to judge and we are in no position to judge."[40]

Beckett's theology, if he can be said to have one, is perhaps best described as a *negative theology*. His writings challenge the presumption of those theologians who would define God in certified or certifiable concepts. His attitude here is, of course, not unprecedented. Kant refuted the traditional proofs for the existence of God, vowing to "establish the limits of reason in order to make way for faith". Kierkegaard also rejected the God of speculative metaphysics and maintained that it was only by a "crucifixion of the understanding" that one could accept the absurd paradox of divine existence; this he called the "leap of faith", echoing Tertullian's *credo quia absurdum*. But perhaps the most remarkable attempt in recent times to distinguish between the God of reason and the God of faith, has been made by Bultmann whose "theology of demythologisation" argues that only by divesting God of the idealist accretions of Greek metaphysics can we recover the original religious experience of the Judeo-Christian scriptures.[41]

*   *   *

Interestingly, most of these demythologising thinkers are, like Beckett himself, of Protestant origin. Even Berkeley, arguably Beckett's favourite philosopher, displayed his reformational credentials in arguing that the spiritual vision of the divine is essentially a matter of religious intuition or faith removed from abstract, scientific rationalism. (Berkeley differed here from such Catholic philosophers as Descartes or Malebranche). At the risk of simplification, one could list the more obvious "Protestant" characteristics of Beckett's portrayal of the God question as follows: (i) God's existence or non-existence is not explicable in terms of the traditional metaphysical proofs of reason; (ii) all that we can know about God is what the perplexing parables of scripture tell us; (iii) God is totally other and transcendent, absent from the workings of the world and of men; (iv) precisely as transcendent, God can only be experienced by a solitary act of faith or by an agonised waiting; (v) God's separation from man is rendered insurmountable by virtue of our inveterate fallibility and fallenness.[42]

But Beckett's borrowings from Protestant theology by no means suggest a sectarian anti-Catholicism. If he indeed explores the "solitary" nature of faith and the "absent" nature of God, he also draws from such Catholic mystics as Meister Eckhart (explicitly referred to in *Murphy* and *Dream*) who held that God was a non-being beyond being who can only be experienced by abandoning the light of reason in favour of a patient, purgative waiting (*Abgeschiedenheit*); or St John of the Cross who wrote that God mystically revealed himself through man's encounter with darkness and death, i.e. "the dark night of the soul" (which Winnie calls the "black night without end").[43]

Although billed by newspaper journalists as "the atheist from Paris", Beckett is, I suggest, more accurately described as an agnostic from Dublin. His works show his attitude to theology to be quite as equivocal as his attitude to metaphysics. When Beckett did allow himself to be drawn into a discussion of his religious upbringing, he was either non-committal or mischievously irreverent.[44] The fact that Beckett was brought up in Catholic Ireland to be "almost a quaker" by an exceptionally devout mother and an Episcopalian father seems, nonetheless, to have been a formative intellectual influence.[45] John Pilling neatly sums up Beckett's singular brand of non-believing belief, "inescapably attracted to the forms he seeks to subvert", in his study of *The Intellectual and Cultural Background to Beckett*: "he has con-continued to be obsessed, personally, by the fundamental religious questions concerning the existence of God, His justice and mercy and the after-life. The excessive literalism of traditional theology, especially of certain thinkers still revered in the Catholic Ireland he has exiled himself from, he is quick to scorn; although his familiarity with it all suggests he was momentarily attracted by it . . . What unbeliever would one expect to be familiar with Caugiamila's *Sacred Embryology* and Pope Benedict XIV's *Diocesan Synod* (quoted in addenda to *Watt*)? At the same time what believer would allow his path to be (even momentarily) halted by the occasional absurdities of Comestor and Adobard (medieval historians referred to by Moran)?"[46]

The dissenting character of Beckett's theology approximates at times to a Gnostic view of the world. According to the heretical Gnostics, the creation of the world signified a fall from light into darkness: "The world is extinguished," Clov muses, "though I never saw it lit." This fall into the cycle of sin and punishment is a conspicuous theme in Beckett's oeuvre. We see, for example, how the Cartesian *cogito ergo sum* and the Augustinian *fallor ergo sum* are ultimately transmuted into a Beckettian *patio ergo sum* (I suffer/wait therefore I am). "He weeps therefore he lives," Hamm says of his father, Nagg, in *Endgame*. Quite clearly, in Beckett's world, to be is to suffer for one's sins. Clov repeats this punitive lesson to himself: "You must learn to suffer better than that."[47]

This Gnostic-cum-Lutheran suspicion of the fallen, created world is manifest in Beckett's treatment of sexuality and women. Woman as the maternal procreator who perpetuates the corrupt cycle of creation is often reviled by Beckett's male narrators: this is true of Murphy's Celia, Nagg's Nell, Mr Rooney's Mrs Rooney, Malone's mistresses and the Unnamable's mother. "I look for my mother," confesses the Unnamable narrator, "in order to kill her." One could hardly be further from the romantic literature of the eternal feminine![48] In *Molloy*, Beckett caricatures human sexuality as the "fatal pleasure principle" represented by the ludicrous Obidil (an anagramatic inversion of the Freudian Libido).[49] Birth itself is at best a forceps delivery (as in *Endgame*), at worst an aborted mess ("the old impotent foetus . . . born in death" of *Malone Dies*). And this revulsion from life's procreative cycle is also manifest in the infanticidal tendencies of several Beckettian characters, notably Hamm, Malone and Mr Rooney.

Several critics have remarked on Beckett's dramatic use of the "puritanism" he experienced during his days in Portora Royal School in Northern Ireland, and during his early Foxrock childhood with a moralistic mother.[50] "To be is to be guilty," says the "wordshit" narrator of *Texts for Nothing*, whose scatological ridicule of mankind is perhaps equalled only by Beckett's Irish Protestant predecessor, Jonathan Swift. Beckett and Swift both write as disillusioned idealists, once so exigent in their search for a transcendent purity that they now recoil in horror from this decadent world of mortals.[51] Beckett's ailing and excrement-obsessed clowns find their literary ancestry in Swift's Struldbruggs and Yahoos.[52] Moreover Beckett's characters are often so disgusted by the alimentary, sexual and defecatory functions of their human condition that they are reduced to sterile impotence and immobility: Nagg and Nell are confined to dustbins, the protagonists of *Play* to urns, Murphy to an asylum, Lucky to the end of a rope and the Lost Ones to a hole in the mud. What Hamlet called the "craven scruple of thinking too precisely on the event" becomes for Beckett's over-intellectualised puritans a source of tortuous paralysis. This iconoclastic view of the human species is comically summed-up in Hamm's suggestion that a post-apocalyptic mankind could be reconstituted from one surviving flea![53]

*   *   *

Some of Beckett's most provocative allusions to religious thought are to be found in his plays. *Godot*, as its title suggests, is at once a comic and compassionate portrayal of man's search for God as he "pines and wastes . . . towards the great dark" of death. The clowns of *Godot* share the same quest for absolute meaning as the intellectuals of *Murphy*. (Beckett admitted to Colin Duckworth: "If you want to find the origins of *En Attendant Godot* look at *Murphy*.")[54] The essential difference between the novel of the 1940s and the play of the 1960s is that Beckett's focus has turned from a metaphysical to a theological perspective. (The Cartesian rationalisations of divine being are hilariously derided in Lucky's "think" about "God quaquaquaqua with white beard quaquaquaquaqua outside time without extension" etc.) *Godot* is, amongst other things, a play about the Judeo-

Christian hope for an eschatological God, the waiting for the coming, or second coming, of a Messiah. Several commentators have suggested that Estragon and Vladimir represent Judaism and Christianity respectively;[55] and while remembering Beckett's warning against the "neat identifications" of the analogymongers it is perhaps unwise to completely dismiss the innumerable theological suggestions to this effect in the play.[56]

Beckett has stated that his use of St Augustine's interpretation of the two crucified thieves in *Godot* epitomises the drama of choice.[57] But if the choices of the Judaic Estragon and the Christian Vladimir are as mutually exclusive as those of the two thieves, the *unknown* nature of Godot's identity (Jehovah or Christ or simply an absurd joke?)[58], means that both share the same human condition of hoping against hope. Their shared agnosticism is a shared paralysis: they cannot hang each other and yet cannot justify their existence; they cannot communicate and yet cannot go silent; they cannot stay together and yet cannot separate. Their relationship is sustained by the fact that they *both* need Godot: "In this immense confusion one thing alone is clear. We are waiting for Godot to come – or for night to fall. We are not saints, but we have kept our appointment."[59]

"Christianity is a mythology with which I am perfectly familiar," Beckett once confessed to Jack McGowran, "and so I used it."[60] *Endgame* is probably Beckett's most concentrated exploration of "Christian mystology" and certainly his most uncompromising attempt to demythologise some of its more dogmatic interpretations. Now of course *Endgame* operates at numerous levels of meaning, none of which is privileged; and we must take Beckett's comment on the play seriously: "no symbols where none intended." Nonetheless, it is undeniable that even the title of the play refers not only to a technical chess position (where play comes to a halt because of diminished forces which cannot culminate in checkmate) but also to the Christian apocalyptic theme of the "ending of the world." The play is mined with scriptural allusions – especially to the *Book of Revelation* – suggesting that Beckett intended a parallel with the eschatological drama between Christ and mankind. Already in *Murphy* Beckett had played with possibilities for such a parallel (the novel is replete with quasi-quotations from *Revelation* and Murphy himself is cheekily attributed with qualities of the apocalyptic Christ[61]), but it was not until *Godot* and more particularly *Endgame* that these possibilities materialised into a sustained parody.

The first scene of the play may be interpreted as a pseudo-re-enactment of the crucifixion with Clov as Christ, erecting and mounting his stepladder-crucifix. Clov's opening lines echo Christ's *consummatum est:* "Finished, its finished, nearly finished, its nearly finished. . .". But the tragedy of Golgotha becomes with Beckett a tragic-comedy that can never be terminated or transcended. Clov hopes that despite the "old Greek's" argument about the grain of millet, time will at last come to an end and sin be fully expiated: "Grain upon grain and one day, suddenly, there's a heap, a little heap, the impossible heap. I can't be punished anymore." But the play is precisely a continuation of Clov's punishment, an endgame which cannot be ended.

Hamm (possibly an amalgamation of the French *Homme* and the Hebrew *Ha-am* meaning man or mankind) admits his guilt in having contributed to Clov's (from the French *clou* or nail?) pain and punishment: "I've made you suffer too much." But just as Vladimir could not leave Estragon, Clov cannot resolve to leave Hamm in spite of his ingratitude and ill-treatment. "I come . . . and go," says Clov, without ever going. Hamm relates how Clov came in to his house (the world?) as a new born child one "Christmas eve". He was brought by his father who begged Hamm to feed and shelter him. But Hamm was irritated by this "invasion" and mistrusted the millennial promise of Clov's arrival: "What in God's name do you imagine? That the earth will awake in spring? That the rivers and seas will run with fish again? That there's manna in heaven still for imbeciles like you?" Now Clov is a grown man and the world is still as unredeemed as ever. A pseudo-eschatological saviour, he acknowledges that he can bring no lasting light into the world ("I see my light dying"); and as the darkness descends, Hamm testifies to the apocalyptic ending of a covenant: "Then let it end! with a bang! of darkness! . . . . It's the end, Clov, we've come to the end. I don't need you any more . . . You cried for night; it falls; now cry in darkness."[62]

The Christ-like Clov is ultimately compelled to acknowledge that his departure from his sepulchre-cell is less a resurrection into light than a return to dust: "I open the door of the cell and go. I am so bowed I only see my feet, if I open my eyes, and between my legs a little trail of black dust. I say to myself that the earth is extinguished, though I never saw it lit." Furthermore, Hamm's suggestion that the "little boy" might be a "potential progenitor" could be a reference to the symmetrical return of the anti-Christ; his quote from *Revelation* that "the end is in the beginning . . .", in addition to Clov's mention of the "brute beast", would certainly seem to confirm such an interpretation. But then again it could also be read as a subversion of eschatological linearity altogether by what Nietzsche, in opposition to Christian eschatology, called "the eternal return of the same".[63] Appropriately, it is also impossible to tell whether Clov himself actually leaves the stage, having delivered his farewell address, at the end of the play.[64] Beckett leaves his audience in excruciating doubt. We may choose to recall Dostoyevsky's maxim that "true faith comes forth from the crucible of doubt." But then again we may not. It is up to us to wager whether Clov's final "weeping for happiness" is a token of salvation or despair. Either way, *Endgame* can be interpreted as a further attempt by Beckett to demythologise any lazy or complacent assumptions we may have about Christianity, or any other messianic religion, as a guaranteed panacea to life's suffering.

*   *   *

Theological references to an unnamable God who sends inscrutable messages to a guilt-ridden and uncomprehending mankind are also frequent throughout Beckett's novels.

Molloy is a writer who receives orders from an unknown master with a stick, "who gives (him) money and takes away the pages". Though rapidly becoming deaf and blind, Molloy feels such punishment to be his due: "It's my fault. Fault? That was the word." He ridicules his early fascination for the images of the "old Geulincx", but still persists in his conviction that "all things hang together, by the operation of the Holy Ghost." In the second half of the novel, the master, now named Youdi (a pseudo Yahweh?) sends his "messenger" Gaber (a pseudo angel Gabriel?: the Greek for messenger being *Angelos*) to another human "agent", Moran, commissioning him to go in search of his "protegé" Molloy. Both Gaber and Moran insist that they are "members of a vast organisation" and refuse to "conjure away the Chief;" for to do so would be to accept that they are "solely responsible for (their) wretched existence".

Moran is tortured by the fear that the Chief and even Molloy are merely his own fictions: "ready made in my head." Though he continues to "obey orders" he cannot be sure whether the voice which utters them is of some transcendent being or his own imagination.[65]

Faithful to this "ambiguous voice", the novel ends with Moran returning home covered with "deep lesions and wounds", acknowledging "the wrong I had done my God, to whom I had been taught to ascribe my angers, fears, desires and even my body". Moran remains as determined as ever to find Molloy who might help him to understand "what I had to do, so that Youdi would not punish me"; but his final word remains agnostic, a confession of ignorance: "I have spoken of a voice telling me things . . . It told me to write the report. Does this mean I am freer now than I was? I do not know."

In the remaining novels of the trilogy, *Malone Dies* and *The Unnamable*, Beckett relentlessly pursues the question of divine existence, but he now approaches it less from the scriptural angle of dogma and revelation than from the mystical angle of a *via negativa*. The mystical way of "negative theology" operates on the assumption that it is only by divesting God of all anthropomorphic attributes (i.e. by accepting his unnamability) and by divesting our human selves of all desires, fears and hopes, that we may experience the *mysterium tremendum et fascinans* of God. Or, as Beckett put it in his *Proust* essay: "The wisdom of the sages . . . is the wisdom that consists not in the satisfaction but in the ablation of desire". This mystical way of dispossession is habitually identified with such Christian thinkers as Meister Eck-hart, Boehme and St John of the Cross, all of whom Beckett mentions in his works.[66] In *Four Quartets* T.S. Eliot expressed the *via negativa*, which he felt best corresponded to modern man's critical quest for the absolute, in terms frequently echoed in Beckett's mature writing:

> ... the mind is conscious but conscious of
>   nothing —
> I said to my soul, be still, and wait without hope
> For hope would be hope for the wrong things; wait without
>   love
> For love would be love of the wrong thing; there is yet faith
> But the faith and the love and the hope are all in the
>   waiting.
> Wait without thought, for you are not ready for thought:
>   . . .

> ... In order to arrive there,
> To arrive where you are, to get from where you are not,
>   You must go by a way wherein there is no ecstasy.
> In order to arrive at what you do not know
>   You must go by a way which is the way of ignorance.
> In order to possess what you do not possess
>   You must go by the way of dispossession.
> In order to arrive at what you are not
>   You must go through the way in which you are not.
> And what you do not know is the only thing you know
> And what you own is what you do not own
> And where you are is where you are not.

In *Malone Dies*, the narrator—Malone—resembles his predecessors in being crippled by religious sentiments of "punishment and sin". He is as ignorant of the source of this culpability as he is of the source of its possible remission: "not knowing what my prayer should be nor to whom." Yet by narrating one story after another, four in all, each one with new characters (Saposcat, MacMann, Lambert, Jackson etc.), Malone intends to dispossess himself, to go by the way in which he is not: "I shall be I no more." Malone cites Democritus' tag that "nothing is more real than nothing", believing that this *via negativa* will lead to an absolute vision of things. Ironically, one of Malone's fictional characters teaches his parrot to say *nihil in intellectu*, a telling dis-tortion of the Scholastic-Aristotelian dictum *nihil in intellectu quod non prius fuerit in sensu* (there is nothing in the mind, that was not first in the senses).

But the narrator gradually comes to realise that all his stories are no more than an innumerable babble of voices barring access to mystical silence: "He could make no meaning of the babel raging in his head, the doubts, desires, imaginings and dread." And so he resolves to renounce all efforts of active will, even "the last effort to understand . . . No I want nothing." If only he can "die alive", thereby experiencing the nothingness of death, he will achieve illumination. But this paradoxical consciousness-in-unconsciousness is a typical ploy of Beckettian irony. As soon as the narrator thinks he has reached silence, the voices return to plague him. As long as he seeks silence through words he can "never get dead". He cannot write himself into silence: "When I stop, as just now, the noises begin again, strangely loud, those whose turn it is."

This attempt to reach, through language, to some miraculous silence is playfully re-explored in *The Unnamable*. Here the narrator speaks of strange "delegates" delivering "lectures" to him about the nature of God: they "gave me the low-down on God. They told me I depended on him, in the last analysis. They had it on the reliable authority of his agents at Bally I forget what, this being the place, according to them, where the inestimable gift of life had been rammed down my gullet." The unnamable narrator develops the mystical doctrine that dependency on God is meaningful only when one has ceased to seek, desire, think or speak about him. "Doubt no more, seek no more", urges the author. "Overcome, that goes without saying, the fatal leaning towards expressiveness." Even hope must be banished — "none of your hoping here, that would spoil everything."

The divine, it appears, can only be revealed if our transcendence of ourselves "opens on the void, on the silence". Thus the unnamable narrator decides to terminate "the frenzy of utterances" he has begun. "If only this voice could stop," he murmurs, "this meaningless voice which prevents you from being nothing." But the search for a verbal means to put an end to speech is of course self-defeating; for it is precisely the search in and through words that obliges the discourse to continue. "It is impossible," the narrator admits, "to speak and yet say nothing."

Beckett is not unmindful of the implications of this incommunicability of transcendent meaning for scriptural hermeneutics. "I am Mathew and I am the Angel," boasts the unnamable, reminding us that the angels and evangelists before him had also a duty to say the unsayable, or as Beckett puts it "to eff the ineffable". The very hermeneutical notions of a "truth to recover" or a "labour to accomplish" are themselves symptoms of "the mad need to speak, to think, to know", symptoms which ultimately subvert the mystical transcendence of the divine. The peace of the biblical God-beyond-being surpasses understanding. "Dear incomprehension," declares the ascetic aspirant of nonbeing, "it's thanks to you I'll be myself, in the end. Nothing will remain of all the lies they have glutted me with. And I'll be myself at last, as a starvling belches his odourless wind, before the bliss of coma." Only when, and if, he is "let loose alone in the unthinkable, unspeakable," will he be able to encounter God at the heart of darkness.[67]

The God of the unnamable narrator appears to be an absent God who chastises him until, like Job, he becomes a "worm in the sight of the Lord". Transposing Eliot's version of the *via negativa*, Beckett pens one of his most trenchant parodies of religious optimism: "The essential is never to arrive anywhere, never to be anywhere . . . The essential is to go on squirming forever at the end of the line, as long as there are waters and banks and ravening in heaven and a sporting God to plague his creature, per pro his chosen shits. I've swallowed three hooks and am still hungry? Hence the howls . . . nothing to do but stretch out comfortably on the rack, in the blissful knowledge you are nobody for eternity."[68]

But Beckett's explorations of negative theology are nowhere more radical and penetrating than in *Watt*. The novel recounts the sojourn of the rationalist Mr Watt in the house of the elusive Mr Knott, appropriately so named. Mr Knott represents the immutable and immortal condition sought by numerous Beckettian characters: "nothing changed in Mr Knott's house." All Watt's attempts to impose a scientific mould on the "nothingness" he encounters are thwarted and he is forced to the "mystical" conclusion that true knowledge is non-knowledge, that the truth of being is non-being.[69] A salient theme in *Watt* is, consequently, the demise of rationalism. In his working plans for the novel, Beckett develops the plot by means of Aristotle's ten logical categories and his termination of the text with a note on the pessimistic deathbed words of Aristotle, "master of those who know", intimates the futility of Watt's invocation of rationalist principles.

Watt cannot fail to see the patent contradiction in his anthropomorphic definitions of nothingness and God: "the only way one can speak of nothing is to speak of it as though it were something, just as the only way to speak of God is to speak of him as though he were a man, which to be sure he was, in a sense, for a time . . ." As the novel progresses, Watt's positivistic endeavour to encapsulate the meaning of Mr Knott in words and names becomes a *reductio ad absurdum* and he finally "abandon(s) all hope, all fear, of ever seeing Mr. Knott face to face."

Like Godot, as described by the "small boy", Mr Knott "does nothing". Mr Knott's abode remains an indefinable nothing, an "empty husk in airless gloom". So Watt eventually consents to ask no more questions, to "like the fact that it has no meaning". He espouses a position of total abandonment: "this mind ignoring. These emptied hands. This emptied heart. To him I brought. To the temple. To the Healer. To the source. Of nought." Thus Watt comes to experience the silent infinite spaces, as Pascal put it, of the *Deus Absconditus*. The summary of his stay in Mr Knott's house is, in this respect, expressly equivocal:

What had he learned? Nothing. What did he know of Mr Knott? Nothing. What remained of his passion to understand? Nothing. But is that not already something? He saw himself as small and lacking. But is that not already something? So sick, so alone. And now. Even sicker, even more alone, was that not something?

Watt's dealings with nothingness reiterate Murphy's talk of that "numb peace" which only comes "when the somethings give way, or perhaps simply add up, to the Nothing, than which in the guffaw of the Abderite naught is more real . . . the accidentless One-and-Only conveniently called Nothing."

Is Beckett suggesting then that the *via negativa* is a valid, possibly the only, way to encounter an incomprehensible God? Or is he simply demythologising this negative theology as just another desperate leap towards an non-existent God? It is impossible to tell. As Jean Onimus argues in his perspicacious analysis of Beckett's philosophy of religion: "the revelation of Nothing is ambiguous. According to the instances, it can bring about anguish, anger and despair or the beatific sentiment of liberation."[70] In a passage in *Molloy*, for example, Beckett infers that silence can indeed be taken as a token of revelation: "to remain silent and listen, not one being in a hundred is capable of even conceiving what this means. It is however . . . beyond the absurd fracas the silence of which the universe is made." And yet we have been able to cite numerous passages from Beckett's writings where the condition of will-less abandonment celebrated by mystics such as Eckhart are mercilessly ridiculed. (In *Dream* Beckett even goes so far as to dismiss Eckhart as a "dud mystic".) Similarly, it is impossible to tell whether the voice that assails Beckett's narrators is simply nihilistic nonsense or the "still, small voice" of the hidden God which once spoke to Elijah after forty nights in the desert. In short, when a Beckettian character exclaims that he cannot forgive God for not existing, is he affirming or denying Divine existence?[71]

To answer such questions one way or the other would be to betray the unique ambivalence of Beckett's writing. In an interview in 1974 Beckett returns to his favourite example of the two thieves: "I take no sides . . . There is a wonderful sentence in Augustine: Do not despair; one of the thieves was saved: Do not presume; one of the thieves was damned."[72] And speaking elsewhere of the religious significance of life and death in his work, Beckett elaborates on this impartiality, pronouncing what must be his most conclusive, albeit elusive, word on the subject:

> If life and death did not both present themselves to us, there would be no inscrutability. If there was only darkness, all would be clear. It is because there is not only darkness, but also light that our situation becomes inescapable.

Take St Augustine's doctrine about grace given and grace refused: have you ever reflected on the dramatic quality of this theology? Two thieves are crucified with Christ; one is saved and the other is damned. How can one understand this? In classical drama, such problems do not arise. The destiny of Racine's *Phaedre* is sealed from the beginning . . . there is no doubt that she travels towards darkness. That's the play. According to this conception, clarity is possible, but for us who are neither Greeks nor Jansenists, there exists no such clarity. The question would not exist either if we believed in the opposite, in a guaranteed salvation. But where we have at once darkness and light, there we also have the inexplicable. The key word of my work is *perhaps*.[73]

III. THE MODERN CRITIQUE OF BEING AND LANGUAGE

Beckettt's intellectual preoccupations extend beyond the conundrums of Cartesian idealism and negative theology to include a modernist critique of the classical concepts of self-identity. This third dimension of Beckett's demythologising finds parallels in both the modern philosophies of existence (Heidegger, Sartre, Camus etc.) and of language (Mauthner, Wittgenstein, Derrida).

As the existentialist or absurdist character of Beckett's work has already been documented by numerous critics, I shall advert to it only in passing. When asked if contemporary philosophers had any influence on (his) thought, Beckett testily quipped: "I never understand anything they write."[74] Asked on another occasion about the specific impact of existentialism on his work, Beckett was equally unforthcoming: "When Heidegger and Sartre speak of a contrast between Being and existence, they may be right, I don't know. . ."[75] Yet despite this legitimate resistance to any facile attempt to reduce his complex, playful works to a straightforward philosophical argument, Beckett was clearly familiar with the existentialist philosophy of Heidegger and Sartre. Jean-Paul Sartre was at *L'Ecole normale* in Paris when Beckett lectured there in 1928-30 and Beckett has admitted that they met several times since "without embarrassment".[76] French existentialism took its inspiration from Martin Heidegger's *Sein und Zeit* which defined existence as the solitary anguish (*Angst*) of a "being-towards-death" (*Sein zum Tode*); it was published in 1927 just as Beckett began his travels to Germany and France. "The principal themes of Heidegger often resemble those of Beckett," declares Onimus," both, profoundly Christian at the outset, share the same tragic vision of existence. Beckett discovered in the German philosopher the same phenomenology of anguish, nothingness, boredom and finitude, the same conception of the paradoxical reality of lucid existence that is nothing other than a scattering in dread and in time, finally he found there the same horror of life when it is degraded by the inauthentic."[77]

The existentialists radicalised the presocratic and mystical doctrine that Being is intimately related to non-being. In *Was Ist Metaphysik?* (1933), Heidegger argued that "nothingness is the veil of Being" and that the very formlessness of its experience fills us with dread:

> Nothing is revealed in dread, but not as something that "is". Neither can it be taken as an object . . . dread finds itself completely powerless in the face of what is as a whole . . . Nihilation is not a fortuitous event, but understood as the relegation to the vanishing Being as a whole, it reveals the latter in all its till now undisclosed strangeness as the pure "other" . . . The essence of nothing (*Nichts*) as original nihilation (*Vernichtung*) lies in this: that it alone brings human existence face to face with what is as such.[78]

By thus equating Being with nothingness, Heidegger announced the "deconstruction" (*Überwindung*) of the traditional metaphysical notions of being as fullness, plenitude and self-sufficiency (e.g. as *ens causa sui*). The truth of Being no longer manifests itself as *what is* (a thing), but rather as *what is not* (a no-thing) or as *what may be* (a possibility). In similar fashion, Sartre affirms in *L'être et le néant* (1944) that "nothingness lurks at the heart of Being, coiled up like a worm." He proceeds to define man as a "useless passion" since all his attempts to impose order on reality are merely aesthetic or imaginary projections. Existence precedes essence announces Sartre, meaning that we invent our own identity and can rely on no universal system of inherited values. One can see the overlap between this Sartrean solipsism and Beckett's claim in *Proust* that art is absolute solitude.[79] And we might also recall Beckett's own equation of Being with formless nothingness not only in the various passages cited in the previous two sections, but even more emphatically in his 1961 interview with Tom Driver: "Being is constantly putting form in danger . . . I know of no form that does not violate the nature of Being in the most vulnerable manner . . . If anything new and exciting is going on today, it is the attempt to let Being into art."[80]

For art to embrace formlessness is to acknowledge that life is absurd. If human existence is haunted by nothingness then we have no given identity; the very notion of self-identity is itself no more than one of our own inventions with which we can never fully identify. Man is a being who is what he is not and is not what he is, as Sartre formulates it. Consequently, while negative theology interprets the experience of nothingness as a mystical experience of God, the existentialists interpret it as an experience of the anguish or absurdity of Being.[81]

Beckett has described his art as an "art of failure . . . with nothing to express and no means to express it."[82] To let Being into art, Beckett advises, is to renounce one's will to be oneself and to let the impersonal voices of language speak. The author of *Texts for Nothing* says as much when he confesses that he is "only a ventriloquist's dummy . . . (Who) holds me in his arms and moves my lips"; so that "it is rare that the sentiment of absurdity is not followed by the sentiment of necessity."[83] And this sentiment of necessity is precisely that suffering of being which Beckett first championed in his early *Proust* essay as the "principal condition of aesthetic experience."[84]

Beckett's answer to our existential anguish is humour. His laughter derives from the recognition of ambiguity, from the impossibility of reconciling juxtaposed opposites − be they hope and despair, logic and folly, presence and absence. "In the beginning was the pun," Murphy reveals. The Beckettian laugh is certainly philosophical to the extent that it puts our assured ideas about God or Being in question; but it is also comic for it is a laugh of comfortless wisdom: "The mirthless laugh is the dianoetic laugh, *risus purus*. . . the laugh that laughs—silence please—at that which is unhappy."[85] Camus, another philosopher of the absurd, exclaimed: "*L'absurde n'a de sens que dans la mesure où l'on n'y consent pas.*" Beckett's laughter of wisdom (Gk. *dianoia*) is perhaps less an uncritical submission to nonsense than a waiting for meaning despite its manifestly absurd absence. This stoic defiance is typified by the Beckettian character in *More Pricks than Kicks* who bravely announces that he "would arm his mind with laughter as he stepped smartly into the torture chamber."[86]

Beckett's affinity with the existentialist ethos led naturally to an interest in the modern philosophy of language. Heidegger himself had deconstructed Being not only into nothingness but also into language. "Language is the house of Being," he stated in his *HumanismusBrief* (1947) (a singularly pertinent analogy when one thinks of Watt's linguistic experiments in Mr Knott's house). One of the first modern philosophers to capture Beckett's attention was the Austrian logician Fritz Mauthner, from whose major work, *Beiträge zu einer Kritik der Sprache*, Beckett read to the blind but alert Joyce in the 1930s.[87] Mauthner claimed that there is "no thinking without speaking" and that we could only reach the truth of reality if we transcended the limits of language (which Mauthner considered impossible). The undoing of language requires what Mauthner, in a phrase redolent of Beckettian pathos, termed "the heavenly stillness and gaiety of resignation and renunciation". Such a gaiety would occasion the "suicide of thought" recalling the impossible project of Molloy, Malone, Watt and the unnamable narrator to say the unsayable, to move from speech to silence.

Beckett's critical preoccupation with language also bears a close resemblance to the ideas of another Austrian linguist, Ludwig Wittgenstein. Wittgenstein agreed with Mauthner that there could be no thought without words; and that without words and thought there is only an undifferentiated nothing. The meaning of man's existence is therefore irredeemably linguistic. Since we name and identify our experience through language, our world is commensurate with our words. Beyond words there is only the limitless non-being of silence. Wittgenstein's much quoted conclusion to the *Tractatus* could have been uttered by almost any Beckettian character: "Whereof one cannot speak, thereof one must be silent."

It is easy to see the intimate rapport between the philosophical linguistics of Mauthner and Wittgenstein and Watt's futile efforts to reduce Knott's nothingness to his own little world of words. It is "comforting" for Watt to suppose that if he can name the uncanny events in Mr Knott's house (his dog, his unfinished dinner, his ladder, his stairs, his servant, the comings and goings of his guests, Tom, Dick and Harry etc.), he can take the harm out of them. But *Watt* is a novel about the dual impossibility of reducing reality to words and of transcending words towards reality. Watt's marathon project to turn "disturbances into words" by enumerating endless lists of postulates and calculations, is doomed from the start. He soon recognizes the "old error" of trying to say "what things were in reality".[88] Thinking of "one of Mr Knott's pots", to take just one of Beckett's hilarious examples, "it was in vain that Watt said, Pot, pot . . . It resembled a pot, it was almost a pot, but it was not a pot of which one could say, Pot, pot, and be comforted."[89] By the end of the novel, Watt has said absolutely nothing of significance about Mr Knott or his world.[90] The terrifying *néant* of Mr Knott's house is refractory to the positivistic claims of reason and language. But as always in Beckett we are left undecided as to whether the timeless, spaceless void beyond language is the portal to a mystical experience (Arsène speaks of the bliss of a "situation where to do nothing exclusively would be an act of the highest value") or simply the nothingness of the absurd (Watt's "preestablished arbitrary"). As the author of *Watt* ruefully concludes: "Know not."

*   *   *

Beckett's demythologising of the scientific pretensions of Cartesian idealism, dogmatic theology and linguistic positivism may be seen as a literary counterpart to Jaques Derrida's recent philosophy of *deconstruction*. Derrida develops Heidegger's destruction of the *logos* of Being into a radical deconstruction of the *logos* of language. Heidegger, we observed, dismantled the metaphysical myth of Being as omnipotent presence concluding that its truth can only reveal itself as absence, nothingness or possibility. Following in the footsteps of the master, Derrida sets out to refute the metaphysical myth of language as a transparent *signifier* referring to some meta-linguistic reality (*the signified*). Accordingly, just as Being is demythologised into nothingness, language must be demythologised into unnamability. Derrida sums up his position in terms that could serve as a gloss to Beckett's entire literary corpus: "One cannot attempt to deconstruct this transcendence (of the logos as original presence) without descending, across the inherited concepts, towards the unnamable."[91] In other words, Derrida argues that the founding concepts of metaphysics—*Logos, Arche, Eidos, Nous* etc.—are merely faded linguistic metaphors (of origin, light and presence); he exposes this covert metaphorising at the root of western philosophy and denounces it as a *white mythology:* "It is metaphysics which has effaced in itself that fabulous scene which brought it into being, and which yet remains, active and stirring, inscribed in white ink, an invisible drawing covered over in the palimpsest."[92] Thus Derrida shows that the metaphorising activity of language, far from re-presenting some extra-linguistic origin of meaning (what he calls the "transcendental signified"), is no more than the perpetual supplementation of one signifier/word for another. Beyond the words which signify there is *nothing* signified, no presence of subject or object, only an endless series of other signifying traces — more words.

Several of Beckett's prose works can be read as radical literary exercises in such deconstruction. The metaphorising attempts of Beckettian narrators to transcend language towards some prelinguistic self-identity are continually frustrated. The reality of the self remains forever "absent" and "inexpressible".[93] "Noone will ever know what I am," complains Beckett's unnamable narrator, "noone will ever hear me say it, I won't say it, I can't say it . . ." To the voices of language trying to persuade him he "has an ego all of his own", he replies, "I shall not say I again." At one point he does think he might be able to rediscover himself through a third person, a new fictional character who might serve as a mirror image of his own genesis: "We must first, to begin with, go back to the beginnings and then, to go on with, follow him patiently through the various stages . . . which have made him what *I* am." But the *I* reached through the detour of the *he* is no more than an imagined self, a trace of itself; the I is always deferred.

The narrative I is a split I, a not-I, forever in pursuit of itself, forever falling short of itself. The Beckettian narrator is a victim of the voices he utters and hears, a prey to language. Thus, for example, Beckett discovers in *Malone Dies* that he cannot disengage his authorial voice from the voice of Malone who, in turn, cannot disentangle himself from the other fictive narrators of Beckett's novels. As long as one lives and speaks, one is a slave to the endless differentiation of language. Only death, it seems, can offer a release from the hell of non-identity: "Let us leave these morbid matters," declares the author of *Malone Dies*, "and get on with that of my demise, in two or three days if I remember rightly. Then it will all be over with the Murphys,

Merciers, Morans and Malones, unless it goes on beyond the grave."
But in Beckett's world it does; in the realm of words there is always
an after-world. Language is limbo. We can never finally appropriate
ourselves for we can never experience our own death as a finality.
We can only experience our existence *towards* death (*Sein zum Tode*)
or else our imaginary existence *after* it. For Beckett as for Derrida,
language is a process of *deferring* and *decentring* the subject, a process
which underscores the futility of trying to *be one self*. There can be no
last word on the subject.[94]

The modern author, if we are to take Beckett at his word, is a
nomad condemned to the alienation of language. But if we lose ourselves in words, we will not, for all that, cease to employ them with
joyous abandon and defiance in order to try to recover ourselves.
The Beckettian narrators, even though they can't go on, go on — in
endless search of themselves.

CONCLUSION

Beckett's entire literary oeuvre embodies a modern critique of traditional notions of "identity" — whether it concern the self, being,
language, God or one's sense of national belonging. His aim, I suggest,
is less a nihilistic deconstruction of sense into non-sense than a playful wish to expose the inexhaustible comedy of existence. His writing delights in disrupting all hard-and-fast categories and distinctions
which seek to simplify experience — including those which would
rigidly divide literature and philosophy; it powerfully illustrates how
all our rational concepts are ultimately related to an ongoing process
of artistic rediscovery and revision. By thus challenging the conventional apartheid which isolated intellect and imagination into mutually
exclusive ghettos, Beckett's work might be said to epitomise, to some
degree, a peculiarly Irish cast of mind. In Beckett we witness an Irish
mind less concerned with self-regarding questions of Irish history and
tradition than with the universal concerns of western humanistic culture as a whole, particularly as it combines the founding heritages of
Hellenic idealism and Judeo-Christian theology. Faithful to his specifically Irish experiences of exile, marginality and dissent, Beckett has
brought a sense of critical humour to bear on philosophical questions
of international import. His writing is testimony to the fact that the
Irish mind is no less Irish for dispensing with the mirror of indigenous
self-absorption and embarking on the endless quest for the other.

PART V

14

Gordon L. Herries Davies

IRISH THOUGHT IN SCIENCE

Ireland is proud to be remembered as a land of saints and scholars; almost never is Ireland remembered as a land which has been famed for its scientists. This is unfortunate. Over the centuries Ireland in reality has produced many scientists of the highest international calibre, and it is the task of this essay to draw attention to this scientific component within Ireland's cultural heritage. In achieving our object there must be no suspicion of special pleading. There is, for example, no need to claim as Irish such scientists as John Desmond Bernal, Robert Boyle, Thomas Condon, Lord Kelvin, Sir Frederick McCoy, or John Tyndall, all of whom were Irish by birth but all of whose careers in science were developed far beyond Ireland's shores. Similarly, there is no necessity to claim as Irish those men of science who were nurtured overseas but who then came to Ireland to deploy their scientific skills – men such as George Boole in mathematics, Joseph Beete Jukes in geology, Erwin Schrödinger in physics, Caleb Threlkeld in botany, or Arthur Edward James Went in zoology. The men upon whom we are about to call in exemplification of the achievements of Irish science are neither emigrants nor immigrants; they are scientists who were born in Ireland and who spent the greater part of their lives within the land of their nativity.

It was during the seventeenth century that modern science – the New Philosophy, as it was then termed – took root within the British Isles, events of particular portent being the publication of William Gilbert's *De Magnete* in 1600, the appearance of Francis Bacon's *Novum Organum* in 1620, and the foundation in 1660 of the Royal Society of London for Improving Natural Knowledge. That society soon became the focus for a brilliant circle of savants – men such as Robert Boyle, Edmond Halley, Robert Hooke, Sir Isaac Newton, and John Ray – and this was genius upon a scale that Ireland could hardly be expected to match. But Ireland did have her own virtuosi fascinated by the challenge of the New Philosophy, and in 1683 a group of these scholars in Dublin came together to found an institution in imitation of London's Royal Society. Their society, initially styled the Dublin Society for the Improving of Natural Knowledge, Mathematicks and Mechanicks but later known simply as the Dublin Philosophical Society, was closely associated with Trinity College Dublin, although from April 1684 onwards the society met not within the college but in its own chambers in Crow's Nest, an alley off Dublin's Dame Street.[1] There the society had its herbal garden and museum, and there its members met to conduct their experiments and to discuss each other's scientific discourses.

The founder of the Dublin Philosophical Society was William Molyneux (1656-1698),[2] and among its most eminent Irish members were men such as William Molyneux's brother Sir Thomas Molyneux (1661-1733), St George Ashe (1658? -1717), Swift's tutor when he came up to Trinity in 1682, Samuel Foley (1655-1695), the Bishop of Down and Connor, William King (1650-1729), the Archbishop of Dublin, and Allan Mullen (died 1690), an anatomist who felt it prudent to quit Ireland in 1686 as a result of what was described as 'a discreditable love affair'. William Molyneux's name is familiar to philosophers because of the eponymous 'Molyneux Problem', but as a scientist he is best remembered for his work in astronomy and as the author of a pioneering text in dioptrics. Thomas Molyneux and Samuel Foley were responsible for papers published in the *Philosophical Transactions of the Royal Society* (the Dublin society never had its own organ) on the subject of the Giant's Causeway of County Antrim, papers in which it was argued that the absence of chisel marks upon the hexagonal columns, and of mortar from between the columns, proved that this remarkable feature must be natural rather than man-made. Ashe read at least twenty-eight mathematical papers to the society between 1683 and 1687, and he was responsible, with John Flamsteed's advice, for the establishment of an astronomical observatory within Trinity College in 1685. King was the author of a *Philosophical Transactions* paper of 1685 devoted to the nature of peat, an important subject, he observed, because 'we live in an Island almost infamous for Bogs'. Mullen earned scientific fame for his dissection of a showman's elephant that died in a Dublin fire in June 1681.

Despite all this scientific activity, the New Philosophy had not really taken secure root in Ireland, and by 1708 the Dublin Philosophical Society was dead. It has to be admitted that the period between 1700 and 1780 saw little real Irish achievement in science, but, let it be remembered, that is precisely the period during which science elsewhere in Europe failed to maintain its earlier vitality. Within Ireland a medical school was opened in Trinity College in 1711, and since it offered facilities for instruction in botany, chemistry, and zoology, as well as in the usual medical specialisms, it is to 1711 that the university's modern departments of botany, chemistry, and zoology are pleased to trace their origin.[3] Perhaps, too, the populace of Dublin was not entirely oblivious to the significance of the New Philosophy because in the 1740s there was a tavern in the city's Cork Hill named 'Sir Isaac Newton's Head', although there is the possibility that Cambridge's most famous son was being remembered as the Master of the Mint rather than as the author of *Principia Mathematica*. Disappointing era though it may have been for Irish science, there are two Irish institutions founded during the eighteenth century which deserve attention.

Firstly, there is the Dublin Society for Improving Husbandry, Manufactures and other Useful Arts and Sciences founded in 1731.[4] (It became the Royal Dublin Society in June 1820). The motivation for the establishment of the society came chiefly from Thomas Prior (1681-1751), a former school-mate of George Berkeley and a strenuous advocate of Berkeley's Tar-Water as a cure for a multitude of bodily disorders.[5] Another of the original members was Sir Thomas Molyneux who by 1731 must have been one of the last survivors from the old Dublin Philosophical Society. From the outset the Dublin Society took a keen interest in all aspects of applied science, its activities ranging from the investigation of mineral ores and pottery clays, to the study of fertilizers and experiments in arboriculture. Secondly, there is the Physico-Historical Society of Ireland founded at a meeting held in the Dublin Parliament House on 14 April 1744.[6] The society's object was the sponsorship of a scientific survey of each of the thirty-two Irish counties as a step towards the more efficient exploitation of Ireland's natural resources. To assist them in this important task they employed one Isaac Butler (1689-1755) to travel the countryside collecting plants and geological specimens. The most active member of the society was nevertheless Charles Smith (c. 1715-1762), an apothecary from County Waterford. It was Smith who wrote the only four county surveys ever to have been published under the aegis of the society – the surveys of Down, Waterford, Cork and Kerry – but by the time the last of these volumes – the Kerry survey – had appeared in 1756, the society had lost all its initial enthusiasm and had fallen into abeyance.

Thus far the story of scientific endeavour in Ireland is hardly a story of startling deeds, but as the eighteenth century approached its close Irish science, like science elsewhere within the British Isles, began to display every sign of a remarkable reinvigoration. The popular picture of Ireland during the hundred years between 1780 and 1880 is one of a land of debilitation, of economic stagnation, and of political unrest – a land of starving, rack-rented peasants struggling to escape from the shackles of colonialist oppression and striving to win for themselves a new national identity. The events of the period remembered in our history texts are the '98, Catholic Emancipation, the Famine, the national haemorrhage of massive emigration, the Fenians, and the Land War. But such a view represents merely one perspective upon Irish history during that hundred-year period. To the historian of

Ireland's scientific culture those years appear in an utterly different light. He sees nothing effete, nothing indigent, nothing impoverished. Quite the contrary; the years between 1780 and 1880 can only be hailed as a golden age for Irish science. Virtually all fields of science were then attracting the attention of Irish scientists; those scientists were at grips with research problems of the most fundamental character; and Ireland's leading figures in science were men enjoying the highest of international scientific reputations.

It was within the Dublin Society that around 1780 the new Irish enthusiasm for science first manifested itself upon an appreciable scale, and if we are to understand events within the society it is necessary to remember what was then happening across the water in Britain. There the Industrial Revolution was beginning to transform both the landscape and the national economy, bringing undreamed of wealth to a new class of entrepreneurs — to the mine-owners at Newcastle, to the textile manufacturers of Manchester, and to the potters at Etruria. If this was happening in Britain, then why should the same not come to pass in Ireland? Why should an Irish river not become a Tyne with railways guiding the coal-trucks down to the holds of waiting colliers? Why should some Irish town not become a second Cottonopolis? Why should the kilns of a new Potteries not rise out of the former pastures of some Irish county? In retrospect, with the wisdom of hindsight, such ambitions perhaps appear to have been futile and absurd, but in the late eighteenth century things looked very different. Not until the following century did Ireland come to feel so tragically inferior to a Britain which by then had become both the workshop of the world and the seat of a global empire of unparalleled extent, and in 1780 it still seemed that Ireland might emulate anything that was achieved in Britain. Was Dublin not a gracious and socially glittering capital city second in size within the empire to London alone? Was the population of Ireland not well over half that of England and Wales (the Irish population density was actually greater than that of England and Wales) and over three times that of Scotland? And did the Irish population not contain some men of the highest talent who were already participants in the exciting events taking place in Britain? The Tighe family from County Kilkenny, for instance, was involved in the mines of Cornwall where the deep shafts were now being drained by James Watt's great pumping engines, and Richard Lovell Edgeworth (1744-1817) from County Longford was a member of the famed Lunar Society of Birmingham where he encountered such giants of the age as Watt himself, Matthew Boulton, Erasmus Darwin, and Josiah Wedgwood. Thus in the 1780s there can have seemed no reason to doubt but that what was being so spectacularly accomplished in Britain might just as readily be brought to pass in Ireland. Now clearly if that were to happen — if there were to be triggered an Irish Industrial Revolution — then the principal financial beneficiaries could only be the Irish landowners. Those landowners were the mainstay of the Dublin Society and it was through the society that they now sought to enlist science in the furtherance of their own prosperity and in the cause of a general expansion of the Irish economy. Using their powerful influence within the Irish Parliament, they were able to secure for the society that financial assistance necessary to permit a major expansion of the society's activities in the field of applied science. Enlightened self-interest may have been the motive of the landowners, but the historian of science has to observe that nothing quite like this venture into applied science had occurred anywhere else within the British Isles. Whatever the motives of its advocates, the Dublin Society deserves the very highest credit for its new initiative.

The first clear sign of the society's reinvigorated interest in applied science was the appointment in 1786 of the Scotsman Donald Stewart as the society's Itinerant Mineralogist charged with the task of scouring Ireland in search of minerals possessing economic significance. That work he continued until his death in 1811. Next, and to further the national knowledge of mineralogy, the society in 1792 purchased for £1350 the magnificent mineral collection – it contained 7331 specimens – assembled in Germany by Nathanael Gottfried Leske. Many were the mineralogists who were now attracted to Dublin by the presence of this famed cabinet within the society's museum. In 1795 the society created a chair of chemistry and mineralogy, the new professor being instructed to give courses of public lectures and to conduct research in his laboratory. At the conclusion of some of the lecture-courses public examinations were held with prizes of 50, 30, and 20 guineas for the three best respondents, and such was the public interest in mineralogy that in 1802 one of the society's publications could look forward to the day when they would 'see small mineralogical societies formed in every provincial city in Ireland'.[7]

In the same year – 1795 – the society acquired 16 acres at Glasnevin in the northern suburbs of Dublin and there it founded a botanical garden which was placed in the charge of a professor who was expected to give lectures on botany in connection with diet, medicine, agriculture and rural economy. Five years later the society appointed a committee to compare the Dublin Society's achievements with those of the recently founded Royal Institution in London and from the committee's report it emerged 'that the Dublin Society had taken the lead of it and all other like institutions in Europe in everything except philosophical lectures'. Clearly this deficiency had to be remedied; a chair of natural philosophy was immediately created and lectures in subjects such as hydraulics, mechanics, and optics were arranged. Between 1801 and 1832 the society published scientific surveys of twenty-three of the thirty-two Irish counties, some of the accounts containing remarkably astute interpretations of the local geology.[8] In 1809 (Sir) Richard Griffith (1784-1878) was commissioned to survey the Leinster Coal

District on behalf of the society; in 1812 he was appointed as the society's Mining Engineer and required to deliver regular courses of public lectures on Ireland's geology and mineral resources; and from 1812 until 1829 he was employed to survey all the Irish coal districts and to report from time to time upon other matters of economic geology as they arose.[9] In 1810 (Sir) Humphry Davy was brought over tó Dublin to give a course of lectures upon electro-chemistry and, his prelections having proved enormously popular (337 people were at his first lecture), he returned in 1811 to conduct courses in both chemistry and geology. For that second year's lectures he was paid the substantial fee of £750 and he also received the society's thanks for his having 'materially increased the spirit of philosophical research in Ireland'.

All this was a truly remarkable investment in science on the part of the Dublin Society but we deceive ourselves if we perceive the flowering of Irish science around 1800 as being merely a result of a group of influential establishment figures seeking to line their own pockets through a mastery of the lessons of applied science. In reality there was in Ireland during the hundred years after 1780 a widespread interest in science both pure and applied. This point can hardly be illustrated better than by considering some of the many institutions of a scientific character inaugurated in Ireland during the decades after 1780. In December 1782, for instance, Trinity College signed a contract for the erection of its fine new astronomical observatory at Dunsink using monies bequeathed for the purpose by their former Provost Francis Andrews (died 1774).[10] In 1785 there was founded the Royal Irish Academy for promoting the study of Science, Polite Literature, and Antiquities, and while it was, and remains to this day, a body devoted to the pursuit of all branches of knowledge, it is surely in science that its Members have attained their highest distinction. In 1788 there came into being the Belfast Library and Society for Promoting Knowledge (now known as the Linen Hall Library) and it immediately purchased a substantial number of scientific instruments including a barometer, a rain-gauge, a hygrometer, and a Wedgwood pyrometer.[11] Perhaps envious of Dublin's new astronomical observatory at Dunsink, Archbishop Richard Robinson (1709-1794) of Armagh in 1793 founded the Armagh Observatory endowing it with lands especially purchased for that purpose.[12] In Munster the Royal Cork Institution was founded in 1803 and ten years later Edmund Davy (1785-1857), Humphry Davy's cousin, became the Institution's professor of chemistry.[13] Back in Ulster the Belfast Natural History Society was founded in 1821 at the home of the society's first president, the former naval surgeon James Lawson Drummond (1783-1853).[14] In Dublin in 1830 there was founded the Zoological Society of Dublin which in 1837 assumed the rather more grandiose title of the Royal Zoological Society of Ireland.[15] Another Dublin society possessed of lofty aspirations was the Geological Society of Dublin which was founded at a meeting held in the Provost's House of Trinity College on 29 November 1831 and instituted 'for the purpose of investigating the mineral structure of the earth, and more particularly of Ireland'; in March 1864 it obtained Queen Victoria's permission to restyle itself the Royal Geological Society of Ireland.[16] In Cork in 1835 there was founded the Cork Cuvierian Society, so named in honour of the great French natural historian Georges Cuvier,[17] and a Dublin society with similar objectives was the Natural History Society of Dublin founded in 1838. By 1857 the latter society could boast that its members had discovered and described the following numbers of creatures new to Ireland: two mammals, six birds, one reptile, and six fish.

In 1845 the government established the Geological Survey of Ireland, charging it with the formidable task of mapping in detail the rocks of the whole of Ireland — a task which engaged the Survey until the autumn of 1887.[18] Another government decision of 1845 led to the foundation of the three Queen's Colleges in Belfast, Cork and Galway, each of the colleges offering instruction in a variety of sciences. When Queen's College Galway opened its doors to students in 1849, for instance, they discovered that apart from chairs in medicine and engineering, there were chairs in chemistry, mathematics, mineralogy and geology, natural history, and natural philosophy. Another event of 1849 was the establishment of the Dublin Microscopical Club, one of its founder members and leading lights being William Archer (1830-1897) who was later to become both a Fellow of the Royal Society and the first Librarian of the National Library of Ireland. Finally, there was another government creation: the Museum of Economic Geology founded in 1845 and located in Dublin at 51 St Stephen's Green East. In 1848 this institution became the Museum of Irish Industry and its evolutionary history was taken one stage further in 1867 when it was transformed into the Royal College of Science for Ireland, but whether it was styled as a museum or a college, one of the institute's tasks was to take science to the people through an extensive programme of lectures.[19] Some of the lecture courses — those intended for 'the artisan classes' — were free of charge and a packed lecture-theatre resulted. During the session 1854-55, for instance, a course in botany given by George James Allman (1812-1898) attracted audiences averaging 140, a course in chemistry given by William Kirby Sullivan (c. 1825-1890) attracted audiences of 380, and a course in geology — a slightly risqué and irreligious subject — by Joseph Beete Jukes (1811-1869) attracted average audiences of no less than 410 persons. But it was not merely the citizens of the metropolis who benefited from the lecture programme. Following the establishment of the Department of Science and Art in March 1853, the Museum became responsible for the organisation of a programme of science lecture-courses delivered throughout the length and breadth of Ireland. In 1863, for instance, the Museum was able to offer local organising committees a panel of twenty-eight eminent scientists from which to select their lectures, the panel including such -distinguished figures as J.B. Jukes from the Geological Survey, (Sir) Charles Alexander Cameron (1830-1921) the Dublin Public Analyst, (Sir) Charles Wyville Thomson (1830-1882) from Queen's College Belfast, Robert Harkness (1816-1878) from Queen's College Cork, William King (1809-1886) from Queen's College Galway, William Henry Harvey (1811-1866) and Edward Perceval Wright (1834-1910) from Trinity College Dublin, and W.K. Sullivan from the Museum itself. The subjects on offer for lecture courses that year were as follows: physical geology, palaeontology, physical geography, botany, agricultural botany, zoology, systematic and experimental chemistry, agricultural chemistry, chemistry applied to arts and manufactures, mechanics, hydrostatics and pneumatics, optics and acoustics, heat and the steam engine, electricity and magnetism, and astronomy. Such provincial lectures were well supported; during the session 1860-61 audiences averaging 123 persons had turned out in Londonderry to hear about heat and the steam engine, audiences averaging 270 had attended in Dromore, County Down, for a course in physical geology, and audiences of 82 had been present in Strokestown, County Roscommon, for a course in chemistry.

Clearly during the period 1780 to 1880 Ireland was amply provided with scientific institutions, but the mere existence of such institutions is of course no guarantee that scientific research of high quality will be executed therein. There must in the modern world be many nations possessing on the one hand a fine range of scientific institutes but possessing on the other hand little real hope that some day one of its scientists will be Stockholm-bound on his way to receive one of the coveted Nobel Prizes in science. But no Irishman, no matter how Chauvinistic a patriot he may be, has anything to fear from the scrutiny of the research achievements of his nineteenth-century countrymen and their judgement according to the highest standards of the international scientific community. Quite simply, many of Ireland's scientists of the period 1780 to 1880 were among the world's leading scientific figures. Richard Kirwan (1733-1812), a foremost figure in the Dublin Society and the second president of the Royal Irish Academy, was a remarkable scientific polymath with interests extending far across the spectrum of the sciences.[20] It was his enthusiasm which brought the Leskean cabinet to Dublin in 1792; his greatly respected *Elements of mineralogy* passed through three British editions between 1784 and 1810 and was translated into French, German and Russian; he was a pioneer student of Ireland's meteorology; and as a chemist his contemporaries held him in hardly less esteem than the great Lavoisier himself. It must have been a tragic day for Kirwan when he learned that his friend had been taken to the guillotine on 8 May 1794. Kirwan's contemporary William Higgins (c. 1763-1825), the professor of chemistry and mineralogy at the Dublin Society, has been described as 'a man of eccentric, indolent habits', but he does have some claim to priority over Dalton in the development of the Atomic Theory.[21] Another distinguished Irish chemist was Sir Robert John Kane (1809-1890), the first director of the Museum of Economic Geology in Dublin and the first president of Queen's College Cork.[22] Like Kirwan, Kane was a medallist of the Royal Society, and he was the author of a text-book of chemistry widely used upon both sides of the Atlantic. Sir Richard Griffith, 'the father of Irish geology', spent some thirty years mapping the rocks of Ireland and his work was eventually published in 1839 at a scale of one inch to four miles (1:253,440). Aided by some of his staff in the Valuation Office, Dublin, – aided in particular by Patrick Ganly (c. 1809-1899) who was himself the discoverer of the fact that cross-bedding can be used to demonstrate whether a stratum has been inverted – Griffith continued to revise his map and in the final versions issued during the 1850s the map achieves the status of a true geological masterpiece. To this day it remains one of the finest geological maps ever prepared. It was this map which Griffith personally displayed to Queen Victoria and Prince Albert when they visited the Great Dublin Industrial Exhibition in August 1853 and it was this map which was again featured at the Exposition Universelle in Paris in 1855.[23] Griffith and Ganly had pioneered the art of geological field-mapping at a scale of six inches to the mile (1:10,560), and during the 1850s it was to Ireland – to Bantry and Glengarriff – that a senior officer of the British Geological Survey came to learn the skills developed by his Irish colleagues.

A stroller upon the beach at Killiney, County Dublin, in October 1849 would doubtless have been alarmed to hear the report of an explosion and to see a part of the beach thrown into sudden upheaval. The physical cause of the incident was the explosion of a 25 lbs (11·35 kilos) keg of gunpowder buried in the sand; the human cause of the incident was another of Ireland's eminent scientists devotedly pursuing his researches. He was Robert Mallet (1810-1881), the son of a successful Dublin ironfounder.[24] In 1846 he had already presented a paper on earthquake waves to the Royal Irish Academy – a paper which is today acclaimed as being one of the foundations of modern seismology – and on Killiney beach in 1849 he was measuring the transit times of shock-waves through various types of deposit exposed at the earth's surface. The Killiney beach experiments were shortly to be extended to the granite of nearby Dalkey Island, and then, on the grand scale, to the rocks of Holyhead Mountain in Anglesey where Mallet was able to observe the shock-waves released by blasting operations which sometimes involved the detonation of 12,000 lbs (5,448 kilos) of gunpowder. He studied at first-hand the effects of the Dublin earthquake of 9 November 1852; in 1862 he published a memorable study of the disastrous Neapolitan earthquake of 16 December 1857; and today our dictionaries credit him with having coined no less than eight terms bearing the prefix 'seism-', the terms including such familiar ones as 'seismic', 'seismometry', and 'seismology'.

At least one of Mallet's Irish contemporaries shared his interest in geophysical research: Humphrey Lloyd (1800-1881), the professor of natural and experimental philosophy in Trinity College. Lloyd's interest lay in geomagnetism. During the 1830s, and inspired by the three Germans, Karl Friederich Gauss, Alexander von Humboldt, and William Eduard Weber, there was established an international network of some thirty geomagnetical observatories – der Magnetische Verein – and Lloyd urged Trinity College to participate in the programme through the establishment of its own magnetical observatory. The College agreed; an observatory was built in the Fellows' Garden, and there observations commenced in November 1838. Thus did Ireland become a participant in one of the earliest schemes for international scientific collaboration.

While Griffith, Lloyd, and Mallet were focussing their research activities upon the earth itself, other Irish scientists were gazing towards the heavens and two of these Irish astronomers must hold our attention: William Parsons (1800-1867), third Earl of Rosse, of Birr Castle, County Offaly, and Edward Joshua Cooper (1798-1863) of Markree Castle, County Sligo. It was early in the 1830s that Parsons decided to devote himself to astronomy and, more especially, to the improvement of the reflecting telescope.[25] He worked at Birr producing his own innovative designs; he trained his estate-workers in the crafts of telescope construction and he built in the grounds of Birr Castle all the furnaces and machinery appropriate for the task; and by 1839 he had completed his first reflector incorporating a 36-inch (91·4-centimetre) speculum. But this first instrument failed to satisfy his lordship's ambitions; he wanted a much larger telescope. Between 1842 and 1845 he and his men therefore built a gigantic instrument containing a 72-inch (182·8-centimetre) speculum – an instrument which was very appropriately named 'Leviathan'. Until the commissioning of the Hooker reflector at the Mount Wilson Observatory in California in 1917, the Birr Leviathan remained the world's largest reflecting telescope and the visitor's books at Birr Castle testify to the numbers of distinguished astronomers who flocked to Birr to use the Leviathan or merely to gaze upon it in wonder. Lord Rosse himself employed the telescope chiefly in studies of the nebulae, and through a series of papers presented to the Royal Society (he was the society's president from 1848 until 1854) he became the first to describe and illustrate the spiral structure that so many of the nebulae possess.

Our second observational astronomer – Edward Cooper – assumed responsibility for his family's estate at Markree Castle in 1830 and he immediately resolved to there establish a fully equipped astronomical observatory.[26] Within twenty years he possessed what was widely regarded as the world's finest private observatory, and on 25 April 1848 Cooper and his assistant, Andrew Graham, discovered the new minor planet Metis. Cooper's best-known work, however, was the compilation of a catalogue of stars located within three degrees of the ecliptic, the catalogue being published at government expense in four volumes between 1851 and 1856. It records the position of 60,066 stars only 8,965 of which had previously been known.

Whether mathematics may properly be claimed as a science is a matter that might be debated, but a science or not, there can be no doubt about the proud attainments of the Irish mathematicians during the first half of the last century. Trinity College Dublin then enjoyed a reputation as the home of a mathematical school of the highest distinction. It is significant that in 1846 the *Cambridge Mathematical Journal* restyled itself the *Cambridge and Dublin Mathematical Journal*. The founder of the Trinity College mathematical school was Bartholomew Lloyd (1772-1837) and among its members were James McCullagh (1809-1847) and George Salmon (1819-1904). McCullagh might have achieved a scholarly eminence sufficient to have placed him alongside the unrivalled French mathematicians of the day had he not tragically committed suicide after destroying virtually all his unpublished papers. Salmon was a noted geometrician; his *Treatise on conic sections* of 1848 remained for half a century the standard work upon the subject, and his pioneering *Treatise on the analytic geometry of three dimensions* of 1862 earned a reputation sufficient to ensure the book's translation into a number of European languages. And then there was Sir William Rowan Hamilton (1805-1865), from 1827 until his death Professor of Astronomy in Trinity College and Royal Astronomer of Ireland.[27] Widely recognised as the most outstanding scientific figure ever produced by Ireland, he is today best remembered for the 'Hamilton function', one of the most important functions in theoretical physics, and for his discovery of quaternions, a famed event which took place on 16 October 1843 while Hamilton was walking by Broom Bridge on the Royal Canal on his way from Dunsink in to Dublin. It was very fitting that, thanks to the interest of mathematically inclined Eamon de Valera, the centenary of Hamilton's discovery should have been marked by the issue of a commemorative postage stamp, one of the earliest of Irish stamps commemorating the achievement of a single individual.

This list of distinguished Irish scientists of the period 1780 to 1880 may be impressive but it is by no means exhaustive. To it there might be added Sir Robert Stawell Ball (1840-1913) the astronomer, mathematician, and brilliant populariser of science.[28] Another addition would be Nicholas Joseph Callan (1799-1864) the 'forgotten genius' from St Patrick's College Maynooth who was a pioneering student of electromagnetism.[29] There is the third Earl of Enniskillen (1807-1886) who assembled at Florence Court, County Fermanagh, one of the world's finest collections of fossil fish.[30] There is Thomas Grubb (1800-1878) who in his Rathmines factory designed and built a wide range of optical instruments including telescopes for astronomical observatories the world over.[31] There is Harvey the distinguished Trinity botanist,[32] and there is his colleague Samuel Haughton (1821-1897) whose scientific interests ranged from anatomy and chemistry to climatology and geology,[33] two men, incidentally, who opposed Charles Darwin's views on the origin of species. There was George Johnstone Stoney (1826-1911), Secretary to the Queen's University in Ireland and the man with whom there originated the term 'electron'.[34] But surely this catalogue of distinguished Irish scientists — and the list of Irish scientific institutions which they helped to create — are together entirely sufficient to demonstrate that science did indeed thrive in Ireland during the hundred years following 1780. This flourishing state of Irish science was widely recognised overseas. The British Association for the Advancement of Science, having been founded at York in 1831, visited only Oxford, Cambridge, and Edinburgh before coming to Dublin in 1835 for the fifth of its annual peripatetic gatherings, and thereafter the Association returned to Ireland upon seven occasions before 1909.[35] When the Association returned to Ireland in 1857 for its second Dublin meeting the Association's president was Humphrey Lloyd and every one of the Association's eight sections was presided over by an Irish scientist. In 1875 the Royal Society of London had twenty-five Ordinary Members of the Royal Irish Academy upon its role of Fellows. Foreign scientists of the calibre of Louis Agassiz, Elie de Beaumont, James Dwight Dana, Alexander von Humboldt, and Baron Justus von Liebig were all pleased to be elected to honorary membership of the Academy. Overseas scientists such as Edward Forbes and Thomas Henry Huxley of London, Sir John William Dawson of Montreal, Oswald Heer of Zurich and Henry James Johnston-Lavis of Naples all published papers in Irish journals, and foreign libraries were eager to add those journals to their shelves. In 1864, for instance, the Natural History Society of Dublin sent its journal to 109 libraries outside the British Isles, in 1877 the *Journal of the Royal Geological Society of Ireland* went to 82 libraries outside the British Isles, and in the 1880s the Royal Dublin Society exchanged publications with 374 bodies at home and overseas.

Within the present essay there are recorded the names of some fifty distinguished Irish scientists and it is now time to observe that they almost all share in common one characteristic which has not yet been mentioned: they were overwhelmingly of the Protestant persuasion. Of the fifty scientists, no more than 14 per cent were members of that Roman Catholic church which constitutes by far the largest religious group within the island. It is customary to explain this striking dearth of Irish Roman Catholic scientists in terms of the poor educational opportunities available to Roman Catholics before the middle years of the last century. This explanation must, however, be viewed with some suspicion. Both England and Scotland can offer many striking examples of individuals whose lack of education was little hinderance to their attainment of considerable scientific eminence. Michael Faraday began his career as an errand boy; William Smith came of yeoman stock but so effectively did he tutor himself in the earth sciences that he is today revered internationally as 'the father of English geology'; Hugh Miller, author of that classic *The Old Red Sandstone*, was originally a Cromarty stone-mason; those two Scottish naturalists immortalised by Samuel Smiles — Robert Dick and Thomas Edward — were respectively a baker and a shoemaker; and John Duncan, the weaver-botanist who presented his herbarium to the University of Aberdeen in 1880, lived alone in a tiny thatched cottage, his one room largely filled by his loom and 'his bed resting on some deals laid across the rafters, and reached by means of a ladder'. To place alongside such English and Scots scientists possessed of what the Victorians would have described as 'humble origins', Ireland, so far as is at present known, can muster but two men: Robert Bell (1864-1934) the riveter from Harland and Wolff's shipyard in Belfast who earned local distinction as a geologist,[36] and Samuel Alexander Stewart (1826-1910) the Belfast trunk-maker who in 1888 published a flora of the north-east of Ireland.[37] But neither Bell nor Stewart was a Roman Catholic. It is, of course, possible that there were Irish Roman Catholics who, despite their poor education, did take a keen interest in the natural phenomena around them. Perhaps there was a Lisdoonvarna shopkeeper who studied the vegetation of the Burren or a County Kilkenny quarryman who assembled a large collection of fossils from the famed workings at Kiltorcan. But if such individuals really did exist, then we can only regret that their names and accomplishments are today entirely unknown to us. It is salutary to recollect that the outstanding geological achievements of Patrick Ganly — himself a Roman Catholic — would today be largely unknown had not somebody purchased four volumes of his letters to Sir Richard Griffith at the sale of Griffith's effects in November 1878 and had not three of those four volumes eventually found their way into the library of the Royal Irish Academy. There is thus a possibility that we are today oblivious to the true extent of the interest in things scientific among Ireland's nineteenth-century Roman Catholics, but there does seem no escaping the conclusion that in its higher echelons Irish nineteenth-century science was largely a preserve of the Protestant element within Ireland's population. The problem of Ireland's 'missing' Roman Catholic scientists is one deserving of further attention.

During the 1860s Irish science was in a flourishing condition; by the 1890s Irish science had entered upon a marked decline. That decline persisted down to the middle years of the present century. There were, of course, a few Irish scientists of the period who did keep alive the tradition of Irish excellence in science, and within this category there immediately come to mind the names of the physicist George Francis Fitzgerald (1851-1901), the geophysicist John Joly (1857-1933), and the biochemist Edward Joseph Conway (1894-1968) — names to which there might be added that of Ernest Thomas Sinton Walton, Ireland's solê Nobel laureate in science, although his actual prize-winning work was conducted at the Cavendish Laboratory in Cambridge. But there does seem no avoiding the fact that during the decades after 1880 Irish science lost much of its former sparkle. No longer could Ireland be regarded as a land where scientists were, upon a broad front, grappling with fundamental research problems of wide international significance. The signs of Ireland's changed scientific status are many and varied. In the 1860s the Royal Cork Institution entered upon a decline. In the 1870s the Natural History Society of Dublin withered and died. In 1878 the Birr Leviathan made its last observations of the nebulae and by 1916 all astronomical work at Birr had ceased. In 1883 the now blind Earl of Enniskillen sold his palaeontological treasures to the Trustees of the British Museum. In 1890 the Geological Survey of Ireland was reduced to little more than a care and maintenance basis following the completion of the one-inch geological map of Ireland. Four years later, in 1894, the affairs of the Royal Geological Society of Ireland had to be wound up, and the rate of publication in Irish journals of research papers devoted to the earth sciences dropped from a total of 190 papers in the 1880s to a total of only 34 papers in the 1920s.[38] Similarly, in Irish entomology the total of papers published in 1925 was the lowest for forty years.[39] The Irish scientific periodicals lost their international status as, in areas such as botany, geology, and zoology, they ceased to publish papers devoted to non-Irish themes, and as their international status declined they increasingly failed to attract to their pages contributions from scientists working outside Ireland. In 1899 the Royal Dublin Society's Science Committee set up an enquiry to discover why the teaching of science was being neglected in Irish schools. In 1902 all work at the Markree Castle observatory ceased. In 1922 the government of the newly independent Irish Free State took over the geological gallery of the National Museum in order to provide offices for the Dail's clerical assistants and from that day to this the national geological collection — it includes the Leskean cabinet purchased by the Dublin Society in 1792 — has been hidden from the public view. In about 1925 the Dublin Microscopical Club came to the end of its life of almost eighty years and in 1926 the Royal College of Science for Ireland ceased to exist following its incorporation into the faculty of science of University College Dublin. Individually each of these events was perhaps of small moment; taken in association they surely indicate that after 1880 some deep malaise was sapping the

Irish scientific tradition. In 1875 twenty-five Ordinary Members of the Royal Irish Academy were entitled to the dignity of an F.R.S.; by 1978 the total had dwindled to only ten and of these ten a mere two were resident within the Republic of Ireland.

Only one sector of Irish science showed any real buoyancy during the closing decades of the nineteenth century: field natural history. Indeed, within that area there was a local boom — a boom in which a major inspirational figure was Robert Lloyd Praeger (1865-1953) who from 1893 until his retirement in 1923 was a member of the staff of the National Library of Ireland.[40] Naturalists' field-clubs were founded in Belfast (1863), in Dublin (1885), in Cork (1892), in Limerick (1892), and in Omagh (1906);[41] in Dublin in April 1892 there appeared the first issue of *The Irish Naturalist*, a monthly journal designed to cater for the interests of the field natural historians; and in 1894 the Irish Naturalists' Field Club Union was established to organise triennial national conferences. The natural historians undertook some highly successful enterprises such as the Lambay Island survey (1905-1906), which involved twenty-one naturalists, and the far more ambitious Clare Island survey (1908-1911), which involved about a hundred naturalists and brought to light the existence of 109 animals and 11 plants new to science. But natural history was soon to feel the chill winds that were blowing across other areas of Irish science. As early as the Field Club Union meeting in Cork in 1907 we find Praeger complaining of falling support; the last meeting of the Union was held at Rosapenna in 1910; and the final issue of *The Irish Naturalist* appeared in Dublin in December 1924, although the journal soon re-appeared phoenix-like in the guise of the Belfast-based *Irish Naturalists' Journal*, the first number of which was published in September 1925.

The reasons for this decline of Irish science during the decades following 1880 — decades during which other facets of Irish culture were so obviously blooming — need far closer scholarly attention than they have yet received. All that can at present be hazarded is a few suggestions as to the nature of possible contributory factors. Firstly, after 1845 the population of Ireland declined steadily and by 1936 it stood at only half its 1845 figure. There was thus progressively diminished that population base whence there had to be drawn the talents appropriate to scientific endeavour. Within the Protestant sector of the Irish population — the sector whence there came most of Ireland's scientists — the decline was even more marked. Within the territory of the Twenty-Six counties the Protestant population fell from 468,000 persons in 1861 to only 144,000 persons in 1961. Secondly, selective emigration may also have taken its toll. It has sometimes been suggested that in Scotland the average intelligence of the population has been diminished as a result of the continual emigration of the keenest intellects to England. May Ireland have suffered similarly? Thirdly, new scientific institutions were developing overseas, especially in Germany and the United States, and as international science became increasingly competitive, it followed that the high prestige of Irish science had to face a growing foreign challenge as a part of the natural course of events. Fourthly, scientific research was becoming increasingly expensive, and Ireland — especially after the acquisition of independence in 1922 — was a poor country. In particular, Ireland contained few wealthy industrialists able to fund scientific research on the scale of the assistance offered to the University of Oxford by Lord Nuffield or that offered to the University of Glasgow by the Clyde shipbuilders. In 1903 Lord Iveagh (1847-1927) did present £24,450 to a Science Laboratories Fund in Trinity College Dublin, and he further displayed his munificence by financial gifts to the College upon other and later occasions, but this was small beer as compared with the sums becoming available to universities overseas. Fifthly — and this is a point of particular relevance to the field-sciences — there must be remembered the disturbed state of the country for much of the period from the 'Agrarian Outrages' down to the Civil War. In the 1870s and 1880s officers of the Geological Survey of Ireland felt themselves to be at risk — by the populace they were regarded as government spies — and they therefore took to the field armed with revolvers concealed beneath their coats. Two distinguished English geologists — Charles Irving Gardiner and Sidney Hugh Reynolds — who had been investigating some of Ireland's oldest rocks, abandoned their research because of 'The Troubles' in the aftermath of World War I and transferred their attention to Scotland. Ireland's leading field-geologists of the day — William Bourke Wright (1876-1939) of the Geological Survey of Ireland — was the victim of some 'incident' and in consequence he in March 1921 took a transfer to a Survey post in England. Even today field-studies are being inhibited in certain Border areas of Ireland because of the continuing problem of the scientists' personal security. But it is not only the field-sciences that have suffered from Ireland's political unrest. During World War I the famed manufactory of astronomical instruments founded in Rathmines by Thomas Grubb turned to the making of range-finders, submarine periscopes, and the like. The factory had to be afforded an armed guard and in 1917 the Ministry of Munitions decided that the installation was too valuable a national asset to be located in restless Ireland. New premises were therefore made available to the firm at St Albans in England and by 1922 the Rathmines factory had been closed. A final reason for the decline of Irish science — a reason applicable to the Irish Free State in the years following 1922 — may be that the new nation itself failed to create an atmosphere in which good science could flourish. Perhaps the young state was too introspective to display much enthusiasm for the thoroughgoing internationalism basic to science — too concerned with Irish language revival and literary censorship to be aware of the momentous scientific developments taking place elsewhere. In the spring of 1932 waves of excitement passed through the international scientific community following the announcement that in Cambridge a young graduate of Trinity College Dublin – E.T.S. Walton – and his collaborator, John Douglas Cockcroft, had succeeded in splitting the atom; back in Ireland a far more important event was the arrival of the Papal Legate at Dun Laoghaire on 20 June and the opening of the International Eucharistic Congress in Dublin two days later.

This essay has focussed attention upon the Irish contribution to science as one facet of Ireland's cultural heritage. There remains to be asked one question: why has Ireland chosen largely to ignore the very considerable achievements of those of her sons who have devoted themselves to science? Part of the answer may be simply that our historians have felt more comfortable in discussions of banking, battles and bishops than in dealing with problems concerning basalt, binomials and brachiopods. It is far easier to appreciate Behan's *Quare Fellow* than it is to understand Hamilton's quaternions. But this can hardly be the complete explanation. Surely we are confronted here with an example of that all too common phenomenon, the manipulation of history for political ends. Ireland's scientists were in the past overwhelmingly drawn from the Protestant, Anglo-Irish ascendency stock, and within the Republic of Ireland it has been customary to play down, and even to dismiss as non-Irish, the notable achievements of that particular ethnic group. The nation has rather sought its roots in a Celtic and Roman Catholic past among a people who have contributed little to Ireland's reputation in science. Further than this, many Irish historians of the nationalistic school have been well content with their representation of the nineteenth-century struggle for national independence as having occurred in a downtrodden, impoverished, starving, and underprivileged nation. Any allusion to the flourishing state of Irish science throughout the greater part of the nineteenth-century serves only to raise doubts as to the validity of that well-established picture of nineteenth-century Ireland as the seat of tragedy, gloom, and despair. But times are changing. We need to be reminded of the remarkable attainments of Ireland's scientists in days gone by. Further, it needs to be emphasised that Griffith's geological map of Ireland is just as much a manifestation of the Irish creative genius as is Orpen's *The holy well* – that in Salmon's *Conic sections* we see an Irish mind at work just as surely as we see De Valera's mind at work in Ireland's 1937 constitution. De Valera himself would hardly have been unaware of such facts; let it be remembered that he harboured a deep admiration for that greatest of Irish mathematicians, William Rowan Hamilton.

Notes and References

Richard Kearney
INTRODUCTION

1. There have been several significant studies of Irish cultural history in recent years, in particular *The Celtic Consciousness*, ed. by R. O'Driscoll, 1982, Dolmen Press and *The Crane Bag Book of Irish Studies*, ed. by M.P. Hederman and R. Kearney, 1982, Blackwater Press. But neither of these works focuses specifically on the speculative, conceptual or philosophical achievements of the Irish mind. They are primarily, though not exclusively, concerned with the Irish imagination rather than Irish *thought per se*. The present publication hopes to supplement and complement these works.

2. This stereotype of the *imaginative thoughtless Celt* has been frequently challenged by such critics as Desmond Fennell and Seamus Deane.

3. One of the earliest records of a colonial campaign to promote a strategic stereotype of the 'mindless' Irish was that of Giraldus Cambrensis' *The History and Topography of Ireland*. This work was written c. 1187, two years after the author had visited Ireland in the entourage of Prince John. Although he praises Ireland's temperate climate and admires its inhabitants' ability to play musical instruments and recount fanciful tales of miracle and magic, his overall judgment is a damning one: "They are a wild and inhospitable people. They live on beasts only, and live like beasts. They have not progressed at all from the primitive habits of pastoral living. . . For given only to leisure and devoted only to laziness, they think that the greatest pleasure is not to work and the greatest wealth is to enjoy liberty" (*The History and Topography of Ireland*, Giraldus Cambrensis, translated by John O'Meara, 1982, Dolmen Press). In *Celtic Leinster: towards an historical geography of early Irish Civilisation A.D. 500-1600*, (1983, Irish Academic Press) Dr Alfred Smyth has successfully challenged this view that early Irish society was exclusively pastoral and demonstrates that agriculture played an essential part in the early economy. But one should not be surprised by the historical inaccuracy of the details of Giraldus Cambrensis' *Topography* for one of its primary ideological purposes was to vindicate a program of political invasion. As the Irish historian, Dr Art Cosgrove has observed: "The picture drawn by Gerald was unflattering; the Irish were economically backward, politically fragmented, wild, untrustworthy and semi-pagan, and guilty of sexual immorality. Doubtless the picture was much influenced by the need to justify conquest and dispossession" ('Seeing Ireland First', Art Cosgrove, *Books Ireland*, No. 71, 1983).

4. Cf. G.J. Watson, 1979, *Irish Identity and the Irish Literary Revival*, Croom

Helm, London, pp. 16-17. I am grateful to Timothy Kearney for bringing these passages to my attention.

5. Seamus Deane in *Two Decades of Irish Writing*, ed. by D. Dunn, 1975, Carcanet, Manchester, p. 8.

6. Seamus Heaney, 1980, *Preoccupations*, Faber, London, p. 104.

7. Garrett Barden, 1978, "Image", *The Crane Bag*, vol. 1, nos. 1 and 2, pp. 140-141.

8. W.B. Yeats, 1970, *Uncollected Prose*, Columbia University Press, New York, p. 172.

9. Frank O'Connor, 1967, *The Backward Look*, MacMillan, London, p. 5.

10. Sean O'Faolain, 1981, "Living and Dying in Ireland", *London Review of Books*, vol. 2, no. 14. I am grateful to Nuala O'Farrell for bringing this article to my attention.

11. Sean O'Tuama, "The Gaelic League Idea", *A Thomas Davis Lecture* broadcast by RTE in 1969 and published in 1972. Apart altogether from the important contributions to these fields of conceptual thought documented in this book, one could also mention here the original and influential publications in these areas by such modern Irish philosophers and thinkers as Conor Cruise O'Brien (*Writers and Politics*), Arland Ussher (*Journey into Dread*), Enda MacDonagh (*Towards a Christian Theology of Morality: Gift and Call*), Patrick Masterson (*Atheism and Alienation*), John Bernal (*The Social Function of Science*), Eiléan Ní Chuilleanáin (*Irish Women: Images and Achievements*), James White (*Church and State in Modern Ireland*), Denis Donoghue (*Ferocious Alphabets*), Anthony Cronin (*Heritage Now*), Seamus Deane (*Essays in Anglo-Irish Literature*), John Maguire (*Marx's theory of Politics*), Bernard Cullen (*Hegel's Social and Political Thought*), Oliver McDonagh (*States of Mind*) and many others.

12. See also the recent debates on the role of the intellectual in Irish culture — Declan Kiberd, 1981, "Aosdána: A Comment", *The Crane Bag*, vol. 5, no. 1, pp. 44-46; and Desmond Fennell, 1982, "Making Aosdána What it's Meant to be", *Sunday Press*, April 18: "Everyone is agreed that the Aosdána scheme (set up by the Irish Government and Irish Arts Council in 1981 to assist and to promote Irish creative writers) is excellent in principle but it has one serious defect which could make it, in practice, a botched job, surrounded continually by embarrassing controversy. . . The trouble lies in that absurd definition of literature — limiting it to fiction, plays and poetry — and partly in the exclusion of all works of creative thought, no matter how brilliant, original or inspiring. . . This discrimination will maintain and intensify the poverty of creative thought in modern Irish culture. . . It will make us continue to live up to the colonial stereotype of the *imaginative, thoughtless Celts.*"

13. This logic expressed itself according to the following three principles: (i) A is A (the principle of Identity); (ii) A is either A or non-A (the principle of the Excluded Middle); (iii) If A is A it cannot be non-A (the principle of Contradiction).

14 Thomas Kinsella, 1972, "The Divided Mind", *Irish Poetry in English*, Mercier Press, Cork, particularly the first chapter; and Declan Kiberd, 1977, "Writers in Quarantine? The Case for Irish Studies," *The Crane Bag*, vol. 3, no. 1, pp. 11f.

15. Vivian Mercier, 1962, *The Irish Comic Tradition*, Faber; cf. also, Andrew Carpenter, 1979, "Double Vision in Anglo Irish Literature", *Place, Person-*

ality and the Irish Writer, Colin Smythe, pp. 173-191

16. Cf. Richard Ellman, 1982, "An Irish European Art", *James Joyce Centenary Issue of Ireland of the Welcomes*, vol. 31 no. 3, pp. 5-6.

17. John Montague, 1978, "Jawseyes", *The Crane Bag*, vol. 2, nos. 1 and 2, pp. 9-10.

18. Seamus Heaney and Seamus Deane, 1977, "Unhappy and at Home", *The Crane Bag*, vol. 1, no. 1, p. 65 *et seq*. Brian Friel affirms a similar position of double allegiance with regard to Irish theatre. Referring to his own work as an Irish dramatist he speaks of being at once "in exile" and "at home" and relates this feeling of dislocation to the problem of writing of the Irish experience in the English language: "It's our proximity to England, its how we have been pigmented in our theatre with the English experience, the use of the English language, the understanding of words, the whole cultural burden that every word in the English language carries is slightly *different* to our burden." (Interview with Fintan O'Toole, 1982, *In Dublin*, no. 165, pp. 20ff).

19. Derek Mahon, 1983, "Lettre Ouvert à Serge Fauchereau", *Digraphe*, Paris, June, no. 27, p. 70.

20. Louis le Brocquy, 1977, "A Painter's Notes on Awareness", *The Crane Bag*, vol. 1, no. 2, pp. 68-9.

21. See Dorothy Walker, 1982, "Traditional Structures in Recent Irish Art", *The Crane Bag*, vol. 6, no. 1, pp. 41f.

22. K. Scherman, 1981, *The Flowering of Ireland: Saints, Scholars and Kings*, Gollancz, London; also Heinz Löwe, *Die Iren und Europa im Früheren Mittelalter*, Klett-Cotta, Stuttgart, 1982.

23. The early Irish missionaries called this voluntary journey into exile a *peregrinatio pro Christi*. The celebrated *Navigatio Sancti Brendani*, St. Brendan's tale of maritime adventure in search of the Isles of the Blest, gave rise to the Gaelic literary genre called *Immram*. Another thinker who might be mentioned here is Pelagius, the fifth century secular monk and heretical theologian who disputed the orthodox Roman doctrine of original sin, affirming that man, like Adam, is created innocent by God and becomes good or evil by his own free will. Pelagius's theory of the essential goodness of human nature, summed up in his teaching: "Man can live without sin" (*Hominem posse esse sine peccato*), was vigorously attacked by St Augustine (*De Gestis Pelagii*) and by St Jerome (*Dialogi adversus Pelagianos*). His writings, particularly *De Libero Arbitrio*, were condemned as heresy by Pope Innocent I in 417 and again by the Second Council of Orange in 529. "Pelagius" means "son of the open sea", a name derived from the original Celtic "Morgan". There is some debate about his origins, some scholars arguing that he was born in Britain or Brittany, others that he was Irish (H. Zimmer, *Pelagius in Irland* and St Jerome who referred to him as an "Irish heretic bloated with porridge"). In general, however, Pelagius was never considered to be a representative Irish thinker in the same manner as Eriugena or Berkeley. But it is fair to say that he did share with these Irish philosophers a distinctive proclivity towards unorthodox speculation, and certainly matched Eriugena's record as a travelling scholar (arriving in Rome in 400 and in North Africa in 412; he died in Jerusalem). Cf. *The Oxford Dictionary of the Christian Church* ed. F.L. Cross, 1958, Oxford University Press, p. 1040, and *The Catholic Dictionary*, Addis and Arnold, 1959, Routledge and Kegan Paul, p. 631.

24. Mircea Eliade, 1968, Myths, Dreams and Mysteries, Fontana, p. 27.

25. Although the writings of the Pseudo-Dionysius had been translated by Hilduin, Abbot of St. Denis (832-5), his version was considered to be so unsatisfactory that it was only with Eriugena's "successful" translation (c. 860) that the Dionysian *corpus* first secured recognition and currency in Western European spirituality.

26. On Shaw and Eriugena see John Jordan's quotation from Borges in this volume; also R. Kearney's interview with Borges and Heaney, 1982, *The Crane Bag*, vol. 6, no. 2.

27. For further studies on Irish scientists see in particular the recent Royal Society of Dublin publication on Tyndall which has as its aim "to restore Irish science to its proper place in the history of the country"; the recent series by Sean O'Donnell on Irish scientific thought in *Technology Ireland*, and Roy Johnston's *Science and Technology in Irish National Culture* in *The Crane Bag*, vol. 7, no. 2, 1983; and especially pages 294-310 of this book.

28. Charles Usher, 1769, *Clio or A Discourse on Taste*, London, p. 110.

29. Usher, *op.cit.*, pp. 113, 116.

30. In another remarkable passage, as far removed from British empiricism as one could imagine, Usher praises the fine arts as "indubitable proofs of the unspeakable sublimity of the soul of man," and concludes: "The arts bear witness, by their fictions, to the fact that the confused ideas of the mind are still infinitely superior, and beyond the reach of all description. It is this divine spirit . . . that stamps upon marble or canvas the figures of gods and heroes, that inspires them with an air of humanity, and leads the soul through the enchanting meanders of music in a waking vision, through which it cannot break to discover the near objects that charm it." Usher, *op.cit*, p. 190. Cf. also Usher, 1771, *Introduction to the Theory of the Human Mind*, London. I am grateful to Kevin Barry for bringing these passages to my attention.

31. On the relationship between Swift's philosophical and literary concerns see also Denis Donoghue's *Jonathan Swift*, 1969.

32. *The Journals of Arland Ussher*, ed. A. Kenny, 1981, Raven Arts, Dublin, p. 5.

33. *Ibid.*, pp. 12-13.

34. See, for example, C.B. Macpherson, 1980, *Burke*, Oxford University Press, or *The Philosophy of Edmund Burke*, 1960, edited with an introduction by L. Bredvold and R. Ross, Ann Arbor, The University of Michigan Press.

35. While Burke's "conservative liberalism" tended towards decentralisation in its opposition to "centralised, authoritarian power" – a sentiment shared by many other Irish political theorists, Thompson, A.E., Connolly etc. – O'Connell's "Benthamite liberalism" tended towards centralisation. The fact that it was O'Connell's version of liberalism which prevailed in Ireland at the level of political *practice* has meant that Ireland has become one of the most centralised modern states in Europe. I employ the term "Benthamite liberalism" because O'Connell was both a Liberal and a disciple of Jeremy Bentham – the English Utilitarian philosopher. The first influential Liberal clubs in Ireland were founded under his aegis. From O'Connell's time on, in Ireland – as in Wales and Scotland – liberalism became the mainstream political ideology and political party (the Conservatives having a majority only in England). The later Irish Party at Westminster was constantly allied with the Liberals, so much so that one could describe it as a Liberal party in disguise.

But its liberalism remained of a decidedly centralist or Benthamite kind. The emphasis on "nationalism," and its various strands, in our nineteenth and twentieth century history has obscured this for many people.

36. Cf. J. Connolly, 1910, "The argument for the compatibility of Irish socialism and the Christian religion" in *Labour, Nationality and Religion.*

37. AE (George Russell), 1982, *Co-operation and Nationality*, Irish Academic Press (Introduction by Patrick Bolger); see also *The National Being: Some Thoughts on Irish Polity*, 1982, Irish Academic Press.

38. E.P. Thompson, 1982, *The Irish Times*, Feb. 27. This internationalist position has been perhaps best represented over the years by the Irish thinker and critic, Sean MacBride.

39. To entertain the hypothesis of recurring characteristics of the Irish mind does not necessitate a belief in a Jungian Collective Unconscious, Herderian Racial Memory or a Yeatsian-mystical-pan-Celtic *Anima Mundi*. It is sufficient that the various generations of Irish writers and intellectuals have heard of, read, or been influenced, in some direct or indirect way, by each other.

40. Quoted by John Jordan in his essay in this book, from Borges, 1952, "A Note on Bernard Shaw," *Otras Inquisiciones.*

41. Quoted by R. Ellmann, 1959, *James Joyce*, Oxford University Press, London, p. 559.

42. Borges, 1952, *op.cit.*

43. J. Joyce, 1973, *Finnegans Wake*, Viking Press, New York, 14th edition, p. 531.

44. "Ireland, Island of Saints and Sages," in *James Joyce. The Critical Writings*, ed. by E. Mason and R. Ellmann, 1964, Viking Press, New York, pp. 160-161.

45. Paul Ricoeur, 1969, *Le Conflit des Interprétations: Essaies d'Herméneutique*, Editions de Seuil, Paris, and *The Symbolism of Evil*, translated by E. Buchanan, 1967, Beacon, Boston; also Don Ihde, 1971, *Hermeneutic Phenomenology*, Northwestern University Press.

46. A further significant dimension of the contemporary Irish mind which exceeded the brief of this book is the rise of a particularly feminist movement of thought in our own century. In Irish history as in most other European histories, women were intellectually and socially oppressed. One of the consequences of this historical oppression is the regrettable absence of any substantial tradition of philosophical texts authored by Irish women down through the centuries. This absence undoubtedly constitutes a shortcoming of Ireland's intellectual history. Despite this philosophical eclipse, however, women did play an essential, if often "hidden" role in Irish society (e.g. as the transmitters of cultural heritage). In recent decades, Irish feminist thinkers and scholars have done much to retrieve these hidden dimensions from historical oblivion and have made decisive contributions to the development of an Irish feminist ideology. This ideology was inaugurated in the seminal study by Anna Wheeler and William Thompson in the 1820s entitled *An Appeal of One Half of the Human Race, Women, Against the Pretensions Of the Other Half, Men, to Restrain Them in Political and thence in Civil and Domestic Slavery*. Amongst the more recent studies devoted to this critical reappraisal of the role of women in Irish society and culture are *Women in Irish Society: the Historical Dimension* (1978, edited by Margaret MacCurtain and Donnacha O Corrain); *Images of Irish Women* (1980, a special issue of *The Crane Bag*, edited by Christine Nulty); *Irish Women: Images and Achieve-*

ments (1984, by Eiléan ní Chuilleanáin); *Women in Irish legend, Life and Literature* (1983, edited by S.J. Gallagher); *Unmanageable Revolutionaries*, (1983, Margaret Ward); and Eunice McCarthy's studies in social psychology. A sequel to the present volume, dealing more specifically with the contemporary, as opposed to historical, philosophies of the Irish mind might well begin with a comprehensive analysis of this crucial contribution to modern thought made by Irish women. Such a sequel might also include studies of the original contributions to metaphysical, theological, social and aesthetic thought made by other Irish scholars in recent decades.

47. Anne Crookshank, 1978, *Painters of Ireland*; Bruce Arnold, 1969, *A Concise History of Irish Art*; Maurice Craig, 1982, *The Architecture of Ireland*; M. Herity and G. O'Eogan, 1977, *Ireland in Prehistory*; cf. also Roderick Knowles, 1982, *Contemporary Irish Art* and Dorothy Walker, 1981, *Louis le Brocquy*.

48. Seamus Deane, 1977, "The Literary Myths of the Revival: A case for their Abandonment," *Myth and Reality in Irish Literature*, ed. by J. Ronsley, W.L.U.P., Canada, pp. 317-329.

49. W.B. Yeats, 1961, *Essays and Introductions*, London, p. 402, quoted by Deane.

50. R. Kearney's interview with Paul Ricoeur, 1978, "Myth as the Bearer of Possible Worlds," *The Crane Bag*, vol. 2, nos. 1 and 2 in particular the following passage, p. 114: Paul Ricoeur: "You have hit here on a very important and difficult problem: the possibilities of a perversion of myth. This means that we can no longer approach myth at the level of naivety. We must always view it from a critical perspective. It is only by means of a selective reappropriation that we can become aware of myth. We are no longer primitve, living at the immediate level of myth. Myth for us is always mediated and opaque. This is so not only because it expresses itself through a particular apportioning of power functions but also because several of its recurrent forms have become deviant and dangerous, e.g. the myth of absolute power (fascism) and the myth of the sacrificial scapegoat (antisemitism and racism). We are no longer justified in speaking of 'myth in general.' We must critically assess the content of each myth and the basic intentions which animate it. Modern man can neither get rid of myth nor take it at its face value. Myth will always be with us, but we must always approach it critically. And I think it is here that we could speak of the essential connection between "critical instance" and the "mythical foundations." Only those myths are genuine which can be reinterpreted in terms of liberation. And I mean liberation in any sense of the word, personal or collective. Or we should perhaps extend this critical criterion to include only those myths which have as horizon the liberation of mankind as a whole. Liberation cannot be exclusive." For more detailed analysis of this question see Richard Kearney, 1978, "Myth and Terror," *The Crane Bag*, vol. 2, nos. 1 and 2, pp. 125-140 and *La Poétique du Possible: Vers une philosophie de la Figuration*, Beauchesne, Paris, 1984; and also *Myth and Motherland*, Field Day Publications, 5, 1984.

51. Terry Eagleton, 1981, *Walter Benjamin or Towards a Revolutionary Criticism*, Verso, London, NLB, p. 59. I am much indebted to Eagleton's analysis.

52. Historiography is hermeneutic in at least three ways; 1) the events are interpreted in terms of an *aesthetic* narrative or plot; 2) the events are inter-

preted in terms of an *ideological* paradigm of a socio-political or cultural nature; 3) the events are interpreted in terms of an *ethical* choice which determines how the narrative and ideological strategies of shaping the past can be seen as serving a liberating and progressive role in relation to contemporary problems. Hannah Arendt succinctly identifies the ways in which every historical hermeneutic operates when she observes that "tradition puts the past in order, not just chronologically but first of all systematically in that it separates the positive from the negative, the orthodox from the heretical, and that which is obligatory and relevant from the mass of irrelevant or merely interesting opinions and data." (Introduction to *Illuminations*, Jonathan Cape, 1970, p. 44). For a more detailed analysis of this precise question see Paul Ricoeur, 1983, *L'histoire et le recit* in *Temps et recit*, Editions du Seuil, Paris, pp. 137 et seq.

53. Mircea Eliade, 1968, *Myths, Dreams and Mysteries*, Fontàna, pp. 23-39.

54. Seamus Deane, 1977, *op.cit.*, p. 326.

55. Marx himself seemed to have recognised this fundamental point in several of his writings, in particular *The Paris Manuscrips* of the 1840s and the opening chapters of volume I of *Capital*, where he analyses the fetishistic nature of commodities and the labour theory of surplus value, or in his analysis of the role of ideology in *The German Ideology*. Cf. on this question, C. Castoriadis, 1975, *L'institution Imaginaire de la Société*, du Seuil, Paris. Deane's literalist hermeneutic displays its dualist assumptions once again when he praises Kavanagh and other contemporary Irish poets for their "modesty in relation to history," their refusal "to play games with history" or to invent "traditions . . . to liberate the mind." Deane's conclusion reveals that the ultimate aim of his literalist-dualist interpretation of Irish intellectual history is to corroborate a hermeneutic of discontinuity: "It is perhaps more honest and sensible to admit the discontinuity which marks the various achievements of the Irish authors who wrote in the English language during these centuries. Continuity is the invention of the revival . . . Our present dilapidated situation has borne in upon us more fiercely than ever the fact that discontinuity, the discontinuity which is ineluctably an inheritance of colonial history, is more truly the signal feature of our tradition . . . For it is the intractability of our situation, the impossibility of converting it into myth which has at last begun to free poets . . . from the aesthetic and heroic vocabularies of the revival." (S. Deane, 1977, *op. cit.*, p. 325-7). Deane's conclusion is entirely legitimate, but his method and means of reaching it are not always so.

56. O'Connor's translations included *Cúirt an Mhéanoíche, Cill Cais* and *A Golden Treasury of Irish Poetry, AD. 600-1200*, in collaboration with David Greene.

57. Proinsias MacCana, 1968, review of *The Backward Look, Studia Hibernica*, no. 8, pp. 153f.

58. Frank O'Connor, 1967, *The Backward Look, op.cit.*, p. 8.

59. Nor is it claimed that all those Irish intellectuals who managed to surmount the divide between critical and poetic reason, always acknowledged this fact. Deane's analysis has already been referred to in this regard. Mention was also made, at the outset, of O'Connor's statement in *The Backward Look* that the Irish chose imagination rather than intellect — an ironic preface to a work of *imaginative intellect* which belies just this opposition! As MacCana remarks, *op.cit.*, p. 153: "Here is the creative mind looking for the significant

substructure and inner meaning of a tale. He does take cognisance of the philosophical facts, but it is his own artistic intuition which finally counts." The point is simply that such inconsistencies or exceptions do not disprove the general rule that some of Ireland's finest intellectuals display, on occasion, a singular ability to synthesise qualities of the human mind commonly opposed in western culture.

60. Are not the characteristics of *decentredness, paradox, exodus* or *otherness* equally recognizable features of the Jewish mind, a mind which also resisted in large part the hegemony of Greek logocentrism? Contemporary Jewish thinkers such as Levinas, Buber, Scholem, Benjamin or Derrida, would certainly suggest that this is so. Indeed, this is perhaps one of the reasons why Joyce felt such an affinity with the Jewish Bloom and chose him as the nomadic wanderer to parody his Greek prototype in *Ulysses*. Compare also in this regard, our observations on Joyce as a cultural and linguistic exile above (p. 3), with the following passage in which Franz Kafka describes the Jewish writer's approach to the German language as an "overt or covert or possibly self-tormenting, usurpation of an alien property, which has not been acquired but stolen, (relatively) quickly picked up, and which remains someone else's possession, even if not a single linguistic mistake can be pointed out."

61. Sean O'Faolain, *op.cit.* As an example of this "underground stream." O'Faolain cites the "lethal practice" of hunger-striking which has survived in Ireland and India "the two peripheries of the Indo-European world."

62. Quoted by Seamus Deane, 1977, "The Question of Tradition", *The Crane Bag*, vol. 3, no. 1, p. 8. Deane concludes his editorial with the following significant admission: "The idea of an Irish tradition . . . . is not easily dismissed since it has provided a basis for much of the political and cultural activity of this century".

63. W. Benjamin, 1973, *Illuminations*, translated by H. Zohn, edited and introduced by H. Arendt, Fontana, p. 57.

64. Arland Ussher, 1981, *The Journal*, edited by A. Kenny, Raven Arts, Dublin.

65. W. Benjamin, 1979, *One Way Street*, Translated by E. Jephcott and K. Shorter, introduced by S. Sontag, NLB, p. 359; Cf. Eagleton, *op.cit.*, pp. 43 *et seq.*

66. T.S. Eliot, 1919, "Tradition and the Individual Talent", *Selected Essays*, p. 150.

67. W. Benjamin, *One Way Street, op.cit.*, p. 362, quoted by Eagleton, *op.cit.*

68. *Ibid.*, p. 314. See also Heidegger's hermeneutic blueprint in *Kant and The Problem of Metaphysics*, 1962, translated by J. Churchill, Indiana University Press, p. 207: "It is true that in order to wrest from the actual words (myths or images) that which they *intend to say*, every interpretation must necessarily resort to violence. This violence, however, should not be confused with an action that is wholly arbitrary. The interpretation must be animated and guided by the power of an illuminative idea. Only through the power of this idea can interpretation risk that which is always audacious, namely, entrusting itself to the secret *élan* of a work, in order by this *élan* to get through to the unsaid and attempt to find an expression for it. The directive idea itself is confirmed by its own power of illumination". I would like to think that the hermeneutic plan followed in this work could combine the leisurely probings and trial-and-error searchings of Benjamin with the more assertive thrust towards essential, illuminative principles advanced here by Heidegger.

CHAPTER 1

Brendan Purcell

IN SEARCH OF NEWGRANGE: LONG NIGHT'S
JOURNEY INTO DAY

1. For the new discoveries, cf. C. Woodman, 1981, "A Mesolithic Camp in Ireland," *Scientific American*, August, pp. 92-98. On the general background, cf. M. Herity and G. Eogan, 1977, *Ireland in Prehistory*, London, Routledge and Kegan Paul and M. Herity, 1974, *Irish Passage Graves*, Irish Univ. Press, Dublin.
2. M. Herity, 1974, *op. cit.*, p. 185. Nora Chadwick, 1970, *The Celts*, Penguin, Harmondsworth, refers to the continuity of cult and myth from neolithic to Celtic cultures both on mainland Europe (p. 164) and in Ireland (p. 173).
3. S.P. Ó Ríordáin and R. de Valera, 1979[5], Methuen, London, p. 28.
4. Cf. C. O'Kelly, 1978, *Illustrated Guide to Newgrange*, 3rd ed., Cork, and the definitive study, *Newgrange*, by M.J. O'Kelly, 1982, Thames and Hudson, London. (The convention by which the whole Boyne Valley complex is referred to as Newgrange, while New Grange designates one of the tumuli, will be followed here.) G. Eogan, 1968, "Excavations at Knowth, Co. Meath, 1962-5," *P.R.I.A.*, 66C, pp. 299-382; 1974, "Report on the Excavations of some Passage Graves," *P.R.I.A.*, 74C, pp. 11-112; 1984, Excavations at Knowth 1, Dublin, RIA. Dowth still awaits excavation.
5. Excellently summarised in J. Wood, 1978, *Sun, Moon and Standing Stones*, Oxford University Press.
6. M. König, 1973, *Am Anfang der Kultur*, Berlin, Mann; 1980, *Unsere Vergangenheit ist älter*, Frankfurt, Krüger. M. Eliade, 1958, *Patterns in Comparative Religion*, London, Sheed and Ward.
7. E. Voegelin, 1956-74, *Order and History*, vols. 1-4, Baton Rouge, Louisiana University Press.
8. How is it possible to interpret symbols for which there are no written documents? C. O'Kelly, 1975, in her valuable monograph, *Passage-Grave Art in the Boyne Valley*, Cork, p. 13, remarks that "one has become suspicious of postulating expediency in explanation of any feature of the Newgrange tumulus because it is not a characteristic normally to be associated with it. Up to the present our experience has been that every feature, structural, architectural, etc., was carefully thought out." Our working hypothesis is that Newgrange is the deepest expression of the Boyne Culture's quest for attunement with divine-cosmic reality. Given that presupposition of maximal significance, a comment of Voegelin's with regard to the interpretation of the so-called "fragments" of Heraclitus seems apposite: "As a matter of principle, whenever I must decide between two interpretations which both

can be supported philologically I prefer the profounder to the flatter meaning" (Voegelin, 1956-74, *op. cit.* vol. II, p. 228n.) What this means in practice is that, faced with a symbol or group of symbols at Newgrange, we draw on whatever archaic experiences and symbolisations are available which are *possibly* equivalent to those we are seeking to understand. In fact, the range of archaic symbolisations of experience is by no means unlimited, and once it is accepted that the Boyne people, whatever their unique contributions to human history, belong to the same humankind that has developed its self-understanding and expression over some 40,000 years, a comparative method which proceeds cautiously and imaginatively seems the most justifiable in the circumstances. While no breakthrough (such as the Landa *Relacion* has made possible for the Mayan glyphs) could occur, the wealth of apparently calendrical detail on the Knowth stones may lead to a verifiable interpretation of purely calendrical symbols there (cf. S. Morley, 1975, *An Introduction to the Study of the Maya Hieroglyphs*, Dover, New York, and 1975, "Maya Thought," *The Maya*, M. Coe, Penguin.)

9. E. Voegelin, 1967, "Immortality: Experience and Symbol," *Harv. Theol. Rev.*, vol. 60, no. 3, p. 235.

10. E. Voegelin, 1956-74, *op. cit.*, vol. I, pp. 1-11.

11. M. Herity and G. Eogan, 1977, *op. cit.*, p. 253.

12. M. Eliade, 1958, *op. cit.*, pp. 370f; 1969, *Le sacre et le profane*, Gallimard, Paris, *passim*. M. O'Kelly's excavation indicated that the Great Circle was probably built either at the same time as the mound or before it, 1982, *op. cit.*, p. 21f.

13. The total tomb length of New Grange is given as 24 m, of Knowth East as 40 m, and of Knowth West as 34 m. Herity, 1974, *op. cit.*, p. 188.

14. M. Eliade, 1958, *op. cit.*, p. 102.

15. *Ibid.*, p. 381. Cf. M. Herity and G. Eogan, 1977, *op. cit.*, p. 75, on the initiatory design of Knowth West: "The most striking pictures are displayed in the deepest recesses of the tomb . . . As in Brittany, the finest art is reserved for the area beyond the angle of the passage, where its impact on the votaries would be greatest."

16. M. Eliade, 1958, *op. cit.*, pp. 245f.

17. E. Voegelin, 1956-74, *op. cit.*, vol. IV, pp. 81f. The location of Stonehenge seems to have been determined by the fact that only at its latitude, 51°, 17', could the principal solar and lunar alignments be made from four points forming a rectangle "perpendicular to the midsummer sunrise line of the monument," a rectangle today marked by two of a possible four "station-stones" (G. Hawkins, 1977, *Stonehenge Decoded*, Fontana, London, pp. 70f, 193). On the square as an earth-symbol, Eliade notes that in archaic rituals, "The founding of a new town repeats the creation of the world – once the spot has been confirmed by ritual, a square or circular enclosure is put around it with four gates corresponding to the four points of the compass. As Usener had already shown, towns are divided into four in imitation of the Cosmos; in other words, they are a copy of the Universe," M. Eliade, 1958, *op. cit.*, p. 374.

18. M. König, 1973, *op. cit.*, pp. 128-45.

19. N. Chadwick, 1970, *op. cit.*, p. 840.

20. P. Opitz, 1967, *Lao-tzu. Die Ordnungsspekulation im Tao-tê-ching*, List, Munich, pp. 48ff.

21. M. Herity, 1974, *op. cit.*, p. 28.

22. M. König,1973, *op. cit.*, pp. 272-77. M. Herity and G. Eogan, 1977,*op. cit.*, p. 75, mention what might be a variation of this in Knowth West: "A bold design of nested rectangles is repeated three times, on the entrance stone, on the sillstone of the chamber and on the backstone." (M. Herity, 1974, *op. cit.*, pp. 36 and 184 illustrates two of these.)

23. M. Eliade, 1958, *op. cit.*, pp. 100f. To the vertical line on the New Grange entrance stone must be added the wide vertical channel on K52, at the back of the mound, and the vertical lines bisecting both of the Knowth entrance stones (Knowth East illustrated in M. Brennan, 1980, *The Boyne Valley Vision*, Dolmen Press, Portlaoise, p. 95). Regarding Dowth, Herity quotes an excavation report in 1848: "In the Centre of the Mound a curious funnel or Air Shaft was discovered, about 5 Inches in Diameter neatly built with small flat Stones. This was reached about 17 feet from the datum line, and reached to the base of the Tumulus" (250). It could be suggested that these vertical lines represent cosmic Axes, along which all three world-regions intersect.

24. M. Eliade, 1952,*Images et symboles*, Gallimard, Paris, p. 51.

25. *Ibid.*, p. 50.

26. M. Eliade, 1958,*op. cit.*, pp. 216f.

27. J. Wood, 1978, *Sun, Moon and Standing Stones*, p. 98.

28. M. Eliade, 1958, *op. cit.*, p. 149; 1969, *Le mythe de l'éternel retour*, Gallimard, Paris.

29. *Ibid.*, 1958, p. 137.

30. A. Marshack, 1972, *The Roots of Civilisation*, Weidenfeld and Nicolson, London, p. 161.

31. *Ibid.*, Chap. 10.

32. M. König, 1973, *op. cit.*, pp. 146-213. The triangles topped by crescents discovered at Stonehenge in 1953 possibly have a lunar significance (cf. R. Atkinson, 1979, *Stonehenge*, Pelican, pp. 44, 92, plate 11).

33. Cf. G. Hawkins, and J. Wood, *op. cit.* The new appreciation of Stonehenge points towards what may yet be ascertained in the Newgrange complex. The English site is best understood perhaps, not in terms of contemporary priorities, as an "observatory" (Wood) or a giant "computer" (Hawkins), but as a cosmic centre of truly symphonic attunement to the secret but massively reassuring cycles of heavenly recurrence. The resonance of that attunement was amplified when, about the same central axis on midsummer sunrise through the heel stone, there was added c. 2,100 BC the great inner sarsen circle and within that the open ellipse of trilithons. The 12 principal solar and lunar alignments could then be made both from the station-stone rectangle and from the new stone circle and trilithon ellipse.

34. M. Brennan, 1980,*op. cit.*, p. 98.

35. M. König, 1973, *op. cit.*, pp. 112f. Perhaps this is the significance of the "circles, gapped circles and arcs" noted by C. O'Kelly as one of the commonest motifs in the Knowth kerb (*Passage-Grave Art*, no. 26).

36. Cf. M. Eliade, 1958, *op. cit.*, pp. 232f: "The manifold significance of the 'centre stone' is even better preserved in Celtic traditions. Lia Fáil, the 'stone of Fáil' . . . starts singing when anyone worthy of being king sits on it . . . Lia Fáil is a theophany of the soil divinity, the only divinity to recognise his master (the High King of Ireland), the only one who controls the economy of fertility . . . That the Celts saw the religious (and implicitly the political) significance of the centre is evidenced by such words as *medi-*

nemetum, mediolanum [=Milan] which exist even today in French place names."

37. *Passage-Grave Art*, no. 11, p. 28; M. Herity, 1974, *op. cit.*, p. 185.

38. M. Herity, 1974, *op. cit.*, pp. 153f.

39. *Ibid.*, p. 126.

40. *Ibid.*, p. 185.

41. N. Chadwick, 1970, *op. cit.*, p. 181; cf. M. MacNeill, 1962, *The Festival of Lughnasa*, Oxford University Press.

42. M. König, 1973, *op. cit.*, pp. 240-48.

43. M. Eliade, 1958, *op. cit.*, p. 167.

44. M. König, 1973, *op. cit.*, p. 132. One of the diagonals joining the points on the station-stone rectangle at Stonehenge is aligned to lowest moonrise and moonset, and the point of intersection of the diagonals almost coincides with the centre of the original outer circle (Hawkins, 1977, *op. cit.*, p. 71).

45. Beautifully illustrated by the Tedavnet gold disc in *Treasures of Early Irish Art*, New York, Metropolitan Museum of Art, 1977, plate 1.

46. C. O'Kelly, 1971, *op. cit.*, 2nd ed., p. 78.

47. E. Voegelin, 1974, *op. cit.*, vol. 4, p. 72.

48. M. König, 1973, *op. cit.*, p. 38. König suggests that the frequent, apparently cultic positioning of human skulls from Neanderthal times could indicate their use to symbolise the whole (*Unsere Vergangenheit ist älter*, pp. 33f.).

49. M. Herity, 1974, *op. cit.*, p. 136.

50. M. Eliade, 1958, *op. cit.*, pp. 414f.

51. C. O'Kelly, 1978, *op. cit.*, 3rd ed., pp. 116f.

52. M. König, 1973, *op. cit.*, p. 38. König refers to Karl Jaspers' suggestion that, in the archaic experience, for the observer at the centre, the whole cosmos would appear as a spherical vault, while from outside, the same hollow sphere would be ball-shaped. She considers that the linked occurrence of hemispheres and hollows in paleolithic experience may express a differentiation of the whole into the concave/convex polarity of the two regions, heaven above and earth below (pp. 75-83). Could the frequent "cupmarks" at Newgrange have the meaning, then, of earth/underworld as differentiated from the whole?

53. E. Voegelin, 1956, *op. cit.*, vol. 1, p. 5.

54. M. König, 1973, *op. cit.*, pp. 105f. Perhaps the "fern" motif on C4, with its predominantly downward sloping lines, changing to an upward slope at its base, has an equivalent meaning to these chevrons.

55. M. Herity, 1974, *op. cit.*, p. 111.

56. D. Walsh, 1974, *Participation in the Order of Divine Being. A Study of Eric Voegelin's Philosophy of Consciousness.* Unpubl. MA thesis, Univ. Coll. Dublin, p. 89.

57. E. Voegelin, 1957, *op. cit.*, vol. 2, pp. 58f.

58. For Zoroaster, cf. M. Eliade, 1965, *The Two and the One*, London, Harvill, p. 83 (also, *Ibid.*, vol. 4, p. 25n). Eliade refers to the triad of Good and Evil born of Zervan, the god of boundless time. For the Hindu experience, cf. *Bhagavad Gita*, ch. 11, v. 37, where Krishna is addressed as being (*sad*), not-being (*asat*), and what is beyond that (*tatparam yat*). For Lao Tzu, cf. *Tao Te Ching*, I, which is a meditation on the nameless name of *Tao* (the way of heaven), transcending the "names" *Wu* (not-being), and *Yu* (being), and the discussion in P. Opitz, *Lao-tzu*, pp. 94-100. In his "Remarks on religious dualism: Dyads and Polarities," *The Quest*, Chicago University Press, pp. 172ff, Eliade, 1969, suggests the possible background for the

speculation on the *Tao* as a "third term" transcending the archaic polarity of the two basically opposed cosmic rhythms, *Yin* (female) and *Yang* (male).

CHAPTER 2

Prionsias MacCana

EARLY IRISH IDEOLOGY AND THE CONCEPT OF UNITY

1. *Táin Bó Cúalnge* from the *Book of Leinster*, ed. Cecile O'Rahilly, 1970, Dublin, pp. 136. 272.
2. Jean-Pierre Vernant, 1980, *Myth and Society in Ancient Greece*, Brighton, pp. 187-89.
3. *Zeitschrift für celtische Philologie* xvii, 279f.
4. *The Backward Look*, 1967, London, p. 9. I quote O'Connor's translation of Thurneysen's German.
5. G. Dumézil, 1973, *The Destiny of a King*, Chicago and London, pp. 115f, 106 = *Mythe et Epopée*, vol. 2, Paris, pp. 361f, 353.
6. *The Impact of the Scandinavian Invasions on the Celtic-speaking Peoples c. 800-1100 AD*, ed. Brian Ó Cuív, 1962, 1975, Dublin, p. 128.
7. *Ibid.*, p. 129.
8. *Top. Hib.*, ed. Dimock, p. 144. For the idea of Uisnech as the "navel" of Ireland; cf. *ós imlind Usnig* "above Uisnech's navel," *Ériu* 4, 150. 22.
9. F. Lot, 1947, *La Gaule*, Paris, pp. 79f.
10. J. Vendryes, 1948, "La Réligion des Celtes," *Mana: Introduction à l'histoire des religions*, 2, Paris, p. 294.
11. A. Rees, 1966, *Proceedings of the International Congress of Celtic Studies 1963*, Cardiff, pp. 47f.
12. This is how the central message of E. Durkheim, *The Elementary Forms of Religious Life* is summarised by Mary Douglas in her *Purity and Danger*, 1970, Pelican Books, p. 30.
13. C. Lévi-Strauss, 1961, *Race et Histoire*, Paris, p. 84.
14. M. Fortes and E.E. Evans-Pritchard (eds.), 1940, *African Political Systems*, Oxford, pp. 9f, 23.
15. *Oxford History of India*, 1919, p. x.
16. David G. Mandelbaum, 1970, *Society in India*, Univ. of Calif., ii, 401.
17. Louis Dumont, 1970, *Religion, Politics and History in India*, The Hague, p. 78.
18. It has been noted of other pre-modern societies that praise-poetry can fulfil a unifying function. Among the Zulu, for instance, praise of the chief, who personified his tribe, served to build up tribal loyalty and solidarity, and, when the various tribes were joined to form a Zulu nation, it helped to bind them together in a common loyalty. (Cf. Trevor Cope, 1968, *Izibongo: Zulu Praise-poems*, Oxford, pp. 32f.)
19. Eleanor Knott, 1922, *The Bardic Poems of Tadhg Dall Ó Huigin*, London, vol. 1, p. xlv.
20. Standish Hayes O'Grady, 1926, *Catalogue of Irish Mss. in the British Museum*, London, vol. 1, pp. 413f.
21. John C. Mac Erlean, S.J., ed., 1917, *Poems*, London, vol. 3, p. 164.

CHAPTER 3

Tomás Ó Cathasaigh

THE CONCEPT OF THE HERO IN IRISH MYTHOLOGY

1. Quoted by Terence Hawkes, 1977, *Structuralism and Semiotics*, London, p. 12.
2. T.S. Eliot, quoted in F. O. Mathiessen, 1959, *The Achievement of T.S. Eliot*, Galaxy Editions, New York, p. 40.
3. G. Dumézil, 1973, *The Destiny of a King*, Chicago, p. 115.
4. Edmund Leach, 1969, *Genesis as Myth and other essays*, London, p. 11.
5. Text edited by A.G. Van Hamel, 1933, *Compert Con Culainn and other stories*, Dublin. There is a translation by Thomas Kinsella, 1970, in *The Tain*, London, pp. 21-23.
6. Tomás Ó Broin, 1961-63, *Éigse*, vol. 10, pp. 286-99.
7. G. Dumézil, 1970, *The Destiny of a Warrior*, Chicago, p. 16.
8. Text edited by Eleanor Knott, 1963, *Togail Bruidne Da Derga*, Dublin.
9. T.F. O'Rahilly, 1946, *Early Irish History and Mythology*, Dublin, p. 121.
10. G. Dumézil, 1943, *Servius et la Fortune*, pp. 33ff; cf. J.E. Caerwyn Williams, 1971, *The Court Poet in Medieval Ireland*, p. 19.
11. *Éigse*, vol. 17, 1977-79, pp. 137ff.
12. G. Dumézil, 1973, *The Destiny of a King*, pp. 111f.
13. J. Vendryes, 1952, "L'unité en trois personnes chez les Celtes," *Chois d'Études Linguistiques et Celtiques*, Paris, pp. 233-46.
14. Myles Dillon, 1946, *The Cycles of the Kings*, Oxford, pp. 11ff.
15. Edited and translated by Whitley Stokes, 1891, *Revue Celtique*, vol. 12, pp. 56ff.
16. Jan de Vries, 1963, *Heroic Song and Heroic Legend*, Oxford, p. 241.
17. Myles Dillon, 1952, *Ériu*, vol. 16, pp. 61ff., for text and translation.
18. *Ibid.*, p. 72, note 6.

PART II

CHAPTER 4

Dermot Moran

NATURE, MAN AND GOD IN THE PHILOSOPHY OF JOHN SCOTTUS ERIUGENA

1. Jean Potter in Myra Uhlfelder, ed., 1976, *John the Scot. Periphyseon. On the Division of Nature*, Bobbs-Merrill, Indianapolis, p. ix. H. Bett, 1925, *Johannes Scotus Erigena. A Study in Medieval Philosophy*, Cambridge University Press, p. 18. F.A. Staudenmaier, 1834, *Johannes Scottus Erigena und die Wissenschaft seiner Zeit*, Frankfurt. For a complete bibliography of Eriugena scholarship see Mary Brennan, 1977, "A Bibliography of Publications in the Field of Eriugenian Studies 1800-1975," *Studi Medievali*, 3a Series, vol. 18, no. 1, pp. 401-47.
2. E. Gilson, 1954, *History of Christian Philosophy in the Middle Ages*, Random

House, New York, p. 113. However, M. de Wulf, 1926, *History of Medieval Philosophy*, vol. 1, Longman's Green & Co., London, p. 138 holds an opposing view.

3. W. Beierwaltes, 1973, "The Revaluation of John Scottus Eriugena in German Idealism," J.J. O'Meara and L. Bieler, eds., *The Mind of Eriugena*, Irish University Press, Dublin, pp. 190-98.

4. There exists no full critical edition of Eriugena's major work, the *Periphyseon*, although one was begun by I.P. Sheldon-Williams and is in progress under Professors O'Meara and É. Jeauneau. Three volumes have so far been published by the Dublin Institute for Advanced Studies. These volumes contain the Latin text of the first three books of the five-book *Periphyseon* together with an excellent, though literal, English translation. Uhlfelder's translation (*op. cit.*) is very readable but unfortunately incomplete. The commentaries on St John have been translated into French and are published in the Sources Chrétiennes series, vols. 151 and 180.

5. A. Gardner, 1900, *Studies in John the Scot. A Philosopher of the Dark Ages*, Oxford University Press, New York, pp. 1-23; J.J. O'Meara, 1969, *Eriugena*, Cork; and M. Cappuyns, 1933, *Jean Scot Érigène: sa Vie, son Oeuvre, sa Pensée*, Louvain.

6. For the Carolingian *renovatio* see Jean Hubert, 1970, *The Carolingian Renaissance*, Braziller, New York. On the state of Ireland at that time see L. Bieler, 1966, *Ireland. Harbinger of the Middle Ages*, Oxford University Press. For the state of learning in general see M.L.W. Laistner, 1957, *Thought and Letters in Western Europe AD 500-900*, 2nd ed., London. For his cosmological interpretation of Martianus Capella see A.H. Armstrong (ed.), 1970, *The Cambridge History of Late Greek and Early Medieval Philosophy*, Cambridge University Press, pp. 576-79.

7. The history of this controversy over predestination is very complex. Hincmar and Pardulus engaged Eriugena's services to write a rebuttal of Gottschalk's tract, but they in turn withdrew support from Eriugena's *On Predestination*, while bishops defending Gottschalk also attacked Eriugena. His arguments were condemned as *pultes scottica*!

8. A.H. Armstrong (ed.), 1970, *op. cit.*, pp. 579ff. The notion of God's ignorance of evil is retained in the *Periphyseon*, vol. 2, 593b-96d.

9. Dionysius the Areopagite held the view that God is known better by negation than by affirmation, that is, we understand His transcendent nature better by using negative statements such as "God is not a nature" than by affirmative statements which seem to reduce God to a being within our comprehension. See A.H. Armstrong (ed.), 1970, *op. cit.*, pp. 457-72.

10. Eriugena's influence on the twelfth century is still not fully documented. See however É. Jeauneau, 1973, *Lectio Philosophorum: Recherches sur l'École de Chartres*, Amsterdam, and P. Dronke, 1974, *Fabula. Explorations into the Uses of Myth in Medieval Platonism*, Brill, Leiden; also M.D. Chenu, 1968, *Nature, Man and Society in the Twelfth Century*, Chicago.

11. Cappuyns, 1933, *op. cit.*, pp. 247 ff. On Eriugena as a heretic see Dermot Moran, 1978, "Wandering from the Path," *The Crane Bag*, vol. 2, nos. 1 and 2, Dublin, pp. 96-102.

12. The Eriugenian tradition must be seen as influencing Robert Grosseteste, Eckhart, Lull and Cusanus. Cusanus is understood to have possessed a copy of the *Periphyseon* which he annotated. The precise doctrines of Eriugena are rarely followed but the general Neoplatonic scheme of his thought is

current throughout the Renaissance.

13. Cappuyns, 1933, *op. cit.*, pp. 59 ff.

14. L. Bieler, 1973, "Remarks on Eriugena's Original Latin Prose," O'Meara and Bieler, eds., *op. cit.*, pp. 140-46. Evidence of John's knowledge of Irish is suggested by the existence of several manuscripts containing Biblical glosses which include a number of Old Irish words. These glosses are marked IOH which some scholars argue is Johannes Scottus. If the glosses are his, they indicate that Scottus had a number of students in France whose Latin was imperfect thus requiring explanations in Irish. See John J. Contreni, "The Biblical Glosses of Haimo of Auxerre and John Scottus Eriugena", *Speculum* LI (1976), pp. 411-34.

15. É. Jeauneau, 1969, *Homélie sur le Prologue de Jean*, Les Editions du Cerf, Paris, pp. 11-14.

16. J.J. O'Meara, 1969, sums up the main positions in the controversy in his *Eriugena*, Cork. The most recent contribution to the debate is É. Jeauneau, 1979, "John Scot Érigène et le Grec," *Archivium Latinitatis Medii Aevi*, Bulletin du Cange, no. 41, pp. 5-50; also W.B. Stanford, 1976, *Ireland and the Classical Tradition*, Allen Figgis and Co., Dublin.

17. See I.P. Sheldon-Williams, 1973, "Eriugena's Greek Sources," O'Meara and Bieler, eds., *op. cit.*, pp. 1-15.

18. The liberal arts became the basis of the school curriculum as a result of a decree from Charlemagne. Eriugena's understanding of the arts saw them essentially as roads which lead the mind from sensible phantasies to contemplation of God. For him, the arts were innate powers of the mind. Eriugena's knowledge of the arts was derived largely from his reading of Martianus Capella, see W.H. Stahl, R. Johnson and E.L. Burge, eds., 1971 and 1977, *Martianus Capella and the Seven Liberal Arts*, 2 vols., Columbia University Press, New York; also G. Mathon, 1967, "Les Formes et la Signification des Arts Libéraux au Milieu du IXe Siècle. L'Enseignement Palatin de Jean Scot Érigène," *Actes du IVe Congrès de la Société Internationale pour l'Étude de la Philosophie Médiévale*, Montreal, pp. 47-64.

19. E. Panofsky, 1960, *Renaissance and Renascences in Western Art*, Stockholm.

20. A.O. Lovejoy, 1976, *The Great Chain of Being*, Harvard University Press, Cambridge, Mass.; also P. Duhem, 1954, *Le système du monde*, vol. 3, Paris.

21. A. Koyré, 1968, *From the Closed World to the Infinite Universe*, John Hopkins University, Baltimore.

22. E. Cassirer, 1972, *The Individual and the Cosmos in Renaissance Philosophy*, University of Pennsylvania Press, Philadelphia.

23. *Ibid.*, p. 10.

24. Pico della Mirandola, 1965, *On the Dignity of Man*, trans. by C. Glenn Wallis, P. Miller and D. Carmichael, Bobbs-Merrill, New York, p. 5.

25. *Theosis* means deification, and it is a central doctrine of the Greek Christian writers – Dionysius, Gregory of Nyssa, Maximus. It proclaims that God became man so that man could become God (as Augustine puts it). It is closely tied up with the notion that man is made in God's image and likeness, see for example, V. Lossky, 1975, *In the Image and Likeness of God*, Mowbrays, London and Oxford; and also with the Neoplatonic doctrine which states that the highest contemplation (*theoria*) of God is actually unity with Him, since contemplation involves an identity of knower and known, for the Greeks. There is little written in English on the concept of *theoria* leading to *theosis*, but in French see the article, "Contemplation," 1953 in *Dictionnaire*

de spiritualité, 2.2, Paris, cols. 1643-2196. In the Thomistic tradition identity with God is exchanged for "likeness" which seeks to preserve the transcendence of God.

26. J.P. Sartre, 1957, *Being and Nothingness*, Methuen and Co., London, p. 566.

27. On the polemical character of Renaissance thought in general see Agnes Heller, 1978, *Renaissance Man*, Routledge and Kegan Paul, London, p. 12. It was the Renaissance which gave rise to the term "middle ages" in the first place.

28. Eckhart is usually depicted in this light, see Reiner Schuermann, 1978, *Meister Eckhart, Mystic and Philosopher*, Indiana University Press, Bloomington. Eriugena is seen as a forerunner of Hegelian-Marxist dialectic in L. Kolakowski's *Main Currents of Marxism*, vol. 1, Clarendon Press, Oxford; also W. Ullmann, 1977, *Medieval Foundations of Renaissance Humanism*, London. To date there exists no single study which tries to show clearly the lines of influence from Scottus through the school of Chartres to the Renaissance writers such as Cusanus and Bruno. For medieval humanism in general see R.W. Southern, 1970, *Medieval Humanism and Other Essays*, Blackwell, Oxford.

29. For a fuller discussion of the blending of hierarchical-authoritative thought with anarchic thought in Eriugena see Dermot Moran, 1980, *"Natura Quadriformata*: The Understanding of Nature in the *Periphyseon* of John the Scot," *Paideia*, special medieval volume, 9th annual issue, New York.

30. On Eriugena's understanding of negative theology see B. McGinn, 1977, "The Negative Element in the Anthropology of John the Scot," in R. Roques, ed., *John Scot Érigène et l'Histoire de la Philosophie*, Paris; B. McGinn, 1975, "Negative Theology in John the Scot", *Studia Patristica*, vol. 13, pp. 232-38. On Eriugena's theory of human knowledge see B. Stock, 1967, "The Philosophical Anthropology of Johannes Scottus Eriugena," *Studia Medievali*, 3a series, vol. 8, pp. 1-57, and J. Trouillard, 1957, "L'Unité Humaine selon John Scot Érigène," *L'Homme et son prochain*, Actes du VIIIe Congrès des Sociétés de Philosophie de Langue Française, Presses Universitaires de France, pp. 298-301; also, T. Tomasic, 1969, "Negative Theology and Subjectivity. An Approach to the Tradition of the Pseudo-Dionysius," *International Philosophical Quarterly*, vol. 9, pp. 406-30.

31. Eriugena is often seen as a rationalist in the sense that he raises reason up to a level higher than faith or church authority. His position is more complex however, he does accept that knowledge begins in faith but he prefers to see true salvation coming about through the liberating knowledge of contemplation. This is why he says in an early work that "no one enters heaven except through philosophy." In matters of authority he was not talking about church authority but about the reliability of scripture (the work of *auctores*) and of scriptural commentators. Here he remarks that "true authority is nothing other than right reason," meaning that the only force that authority has is its truth. Nevertheless he is a rationalist in that he assumes that knowledge in its highest form will lead to salvation and intellectual liberation.

32. For a discussion of Eriugena's *cogito* which derives from the Augustinian *cogito* see B. Stock, 1977, *"Intelligo me esse*: Eriugena's *Cogito*," R. Roques, ed., *op. cit.*, pp. 327-36.

33. This abrupt introduction of the difficult concept of non-being is characteristic of Eriugena's style. Actually, non-being (*nihil*) is understood by him in two main ways: (a) non-being signifies total absence of any substance.

For example, we may think of the state of the world before it was created as being in the state of non-being; (b) non-being signifies those things which the intellect cannot comprehend within its own categories. Thus God, conceived of as transcending the mind, cannot be described by our category of substance or existence, and he thus may be said to be non-being. Eriugena complicates these two basic meanings in his dialogue by suggesting that those things which are merely potential (such as my knowledge of mathematics when I am not actually doing maths) may be said to be non-being. In recent times continental philosophers such as Heidegger and Sartre have been quite happy to use the concept of non-being whereas empiricists in general follow Carnap in arguing that the concept is an illegitimate hypostatisation of the concept of negation., i.e. the noun "nothing" does not refer to anything, but the particle "not" does refer to the logical act of negation.

34. These four levels of nature are Eriugena's most famous contribution to philosophy and are mentioned in all histories of medieval thought. However the business of interpreting them is far from simple, see Dermot Moran, 1979, "Natura quadriformata and the Beginnings of Physiologia in the Philosophy of Johannes Scottus Eriugena," Bulletin de Philosophie Médiévale, vol. 21, pp. 41-46.

35. The Neoplatonists had a dynamic conception of the world. They understood it to consist of a series of pulsations (or expansions) and contractions around an immobile One. The eternal immutable one which is beyond being and beyond intelligence expands (descends, explicates itself) through a series of levels until it rests at the level of the material sensible world. The material world depends on the one and attempts to return to it by gradually spiritualising itself through the activity of soul and intelligence. For a precise explanation of this doctrine as it pertains to Eriugena see S. Gersh, 1978, From Iamblichus to Eriugena, Brill, Leiden. In the twentieth century thinkers such as Whitehead and Teilhard de Chardin saw in this theory a means of explaining in philosophical terms the scientific theories of Einstein and quantum physicists.

36. The first level of nature is God. The second level is God the Son understood as a "cosmic" principle of wisdom, intelligence, the very incarnation of rationality. Hence the Son or Logos is understood as containing in Himself the intelligible principles which go to make up all things. These highest intelligible principles are called by Eriugena, following Augustine, the primary causes. They are considered to be the thoughts of God (following Philo and Plotinus) and are direct descendants of the Platonic Ideas. Eriugena calls them ideas, forms, causes, reasons and divine volitions indifferently.

37. According to the Neoplatonists all effects depend on and return towards their causes. Proclus inspired Dionysius here, and Eriugena follows the latter. The highest form of return or reversion of an effect upon a cause is the manner in which the thoughts produced by the intellect return to contemplate their own nature and the nature of the intellect that produced them. This self-conscious dialectic is the best example of Neoplatonic causation and reversion. See S. Gersh, 1977, "Per se ipsum: The Problem of Immediate and Mediate Causation in Eriugena and his Neoplatonic Predecessors," in R. Roques, ed., op. cit., pp. 367-76.

38. Strictly speaking of course, this realm of non-being does not exist, it is really a privation of being, and Eriugena terms it nihil per privationem to distinguish it from the non-being of God which he calls nihil per excellentiam. See I.P.

Sheldon-Williams, 1981, introduction to the *Periphyseon*, vol. 3, The Dublin Institute for Advanced Studies, Dublin, pp. 5-10.

39. Time is understood by Eriugena, in the manner of the Platonists, as an illusory form of existence, scarcely fully real. Eriugena went much further than Augustine in his analysis of time, and makes it merely a category of the human mind in its fallen state. Once the return of man to a state of grace or deification has been achieved then time will have a new mystical significance, expressing the endless nature of man's circuling about God. *Periphyseon*, vol. 1, 483a-b. The soul, once dominated by time's inexorable succession, will now experience the freedom of the anarchic spiral which is human contemplation in its endless experiencing of the *theophanies* or appearance of the divine.

40. On Christian Neoplatonism in general see A.H. Armstrong (ed.), 1970, *op. cit.*, pp. 272ff. On creation see J.H. Gay, 1963, "Four Medieval Views of Creation," *Harvard, Theological Review*, vol. 56, pp. 253-58.

41. Hegel remarks in his *Lectures on the Philosophy of Religion* that the history of philosophy is really a history of differing conceptions of unity.

42. The medievals inherited from the Platonists the desire to order everything in triads. An extreme example of this fascination with triadic structure is Alain of Lille's sermon on the Trinity, but Augustine's speculation on the image of the Trinity in the mind is a case in point.

43. Compare Hegel's interpretation of the fall as the awakening of free self-conscious life in *The Logic*, trans. by W. Wallace, 1968, 2nd ed., Oxford University Press, London, pp. 54ff.

44. "Do you not see how the Creator of the whole universe takes the first place? . . . For in Him are all things immutably and essentially and He is the division and collection of the universal creature, and genus and species and whole and part . . . For the monad also is the beginning of numbers and the leader of their progression, and from it the plurality of all numbers begins and in it is consummated the return and collection of the same." *Periphyseon*, vol. 3, 621b-c. Eriugena does not clearly distinguish the creation of all things in their causes and the generation of the "word," and indeed the two are one for him, since the word is the coming together in wisdom of the principles of all things: "For to the human intellect which Christ assumed all the intellectual essences adhere." *Periphyseon*, vol. 2, 542a-b.

45. The Holy Spirit acts as a kind of individuating principle in Eriugena's scheme, Eriugena conceives of Him mythically as brooding over and hatching the cosmic egg: "For the Holy Spirit fermented . . . the primordial causes which the Father had made in the beginning, that is, in his Son, so that they might proceed into those things of which they are the causes. For to this end are eggs fermented by birds, from whom this metaphor is drawn . . ." *Periphyseon*, vol. 2, 554b-c. For a discussion of this image see P. Dronke, 1974, *Fabula*, Brill, Leiden.

46. God's act of self-manifestation is at the same time the creation of all things: "For the creation of itself, that is, the manifestation of itself in something, is surely that by which all things subsist." *Periphyseon*, vol. 1, 455b.

47. Eriugena frequently stresses that God is *anarchos*: "Deus autem anarchos, hoc est sine principio," *Periphyseon*, vol. 1, 516a.

48. Uhlfelder, *op. cit.*, p. 244.

49. *Ibid.*, p. 252.

50. See J.E. Gracia, 1978, "Ontological Characterisation of the Relation between

Man and Created Nature in Eriugena," *Journal of the History of Philosophy*, vol. 16, no. 2, pp. 155-66. On omnipresence see S. Gersh, 1980, "Omnipresence in Eriugena. Some Reflections on Augustino-Maximian Elements in the *Periphyseon*," in W. Beierwaltes (ed.), *Eriugena. Studien zu seinem Quellen*, Heidelberg, pp. 55-74.

51. Trans. by Dermot Moran.

52. The mind has a triadic structure, according to Eriugena, consisting of intellect-reason-inner sense, which Eriugena sees as linked according to the Neoplatonic scheme of essence-power-operation. In the perfect man the three aspects of mind are so united that they are one. *Nous* is "whole in the whole and whole in each of the parts" as Eriugena would say.

53. Eriugena understands the division of human nature into sexes as a consequence of the fall. See É. Jeauneau, 1980, "La division des sexes chez Grégoire de Nysse et chez Jean Scot Érigène, in W. Beierwaltes, ed., *Eriugena*, Heidelberg, pp. 33-54. If man had not fallen he would have propagated his race according to the angelic manner, by thought alone. Eriugena's conception of the ultimate unity of all minds in the one essence (or *ousia*) is not fully clear or consistent. He held that all minds were one just as all lights merge to give just one light, they become one without losing their individual difference. However, if minds are not embodied it is difficult to see how they could be distinguished. The impact of Eriugena's thought on Latin Averroism which taught the same concept of a universal intellect for all men has never been adequately explored.

54. I.P. Sheldon-Williams, 1968, *Periphyseon*, vol. 2, Dublin, p. 107. The highest nature of the soul is simple and it merges with the One in a purely intellectual way (based on its contemplation or *theoria*) such that reason cannot analyse it. This part of the soul in Eriugena is very close to Eckhart's conception of the ground of the soul. See Eckhart's sermon *Intravit Jesus in Quoddam Castellum* in M. O'C. Walshe, ed., 1979, *Meister Eckhart Sermons and Treatises*, Watkins, London, p. 76.

55. This level of the soul defines God as cause (*Periphyseon*, vol. 2, 573a) and understands things in terms of the primary causes contained within itself. It is closely associated with the intellect, and is best understood as the outward manifestation of the inner simplicity of the intellect.

56. Sheldon-Williams's translation. Eriugena sees all things as subsumed under the categories of the liberal arts, which are themselves aspects of reason itself. When reason manifests itself outside of the intellect, it displays all other things also. Eriugena generally speaks of this process as having two aspects — one of division and one of collection. The aim of the study of the arts is to bring all knowledge back to its unitary source.

57. This third motion is complex. It both moves outwards into the world, clothing the intellect with the visible garment of speech and bodily action and it also receives data from the outer senses. Eriugena calls these received data *phantasiai* or fantasies. In actual fact these phantasies are also theophanies or divine apparitions, but it requires a conversion of the mind away from its tendency towards materialism for these theophanies to be seen. Eriugena gives us to understand that the wise man will experience the whole world as a theophany of God.

58. Eriugena actually uses the word *creat*, creates, in association with the activity of the human mind. The body is formed by the various accidental qualities of colour, texture etc. being "commingled" with quantity to give the impres-

sion of a solid substance. In reality however the body is just a bundle of sensible phantasies assembled around the soul.

59. Eriugena will go on to say that man can be considered a rational animal but it can also be denied that he is a rational animal. The application of affirmative and negative dialectic to man (instead of God) is a highly original move on Scottus's part.

60. *Periphyseon*, vol. 2, 531a-c.

61. R.C. Dales, 1977, "A Medieval View of Human Dignity," *Journal of the History of Ideas*, vol. 47, pp. 557-72.

62. Donald F. Duclow, 1980, "Dialectic and Christology in Eriugena's *Periphyseon*," *Dionysius*, vol. 4, (Dec.) pp. 99-117. The assertion that the perfect man is Christ in *Periphyseon*, vol. 4, 743a coupled with the assertion at vol. 2, 544d that Christ *is* the intelligising of all things (*omnium intellectus*) make Christ to be the attainable ideal of the human mind, not simply a historical figure.

63. Eriugena, like Hegel, sees that what is actual is rational and what is rational is actual. However the rational is only the explication of the intellectual level of the universe, and is not something complete in itself. It is part of the Neoplatonic heritage to think of the domain of *nous* and *logos* as higher than the domain of spatio-temporal existence.

64. See Plotinus, *Ennead* V.i in J. Katz, 1950, *The Philosophy of Plotinus*, Appleton-Century-Crofts, New York.

65. Eriugena's understanding of place and time as categories of the mind has been seen as a precursor of Kantianism, and is certainly the most rationalist interpretation of space and time in the middle ages. See J.F. Courtine, 1980, "La dimension spatio-temporelle dans la problématique catégoriale du De Divisione Naturae de Jean Scot Érigène," *Les Études Philosphiques*, vol. 3, pp. 343-67.

66. *Periphyseon*, vol. 1, 483c.

67. Eriugena correctly recognises that the so-called "formless matter" of the philosophers can be perceived only by the intellect and hence is incorporeal. (*Periphyseon*, vol. 1, 500d ff). The four elements themselves are simple and incorruptible but they are mingled together by the senses to give the impression that the pure essences of creation have corporeal being, see *Periphyseon*, vol. 1, 503c-d.

68. This is the means by which we recognise others, God and ourselves. It is a kind of openness and receptiveness, Hegel's "mutual recognition" perhaps, a form of undistorted communication between minds, rather than a form of domination or circumscription. This kind of knowledge is recognised by contemporary philosophers as the ideal intersubjectivity.

69. The self's knowing that it is, its *cogito*, reveals to it that it is a trinity of essence, power and operation, because it knows that it is, and therefore that it can be, and that it actually is. See B. Stock, 1977, *op. cit*. By this cogito then it also grasps that it is made in the image of God (Uhlfelder, *op. cit*., p. 243). Eriugena's recognition of the unique status of existential knowledge contradicts the portrayal of him as an essentialist by E. Gilson, 1952, *Being and Some Philosophers*, 2nd ed. Pontifical Institute of Medieval Studies, Toronto.

70. B. McGinn, 1977, *op. cit*., pp. 315-25. This higher form of self-ignorance is taken up by Nicholas of Cusa in his *Of Learned Ignorance*, trans. by G. Heron, 1954, Routledge and Kegan Paul, London.

71. *Periphyseon*, vol. 4, trans. by M. Uhlfelder, *op. cit.*, p. 240.

72. See the translation of Maximus's *Ambigua* in J.P. Migne (ed.), *Patrologia Latina*, vol. 122. This idea is developed by Feuerbach, *The Essence of Christianity*, trans. by George Eliot, 1957, Harper and Row, New York, p. 13, religion as consciousness of God comes to be understood as the self-consciousness of man.

73. See above note 59. *Periphyseon*, vol. 4, trans. by Uhlfelder, *op. cit.*, p. 220.

74. Eckhart also sees man as self-creating, as *causa sui*. See Eckhart's Sermon, *Beati pauperes spiritu*, trans. by R. Schuermann, 1978, *Meister Eckhart. Mystic and Philosopher*, Indiana University Press, pp. 214-20. Both Hegel and Marx understand man as creating himself through his work.

75. Trans. by Dermot Moran.

76. Eriugena sees man as stretching across all four divisions of nature, he is both created and creating (and thus identical with the *verbum* or second level of nature), and created and not creating, (the rational animal or third level of creation). But also he is uncreated in that he exists as a kind of formless non-being in God which allows him to share in both the first and the fourth levels of nature. The four levels of nature are only an explication of the man-God relationship.

77. Sheldon-Williams's translation. The opening up of the human will to allow the divine will to act through it is a central feature of medieval mysticism, as for example expressed in *The Cloud of Unknowing* or Eckhart's sermon *Beati pauperes spiritu, op. cit.* Eriugena gives it an intellectual twist by linking it directly with self-knowledge in its highest sense as knowledge that man creates himself.

CHAPTER 5

Harry M. Bracken

GEORGE BERKELEY, THE IRISH CARTESIAN

1. See the discussions by Noam Chomsky, 1975, *Reflections on Language*, New York, chap. 3, and 1977, *Language and Responsibility*, New York, part 2. "Empiricist" and "rationalist" are very general classification terms. At issue are the grounds for our claims to knowledge. Some scholastics, for example, hold that there is "nothing in the intellect which is not first in the senses." Rationalists (including the Cartesians), on the other hand, argue that our sensory data is neither extensive nor rich enough to provide the basis for knowledge which we in fact possess (rationalists often cite mathematics as a case in point). What may seem like an abstract philosophical issue takes on quite practical importance when this disagreement is seen to reflect two very different doctrines about human nature. Crudely, the empiricist doctrine is that humans are plastic and malleable. That means they are "programmable" by environmental factors and fit objects for (bureaucratic) control. The rationalist doctrine is that humans have autonomous, creative minds whose structures are largely innate and immaterial. It is this "political" component that raises the stakes in discussions of empiricism/rationalism both in the seventeenth and eighteenth centuries and in our own times.

2. George Berkeley, *Philosophical Commentaries*, ed. A.A. Luce, 1944, London. Luce makes similar remarks in his notes to the *Commentaries* in *The Works*

of George Berkeley Bishop of Cloyne, 1715, A.A. Luce and T.E. Jessop, eds., 1948-57, London, vols. 1-9.

3. A.A. Luce, 1934, *Berkeley and Malebranche*, Oxford, p. 43. It is not new to suggest that considering Berkeley an "idealist" is anachronistic. The *modern* philosophical meaning of that term is derived from considerations of both logic and knowledge advanced first by Hegel a century later. To help break the spells of the labels "idealist" and "empiricist", Luce wrote that "my aim is to show that the way to the heart of Berkeleinism lies through Malebranche." Nevertheless, philosophers who should now certainly know better, continue to treat Berkeley as a product of Locke.

4. AA. Luce, 1949, *Life of George Berkeley*, London, is the best biography of Berkeley. On Malebranche, cf. pp. 70-71.

5. The definitive edition is that prepared under the general direction of André Robinet, 1958-65, *Oeuvres complètes de Malebranche*, Paris, 20 vols., Geneviève Rodis-Lewis edited the *Recherche* plus the *Éclaircissements* in vols. 1-3. A new English version of the *Search After Truth* plus the *Elucidations* and a *Philosophical Commentary* by Thomas M. Lennon, co-translated by Paul J. Olscamp, 1980, has just appeared. (Ohio State University Press, Columbus.) See also D. Connell, 1967, *The Vision in God, Malebranche's Scholastic Sources*, Leuven.

6. A.A. Luce, 1934, *op. cit.*, p. 77.

7. George Berkeley, *Philosophical Commentaries*, ed. George H. Thomas, 1976, Mount Union College, Alliance, Ohio.

8. Cf. Berkeley, *Principles*, para. 148.

9. Letter to S. Johnson, Connecticut, G. Berkeley, 1715, ed. by A.A. Luce and T.E. Jessop, 1948-57, *op. cit.*, vol. 2, p. 282.

10. Pierre Bayle, 1647-1706. French Calvinist refugee, resident in Rotterdam; a philosopher, teacher, editor and polemicist. His *Dictionnaire historique et Critique* was a major source of philosophical discussions on, e.g., primary/secondary qualities, scepticism, Bible criticism, faith/reason, the problem of evil, Zeno's paradoxes. His *Commentaire Philosophique* is a defense of virtually complete religious toleration. Although often sceptical, Bayle also advances the positions of Descartes and Malebranche. Cf. H. Bracken, 1974, *Berkeley*, London.

11. See H. Bracken, 1965, *Early Reception of Berkeley's Immaterialism: 1710-1733*, 2nd ed., Den Haag.

12. Muriel McCarthy, 1980, *All Graduates and Gentlemen: Marsh's Library*, The O'Brien Press, Dublin, p. 168.

13. G. Berkeley, ed. A.A. Luce, 1944, *op. cit.*, entry 887.

14. John Locke, *An Essay Concerning Human Understanding*, ed. Peter H. Nidditch, 1975, Bk. 2, ch. 8, para. 9.

15. *Ibid.*, Bk. 2, ch. 8, para. 15.

16. Essays on Berkeley in Richard H. Popkin, 1980, *The High Road to Pyrrhonism*, eds. Richard A. Watson and James E. Force, Austin Hill Press, San Diego. See also H. Bracken, 1976, "Berkeley: Irish Cartesian," *Philosophical Studies*, Dublin, vol. 24, pp. 39-51.

17. G. Berkeley, *Principles*, para. 86.

18. Entry no. 18. Both the finite/infinite divisibility question and the mental or "ideal" status of extension are matters which Bayle discusses at great length in his *Dictionary* article, Zeno of Elea (Bayle is cited in the *Philosophical Commentaries*.)

19. G. Berkeley, 1715, ed. by A.A. Luce and T.E. Jessop, 1948-57, *op. cit.*, vol. 2, pp. 235-36.
20. J. Locke, *Essay*, vol. 2, p. vi.
21. *Ibid.*, vol. 4, pp. vi and x.
22. *Ibid.*, vol. 2, pp. xxiii, para. 26.
23. G. Berkeley, *Principles*, para. 142.
24. Cf. G. Berkeley, ed. by A.A. Luce and T.E. Jessop, 1948-57, *op. cit.*, vol. 5, pp. 142-43, vol. 7, p. 130.
25. Personal communication.
26. Cf. David Berman, 1972, "On Missing the Wrong Target. A Criticismsof Some Chapters in Jonathan Bennett's Locke, Berkeley, Hume: Central Themes," *Hermathena*, vol. 113, pp. 54-67.
27. Pfaff, C.M., 1722, *Oratio de Egoismo, Nova Philosophica Haeresi*, Tübingen.
28. Willy Kabitz, 1932, "Leibniz und Berkeley," *Sitzungsberichte der Preussischen Akademie der Wissenschaften*, (Philosophisch-Historische Klasse), Berlin, pp. 623-636.
29. A.A. Luce, 1949, *op. cit.*, p. 169.
30. G. Berkeley, 1712, ed. by A.A. Luce and T.E. Jessop, 1948-57, *op. cit.*, vol. 6.
31. G. Berkeley, 1712, *Passive Obedience*, para. 30. Berkeley also makes an interesting distinction between positive and negative precepts. See the discussion by Joseph Tussman, 1957, "Berkeley as a Political Philosopher," *University of California Publications in Philosophy*, vol. 29.
32. G. Berkeley, 1712, *op. cit.*, para. 52.
33. Jeremiah, xvii, 1.
34. G. Berkeley, 1712, *op. cit.*, para. 12.
35. G. Berkeley, ed. by A.A. Luce and T.E. Jessop, 1948-57, *op. cit.*, vol. 6, p. 4.
36. *Ibid.*, p. 57.
37. *Ibid.*, vol. 7, p. 122.
38. *Ibid.*, p. 346.
39. *Ibid.*, vol. 6, p. 235.
40. *Ibid.*, p. 240.
41. *Ibid.*, p. 127, query 265. Cf. Joseph Johnston, 1970, *Bishop Berkeley's Querist in Historical Perspective*, Dundalgan Press, Dundalk.
42. G. Berkeley, 1735, ed. by A.A. Luce and T.E. Jessop, 1948-57, *op. cit.*, vol. 6, p. 120, query 191.
43. *Ibid.*, p. 160, query 297.
44. *Ibid.*, p. 127, query 261.
45. George E. Davie, 1979, "Berkeley, Hume, and the Central Problem of Scottish Philosophy," in *McGill Hume Studies*, ed. David Fate Norton, N. Capaldi and W.L. Robison, San Diego, p. 44.
46. *Ibid.*, pp. 43-44.
47. *Ibid.*, pp. 61-62.

CHAPTER 6

David Berman

THE IRISH COUNTER-ENLIGHTENMENT

1. John Toland, 1697, *Apology . . . in a Letter from Himself to a Member of the House of Commons in Ireland*, p. 36.
2. Peter Browne, 1697, *A Letter in Answer to . . . Christianity Not Mysterious*, p. 50.
3. George Berkeley, 1733, *The Theory of Vision Vindicated*, sect. 6. For Burke's affirmative answer to a Molyneux-type question, see his *Philosophical Enquiry*, part 3, sect. 24. In David Berman, 1974, "Francis Hutcheson on Berkeley and the Molyneux problem," *Proceedings of the Royal Irish Academy*, pp. 259-65, the Irish answers to the problem are discussed.
4. William King, 1709, *Sermon on Predestination*, sects. 12 and 13.
5. This letter is in the King Correspondence, Trinity College Library; in another letter, to Arthur Charlett, written ten years later, King says that he is "sorry those heathens . . . should be so numerous . . . [yet] our treating of Toland and Emlyn shows how little [we] favour them."
6. W. King, 1709, *op. cit.*, sect. 15.
7. *Ibid.*, sect. 15.
8. *Ibid.*, sect. 24.
9. *Ibid.*, sect. 28.
10. *Ibid.*, sect. 28.
11. *Ibid.*, sect. 13.
12. *Ibid.*, sect. 9.
13. *Ibid.*, sect. 22.
14. *Ibid.*, especially sect. 22.
15. Peter Browne, 1728, *Procedure*, p. 388.
16. *Ibid.*, p. 388.
17. *Ibid.*, p. 389.
18. *Ibid.*, pp. 64, 387, 414.
19. *Ibid.*, pp. 413-14.
20. *Ibid.*, p. 178.
21. *Ibid.*, p. 416.
22. *Ibid.*, p. 97.
23. *Ibid.*, p. 412.
24. *Ibid.*, p. 67.
25. *Ibid.*, p. 149, and also pp. 77, 153, 367-68.
26. *Ibid.*, pp. 150.153.
27. On Dodwell and Browne, see D. Berman, 1980, "Poverty of mortalism and superfluity of immortalism," *Freethinker*, pp. 3, 14, 35-36 and A.R. Winnett, 1974, *Peter Browne: Provost, Bishop and Metaphysician*.
28. G. Berkeley, 1732, *Alciphron*, dialogue IV, sects. 16-22.
29. J-P. Pittion, A.A. Luce and D. Berman, 1969, "A new Letter by Berkeley to Browne on Divine Analogy," *Mind*, pp. 375-92. For a fuller view of the analogy controversy, see D. Berman, 1976, "Introduction," *Archbishop King's Sermon on Predestination*.
30. G. Berkeley, 1732, *op. cit.*, dialogue IV, sect. 17.
31. G. Berkeley, *Principles*, sect. 77.

32. *Ibid.*, sect. 20.
33. G. Berkeley, 1732, *op. cit.*, dialogue VII, sects. 5-16.
34. R. Molesworth, 1723, *Some Considerations for the Promoting of Agriculture*, p. 31.
35. In Francis Hutcheson, 1729, *An Inquiry into the Original of our Ideas of Beauty and Virtue*, 3rd ed., the author acknowledges his "obligations" to Synge "for revising these papers;" he also says that he "was much confirmed in his opinion of the justness of these thoughts, upon finding that this gentleman had fallen into the same way of thinking before him . . .," p. xix.
36. R. Clayton, 1750, *Essay on Spirit*, sect. 28.
37. *Ibid.*, sect. 23.
38. Because of Clayton's unorthodox statements on the Trinity, the Irish House of Lords "summoned him to appear before them. He then consulted a great lawyer on the subject, and asked him, if he thought he would lose his bishoprick? 'My Lord,' answered he, 'I believe you will.' 'Sir,' he replied, 'You have given me a stroke I'll never get the better of.' His apprehensions were unfortunately too true; for he was instantly seized with a disorder, and soon after died in 1758." (Samuel Burdy, 1792, *Life of Skelton*, ed. 1914, p. 138.)
39. R. Clayton, 1757, *Vindication of the Old and New Testament*, part 3, pp. 23-26.
40. *Ibid.*, p. 26.
41. G. Berkeley, 1732, *op. cit.*, dialogue IV, sects. 16-22.
42. D. Berman, 1971, "Berkeley, Clayton and *An Essay on Spirit*," *Journal of the History of Ideas*, pp. 367-78, where the letter is reprinted and Clayton's *Essay* is discussed.
43. Footnote in R. Clayton, 1753, *Some Thoughts on Self-love.* p. 9."
44. Philip Skelton, 1749, *Ophiomaches: or Deism Revealed*, vol. 1, p. 83.
45. John Ellis, 1743, *Knowledge of Divine Things from Revelation and not from Reason or Nature*, p. 86.
46. *Ibid.*, p. 46.
47. *Ibid.*, p. 99.
48. *Ibid.*, p. 105.
49. *Ibid.*, p. 106.
50. *Ibid.*, p. 104.
51. *Ibid.*, p. 107.
52. G. Berkeley, 1732, *op. cit.*, dialogue IV.
53. *Literary Journal*, 1745, Dublin, vol. 2, part I, p. 146, (my italics).
54. E. Burke, 1747 and 1748, *Reformer*, no. 12 (italics – author's emphasis).
55. E. Burke, 1757, *Philosophical Enquiry into the Origin of our Ideas of the Beautiful and Sublime*, part 2, sect. 5.
56. Collins, 1713, *Discourse of Free-thinking*, pp. 54-55.
57. "You must flatter [Browne, writes Swift,] monstrously upon his learning and his writing; that you have read his book against Toland a hundred times . . ." However, Swift also spoke of Browne as "the most speculative writer of his age." (See Irwin Ehrenpreis, 1962, *Swift: the Man, his Works and the Age*, pp. 74-75).
58. Jonathan Swift, 1726, *Gulliver's Travels*, part 3, chap. 5.
59. J. Swift *et. al.*, 1741, *Memoirs of Martinus Scriblerus*, chap. 14.
60. In 1714 and 1715 Swift's allegory of the coats in the *Tale of a Tub* was at the centre of a debate between Synge and Browne, although neither party

mentioned Swift or his book. In his 1714 sermon, *Eternal Salvation the Only End of Religion*, Synge compared the essential articles of religion – such as loving God – to the vital parts of our body, and the inessentials – such as when and where a congregation meets – to the clothes we wear. The latter is subject to fashion, he argued, but not the former. In P. Browne, 1715, *The Doctrine of Parts and Circumstances in Religion Laid Open*, Synge's "injurious similitude" is attacked because it suggested that "all rites and ceremonies are mean and despicable . . . [since] man is perfect without his clothes."

61. J. Swift, 1726, *op. cit.*, part 3.
62. *Ibid.*, chap. 5.
63. J. Locke, 1690, *Essay*, Bk. 3.
64. E. Burke, 1757, *op. cit.*, part 5.
65. Treaty of Limerick.
66. R. Dunlop, 1909, *Cambridge Modern History*, vol. 6, p. 486; also see J.C. Beckett, *Making of Modern Ireland*, p. 213, and J.M. Robertson, 1936, *History of Freethought*, pp. 747-48.
67. W. King, 1702, *De Origine Mali*, translated by E. Law, 1739, preface pp. xxiii-xxiv.
68. *Ibid.*, p. xix.
69. *Ibid.*, p. xxii.
70. *Ibid.*, p. xxiv.
71. W. King, 1691, *State of the Protestants of Ireland*, p. 239.
72. P. Skelton, 1750, *Censor Censured*, p. 21.
73. P. Skelton, 1749, *op. cit.*, vol. 2, pp. 400-10.
74. G. Berkeley, 1732, *op. cit.*, dialogue II, sect. 26.
75. Anon., 1757, *A Protestant's Address to the Protestants of Ireland*, p. 53.
76. *Apology for Mr Toland*, p. 14.
77. *Ibid.*, p. 16.
78. P. des Maizeaux, 1726, *Memoir of Toland*, p. 22.

PART III

CHAPTER 7

Seamus Deane

EDMUND BURKE AND THE IDEOLOGY OF IRISH LIBERALISM

1. Quoted in Franco Venturi, 1971, *Utopia and Reform in the Enlightenment*, Cambridge, p. 52. Also Albert Goodwin, 1979, *The Friends of Liberty*, London, pp. 34-37.
2. E. Burke, 1877, *Complete Works*, London, vol. 2, pp. 361-62.
3. *Ibid. (Letter to a Member of the National Assembly)*, p. 536.
4. *Ibid.*, p. 382.
5. See, for instance, C.P. Courtney, 1963, *Montesquieu and Burke*, Oxford; F.T.H. Fletcher, 1939, *Montesquieu and English Politics, 1750-1800*, London.
6. This was also very close to Montesquieu and closely linked with the whole eighteenth century debate on the relationships between luxury, decadence

and despotism. Cf. Badreddine Kassem, 1960, *Decadence et Absolutisme dans l'Oeuvre de Montesquieu*, Geneva and Paris.

7. See Acton Mss. in Cambridge University Library, Acton Room, Add. Mss. Burke, 4967. Also Seamus Deane, 1972, "Lord Acton and Edmund Burke," *Journal of the History of Ideas*, vol. 33, April-June, pp. 325-35.

8. E. Burke, 1877, *op. cit.*, vol. 6, p. 27.

9. *Ibid.*, vol. 3, p. 296.

10. *Ibid.*, pp. 304-5.

11. *Ibid.*, vol. 6, p. 58.

12. *Ibid.*, p. 63-64.

13. *Ibid.*, vol. 5, p. 254.

14. *Ibid.*, p. 220.

15. *Ibid.*, vol. 3, pp. 414-15.

16. O. Goldsmith, 1770, "The Life of Henry St. John, Lord Viscount Bolingbroke," *Collected Works of Oliver Goldsmith*, ed. by A. Friedman, 1966, Oxford, 5 vols., vol. 3, pp. 472-73.

17. Matthew Arnold, 1880, "The Future of Liberalism," *The Complete Prose Works of Matthew Arnold* ed. by R.H. Super, 1973, Ann Arbor, vol. 9, p. 137.

18. *Ibid.*, pp. 277-78.

19. Padraig Pearse, *Collected Works, Political Writings and Speeches*, n.d. Dublin, p. 246.

CHAPTER 8

Liam de Paor

THE REBEL MIND: REPUBLICAN AND LOYALIST

1. Circular letter from the Society of United Irishmen of Dublin, 30 December 1791. *Report from the Secret Committee of the House of Commons*, 1798, Dublin, p. 94.

2. *The Correspondence of Edmund Burke*, 1958-70, Cambridge, vol. IX, p. 162.

3. Attributed to Eoghan Rua Ó Súilleabháin. See Seán Ó Tuama and Thomas Kinsella, 1981, *An Duanaire 1600-1900: Poems of the Dispossessed*, Mountrath, pp. 196-7. Thomas Kinsella's translation reads:
   Being sunk at all times in misery is not the worst
   but the scorn that pursues us, now that the lions are gone.

4. By Fear Dorcha Ó Mealláin: *In ainm an Athar go mbuaidh* . . . Thomas Kinsella's translation in *An Duanaire*, p. 105.

5. Arthur Young, 1780, *Tour of Ireland*, Dublin, vol. 2, p. 37.

6. K. Marx, with F. Engels, 1848, *Communist Manifesto*, London, Ch. 1.

7. See the discussion of Catholics and the United Irishmen in P.J. Corish, 1981, *The Catholic Community in the Seventeenth and Eighteenth Centuries*, Dublin, pp. 135-39.

8. Paper circulated in Dublin, June 1791. *Report from the Secret Committee of the House of Commons*, pp. 86-88.

9. For a detailed discussion of the growth and meaning of this usage, see Richard Koebner, 1961, *Empire*, Cambridge.

10. Address to the 'Friends of the People' at London, from the Society of United Irishmen of Dublin, October 26, 1792. *Proceedings of the Society of United Irishmen of Dublin*, 1795, Philadelphia.

11. Address to the Delegates for promoting a reform in Scotland, 23 November 1792. *Proceedings of the Society of United Irishmen of Dublin*.

12. Address to the Volunteers of Ireland, 14 December 1792. *Proceedings of the Society of United Irishmen of Dublin*.

13. *Report from the Secret Committee of the House of Commons*, pp. 253-55.

14. Marianne Elliott, 1982, *Partners in Revolution: the United Irishmen and France*, New Haven, pp. 40, 42.

15. Tomás Ó Míocháin, *Le Geugaibh gníomhach Chuin is Eoguin* ... RIA MS 24.L.22, pp. 15-16. My translation. Conor Cruise O'Brien, in a penetrating article reviewing Seán Cronin's *Irish Nationalism* (29 April 1982, 'Ireland: The Shirt of Nessus', *New York Review*, pp. 30-33) is mistaken when he writes (p. 30) that 'Gaelic literature of the period does not contain any reference to the American Revolution'. The references are few, and it is doubtful if they merit the description 'literature' but their existence is interesting in itself, since the usual range of the generally highly conventional material is very limited.

16. See D. Hyde, 1902, *Irish Poetry*, Dublin, pp. 136-37, where this poem is quoted. My translation.

17. See Marianne Elliott's further remarks on the Defenders, *Partners in Revolution*, p. 31.

18. John O'Leary, 1896, *Recollections of Fenians and Fenianism*, London, vol. 1, pp. 30-31.

19. P.H. Pearse, 1924, *Collected Works, Political Writings and Speeches*, Dublin, 'The Sovereign People', p. 335.

20. William Rooney, 1909, 'Emigration — How to stay it', *Prose Writings*, Dublin, p. 217.

21. M. Moynihan, ed., 1980, *Speeches and Statements by Éamon de Valera 1917-1973*, Dublin, p. 466.

22. J.B. Woodburn, 1914, *The Ulster Scot*, London, pp. 396-400.

23. David W. Miller, 1978, *Queen's Rebels: Ulster Loyalism in Historical Perspective*, Dublin, pp. 119-20.

24. *Minutes of Proceedings of the First Parliament of the Republic of Ireland 1919-1921* (Dublin), First day, 21 January 1919, 'Democratic Programme', pp. 22-3.

25. In his book *The New Poetic* (Penguin edition, Harmondsworth 1967) G.K. Stead comments, p. 39, on these lines of Yeats: "The nationalists have transcended the mutable world, but only by the destruction of normal human values, by a single-mindedness that turns the heart to stone. The movement of this section imparts the joy of life, which throws a new light on the 'terrible beauty', emphasizing terror over beauty."

CHAPTER 9

Desmond Fennell

IRISH SOCIALIST THOUGHT

A short bibliography

Richard K.P. Pankhurst, 1954, *William Thompson*, Watts and Co., London.
R.G. Garnett, 1972, *Co-operation and the Owenite Socialist Communities in Britain*, Manchester University Press.

Michael Davitt, 1895, *Leaves from a Prison Diary*, vol. 2, Chapman and Hall, London.

A.E., 1917, *The Nationalist Being*, Maunsel and Co. Ltd., Dublin.

C. Desmond Greaves, 1961, *The Life and Times of James Connolly*, Lawrence and Wishardt, London.

P. Berresford Ellis, 1975, *James Connolly: Selected Writings*, Penguin, London.

Patrick Bolger, 1977, *The Irish Co-operative Movement: Its History and Development*, Institute of Public Administration, Dublin.

G.D.H. Cole, 1956-67, *A History of Socialist Thought*, Macmillan.

P. Berresford Ellis, 1972, *A History of the Irish Working Class*, Gollancz, London.

C. Desmond Greaves, 1971, *Liam Mellows and the Irish Revolution*, Lawrence and Wishardt, London.

J. Bowyer Bell, 1979, *The IRA*, The Academy Press, Dublin.

E. Rumpf and A.C. Hepburn, 1977, *Nationalism and Socialism in 20th Century Ireland*, Liverpool University Press.

Arthur Mitchell, 1974, *Labour in Irish Politics, 1890-1930*, Irish University Press, Dublin.

J.W. Boyle, 1972, *The Rise of the Irish Trade Unions, 1729-1970*, Anvil Books.

Michael McInerney, 1974, *Peadar O'Donnell, Irish Social Rebel*, O'Brien Press, Dublin.

Anton Menger, 1899, *The Right to the Whole Produce of Labour*, Macmillan, London.

Leaders and Workers, ed. by J.W. Boyle, 1966, Mercier Press, Cork.

R.M. Fox, 1957, *Jim Larkin*, International Publishers, N. York.

Connolly's selected writings 1948-55, *Labour in Ireland, The Workers' Republic Socialism and Nationalism, Labour in Easter Week 1916*, Three Candles, Dublin.

Ruth Dudley Edwards, 1981, *James Connolly*, Gill, Dublin.

Michael Gallagher, 1982, *The Irish Labour Party in Transition* (1957-82), Gill and Macmillan, Dublin.

PART IV

CHAPTER 10

John Jordan

IDEAS, EPIGRAMS, BLACKBERRIES and CHASSIS

1. Alfred Turco, Jr., 1976, *Shaw's Moral Vision*, p. 150.
2. v. Peter Ure, 1963, *Yeats the Playwright*, Ch. 5, *passim*.
3. The author omits Congreve, since contrary to popular opinion, he was not Irish-born.
4. This will be qualified later.
5. Una Ellis-Fermor, 1939, *The Irish Dramatic Movement*.
6. A revised and enlarged edition appeared in 1912, with a section covering Ibsen's plays after 1891.
7. Stanley Weintraub, ed., 1962, *Shaw: An Autobiography 1856-1898*, p. 132.
8. *Ibid.*, p. 236.
9. *The Complete Prefaces of Bernard Shaw*, 1965, pp. 704-45.

10. Frederick Copleston, 1975, *Arthur Schopenhauer: Philosopher of Pessimism*, 2nd ed., pp. 39-40.

11. Bernard Shaw, 1962, *Complete Plays with Prefaces*, 6 vols., New York, vol. 1, pp. 302-3.

12. *Ibid*., p. 303.

13. *Nietzsche: The Man and his Philosophy*, 1965, Baton Rouge, p. 302.

14. *Op. cit*., pp. 303-5.

15. Turco, 1976, *op. cit*., p. 145.

16. *Ibid*., p. 160.

17. B. Shaw, 1962, *op. cit*., vol. 3, p. 507. By an uncharacteristic slip Shaw includes Turner and Hogarth among "the writers." The inclusion of Wagner is dubious, if justifiable.

18. *Ibid*., p. 511.

19. "*John Bull's Other Island* was written in 1904 at the request of Mr William Butler Yeats as a patriotic contribution to the repertory of the Irish Literary Theatre . . . The play was at that time beyond the resources of the new Abbey Theatre . . . There was another reason for changing the destination of *John Bull's Other Island* . . . It was uncongenial to the whole spirit of the neo-Gaelic movement which is bent on creating a new Ireland after its own ideal, whereas my play is a very uncompromising presentment of the real old Ireland." B. Shaw, 1962, *op. cit*., vol. 2, p. 443. Shaw wrote only one other play, the one-act *O'Flaherty V.C.*, set wholly in Ireland. Act I of Part 4 of *Back to Methusaleh* (1921) is set in the Burren.

20. B. Shaw, 1962, *Complete Plays*, vol. 2, p. x.

21. Jorge Luis Borges, *Labyrinths: Selected Stories and Other Writings*, ed. Donald A. Yates and James E. Irby, 1964, New York. "A Note on (toward) Bernard Shaw" was collected in *Otras Inquisiciones*, 1952.

22. H. Montgomery Hyde, 1976, *Oscar Wilde*, p. 5.

23. Lloyd Lewis and Henry Justin Smith, 1936, *Oscar Wilde Discovers America*, New York, p. 168.

24. Hyde, 1976, *op. cit*., pp. 68-69.

25. *Autobiography*, pp. 116-17.

26. Hyde, 1976, *op. cit*., p. 89.

27. *Ibid*., p. 125.

28. *Ibid*., p. 381.

29. *Oscar Wilde: the Critical Heritage*, ed. Karl Beckson, 1970, p. 372.

30. *Ibid*., p. 392.

31. Dominic Mangraniello, *Joyce's Politics*, 1980.

32. Benjamin Tucker, 1897, *Instead of a Book by a Man too Busy to Write One*.

33. Manganiello, *op. cit*., pp. 219-20.

34. *Ibid*., p. 220.

35. *Ibid*., p. 220.

36. George Woodcock, 1975, *Anarchism*, p. 30.

37. *De Profundis*, in *Selected Letters of Oscar Wilde*, ed. Rupert Hart-Davis, 1979, p. 216.

38. Hyde, 1976, *op. cit*., pp. 83-84.

39. James W. Hulse, 1970, *A Study of Revolutionists in London*, p. 99.

40. *Ibid*., p. 99.

41. Manganiello, *op. cit*., p. 220.

42. Michael Wilding, 1980, *Political Fictions*, p. 48.

43. "The Soul of Man Under Socialism," *The Works of Oscar Wilde*, ed. G.F. Maine, 1961, p. 1018.
44. *Ibid.*, p. 1020.
45. *Ibid.*, p. 1026.
46. Manganiello, *op. cit.*, p. 221.
47. Ed. G.F. Maine, 1961, *op. cit.*, p. 1038.
48. Manganiello, *op. cit.*, p. 221.
49. Ed. G.F. Maine, 1961, *op. cit.*, p. 1043.
50. *Oscar Wilde*, (Columbia Essays on Modern Writers), 1972, p. 21.
51. Hyde, 1976, *op. cit.*, p. 140.
52. *The Critical Writings of James Joyce*, ed. Ellsworth Mason and Richard Ellmann, 1964, New York, p. 70.
53. *Ibid.*, p. 72.
54. But his influence was to be found in the so-called Cork Realists, Lennox Robinson (1886-1958) and T.C. Murray (1873-1959) and, we are told, the mysterious R.J. Ray.
55. *The Plays and Poems of J.M. Synge*, ed. T.R. Henn, 1963, p. 108.
56. *Ibid.*, p. 174.
57. *Ibid.*
58. *Ibid.*
59. *Ibid.*
60. *Ibid.*, pp. 174-75.
61. *Ibid*, p. 175.
62. *Ibid.*, p. 108.
63. *Ibid.*
64. Michael Meyer, 1967, *Henrik Ibsen: The Making of a Dramatist 1828-1864*, p. 124.
65. *Theatre in Ireland*, 1974, p. 48.
66. Sean O'Casey, 1963 (originally 1949), *Collected Plays*, 4 vols., vol. 1, p. 23.
67. Collected in two volumes as *Autobiographies*, 1963. See the *Letters of Sean O'Casey*, ed. David Krause, 1975, vol. 1, 1910-41; 1980, vol. 2, 1942-54.
68. "Sean O'Casey as a Socialist Artist," *Sean O'Casey: Modern Judgements*, ed. Ronald Ayling, 1969, p. 192.
69. "Ireland After Yeats", *The Bell*, vol. 18, no. 2, summer 1953, pp. 37-48.
70. *Letters*, vol. 1, p. 131, (to *Irish Statesman* February 7, 1925).
71. Cf. John Jordan, Spring 1980, "The Passionate Antodidact: The Importance of *litera scripta* for Sean O'Casey," *Irish University Review*, vol. 10, no. 1, pp. 70-71.
72. John Jordan, "Illusion and Actuality in the Later O'Casey," *Modern Judgements op. cit.*, pp. 146-47.
73. *Collected Plays*, vol. 2, p. 333.
74. See for instance Denis Johnston, 1931, *The Moon in the Yellow River*, Conor Cruise O'Brien, 1969, *Murderous Angels*, Brian Friel, 1981, *Faith Healer*.
75. See *The Plays of George Fitzmaurice*, 3 vols., 1967-70, Dublin.

CHAPTER 11

Elizabeth Cullingford

THE UNKNOWN THOUGHT OF W.B. YEATS

1. W.B. Yeats, 1955, *Autobiographies*, Macmillan, London, p. 33.
2. W.B. Yeats, 1950, *Collected Poems*, 2nd ed., Macmillan, London, p. 169.
3. *Ibid.*, p. 167.
4. W.B. Yeats, *Letters*, 1954, ed. Allan Wade, Hart-Davis, London, p. 35.
5. W.B. Yeats, 1955, *op. cit.*, p. 31.
6. W.B. Yeats, 1961, *Essays and Introductions*, Macmillan, London, p. 176.
7. W.B. Yeats, 1962, *Explorations*, Macmillan, New York, p. 31.
8. W.B. Yeats, 1955, *op. cit.*, p. 82.
9. W.B. Yeats, 1954, *op. cit.*, p. 921.
10. W.B. Yeats, 1955, *op. cit.*, p. 166.
11. *Ibid.*, p. 188.
12. W.B. Yeats, 1954, *op. cit.*, p. 549.
13. W.B. Yeats, 1955, *op. cit.*, p. 65.
14. *Samhain*, ed. W.B. Yeats, 1908, Maunsell, Dublin, p. 8.
15. W.B. Yeats, 1962, *op. cit.*, p. 390.
16. W.B. Yeats, 1950, *op. cit.*, p. 370.
17. Hans Eichner, 1982, "The Rise of Modern Science and the Genesis of Romanticism," *PMLA*, no. 97, p. 15.
18. W.B. Yeats, *Letters to the New Island*, ed. Horace Reynolds, 1934, Harvard University Press, Cambridge, Mass., p. 174.
19. W.B. Yeats, 1962, *op. cit.*, p. 435.
20. W.B. Yeats, 1950, *op. cit.*, p. 159.
21. W.B. Yeats, *Uncollected Prose*, ed. John P. Frayne, 1970, Columbia University Press, New York, vol. 1, p. 147.
22. *Ibid.*, p. 172.
23. W.B. Yeats, 1950, *op. cit.*, p. 319.
24. W.B. Yeats, 1955, *op. cit.*, p. 469.
25. *Ibid.*, p. 189.
26. W.B. Yeats, 1962, *op. cit.*, p. 310.
27. *W.B. Yeats and T. Sturge Moore: Their Correspondence*, ed. Ursula Bridge, 1953, O.U.P., New York, p. 106.
28. "The Public v. the Late Mr. William Butler Yeats," in *W.B. Yeats: A Critical Anthology*, ed. W.H. Pritchard, 1972, Penguin, Harmondsworth, pp. 138-39.
29. W.B. Yeats, 1955, *op. cit.*, p. 116.
30. *Ibid.*
31. For a brief account of Madame Blavatsky, see Richard Ellman, 1961, *Yeats: The Man and the Masks*, 2nd ed., Faber, London, chap. 5.
32. W.B. Yeats, *Memoirs*, ed. Denis Donoghue, 1972, Macmillan, London, p. 23.
33. W.B. Yeats, 1955, *op. cit.*, p. 181.
34. W.B. Yeats, 1972, *op. cit.*, p. 23.
35. See George Mills Harper, 1974, *Yeats's Golden Dawn*, Macmillan, London.
36. W.B. Yeats, 1972, *op. cit.*, p. 27.
37. W.B. Yeats, 1961, *op. cit.*, p. 28.
38. *The Rhizome and the Flower*, 1980, University of California Press, Berkeley, *passim*.

39. W.B. Yeats, 1954, *op. cit.*, p. 379.
40. *Ibid.*
41. W.B. Yeats, 1961, *op. cit.*, p. 130.
42. Denis Donoghue, 1971, *Yeats*, Collins, London, p. 47.
43. *Ibid.*, p. 48.
44. W.B. Yeats, 1950, *op. cit.*, p. 274.
45. *Ibid.*, p. 185.
46. In the margin of *Nietzsche as Critic, Philosopher, Poet and Prophet*, ed. Thomas Common, 1901, Grant Richards, London, p. 129.
47. *Ibid.*, p. 113.
48. W.B. Yeats, 1950, *op. cit.*, p. 339.
49. W.B. Yeats, 1955, *op. cit.*, p. 189.
50. W.B. Yeats, 1929, *A Packet for Ezra Pound*, Cuala Press, Dublin, pp. 32-33.
51. W.B. Yeats, 1962, *A Vision*, rev. ed., Macmillan, London, p. 40; see also Thomas Whitaker, 1964, *Swan and Shadow*, University of North Carolina Press, Chapel Hill, *passim.*, for discussions of *A Vision* and history.
52. W.B. Yeats, 1962, *A Vision, op. cit.*, p. 68.
53. W.B. Yeats, 1962, *Explorations, op. cit.*, p. 305.
54. W.B. Yeats, 1950, *op. cit.*, p. 286.
55. W.B. Yeats, 1962, *A Vision, op. cit.*, p. 72.
56. For a discussion of Yeats and Kant, see Robert Snukal, 1973, *High Talk*, Cambridge University Press, chap. 1.
57. Ursula Bridge, ed., 1953, *op. cit.*, p. 146.
58. W.B. Yeats, 1962, *A Vision, op. cit.*, p. 52.
59. *Ibid.*, pp. 262-63.
60. *Ibid.*, p. 271.
61. W.B. Yeats, 1950, *op. cit.*, p. 244.
62. *Ibid.*, p. 245.
63. *Ibid.*, p. 218.
64. B. Russell, 1912, *The Problems of Philosophy*, Galaxy Books, New York, p. 100.
65. W.B. Yeats, 1950, *op. cit.*, pp. 218-19.
66. *Ibid.*, p. 223.
67. *Ibid.*, p. 533.
68. Ursula Bridge, ed., 1953, *op. cit.*, p. 67.
69. W.B. Yeats, 1962, *Explorations, op. cit.*, p. 368.
70. Ursula Bridge, ed., 1953, *op. cit.*, p. 80.
71. First quoted in Richard Ellmann, 1964, *The Identity of Yeats*, 2nd ed., Faber, London, p. 236.
72. *Variorum Poems*, ed. Russell K. Alspach and Catherine C. Alspach, 1957, Macmillan, New York, p. 825.
73. Ursula Bridge, ed., 1953, *op. cit.*, p. 149.
74. W.B. Yeats, 1962, *Explorations, op. cit.*, pp. 333-34; for a discussion of Yeats and Berkeley, see Donald Torchiana, 1966, *W.B. Yeats and Georgian Ireland*, Northwestern University Press, Evanston, chap. 6.
75. W.B. Yeats, 1962, *Explorations, op. cit.*, p. 435.
76. *Ibid.*, p. 325.
77. W.B. Yeats, 1961, *op. cit.*, p. 401.
78. W.B. Yeats, 1950, *op. cit.*, p. 240.
79. W.B. Yeats, 1961, *op. cit.*, p. 401.
80. W.B. Yeats, 1962, *Explorations, op. cit.*, p. 435.

81. W.B. Yeats, 1954, *op. cit.*, p. 656.
82. "Michael Robartes: Two Occult Manuscripts," ed. W.K. Hood, 1976, *Yeats and the Occult*, ed. G.M. Harper, Macmillan, London, p. 221.
83. Quoted in A.N. Jeffares, 1962, *W.B. Yeats: Man and Poet*, 2nd ed., Routledge and Kegan Paul, London, p. 351.
84. For a fuller discussion of this topic, see Elizabeth Cullingford, 1981, *Yeats, Ireland and Fascism*, Macmillan, London, chap. 8.
85. W.B. Yeats, 1962, *Explorations, op. cit.*, pp. 435-36.
86. B. Russell, 1927, *Outline of Philosophy*, Allen and Unwin, London, pp. 104 and 112.
87. W.B. Yeats, 1961, *op. cit.*, p. 461.
88. Reported in Lady Gregory's unpublished journal, June 1923, and quoted in Donald Torchiana, 1979, "Yeats and Plato," *Modern British Literature*, vol. 4, no. 1, p. 12.
89. W.B. Yeats, 1962, *Explorations, op. cit.*, p. 429.
90. "Yeats – and Philosophy," *Cronos*, 1947, vol. 1, no. 3, p. 19.
91. W.B. Yeats, 1950, *op. cit.*, p. 394.
92. W.B. Yeats, 1962, *Explorations, op. cit.*, pp. 449-50.
93. W.B. Yeats, 1954, *op. cit.*, p. 922.

CHAPTER 12

Mark Patrick Hederman

THE "MIND" OF JOYCE: FROM PATERNALISM TO PATERNITY

1. Denis Donoghue, Spring 1960, "Joyce and the Finite Order," *Sewanee Review*, no. 68, p. 256.
2. M.P. Hederman, 1982, "James Joyce: Priest & Poet," *The Crane Bag*, vol. 6, no. 1.
3. T.S. Eliot, 1920, "Hamlet and His Problems," *The Sacred Wood*, Methuen, London, pp. 87-94.
4. This theory re-echoes similar ones in both Bruno and the German romantic tradition, whose idealistic estheticism was fashionable at the turn of the century. As a renaissance philosopher who fuses classical and Christian thought, Bruno seeks the "real" world of Plato in our imperfect world which holds its reverberations. In *Ars Memoriae* he suggests that certain sounds are reminiscent of this lost reality. The *Anima mundi* infuses our world and to invoke this special power, Bruno composed a list of one hundred and fifty sounds which recall parts of some one word or Logos, which evokes the Godhead.

   The Hegelians of the German romantic school thought of art as a process of self-expression by the cosmic mind. The thoughts of the individual artist are simply parts of this process of divine expression. Benedetto Croce, who belonged to this school and was almost a contemporary of Joyce (1866-1952), regarded art as vision or intuition and not a physical fact, since physical facts do not possess reality. All these reflections are re-echoed in Stephen's attempt to read the signature of things in the proteus episode of *Ulysses* and are taken up again in a novel way in *Finnegans Wake*.
5. James Joyce, 1958, *Ulysses*, London, p. 196.
6. *Ibid.*, p. 194.

7. Cf. for example: De Wulf, 1894, "Les théories esthétiques propres à Saint Thomas," *Revue néoscolastique*, vol. 1, p. 191ff; see also D. Mercier, 1895, "Du Beau dans la nature et dans l'art," *Ibid*. vol. 1, p. 359.

8. William T. Noon, S.J., 1957, *Joyce and Aquinas*, Yale University Press.

9. *Ibid*., p. 105ff.

10. *Summa Theologiae* I, q. 39, a. 8.

11. Louis Gillet, 1949, "Stele for James Joyce," *James Joyce Yearbook*, Paris, pp. 42-43.

12. J. Joyce, 1958, *op. cit*., p. 18.

13. Lionel Trilling, 1951, *The Liberal Imagination*, London, p. 40.

14. *Ibid*., p. 35.

15. *Ibid*., p. 34.

16. Richard Ellmann, 1959, *James Joyce*, Oxford University Press, p. 393.

17. Frank Budgen, 1934, *James Joyce and the making of Ulysses*, London, p. 8.

18. R. Ellmann, 1959, *op. cit*., p. 450.

19. *Ibid*., p. 538.

20. R. Ellmann, 1959, *op. cit*., p. 706.

21. C.G. Jung, 1966, "*Ulysses*: a Monologue," *Collected Works*, Bollingen XX, New York, vol. 15, pp. 122-23.

22. *Selected Joyce Letters*, ed. Richard Ellmann, 1975, New York, p. 360.

23. *Ibid*., p. 361.

24. *Ibid*.

25. C.G. Jung, 1966, *op. cit*., p. 119.

26. R. Ellmann, ed., 1975, *op. cit*., p. 25.

27. *Ibid*.

28. R. Ellmann, 1959, *op. cit*., p. 692.

29. Colin McCabe, 1978, *James Joyce and the Revolution of the Word*, London. The writer is greatly indebted to this work for what I say about Joyce's destruction of the novel form in *Ulysses* and *Dubliners*.

30. *Ibid*., p. 54.

31. J. Joyce, 1958, *op. cit*., p. 199.

32. Sheldon R. Brivic, 1980, *Joyce between Freud and Jung*, NUP, New York, p. 34. I have used this work extensively when treating of the sexual implications of the various relationships in *Ulysses*.

33. *Ibid*., p. 141 and 148.

34. R. Ellmann, 1959, *op. cit*., p. 706.

35. Herman Broch, 1949, "Joyce and the Present Age," *Yearbook*, ed. Maria Jolas, Paris, pp. 106-7.

36. J. Joyce, 1958, *op. cit*., p. 172.

37. *Ibid*., p. 206.

38. *Ibid*., p. 203.

39. *Ibid*., p. 179.

40. Cf. Sheldon Brivic, 1980, *op. cit*., p. 136.

41. J. Joyce, 1958, *op. cit*., p. 190.

42. *Ibid*., p. 266.

43. R. Ellmann, 1959, *op. cit*., pp. 562-63.

44. C.G. Jung, 1960, *The Collected Works*, Bollingen XX, New York, vol. 8, pp. 419-531.

45. R. Ellmann, 1959, *op. cit*., p. 563.

46. C.G. Jung, 1960, *op. cit*., pp. 509-11.

47. *Ibid*., p. 513.

48. *Ibid.*, p. 510.
49. *Ibid.*, p. 511.
50. C.G. Jung, 1966, *op. cit.*, p. 119.
51. J. Joyce, 1939, *Finnegans Wake*, p. 181.
52. *Ibid.*, p. 18.
53. Herman Broch, 1949, *op. cit.*, p. 106-7.
54. C.G. Jung, 1960, *op. cit.*, p. 513.
55. J. Joyce, 1939, *op. cit.*, p. 186.
56. *Ibid.*, pp. 186-87.
57. *Ibid.*, pp. 181-82.
58. R. Ellmann, 1959, *op. cit.*, p. 559.
59. *Ibid.*
60. J. Joyce, 1939, *op. cit.*, p. 598.
61. *Ibid.*, p. 460.
62. *Ibid.*, p. 485.
63. *Ibid.*, p. 98.
64. *Ibid.*, p. 473.
65. *Ibid.*, p. 242.
66. *Ibid.*, p. 109.
67. *Ibid.*, p. 583.
68. *Ibid.*, p. 626.
69. *Ibid.*, p. 613.
70. *Ibid.*, p. 120.
71. *Ibid.*, p. 623.
72. *Ibid.*, p. 615.
73. *Ibid.*, pp. 184-89.
74. *Ibid.*, p. 444.
75. *Ibid.*, p. 415.
76. *Ibid.*, p. 602.
77. *Ibid.*, p. 452.
78. *Ibid.*, p. 472.
79. *Ibid.*, p. 378.

CHAPTER 13

Richard Kearney

BECKETT: THE DEMYTHOLOGISING INTELLECT

1. S. Beckett, 1929, "Dante . . . Bruno. Vico . . . Joyce," *Our Exagmination round'his Factification for Incamination of Work in Progress*, Paris.
2. S. Beckett, 1931, *Proust*, Chatto and Windus, London.
3. S. Beckett, 1949, "Three Dialogues with Georges Duthuit," *Transition*, no. 5.
4. G. d'Aubarède, 1961, "Waiting for Beckett," *Trace*, no. 42.
5. Interview with Lawrence Harvey, 1962 quoted by John Pilling, 1976, *Samuel Beckett*, Routledge and Kegan Paul, London, p. 124.
6. Quoted by Vivian Mercier, 1977, *Beckett/Beckett*, Oxford University Press.
7. Deirdre Bair, 1978, *Samuel Beckett, a Biography*, Jonathan Cape, p. 91.
8. S. Beckett, 1938, "Denis Devlin," *Transition*, no. 27, p. 289.
9. S. Beckett, 1934, "Recent Irish Poetry," *The Bookman*, no. 86.

10. *Ibid.*; see also R. Kearney, 1982, "Samuel Beckett: The End of the Story," *Anglo-Irish Literature*, Academy Press, Dublin, 1985, particularly the section "Beckett the Irish Writer, A Contradiction in Terms;" and J.C.C. Mays, 1977, "Mythologised Presences: *Murphy* in its Time," *Myth and Reality in Irish Literature*, ed. J. Ronsley, Laurier University Press, pp. 202-3: "The staking out of critical principles and of a relationship to the traditions he inherits or is aware of is an almost inevitable preliminary to any Irish writer's career, and one that at the same time involves him in predicaments of national and personal identity ... his understanding of the situation in more than national terms, in feeling the alternative to Yeats lies not in realism but, following the example of Joyce, in European writers of a quite different ambience."

11. S. Beckett, Apr. 1954, "*Hommage à Jack. B. Yeats*," *Les Lettres Nouvelles*, p. 619, quoted Mays, 1977, *op. cit.*

12. S. Beckett, 1934a, "The Essential and the Incidental," *The Bookman*, no. 87.

13. S. Beckett, 1934b, *Murphy*, Routledge and Kegan Paul, London, p. 63.

14. J. Mays, 1977, *op. cit.*, p. 208: "(Beckett's) satire is at random at the expense of all things Irish, from Junior Fellows to Irish virgins, as well as at life at large."

15. Interview with Israel Shenker, *New York Times*, May 6, 1956.

16. D. Bair, 1978, *op. cit.*, p. 104.

17. On Beckett's references to Cartesianism cf. J. Onimus, 1968, *Beckett*, Desclée de Brouwer, pp. 40f; J. Pilling, 1976, *op. cit.*, pp. 112f; E. Levy, 1980, *Beckett and the Voice of Species*, Gill and Macmillan, pp. 18f; R. Coe, 1965, *Beckett*, Rives and Boyd, pp. 20f.

18. S. Beckett, 1934b, *op. cit.*, p. 107.

19. *Ibid.*, p. 8.

20. See D. Bair, 1978, p. 220: "All Murphy's seemingly random actions are set within a specific period, and every date is presented with information about the heavenly bodies ... the reader knows exactly what time and date it is throughout the novel." The frequent allusions to chess and mathematical calculations further confirm the sense of predetermined unfreedom in the novel.

21. S. Beckett, 1934b, *op. cit.*, p. 275. Joyce so admired this passage that he committed it to memory.

22. *Ibid.*, p. 178. See D. Bair, 1978, *op. cit.*, p. 92: "Geulincx's philosophy had the most powerful and lasting effect on Beckett of anything he had read to date. So impressive was it that he made it the key of his novel, *Murphy*, written in 1935."

23. The Zeno example also recurs in *Lost Ones* and *Happy Days*; cf. J. Pilling, 1976, *op. cit.*, p. 125.

24. For Aristotle's critique of Zeno see *Metaphysics*, p. 160b, *De Sophisticis Elenchis*, pp. 172a, 179b and *Physics*, vol. 5, pp. 204a, 206a.

25. J. Pilling, 1976, *op. cit.*, pp. 89, 138, 167 and E. Levy, 1980, *op. cit.*, pp. 64-65, 77-79. In *More Pricks than Kicks* Beckett mocked Duns Scotus' definition of the divine being as a "haecceity of puffect love."

26. S. Beckett, 1931, *op. cit.*, p. 1.

27. S. Beckett, 1959, *Watt*, Grove Press, New York, p. 48.

28. S. Beckett, 1934b, *op. cit.*, p. 109.

29. S. Beckett, 1934, *More Pricks than Kicks*, Calder, London, pp. 31, 41.

30. Several of Beckett's characters suffer from a total lack of synchrony between

thought and action; they will to do one thing but in fact do the opposite, e.g. Estragon and Vladimir, Malone, Molloy, Moran and Clov.

31. See J. Pilling, 1976, on Beckett and Leibniz, *op. cit.*, p. 185.
32. S. Beckett, 1934b, *op. cit.*, p. 185.
33. S. Beckett, 1931, *op. cit.*, p. 64.
34. Berkeley met Malebranche in Paris and Beckett refers to him by name on several occasions, e.g. S. Beckett, 1964, *How It Is*, London, p. 33; cf. also J. Pilling, 1976, *op. cit.*, p. 116.
35. H. Bracken, 1974, *Berkeley*, Macmillan, p. 18; cf. Dr. Bracken's essay on Berkeley in the present collection.
36. S. Beckett, 1934b, p. 246.
37. *Ibid.*, p. 190. For other commentaries on the influence of Berkeley on Beckett see V. Mercier, 1977, *op. cit.*, pp. 101, 161, 194; J. Pilling, 1976, *op. cit.*, pp. 2, 116, 117.
38. S. Beckett, 1972, *Film*, Faber and Faber, p. 11.
39. *Ibid.*, p. 12; cf. Alec Reid, 1977, "Beckett, The Camera and Jack McGowan," *Myth and Reality in Irish Literature, op. cit.*, p. 224.
40. Quoted by V. Mercier, 1977, *op. cit.*, p. 175.
41. See Kant, 1781, *Critique of Pure Reason*, preface; Kierkegaard, 1883, *Fear and Trembling*, and Bultmann, 1954, *The Christian Hope and the Problem of Demythologising*.
42. For the most suggestive analysis of the influence of Protestant thinking on Beckett's writing see, J. Onimus, 1968, *op. cit.*, pp. 88-98: "Lorsque le dualisme cartésien vient s'articular sur une théologie aussi tragique que de Luther, Dieu s'éloigne. La sensibilité et l'imagination (qui jouent en ce domaine un rôle si important) s'accoutument à un 'extrincésisme' séparateur qui exile Dieu par delà tout horizon. Dieu n'est *plus que* le 'Tout Autre', l'étranger par excellence, celui qui est radicalement en dehors (p. 88). Qui sait si les supplices de la dépossession, de l'impuissance, de la claustration ne sont pas des tentatives de l'au-delà pour entrer en communication avec ses créatures? ... Peut-être l'engloutissement de Winnie par une suffocante chaleur est-il un bien – comme la marche errante de Molloy et la longue agonie de Malone? Peut-être le malheur même est-il orienté vers une plénitude – comme cette foule misérable qui, dans *l'Innomable*, avance lentement par bonds dérisoires, dans la boue, mais avance quand même, obstinément en direction de l'Orient, vers la lumière du matin (pp. 92-6) ... Le Tout n'est séparé du Rien que par un *presque*, un *peut-être*, l'espace d'un hésitation. Mais toute l'oeuvre de Beckett n'est-elle pas faite de cette hésitation?" (p. 98).
43. On Beckett and negative theology see J. Onimus, 1968, *op. cit.*, pp. 111-20; R. Coe, 1965, *op. cit.*, pp. 12-34; H. Deyle, 1960, *Samuel Beckett*, (Aix-en-Provence), pp. 27-71; S. Kennedy, 1971, *Murphy's Bed*, Bucknell University Press, particularly on the negative theology of the Pseudo-Dionysius, pp. 38-40, 58-59, 83-84, 93-94, 155-56, 162-63, 294-95. One should also keep in mind the similarities between Beckett's exploration of nothingness and the negative theology of Meister Eckhart who claimed that the mystical experience returns us "to the calm desert, the bottomless abyss of God in which we must eternally submerge ourselves, as one nothingness to another nothingness." (*Deutsche Werke*, vol. 1, p. 281).
44. "My family was Protestant," says Beckett, "but for me it was only a nuisance and I left it ... Irish Catholicism is not seductive but it is more profound.

When an Irish bus passes a church all hands make a quick sign of the cross. One day, the dogs in the street will do likewise, perhaps even the pigs." (Interview with Tom Driver in *Columbia University Forum*, 1961.)

45. J. Onimus, 1968, *op. cit.*, p. 19. Beckett's description of Belacqua Shuah as a "low-down Low Church Protestant" of Huguenot stock (*More Pricks than Kicks*) may be a comic reference to himself.

46. J. Pilling, 1976, *op. cit.*, pp. 117-18. It is also worth noting that Beckett frequently makes humorous allusion to several dogmas of traditional Catholic theology; in *Whoroscope* and *Watt*, for example, he parodies the "Jesuitasters" teaching of the "real presence" of Christ in the Eucharist; in *First Love* he mocks at the Irish Catholic ruling on censorship and contraception, and so on.

47. On the theological motif of suffering and sin in Beckett, see H. Deyle, 1960, *op. cit.*, pp. 27-47; and J. Onimus, 1968, *op. cit.*, pp. 102, 108-9: "Dieu est en dehors; son action sur les consciences ne peut s'excercer que de loin et pour ainsi dire mécaniquement. Il n'y a pas de "co-naissance" possible entre des êtres si totalement étrangers. Dieu a été rejeté sur l'autre versant de l'existence, le versant infernal, et Beckett rejoint spontanément la vieille gnose pour qui le monde ne peut être que l'oeuvre du Malin: tout ce qu'il comporte de positif est, en profondeur, négatif, puisque les êtres n'existent que pour pouvoir se dégrader et souffrir; le désir de vivre, qui est toujours un besoin d'absolu, mène fatalement au désir du néant et à la haine de soi . . . Pour que le mal soit lié à ce point à l'existence on en vient naturellement à croire que l'existence est elle-même une faute, la conséquence d'une erreur, et que l'on paie toute sa vie cette erreur d'être né. Beckett notait déjà une telle angoisse dans son *Proust* et y parlait du péché d'être né."

48. See H. Deyle's analysis of Beckett's treatment of women, 1960, *op. cit.*, pp. 62f: "Beckett assimile la femme au piège de la vie qui nous détourne du grand néant. Joyce identifie A.L. Plurabelle à la vie fluide et féconde."

49. For Beckett's attitude to the psychoanalysis of Freud and Jung, whom he read and admired, see D. Bair, 1978, *op. cit.*, pp. 177-78, 208-12. Beckett attended a lecture of Jung's in 1935 and was fascinated by his theory that consciousness was an illusion and that the complexes of the unconscious could form "little personalities" of their own until "they appear as visions (and) speak in voices which are like the voices of definite people" (quoted Bair, p. 208).

50. See H. Deyle, 1960, *op. cit.*, p. 27. One might add that the Jansenistic Catholicism current in Ireland during Beckett's youth was no less "puritanical" than its Irish Protestant counterpart; one only has to read Joyce or Flann O'Brien to be reminded of this.

51. Cf. H. Deyle, 1960, *op. cit.*, pp. 52f; and V. Mercier, 1977, *op. cit.*, pp. 141, 193-94, 207.

52. The clowns in *Godot*, for example, suffer from swollen feet, diseased prostrates, syphilis etc., while Molloy and Malone are constantly preoccupied by their bowel movements.

53. Cf. S. Beckett, 1959, *op. cit.*, p. 84.

54. Quoted J. Mays, 1977, *op. cit.*, p. 214.

55. See for instance Daniel Stempel, 1976, *History Electrified into Anagogy: A Reading of Waiting for Godot* in *Contemporary Literature*, vol. 17, pp. 266-69. Stempel contends that Estragon and Vladimir represent Judaism and Christianity respectively in a dying Europe. Estragon, he points out, is a type-name referring to both tarragon – in French *estragon* – the "bitter

herb" of the Jewish pass-over supper, and the Spanish-Jewish city of the same name where Christians and Jews debated in 1414 the question of whether the Messiah had come or was yet to come. (Interestingly, in the original manuscript of the play, Estragon is called by the archetypally Jewish name Lévy.) Vladimir, Stempel argues, refers to Duke Vladimir of Kiev who was the first Russian converted to Christianity and to the last famous Russian theologian Vladimir Soloviev whose *War and Christianity* ends with a discussion of the apocalypse to be expected in decadent modern Europe and frequently alludes to the two thieves crucified with Christ (a recurring motif in *Godot*). On the theological motifs in *Godot* see also J. Onimus, 1968, *op. cit.*, particularly pp. 80f, 99f.

56. *Ibid.*, Stempel, p. 8. Estragon admits that he cannot recall when he last read the Bible but vividly revisualises the map of Holy Zion: "The dead sea was pale blue . . . that's where we'll go on our honeymoon" (p. 56). The elder of the two protagonists, Estragon, only quotes Jehovah as an invisible all-seeing eye and interrupts Vladimir's story of the two thieves crucified "at the same time as Our Saviour" to ask – "Our what?" Whereas Estragon calls the plant where Godot promised to meet them a "bush" (recalling the burning bush in which Yahweh appeared to Moses), Vladimir insists that it is a "willow tree" (a crucifix which may serve as a gibbet of despair or a "little leaved" flowering of hope). The temporal axis of Estragon's theology is the Godot of the past – he observes that they were waiting in exactly the same place the "day before;" Vladimir's, by contrast, is the Godot of the future. To Estragon's statement that they are "tied" to Godot (the French *lier* meaning "to tie," having the same root as alliance or covenant), Vladimir retorts "not yet." Estragon as the Wandering Jew has sore feet after all his travelling and wants to go barefoot as his fellow Jew "Christ did." But Vladimir is irritated by such a sacriligious analogy: "Christ! What has Christ to do with it: you're not going to compare yourself to Christ!" Estragon replies, however, that he has compared himself to Christ all his life, taking solace from the idea that "they crucified quick" and adding: "The best thing would be to kill me, like the other." In short, it can be argued that Estragon, who is beaten every night by unknown assailants, identifies with Christ only as a fellow human victim, unlike Vladimir who sees him as a resurrected Saviour who will return. Perhaps this is why Vladimir is so shocked when Godot's messenger informs them that the Master's beard is "white" rather than "blond" for it hints that Godot might indeed be the distant Father of the Old Testament rather than the redemptive Son of the New: "Christ have mercy on us," exclaims Vladimir on hearing the news. On the other hand, Pozzo's allusion to the unexpected arrival of darkness reinforces the apocalyptic notion of Christ returning like a thief in the night: "Behind this veil of gentleness and peace night is charging and will burst upon us pop! . . . just when we least expect it." This would also explain why Vladimir enthuses at the prospect of a Redeemer-Godot arriving: "Its Godot! We're saved," while Estragon reacts: "I'm in hell." For if Christ *is* God then Vladimir is the thief who is saved and Estragon the one who is damned.

57. On Beckett and the Augustinian image of the two thieves (Beckett read Augustine's *Confessions* in 1935) see D. Bair, 1978, *op. cit.*, p. 386 and V. Mercier, 1977, *op. cit.*, pp. 172-73.

58. Godot is the epitome of unknowability as Beckett made quite clear when he replied to critics that if he knew who Godot was he would have said so in

the play!

59. On the conflicting theistic and atheistic readings of *Godot* see H. Deyle, 1960, *op. cit.*, p. 90.

60. D. Bair, 1978, *op. cit.*, p. 386.

61. *Murphy* opens with a paraphrase of the *Book of Ecclesiastes*: "The sun shone on the nothing new" and is replete with references to *Revelation*, e.g. "There should be time no longer" (*Revelation*, chap. 10, v. 6) and "the beginning and the end" (*Revelation*, chap. 21, v. 6) as well as constant allusions to the image of the apocalyptic "nihil" of time as the *Anno Domini*. This apocalyptic theme of the ending of time is strengthened by pointed astrological and calendar references to such Judeo-Christian feasts as Passover and Holy Week. Several other biblical references identify Murphy as a mock-messiah: Friday is called a "day of execution, love and fast;" the epithet of chapter 9 announcing Murphy's entry to the Magdalen Mental Mercy seat: "Il est difficile à celui qui vit hors du monde de ne pas rechercher les siens," is reminiscent of *John*, chap. 1, v. 2 ("He came into his own and his own received him not"). Furthermore, Bom Clinch sees Murphy as a Christ-like fool and the narrator develops the parallel as follows: "Admire Bom feeling dimly for once what you feel acutely so often, Pilate's hands rustling in his mind. Thus Bom . . . delivered Murphy to his folly." There are also the quasi-quotations from the New Testament which summarise Murphy's relationship with Celia: "The hireling fleeth because he is a hireling" (*John*, chap. 10, v. 13) and "What shall a man give in exchange for Celia" (*Mark*, chap 8, v. 37); as well as echoes of *Job*, chap. 17, v. 16 and *Revelation*, chap 21, vs. 16, 23 all well documented by S. Kennedy, 1971, *op. cit.*, pp. 245 and 265: "In *Revelation*, chap. 21, vs. 16, 23, the City of God is described as standing "foursquare," with "no need of the sun, neither of the moon to shine on it." As Cooper rushes away from the supposed deathbed of Murphy, he sees a vision not unlike that of St John. Before him, standing "foursquare" is a "glowing gin-palace . . . that had no need of the sun, neither of the moon, to shine in it" (p. 120)".

62. I wish to acknowledge my debt here to T. Eisele's informative essay, 1976, "The Apocalypse of Beckett's *Endgame*," *Cross Currents*, vol. 26, no. 1, pp. 11-22. As Eisele puts it: "This play offers the most sustained portrayal of Beckett's religious sensibility" (p. 12). He goes on to argue as follows: "The Apocalypse of Beckett's *Endgame* is the revelation of the coming of the Anti-Christ and the leaving of Christ. With that event the world of Christianity ends. So while Beckett's play recalls the New Testament's *Book of Revelation* in its imagery, it produces a startlingly new twist to that iconology. Christianity does not triumph as it does in the New Testament, but dies" (p. 22). The Anti-Christ is presumably the "small boy" seen by Hamm in the deluged ("under water") and "corpsed" wasteland outside his window at the conclusion of the play. The ending of Christianity is heralded by the ending of Clov's relationship with Hamm. Clov declares that he has done his "best to create a little order" in Hamm's house, while Hamm concedes that Clov's arrival "was the moment I was waiting for." Clov's departing speech, with its subtle parodying of Christ's mission, can be read as a statement of disillusionment with the evangelical message of loving sacrifice: "They said to me, that's love, yes, yes, not a doubt . . . They said to me, Here's the place, stop, raise your head and look at all that beauty. That order! They said to me, Come now, you're not a brute beast, think upon

these things and you'll see how all comes clear. And simple! They said to
me, What skilled attention they get. All those dying of their wounds ...
I say to myself – sometimes, Clov, You must learn to suffer better than that
if you want them to weary of punishing you – one day ... It'll never end,
I'll never go. Then one day, suddenly, it ends, it changes, I don't understand, it dies, or it's me, I don't know, I don't understand that either."
There have also been commentaries on the eschatological themes in *Endgame* by such diverse critics as Cavell, Esslin, Cohn and Sheedy: for biblio-
graphical references see Eisele, pp. 31-32.

63. T. Eisele, 1976, *op. cit.*, p. 31. Clov hovers between the hell of Anti-Christ
and the heaven of Christ; he inhabits the purgatory of incertitude and
repetition. But is it the Dantesque purgatory of orthodox redemption or
the Joycean purgatory which Beckett defined in his *Exagmination* essay as
"the absolute absence of the absolute?" Whereas Dante's purgatory ends
in salvation, Joyce's is an endless repetition of the human quest for salvation: "Dante's is conical and consequently implies culmination," explains
Beckett, "Joyce's is spherical and excludes culmination." As Vivian Mercier
comments, 1977, *op. cit.*, p. 178: "Purgatory is another theological concept
that Beckett found extremely useful for structural purposes."

64. Still with Dostoyevsky, we could as easily construe *Endgame* as an enact-
ment of the nihilist's statement in *Notes from the Underground* that "man
is a frivolous and incongruous creature who like a chess player loves the process of the game, not the end of it!"

65. "I am still afraid, but simply from force of habit. And the voice I listen to
needs no Gaber to make it heard. For it is within me and exhorts me to continue to the end the faithful servant I have always been, on a course that is
not mine, and patiently fulfil in all its bitterness my calamitous past ... And
this was with hatred in my heart, and scorn, of my master and his designs.
Yes, it is rather an ambiguous voice and not always easy to follow in its
reasonings and decrees ... And when it ceases, leaving me in doubt and
darkness, I shall wait for it to come back" (*Molloy*, 1955, Picador edition,
p. 121). Pursuing his nomadic journey "in obedience to Youdi's command,"
Moran suddenly embarks on a comic mimicry of the theological dogmas of
divine creation. "Certain questions of a theological nature preoccupied me
strangely," says Moran. "What value," he asks, "is to be attached to the
theory that Eve sprang not from Adam's rib, but from a tumour in the fat
of his leg (arse?)?" Or: "How much longer are we to hang about waiting for
the Anti-Christ?" Or again: "What was God doing with himself before the
creation?" (*Ibid.*, p. 153). Moran's blasphemous buffoonery reaches its
climax in his inversion of the "quietest" Our Father: "God is no longer in
heaven, nor on earth, nor in hell, I do not wish nor desire that Your Name
be hallowed" ... etc.

66. See references to Boehme in *More Pricks than Kicks*, to Eckhart in *Dream*,
to St. John in *Malone Dies* etc. As R. Coe, 1965, points out in his analysis
of Beckett's mysticism, *op. cit.*, p. 20: "To confront the limits of the human
condition is not only the equivalent of facing up to the philosophical basis of
the scientific attitude, it is also a profound mystical experience."

67. J. Onimus, 1968, *op. cit.*, pp. 75f: "Parler de Dieu dans l'oeuvre de Beckett
c'est parler d'un absent. L'absence est tout autre chose que l'inexistence: on
pense à un absent, on peut fictivement s'adresser à lui, on l'attend, on le
désire, on ressent même sa présence comme un manque, un vide pénible,

une blessure . . . c'est la contemplation d'un *Dieu-néant*, d'un être qui, à force de la torturer, a fini par épuiser chez sa créature les réserves d'angoisse qui lui donnaient prise sur elle – et l'abandonne hébétée, le regard figé sur le Rien (p. 76) . . . Nous sommes nés en état d'expectative – peu important nos croyances: nous attendons la plénitude et nous ne pouvons vivre sans elle (p. 81)."

68. Of course, the fundamental irony in Beckett's treatment of this negative theology is that even if one succeeds in suspending one's own interfering will, one is still prevented from attaining the silence of non-being since there are always *other* voices to speak and name us: "Feeling nothing, knowing nothing, he exists nevertheless, but not for himself, for *others*, others conceive him and say, Worm is, since we conceive him, as if there could be no being but being conceived . . . One alone turned towards the all-important, all-nescient, that haunts him, then *others*." The Beckettian purgation of the unnamable differs from the biblical purgation of Job in that it is without issue. Unlike Eliot's fideistic assurances in *Four Quartets* that our salvation lies in the "frigid purgatorial fires of which the flame is roses and the smoke is briars," Beckett's purgatory is endless, its roses and smoke devoid of mystical redemption: "They mentioned roses. I'll smell them before I'm finished. Then they'll put the accent on the thorns. What prodigious variety: the thorns they'll have to come and stick into me, as into their unfortunate Jesus. No, I need nobody, they'll stand sprouting under my arse, unaided . . ." And so the narrator of *The Unnamable* concludes with the horrifying supposition *à la* Hamlet that even the silence of death will be tormented by dreams, by further words: "Perhaps its all a dream . . . I'd wake in the silence and never sleep again . . . dream of a silence, a dream silence, full of murmurs, I don't know." And not knowing, and knowing that he'll never know, he simply vows to go on without end. "I'll go on, you must say words, as long as there are any, until they find me, until they say me, strange pain, strange sin, you must go on . . .".

69. Cf. V. Mercier, 1977, *op. cit.*, p. 167: "I find two dominant philosophical patterns in *Watt*: one ontological, the other epistemological. Watt at Mr Knott's house experiences, however dimly, both the difference between being and non-being, and the difference between knowing and not-knowing . . . The philosopher's quest for "truth" . . . is the comic image that underlies many pages of *Watt* and gives the book whatever unity it possesses."

70. J. Onimus, 1968, *op. cit.*, p. 114.

71. Cf. R. Coe, 1965, *op. cit.*, p. 15.

72. Interview with Alan Schneider, 1974, quoted by V. Mercier, 1977, *op. cit.*, p. 163.

73. Interview with Tom Driver, 1961, *op. cit.*; cf. J. Onimus, 1968, *op. cit.*, pp. 178-79.

74. Interview with G. d'Aubarède, 1961, *op. cit.*

75. Interview with Tom Driver, 1961, *op. cit.*

76. Cf. On Beckett and Sartre: E. Levy, 1980, *op. cit.*, pp. 87, 127; J. Pilling, 1976, *op. cit.*, p. 129; V. Mercier, 1977, *op. cit.*, pp. 84, 161. Sartre himself has adverted to his common cause with Beckett as a dramatist of "scandal" aiming at a "decentralisation of the subject" (Cf. J.P. Sartre, 1973, *Politics and Literature*, Calder Press, pp. 63, 66). Sartre's description of the modernist movement in literature is also particularly relevant to Beckett: "It pushed contestation to the limit, even to the point of contesting itself; it

gives us a glimpse of silence beyond the massacre of words . . . it invites us
to emerge into nothingness by destruction of all myths and all scales of
value; it discloses in man a close and secret relation to the nothing." (J.P.
Sartre, 1969, *Literature and Existentialism*, Citadel Press, p. 146.)

77. J. Onimus, 1968, *op. cit.*, p. 88.
78. Martin Heidegger, *What is Metaphysics?* translated from the German by
W. Brock, 1949, in the collection *Existence and Being*, Vision Press, London,
pp. 368-69. On the relationship between Beckett's writing and existentialist
phenomenology see Eugune F. Kaelin, *The Unhappy Consciousness: The
Poetic Plight of Samuel Beckett. An Inquiry at the Intersection of phenomenology and literature*, D. Reidel Publishing, 1981.
79. S. Beckett, 1931, *op. cit.*, p. 47.
80. J. Pilling, 1976, *op. cit.*, p. 22 citing interviews with L.E. Harvey, 1962 and
T. Driver, 1961.
81. Beckett's leanings towards the existentialist philosophy of the absurd were
certainly nurtured by his reading in the early thirties of Nietzsche and
Schopenhauer, two progenitors of modern existentialism. Nietzsche's declaration that "God is dead" and that the world is really an "eternal return of the
same," an absurd and nihilistic repetition, had a profound impact on Beckett;
he also appears to have been deeply attracted by Schopenhauer's pessimistic
doctrine that wisdom only comes when we accept that there is "no will: no
idea, no world . . . only nothingness". Language itself, Schopenhauer believed,
is condemned to nothingness and can aspire to "being" only by going beyond words towards the mystical condition of music. It is perhaps no accident that both Beckett's *Murphy* and Sartre's *Nausea* culminate with an invocation of the *being* of music beyond the absurd nothingness of words.
82. Interview with Alan Schneider, *op. cit.*
83. S. Beckett, 1959, *op. cit.*, p. 146.
84. S. Beckett, 1931, *op. cit.*, p. 16.
85. S. Beckett, 1959, *op. cit.*, p. 53. On Beckett's humour see H. Deyle, 1960,
op. cit., pp. 75-78.
86. S. Beckett, 1934, *More Pricks than Kicks*, Chatto and Windus, London,
p. 236. This comic stoicism is also typified by Malone's routine cultivation
of potted plants in his dark and airless basement even though he knows their
survival is against all the odds.
87. D. Bair, 1978, *op. cit.*, p. 90; J. Pilling, 1976, *op. cit.*, pp. 127-29.
88. S. Beckett, 1959, *op. cit.*, p. 250.
89. *Ibid.*, pp. 88-89.
90. Watt soon recognises the "old error" of trying to discover "what things were
in reality" (S. Beckett, 1959, *op. cit.*, p. 250). Beckett may be thinking here
of Leibniz's famous attempt to establish an ideal alphabet — *caracteristica
universalis* — which might englobe all of reality, or of the logical positivist
formulation of an equally foolproof *Begriffschrift* advanced by Frege and the
early Wittgenstein. I refer the reader here to Coe's excellent analysis of Watt
as "a living incarnation of the theories of Fritz Mauthner and of Ludwig
Wittgenstein," (1965, *op. cit.*, pp. 39-45). As Coe observes, "Watt is the
first incarnation of what is to be one of the primary themes of Beckett's
later work: the failure of man, in his search for the significance of either
himself or of the cosmos, to penetrate the barrier of language" (p. 41).
Cf. also E. Levy, 1980, *op. cit.*, pp. 27, 33.
91. J. Derrida, 1967, *La Voix et le Phénomène*, P.U.F., translated by D.B.

Alison, 1972, *Speech and Phenomena*, N.Y.; as Derrida explains "The prerogative of Being cannot withstand the deconstruction of the word" (p. 74). See Appendix to these notes.

92. J. Derrida, 1972, "La Mythologie blanche," *Marges de la philosophie* (Les editions de minuit), p. 247f. Derrida bases his argument that the deconstruction of the metaphysical notions of being necessarily entails the deconstruction of the equally metaphysical notions of language as a metaphorizing transcendence from absense to presence, on Heidegger's doctrine that "the metaphorical exists only within the metaphysical." Cf. P. Ricoeur's (1975) lucid critique of this Heidegger-Derrida thesis in "La méta-phore et la méta-physique" in his *La métaphore vive* (Ed. du Seuil), translated by R. Czerny, 1977, *The Rule of Metaphore* (University of Toronto Press), pp. 280f; for a more detailed analysis of the motifs of metaphor and palimpsest in Beckett and Derrida see R. Kearney, 1984, *op. cit.*, and Appendix to these notes.

93. Thus Beckett debunks our habitual approach to language as a representational "expression" (*Ausdruck*) of some self-present subject and reveals it as a perpetually self-deferring "signification" (*Anzeigen*) irreducible to presence. "All speech," Derrida contends, "which does not restore the immediate presence of the signified content, is inexpressive . . . all these "goings-forth" effectively exile this life of self-presence in signification. We know that signification . . . is the process of death at work in signs" (J. Derrida, 1969, trans. D. Alison, 1972, *op. cit.*, p. 40). The temporality of signification cannot be reduced to the expression of a self-identical subject "precisely because it cannot be conceived on the basis of a present or the self-presence of a present being; time defers the presence of self to self *ad infinitum* which means that "my death is structurally necessary to the pronouncing of the I" (*Ibid*, p. 86). Accordingly, "only a relation to my death could make the infinite differing of presence appear" (*Ibid.*, p. 102). Elsewhere, Derrida is even more explicit on this point: "Constituting and dislocating it at the same time, writing is other than the subject . . . Writing can never be thought under the category of the subject . . . And the original absence of the subject of writing is also the absence of the thing or the referent" (J. Derrida, 1976, *Of Grammatology*, Hopkins University Press, pp. 68-69). It is not difficult to see the relevance of Derrida's analysis to the life/death, absence/presence dilemma of the Beckettian narrator.

94. It is remarkable how close Beckett is here to Heidegger's doctrine that the subject is not the master but the servant of language (e.g. "man is the shepherd of language," *Humanismusbrief*, Frankfurt, 1949), or to Lévi-Strauss's theory that language is not an "epistemology" enabling the subject to know truth but a "mythology" which dispenses with the subject as a magisterial author: "Les mythes n'ont pas d'auteur . . . ce n'est pas l'homme qui pense les mythes mais les mythes qui se pensent dans l'homme" (*Mythologiques*, vol. 1, Paris, 1964). "I'm in words, made of words, other's words," howls Beckett's unnamable narrator, "I'm all these words, all these strangers, this dust of words, with no ground for their settling." And as Beckett thus dissolves and ruptures the "I" into a "bloody flux" of words, he significantly compares the writer to both a Prometheus and a Job (Worm) beholden to the anonymous voices of language; in choosing these two examples Beckett is perhaps inferring that the tragic comedy of language is inscribed into the two traditions of western civilisation – Hellenic and Hebraic. One is also reminded of the affinity between Beckett's attempt to "deanthropomor-

phise" the subject through language (D. Bair, 1978, *op. cit.*, p. 191) and Michel Foucault's (1973) theory of the "deanthropologising" role of language in the twentieth century (*The Order of Things*, Random House, N.Y.); Foucault argues that while in the Renaissance *things resemble things*, and in the classical age and nineteenth century *words represent things*, in our own century *words speak themselves* (with no reference to things or ideas beyond themselves) thus undoing the habitual notion of man as the *centre* of language. Lastly, one might mention the relevance of another French thinker of Beckett's generation, Maurice Blanchot, who holds that language has become a neutral, impersonal, interminable voice which expresses itself in modern literature as an "enigmatic space of repetition" (see *L'entretien infini*, Gallimard, 1969, particularly p. 504 where Blanchot speaks explicitly of Beckett). In short, all these contemporary thinkers, including Derrida, share Beckett's determination to expose the *logos* of language as a mere *muthos*, an endgame heralding not only the "end of philosophy" and the "end of the subject" but also "the end of history" as we have known it.

Appendix: Beckett and Derrida

Jacques Derrida's notion of language as "différance" provides us with a valuable key to the understanding of Beckett's critique of writing. Derrida's neologism (difference spelt with an "a") conveys both the sense of "differing" and "deferring" contained in the French verb *différer*. To deconstruct language is, Derrida claims, to discover that it is in fact an endless process of signifying, a "différance" or differentiation wherein the "meaning" signified is forever "different" from itself and forever "deferred" to some ideal but non-existent source of origin. The traditional metaphysical notion of "meaning" as a timeless self-identity or presence is itself a myth produced by language and so the quest of language for an original totalising presence is in truth no more than an endless "play of differences," a "temporalising" by means of ever-receding "traces": "Differance is what makes the movement of signification possible for each element that is said to be "present," appearing on the stage of presence, is related to something *other* than itself . . . a trace that relates no less to what is called the future than to what is called the past, and that constitutes what is called the present by this very relation to what is not, to what it absolutely is not" (Jacques Derrida, 1968, *Différance* in *Bulletin de la Société française de philosophie*, vol. 62, no. 3; reprinted in *Speech and Phenomena, op. cit.*, p. 142.) Every word in language is no more, therefore, than a "supplementation" or "substitution" for another word/trace and thus serves to mask and make up for the absence of an original presence. Hence the irony that word-signs *produce* the very illusory presence which they are supposed to *re-present*. The differentiating play of traces invents presence and consequently can unmask its imposture. As such it allows for the deconstruction of the metaphysical notion of presence, thereby transforming the traditional semiology of *identity* into what Derrida terms a grammatology of *différance*. Language *is* différance or as Derrida puts it: "Language preserves the différance that preserves language." The differential trace itself refers us back to a trace that can never present or re-present itself, that can never appear as such in a transparent phenomenon, in a *name*, in *being*. Each trace functions as a perpetual postponement or deferment of its own origin, as a trace of the effacement of a trace.

Derrida concludes accordingly that "older than being itself, our language has no name for such a differance . . . what is *unnamable* here is not some ineffable being that cannot be approached by a name . . . what is unnamable is the play (of language itself) that brings about the nominal effects, the relatively unitary or atomic structures we call names, or chains or substitutions for names. In these, for example, the nominal effect of "différance" is itself involved, carried off, and reinscribed, just as the false beginning or end of a game is still part of the game, a function of the system . . . There will be no unique name". The critical project of Beckett's writing is, I suggest, readily recognizable in terms of this grammatology of unnamable *différance*.

Already in the early nouvelles, Beckett's "deconstructing" scalpel had left its scar. The *Expelled*, written in concise, unsentimental prose, concludes with a statement which annuls its very raison-d'être: "I don't know why I told this story. I could just as well have told another." *The End*, stacatto and hesitant from the outset, breaks off just at that point where the narrator discovers that the projected "story in the likeness of my life" is not the story he has told but a "story I *might* have told." And this obsessional search for some original selfhood through language is taken up again in *The Calmative*: "I'll tell my story in the past none the less, as though it were a myth, or an old fable, for this evening I need another age, that age to become another age in which I become what I was."

In *Texts for Nothing*, (1947-1952), one of his more mature prose writings, Beckett pursues his deconstruction with unprecedented ruthlessness. In the first of the thirteen splendidly composed texts, the author establishes the fact that the voices which haunt him are the different time tenses of language, continually overlapping each other and thereby obstructing the quest for an original univocal subject: "All angles, times and tenses, at first I only had been here, now I'm here still, soon I won't be here yet . . . I was my father and I was my son." In the second, the author tries to reconstitute a "far memory" of his youth which the third text cancels out as "only voices, only lies". The futility of the narrator's desire "to get into my story in order to get out of it" by discovering his true self, becomes patently evident: there is no way out of the vicious circle of language. In the fourth text the author consents to embrace the play of words so as to console himself with some fictional persona; for even as victim of an impersonal voice there is the solace that, at least, "accusative I exist". But remembering his miserable anterior existences as Molloy and Malone, the narrator regrets having allowed his "figments talk" and convince him to invent a "story for myself". It is already too late to escape from his story, nevertheless, or even to decide to end it, for the interminable voice cannot, he realises, "be mine". So that in the fifth text, he resigns himself to the dictates of another's words: "I'm the clerk, I'm the scribe, at the hearings of what cause I know not," a Kafkaesque culprit "not understanding what I hear, not knowing what I write." The Beckettian narrator is once more driven to confess that the "phantasms" that appear "to issue from this imaginary head" are in fact not his own but a stranger's.

In the sixth text, the author suddenly hits upon the quasi-divine art of erasure which allows him to subvert language even while he remains its captive: "Blot, words can be blotted and the mad thoughts they invent, the nostalgia for that slime where the eternal breathed and his son wrote, long after, with divine idiotic finger, at the feet of the adulteress, wipe it out, all you have to do is say you said nothing and so say nothing again." But the seemingly messianic erasure of words – explicitly recalling Christ's action – only produces an illusory silence, "a silence that is not silence" but rather the inner abyss of language itself: "This unnamable thing, that I name and name and never wear out, and I call that words." Whence the author's self-defeating question: "with what words shall I name my unnamable words?"

The seven remaining texts elaborate this question, scrutinising it meticulously in all its possible permutations. The unnamable thing is the intangible *I* which the nameless author seeks to reappropriate by means of fiction: "Fantasies and hope of a story for me somehow, of having come from somewhere and of being able to go back." If only he could reach this *I* and name it, he could regain his true identity, the neoplatonic *one* which lost itself in giving voice to all its mimetic *vice-existers*: "I shall know again that I once was, and roughly who, and how to go on, and speak unaided, nicely, about number one and his pale imitations". (*Text*, 10) To name the *I* however is already to invent and such a fictive *I* can be no more than a ventriloquist's medium uttering a ceaseless anonymous language which baulks at self-recovery: "It is for ever the same murmur, flowing unbroken, like a single endless word and therefore meaningless, for it's the end gives the meaning to words." Consequently, the author resolves to subordinate his individual will to represent and possess, to the involuntary suffering of being that language imposes. The tone here is at once belligerent and acquiescent, apocalyptic and calm – a prayer uttered in defiance and despair: "That's right, wordshit, bury me, avalanche, and let there be no more talk of any creature nor of a world to leave, nor of a world to reach, in order to have done, with worlds, with creatures, with words, with misery, misery." (*Text*, 9) By means of such self-effacement, he hopes paradoxically, to be carried beyond (*metapherein*) his suffering state into some "outer", "other" redeemed existence beyond the subterranean cave of language. But language has no reality reference to justify a Platonic journey outwards; and so the author finds himself thrown back upon his words lacking "a body to get there with . . . and the power to get there, and the way to get there, and pass out, and see the beauties of the skies . . ." (*Text*, 9).

If the voice cannot escape from itself through objective reference or self-effacement, then the last possible resort would seem to be the invocation of a voice that would *at once* speak and be silent: "a voice of silence". This ideal of a silent voice constitutes, as Derrida has argued in his remarkable essay *The Voice that keeps Silence*, one of the fundamental projects of the traditional theory of language. This silent voice would be a voice unbound by time and space, that is, a self-referring presence no longer subject to differentiation or deferment. But the possibility of such a silent voice is of course its very impossibility, for such a voice would have to be "at the same time absolutely dead and absolutely alive". Beckett's writings expose the contradictoriness of this ideal voice of presence, or more exactly of immediate at-one-ness of the self with itself. One only appreciates the revolutionary nature of such exposure when one recalls that the contradiction inherent in this mythic voice of presence has remained masked by the western philosophical definitions of being as an atemporal "self-originating principle of principles" (*Arche, Ousia* etc). Husserl and Heidegger first adverted to this contradiction when they demonstrated that language does not represent some pre-existent presence but rather creates and sustains it. Thus Derrida and others were given the lead to deconstruct the conventional view of language as a transparent signifier whose *signified* would be some silent prelinguistic origin of meaning.

The "voice of silence" represents the ideal of a timeless and immaterial subject, what Derrida defines as a "spiritual flesh that continues to speak and to be present to itself." (J. Derrida, 1967, *op. cit.*, pp. 71-87). To acknowledge with

Beckett that language (and more explicitly writing) is a material, spatio-temporal process of signifying is to sound the death knell of the metaphysical fiction of a silent soliloquy of the soul with itself, a fiction which attempts to hide its own *differing activity as signifier* in order to project the "identity of presence as self-presence" (p. 57). The "silent voice" signalling the perfect adequation of language and self is impossible, for language always leaves a wake of irrecuperable traces behind it. Language, as Beckett writes in text 13 of *Texts for Nothing*, is "nothing but a voice murmuring a trace . . . like air leaves among the leaves, among the grass, among the sand." The deconstruction of the word into the trace shows us that "this bending-back is irreductible to presence or to self-presence, that this trace or difference is always older than presence . . . and prevents us from speaking of a simple self-identity" (Derrida, *op. cit.*, p. 58). In fact, the so-called voice of silence is nothing more than "the voice's breath" which "breathes in vain" (*Text* 13), since it can never utter the name of presence. Beckett even wrote a fifteen-second play called *Breath* to prove it!

Beckett's writing masterfully deconstructs itself by directing our attention to itself *as writing*, that is as a system of *sounding* signifiers irretrievably at odds with the ideal of a corresponding *silent* signified. It is only by deconstructing the word's pretension to achieve self-adequation by means of silence, that we can uncover its hidden self-alienation. The irony which Beckett makes such great play of is, of course, that one is obliged to use language to deconstruct language. We can only undo words by means of words: "the same lie lyingly denied . . . no's knife" (Text 13). All that the Beckettian author can conclude is that the *I* is *not-I*, that the coveted original *one* is *no-one*; that there is *no-thing* to be said and *no-where* to be journeyed to: "And it's the same old road I'm trudging, up yes and down no, towards one yet to be named . . . name, no, nothing is namable, tell, no, nothing can be told, what then, I don't know, I shouldn't have begun." (Text 11). The *other I* one seeks to appropriate in words is "merely a babble of homeless mes and untenanted hims . . . without number or person whose abandoned being we haunt, nothing." (Text 12).

In the German Letter, published in *Disjecta: Miscellaneous Writings and a Dramatic Fragment* (Calder, 1983), Beckett makes his deconstructive attitude to language abundantly clear: "More and more my own language appears to me like a veil that must be torn apart in order to get at the things (or the Nothingness) behind it . . . As we cannot eliminate language all at once, we should at least leave nothing undone that might contribute to its falling into disrepute. To bore one hole after another in it, until what lurks behind it — be it something or nothing — begins to seep through; I cannot imagine a higher goal for a writer today."

PART V

CHAPTER 14

Gordon L. Herries Davies

IRISH THOUGHT IN SCIENCE

1. Karl Theodore Hoppen, *The common scientist in the seventeenth century: a study of the Dublin Philosophical Society 1683-1708*, London, 1970, pp. xiv + 298.

2. John Gerald Simms, *William Molyneux of Dublin 1656-1698*, (edited by P.H. Kelly), Dublin, 1982, pp. vii + 176.
3. J.B. Gatenby, "The history of zoology and comparative anatomy in Trinity College, Dublin," *Irish Journal of Medical Science*, 1961, 395-407.
4. Henry Fitzpatrick Berry, *A history of the Royal Dublin Society*, London, 1915, pp. xvi + 456; James Meenan and Desmond Clarke, *RDS: the Royal Dublin Society 1731-1981*, Dublin, 1981, pp. x + 288.
5. Desmond Clarke, *Thomas Prior 1681-1751 founder of the Royal Dublin Society*, Royal Dublin Society, 1951, pp. 60.
6. G.L. Herries Davies, "The making of Irish geography, IV: The Physico-Historical Society of Ireland, 1744-1752," *Irish Geography*, 12, 1979, 92-98; Gordon Leslie Herries Davies, *Sheets of many colours: the mapping of Ireland's rocks 1750-1890*, Royal Dublin Society, 1983, pp. xiv + 242.
7. Herries Davies, *op. cit.*, 1983, 6.
8. D. Clarke, "Dublin Society's statistical surveys," *An Leabharlann*, 15(2), 1957, 47-54.
9. Gordon Leslie Herries Davies and Robert Charles Mollan, *Richard Griffith 1784-1878*, Royal Dublin Society, 1980, pp. vi + 222; Herries Davies, *op. cit.*, 1983.
10. *The book of Trinity College Dublin 1591-1891*, Belfast, 1892, pp. xii + 316.
11. John Anderson, *History of the Belfast Library and Society for Promoting Knowledge*, Belfast, 1888, pp. viii + 128.
12. John Louis Emil Dreyer, *An historical account of the Armagh Observatory*, Armagh, 1883, pp. 20.
13. S.F. Pettit, "The Royal Cork Institution: a reflection of the cultural life of a city," *Journal of the Cork Historical and Archaeological Society*, 81, 1976, 70-90.
14. Arthur Deane (editor), *The Belfast Natural History and Philosophical Society. Centenary volume. 1821-1921*, Belfast, 1924, pp. x + 212.
15. A.E.J. Went, "The Royal Zoological Society of Ireland," *Irish Naturalists' Journal*, 12(7), 1957, 193-195.
16. G.L. Davies, "The Geological Society of Dublin and the Royal Geological Society of Ireland 1831-1890," *Hermathena*, 100, 1965, 66-76.
17. M. MacSweeney and J. Reilly, "The Cork Cuvierian Society," *Journal of the Cork Historical and Archaeological Society*, 63, 1958, 9-14.
18. Herries Davies, *op. cit.*, 1983.
19. B.B. Kelham, "The Royal College of Science for Ireland (1867-1926)," *Studies*, 56, Autumn 1967, 297-309; Thomas Sherlock Wheeler, *et al.*, *The natural resources of Ireland*, Royal Dublin Society, [1944], pp. 90.
20. P.J. McLaughlin, "Richard Kirwan," *Studies*, 28, 1939, 461-474, 593-605, 29, 1940, 71-83, 281-300; F.E. Dixon, "Richard Kirwan: the Dublin philosopher," *Dublin Historical Record*, 24(3), 1971, 53-64.
21. T.S. Wheeler, "William Higgins, chemist (1763-1825)," *Studies*, 43, 1954, 78-91, 207-218, 327-338.
22. T.S. Wheeler, *et al., op. cit.*, [1944].
23. Herries Davies, *op. cit.*, 1983, 75.
24. Ronald Charles Cox (editor), *Robert Mallet, F.R.S. 1810-1881*, Institution of Engineers of Ireland, Dublin, 1982, pp. vi + 146.
25. Patrick Moore, *The astronomy of Birr Castle*, London, 1971, pp. xii + 82.
26. S.M.P. McKenna, "Astronomy in Ireland from 1780," *Vistas in Astronomy*, 9, 1968, 283-296.

27. Thomas L. Hankins, *Sir William Rowan Hamilton*, Baltimore, 1980, pp. xxii + 474.
28. William Valentine Ball (editor), *Reminiscences and letters of Sir Robert Ball*, London, 1915, pp. xvi + 406.
29. Patrick John McLaughlin, *Nicholas Callan: priest-scientist 1799-1864*, Dublin and London, 1965, pp. 128.
30. G.L. Herries Davies, "The palaeontological collection of Lord Cole, third Earl of Enniskillen (1807-1886), at Florence Court, Co. Fermanagh," *Irish Naturalists' Journal*, 16(12), 1970, 379-381.
31. T.H. Mason, 'Dublin opticians and instrument makers," *Dublin Historical Record*, 6(4), 1944, 133-149.
32. D.A. Webb, "William Henry Harvey 1811-1866 and the tradition of systematic botany," *Hermathena*, 103, 1966, 32-45.
33. W.J.E. Jessop, "Samuel Haughton: a Victorian polymath," *Hermathena*, 116, 1973, 5-26.
34. J.G. O'Hara, "George Johnstone Stoney, F.R.S., and the concept of the electron," *Notes and Records of the Royal Society of London*, 29(2), 1975, 265-276.
35. Jack Morrell and Arnold Thackray, *Gentlemen of science: early years of the British Association for the Advancement of Science*, Oxford, 1981, pp. xxiv + 592.
36. Jesse Austin Sidney Stendall, *Robert Bell: geologist. A biographical sketch*, Belfast, 1938, pp. 100.
37. Robert Lloyd Praeger, *Some Irish naturalists: a biographical note-book*, Dundalk, 1949, 159-160.
38. G.L. Herries Davies, "The earth sciences in Irish serial publications 1787-1977," *Journal of Earth Sciences: Royal Dublin Society*, 1(1), 1978, 1-23.
39. B.P. Beirne, "The development of Irish entomology," *Irish Naturalists' Journal*, 9(4), 1947, 81-84.
40. "Robert Lloyd Praeger, 1865-1953," *Irish Naturalists' Journal*, 11(6), 1954, 141-171.
41. R. Ll. Praeger, "The Irish field clubs," *Irish Naturalist*, 3, 1894, 141-145, 211-215, 247-252.

CONTRIBUTORS

RICHARD KEARNEY, Ph.D.

From Cork. Received Masters Degree from McGill University, Montreal, Canada and Doctorate from University of Paris. Lecturer in Philosophy in University College, Dublin. Co-editor of *The Crane Bag: Journal of Irish Studies* since its foundation in 1977. Author or editor of several books on philosophy and literature including *Heidegger et la Question de Dieu* (Grasset, 1979), *La Poetique du Possible* (Beauchesne, 1984), *Dialogues with Contemporary Continental Thinkers* (Manchester University Press, 1984).

BRENDAN PURCELL, Ph.D.

From Dublin. Received Doctorate from University College, Dublin. Lecturer in Philosophy and Psychology at University College, Dublin.

PROINSIAS MacCANA, Ph.D.

From Belfast. Received Doctorate from Queen's University, Belfast. Professor of Early (including Medieval) Irish Language and Literature at University College, Dublin. His many works include *Branwen Daughter of Llyr* (University of Wales Press, 1958), *Celtic Mythology* (Hamlyn Press, 1970, Newnes Books, 1983), *The Mabinogi* (University of Wales Press, 1977) and *The Learned Tales of Medieval Ireland* (Dublin Institute for Advanced Studies 1980).

TOMÁS Ó CATHASAIGH, M.A.

From Waterford. Received Masters Degree from National University of Ireland. Lecturer in Early (including Medieval) Irish Language and Literature at University College, Dublin. Author of *The Heroic Biography of Cormac Mac Airt* (Dublin Institute for Advanced Studies 1977) and articles on early Irish mythology and literature.

DERMOT MORAN, M.A.

From Dublin. Studied at University College, Dublin and Yale University. Has lectured in Philosophy at Queen's University, Belfast, and is currently lecturer in the Philosophy Department of St. Patrick's College, Maynooth. Author of studies on medieval and contemporary European philosophy.

HARRY M. BRACKEN, Ph.D.

From New York. Received Doctorate from University of Iowa. Professor of Philosophy at McGill University, Montreal, Canada. Author of *The Early Reception of Berkeley's Immaterialism: 1710-1733* (Den Haag: Martinus Nijhoff, 1965), *Berkeley* (London: MacMillan, 1974), *Mind and Language: Essays on Descartes and Chomsky* (Dordrecht: Foris 1984: at press).

DAVID BERMAN, Ph.D.

From New York. Senior Lecturer in Philosophy in Trinity College, Dublin. A specialist on eighteenth century intellectual history.

SEAMUS DEANE, Ph.D.

From Derry. Received Doctorate from Cambridge. Fulbright and Woodrow Wilson Scholar and Visiting Professor at University of California, Reed College, Notre Dame. Professor of Modern English at University College, Dublin. Poet, editor and leading Irish literary critic. A director of Field Day. His most recent publication is *History Lessons* (Gallery Press, 1983).

LIAM de PAOR, M.A., M.R.I.A.

From Dublin. Educated at University College, Dublin. Lecturer in History at University College, Dublin. He has published many books on Irish history and culture, including *Divided Ulster* (Penguin, 1970).

DESMOND FENNELL, M.A.

From Dublin. Educated at U.C.D. Teaches Communications at Rathmines College of Commerce, Dublin. Author of political and historical studies including *Sketches of the New Ireland* (New Ireland Association for the Advancement of Self Government 1973), *The State of the Nation* (Ward River, 1983) and *Beyond Nationalism* (Ward River: at press).

JOHN JORDAN, M.A., B. Litt. (Oxon)

From Dublin. Educated at University College, Dublin and Pembroke College, Oxford. Poet, short-story writer, critic. Published works include *A Raft from Flotsam* (Gallery Press, 1975), *Blood and Stations* (Gallery Press, 1976), *Yarns* (Poolbeg, 1977), *With Whom Did I Share the Crystal?* (Owner's Press, 1980), *Patrician Stations* (New Writers' Press, 1973) and many critical essays on Irish writers, including Sean O'Casey, Patrick Kavanagh, Padraic Ó Conaire, Aogán Ó Rathaille, and on the Irish Theatre.

ELIZABETH CULLINGFORD, Ph.D. (Oxon.)

From Lancaster, England. Educated at Oxford. Assistant Professor of English at University of Texas, Austin. Author of *Yeats, Ireland and Fascism* (Macmillan, 1981).

MARK PATRICK HEDERMAN, Ph.D.

From Limerick. Received Doctorate from the National University of Ireland. Prior of the Benedictine Abbey at Glenstal, Co. Limerick. Co-editor of *The Crane Bag, Journal of Irish Studies* and author of several articles on philosophy, theology and literature.

GORDON L. HERRIES DAVIES, M.A., Ph.D., F.T.C.D., M.R.I.A.

From Lancashire, England. Received Doctorate from University of Dublin. Associate Professor of Geography at Trinity College, Dublin. Author of many papers in the earth sciences and the history of science. He has written for television and his published books include *The Earth in Decay: A History of British Geomorphology* (MacDonald, 1969) and *Sheets of Many Colours: The Mapping of Ireland's Rocks* (Royal Dublin Society, 1983).